BUSINESS PSYCHOLOGY IN ACTION

BUSINESS PSYCHOLOGY IN ACTION

creating flourishing organisations through evidence-based and emerging practices

Edited by Pauline Grant

with Uzma Afridi, Juliane Sternemann and Emma Wilson

Association for Business Psychology

Matador
9 Priory Business Park,
Wistow Road, Kibworth Beauchamp,
Leicestershire. LE8 0RX
Tel: 0116 279 2299
Email: books@troubador.co.uk
Web: www.troubador.co.uk/matador
Twitter: @matadorbooks

ISBN 978 1784625 481

British Library Cataloguing in Publication Data.
A catalogue record for this book is available from the British Library.

Printed and bound by CPI Group (UK) Ltd, Croydon, CR0 4YY
Typeset in Aldine by Troubador Publishing Ltd, Leicester, UK

Matador is an imprint of Troubador Publishing Ltd

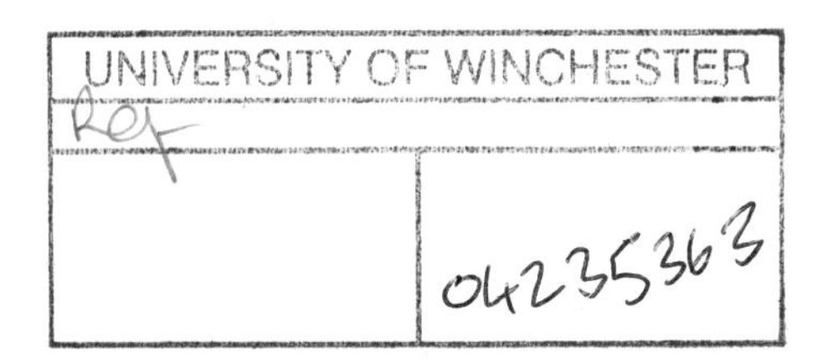

CONTENTS

ACKNOWLEDGEMENTS

Pauline Grant – Editor

Those who have been instrumental in creating *Business Psychology in Action* are numerous, with various different kinds of contribution to the final result. What unites them is that this discretionary effort has been alongside their many other commitments, and in some cases accompanying some significant personal challenges.

I would like to pay tribute to the authors whose work is contained within *Business Psychology in Action*. It is always a joy to work with people who are on the one hand enthusiastic and motivated and on the other responsive and co-operative, and this is what I have experienced in our collaboration. I am therefore proud to present our authors, who have interesting (and sometimes inspiring) things to say about the status and future direction of Business Psychology, and whom I commend to you as worthy of your attention.

One of the priorities of the Association for Business Psychology is 'thought leadership' and this book was commissioned with that in mind. The support of the ABP Management Board has gone far beyond agreeing that the book fits with their strategic objectives. I am sure the Board members will forgive me for particularly acknowledging the contributions of Clodagh O'Reilly, Steve Apps and Maria Gardner, all of whom have eased our journey.

There is no doubt about the value of great teamwork. I was privileged to be joined by Uzma Afridi, Juliane Sternemann and Emma Wilson in bringing this book to fruition. As well as their energy, resourcefulness and dedication, they have been a delight to work with.

Finally, I would like to acknowledge others who have provided their guidance, time and assistance. These include Dawn Beadle, Michael Bloomfield, Bill Fear, Sam Keyne, Josette Lesser, Jessica Pryce-Jones and Paul Thorne.

MEET THE EDITORIAL TEAM

Pauline Grant is a freelance Business Psychologist, Executive Coach and Facilitator who has previously been a Director at YSC Ltd and Business Director at Ashridge, where she developed her liking for international assignments. She sees businesses as the communities in which people spend much of their time, so consulting is her way of 'making a difference' by helping leaders and decision-makers improve those communities. Prior to business consulting, Pauline worked as an Educational Psychologist. She was the Founding Vice Chair of the ABP, has presented at their conferences and edited Business Psychology in Practice.

Uzma Afridi is a Business Psychologist passionate about implementing and effecting positive change. Having worked for public and private sectors, she is particularly interested in how company culture, team dynamics and leadership contribute to a successful business environment, and she is a strong advocate for equality and diversity in the workplace. With a background in HR, Uzma worked for a large advertising agency and now provides executive coaching in the media industry via the National Advertising Benevolent Society. Uzma believes that the right resources and guidance give everyone the opportunity to fulfil their potential, for themselves and their employer.

Juliane Sternemann is a Business Psychologist and Facilitator at Criterion Partnership, having previously worked for an international professional services company. Combining five years business experience across a number of different sectors with expertise in assessment and development, she feels that building strong relationships and collaborating with her clients can deliver flexible solutions and make a difference to their organisational success. To promote the continued growth of our profession and actively support knowledge sharing, she has been involved as a member at the ABP conference and DOP Awards and facilitated at an ABP training event.

Emma Wilson is a Business Psychologist and Researcher experienced in providing evidence-based insight for private and public sector organisations internationally. Previously a Research Consultant for YSC Ltd, she has also conducted business and social psychological research with Prof. Adrian Furnham at University College London, where she gained her First Class Psychology degree. She also has a Masters in Organisational Psychology from City University, London. Passionate about aligning industry practice with academic research and advocating their mutual value, her main research interests lie in differential psychology and health & well-being at work. She has a number of peer-reviewed publications in academic journals.

FOREWORD

by Peter Cheese, Chief Executive, CIPD

We live in interesting and challenging times. Economies are uncertain and unpredictable, technology continues to advance and disrupt, and businesses everywhere are trying to respond. Rapid innovation, agility, and resilience are the new watchwords, but we also need new thinking, new capabilities, and even new ways of organising and managing work. What got us to where we are today won't necessarily get us to where we need to go.

At the same time, there are many changing dynamics and challenges with our workforces. Workforces are much more diverse due in part to emerging generational differences in expectations and aspirations. There is also more diversity in the ways in which people want to work, with growing proportions of our workforces working for themselves or flexi-working. Across Europe we have ageing workforces and high youth unemployment. Education and the demands of the world of work are not well aligned, so we have increasing skills mismatches with the changing nature of work. The result is that globalisation and growth of economies everywhere are now being seen much more clearly as constrained, or enabled, by access to skills and talent.

In case we needed reminding, most failures of the past, whether they be the banking crisis, crises in the NHS, oil company disasters, corruption scandals, cyber security attacks or whatever else, come down to people and the actions and decisions they take.

These huge contextual shifts, perhaps together with a major shock like the Global Financial Crisis, have created what can be seen as an inflection point in thinking about the real fundamentals of business.

This is not just about how businesses need to become more agile, or how new organisational models are emerging, but also about the role and responsibilities that businesses have in society at large. People and the nature of organisations are now much more at the centre of the business debate, and the political and policy debates as well. In even the most analytical and numbers-driven environments such as the financial services sector, the discussion is now, more than it ever has been, about behaviours, about leadership, about trust, and about capabilities and cultures.

People, how they work, how they learn, what engages them, how they respond to change, how and why they behave in certain ways, should always have been at the centre of what makes good business. We have for years talked about people being our most important assets. In reality it is hard to see how this has manifested itself, with many leading indicators such as engagement levels, degrees of trust, productivity, and employment rates all seemingly having declined.

These understandings are of course the knowledge and craft of Business Psychologists, and also the roots of the Human Resources (HR) function and of people management and development. In the last few decades, management and HR thinking has been very focused on processes, policies, structures and models of efficiency. This has been encouraged by management trends such as lean, six sigma, process reengineering and shared services models, and the 'rational man' thinking of economics in the past. Focus has been lost on the fundamentals of understanding people and organisational behaviours. The many new insights and thinking that have been emerging in recent years from fields such as neuroscience, behavioural science, positive psychology, systems thinking and the understanding of morals and ethics have yet to be fully incorporated into business practice.

It is vital now that the practitioners, researchers, consultants, and academics who bring these deeper insights and understanding of people and organisational behaviour, step up together and more strongly influence the direction of business and management thinking. It is certainly a key part of what we at the CIPD see as the development of HR and Learning & Development thinking and capabilities for the future. We have to challenge some of the old paradigms and models, for example in learning, motivation, leadership development or the management of change, that have been around too long, and that with the newer insights from areas like neuroscience we can now better understand. This should lead to better outcomes and value from the interventions that we make.

There is no doubt that things are beginning to change, and the ideas and understanding that Business Psychologists bring are becoming better recognised. Behavioural science and behavioural economics are becoming embedded much more in policy and governmental thinking, mindfulness ideas are much more prevalent in management coaching and development, wellbeing is a big area of focus for organisations and for health systems and society more broadly, and neuroscience seems to be appearing everywhere. Even happiness is now a legitimate business topic.

So now is the time to get serious, to put the human into human resources and into the heart of business thinking. This book is a great collection of insights, practical advice and research evidence from a wide range of consultants, researchers, and practitioners. Themes that are covered include implementing business psychology in practice, tools, technologies, and techniques. New ideas and thinking in managing and understanding diversity, conflict, cultural differences and alignment to organisational cultures are presented. Leadership development and coaching is a critical theme within several essays, as well as understanding risk behaviours and a focus on wellbeing.

We can all learn from these insights and, hopefully, as a result, help to better equip leaders, employees and organisations to be effective, productive, and resilient in these fast changing times.

SECTION 1

Leadership

LEADERSHIP INTRODUCTION

Pauline Grant

Most Business Psychologists would say that leadership is a key part of their work. It therefore seems fitting that we start this book with some perspectives on leadership, a theme that you will also find cropping up in other sections. For me, the term 'leadership' makes sense when two criteria are satisfied. The first is that there is a destination, an aspiration or goal. If there is no answer to the question 'What are you leading us towards?', then leadership makes no sense. The second criterion is that there are followers. An individual can have personal aspirations and objectives without being a leader. It is only when they have followers that they are exercising leadership.

Whilst very simple, this encapsulates the major challenges for our business leaders. Some people are known to be good organisers. They feel a natural tendency to take charge which might be accompanied by an unusually strong ability to rally people around. They might become known for getting things done, albeit that their goals have been articulated by others rather than being destinations that they have defined for themselves. Many leaders in business are in this position, selected to lead teams, functions or enterprises because they have 'good people skills'. When we work with those leaders we often find that the stated goals (e.g. to increase their market share, make an imprint somewhere new or deliver a project) are seldom the aspirations that inspire them and their followers.

Others have a burning desire to 'make a difference', and can articulate it in terms that transcend business metrics. Their challenge is that it cannot be achieved by them alone, yet can appear hazy and unrealistic to colleagues or even a distraction from the day to day activities of the business. Gathering followers is different from supervising routine tasks, and involves harvesting and deploying discretionary effort, intellectual, imaginative and practical. When is such resource utilisation appropriate, and when does it stray into being manipulative or self-serving? Such questions take us to leaders' values which, as you will see in this section, become at least as important as skills when considering leadership.

We begin with an overview of leadership theory provided by Tom Hopton and Peter Saville. They draw together the history that brings us to more contemporary perspectives and offer their conclusions about leadership today. Peter Hamill takes us on a very different journey, to look inward to the unconscious drivers of behaviour. These are of course relevant beyond leadership; in looking at them we get a glimpse of how, through a more intense level of self-awareness, leaders might re-think their approach to the challenges of destination and followership. Finally Scott Lichtenstein and Paul Aitken offer a radical and bold stance on the role of leadership for the good of all.

LEADERSHIP – MEET THE AUTHORS

Tom Hopton is Principal Consultant at Saville Consulting and a Visiting Fellow of Kingston University, London. He graduated from Oxford University as an Experimental Psychologist and is a consultant and trainer to a range of global clients. Tom managed the development of numerous psychometric models and tools, including many of Saville Consulting's aptitude tests. He has also managed a variety of research activities including Project Epsom, a major validation study of personality questionnaires. In addition, Tom is a frequent presenter and a published author whose work features internationally.

Peter Saville, Professor, Founder and Chair of Saville Consulting, previously also of SHL which he took to flotation on the London Stock Exchange in 1997, is acknowledged worldwide as an 'assessment guru'. In1998 he was voted one of the UK's top entrepreneurs. In 2000 he became the first Work Psychologist to be awarded the British Psychological Society's Centenary Life Time Achievement Award for Distinguished Contributions to Professional Psychology. Peter was awarded Honorary Fellowship of the BPS in 2012, the highest honour the BPS can confer.

Peter Hamill is a consultant, coach and author who specialises in leadership and personal development, working with individuals within organisations to help them achieve their potential. Pete is an expert on embodied approaches to leadership development, on which he has written a book (entitled Embodied Leadership). He also works with clients on Leadership Development, Organisational and Individual Change, Organisational Development, Culture Change, and Corporate Social Responsibility. He lives in Brighton, UK with his wife and young daughter, and loves travel, good food and fine wines.

Scott Lichtenstein is a founding Director of EVS Consulting and Senior Lecturer at Birmingham City Business School. He also researches, publishes and facilitates leaders to be more effective through understanding their motives for action and personal values. He co-authored 'From Recession to Recovery: A Leadership Guide for Good and Bad Times', and 'Integrity in the Boardroom: A Case for Further Research', in A. Brink (Ed.) *Corporate Governance and Business Ethics*, and has academic and practitioner articles in the area of Leadership, Strategy, Organisational Behaviour and Corporate Governance.

Paul Aitken is a leadership learning and development entrepreneur and Founder/CEO of Mastering Leadership Agility (MLA) Ltd. Paul has worked as a senior human resource manager/internal consultant and professional lead in the private utility and public sectors, including a Business School. In addition, Paul is Co-Founder (with Ludovic Odier) and MD of HELIOS ('Heart of Enterprise for Organisations and Schools'), operating globally from the Asia-Pacific learning hub which is Singapore, with a mission to create powerful regenerative human experiences through leadership.

UNIVERSAL LEADERSHIP: THE EVOLUTION OF LEADERSHIP THEORY

Professor Peter Saville & Tom Hopton

From the 19th century to the present day, psychology as a modern discipline has examined leadership from a range of different angles. Here we consolidate a wide range of leadership research to provide an up-to-date topic review culminating in an overview of the development and validation of Saville Consulting's 3P (Professional, People & Pioneering) model of leadership.

In developing the 3P model as part of a team at Saville Consulting, we've recently had a chance to reacquaint ourselves with the rich body of leadership literature and to carry out some fascinating research. In essence, this work suggests that many existing leadership models tend to focus on Professional and People Leadership, while neglecting the entrepreneurial and revolutionary behaviours which underpin some of the most effective forms of Pioneering Leadership.

However, before we discuss the most up-to-date models and theories, we want to begin by reflecting how far leadership research has come, starting our enquiry before psychology existed as a modern scientific discipline.

The Great Person Approach

Before the advent of modern psychological enquiry, views on leadership can be loosely categorised into two broad classes. The first contains stories of lowly people rising to positions of leadership and the second refers to so-called 'Great People', that is, individuals (invariably white, European males) who were 'born to be leaders'. The distinction between these two broad classes persists to the present day in discussions about the extent to which leadership is innate or a set of characteristics and skills that can be taught or developed.

Even though there have clearly been contrasting views on leadership throughout human history, those held by the ruling classes have tended to exert the greater influence. It is therefore no surprise to see many instances where the ruling class was able to convince itself (if not everyone) that leadership was simply a matter of belonging to their own 'right' class! As such, many so-called 'Great People' have taken on an almost mythical, revered status. Looking back, we can generally only speculate how other individuals would have fared in the same privileged circumstances.

However, it is worth bearing in mind that this was before there was agreement on the structure of personality, and so personality, intelligence and other factors such as social class were not seen as distinct from one another. More modern research has suggested that there are clear links to leadership from such variables.

People–Task Differentiation, The Ohio Studies

In the 1950s, a series of studies carried out at the Ohio State University identified two independent and critical characteristics of leaders: 'consideration' towards subordinates and 'initiating structure' to promote the achievement of goals. This frequently has been rendered as the 'people–task' division in leadership, which is seen today in a number of different leadership models.

For example, Blake and Mouton (1964) produced the managerial grid model which considered the two variables *concern for people* and *concern for production*. Different scores on the two variables identified five distinct leadership types.

The 'people–task' distinction is a useful one, though it does not typically take account of context or offer great detail about different leadership styles. When developing our own leadership model the team advanced the concept of 'Pioneering Leadership'. This looks at the impact of the leader at the broader organisational level in terms of their potential to grow and develop a business. We shall discuss this new concept in greater detail later on as we feel it adds a useful third factor to the 'people' and 'task' concepts in leadership theory.

Situational Leadership and Contingency Theories

By the late 1960s researchers were frequently focusing on what came to be known as 'contingency theory'. This approach suggests that leadership is dependent upon both internal and external situational factors. The several different contingency models generally agree that much of the previous leadership research had neglected the influence of environmental (contingency) factors on leadership effectiveness. Contingency theory is still widely used today and modern versions integrate concepts such as organisational culture as contingency factors (Schimmoeller, 2010).

The importance of the leadership context is demonstrated by situational leadership theory, one example being Hersey and Blanchard's model (1969). This proposed that there is no single 'best' style of leadership and that the most effective leaders adapt their style to the task at hand. Furthermore, these researchers characterised leadership styles in terms of Task Behaviour and Relationship Behaviour, building on the established people–task distinction.

In proposing that the context for leadership can inform the type of leadership that is most effective, situational and contingency theories went some way to undermining the earlier Great Person idea. This stated that certain people were likely to be effective leaders across all situations merely by virtue of their 'greatness'. However, focusing too much on the situational and contingency factors can ignore the finding that people often do behave consistently across situations (e.g. Furr & Funder, 2004; Mischel et al., 2002). There is also evidence showing that combinations of behaviours and attributes can reflect a stable tendency to lead across dissimilar situations (Zaccaro, 2007). While leadership research on the whole has tended to move away from 'heroic leadership' to situational approaches, it seems that some aspects of personality, to a certain extent, do offer a stable means of predicting leadership potential.

At their extreme, situational and contingency leadership theories have been taken to suggest that anyone can become an effective leader provided they are put in the right situation, and given the necessary training and resources to perform appropriately. Yet many individuals do fail as leaders when it appears that all conditions are favorable to them; equally, there are people who can still be effective leaders when the situation is not in their favour. As an example, David Moyes was Sir Alex Ferguson's choice to replace him as manager of the English Premier League football club Manchester United. Inheriting a talented team and strong financial resources he nevertheless left after a brief tenure, which was viewed by many as unsuccessful. We also tend to think that situational and contingency theories of leadership sometimes do not consider in sufficient depth how leaders can adapt their approach to fit the situation they are in, or how they might go about changing the situation itself.

Emergent and Servant Leadership

Emergent leadership research focuses on how leaders surface from their peer group. There are different ways a leader can emerge. It may be through a conscious attempt to dominate their peer group, while at other times it may be by merit of their performance and the respect of their peers. The central emergent leader approach relates closely to the concept of 'servant leadership' (Greenleaf, 1977) which identifies two different kinds of leaders: 'strong natural leaders' (who are assertive and driven by a need for dominance) and 'strong natural servants' (who are driven by the need to serve a cause).

Bolden (2004) argues that the servant leader is a servant first and leader second. Servant leaders want to serve a cause and often this means they need to represent other people. A good example would be a leader heading a charity or organisation that engages in humanitarian work.

For such individuals leading may be a secondary and necessary aspect to achieve an overall goal, rather than arising out of a desire to control and dominate others *per se*. Servant leaders can sometimes take the role of a partner or confidant to his or her followers.

This view also relates to the concept of 'authentic leadership', which focuses on the shared values between the leaders and their followers (Avolio, 2007). While servant leadership is effective as a style in certain situations, its wide generalisability and the effectiveness of servant leadership is more contentious in some contexts. For example, in a crisis situation, having a more authoritarian style of leadership may be more effective over a short duration, particularly when people simply need to be told what to do and to do it without any available time for debate. Nevertheless, regardless of any discussions about the importance, validity or generalisability of the servant leader concept, it does remind us of a very important point about leadership. In our view, leadership isn't necessarily about people who have been formally appointed as leaders, or who have the appropriate status and reputation. Effective leadership qualities *can* be displayed by people who don't have the official status or recognition and this is very important to remember.

For practitioners, this subtlety between officially designated leaders and *de facto* non-appointed leaders is sometimes overlooked. Understanding the behavioural characteristics which increase the likelihood of someone being an effective leader is crucial regardless of whether you're working with someone with an official leadership role or not. We would recommend that practitioners are mindful of this; the individual you are working with may not have the official designation of a leader, but this doesn't mean that they couldn't or wouldn't show leadership qualities in the right context. Similarly, just because somebody reaps the benefits of their leader status, it doesn't necessarily mean that they will display the characteristics to lead effectively!

Transformational and Transactional Leadership

One of the prevailing modern approaches to leadership is based on the concepts of 'transformational' and 'transactional' leadership. In broad terms Transformers tend to favour a leadership style which brings about change, whereas Transactors focus more on existing goals. Transformers tend to engender success by inspiring their followers, enhancing motivation and promoting individual responsibility and ownership of work. They also give individualised consideration to the strengths and weaknesses of the people who work for them. Transactors focus on achieving success by exchanging and negotiating benefits with their followers, as well as clarifying their role and responsibilities through a reward and punishment system.

In one of the most widely used transformational leadership models, Bass and Avolio (1989) include the transactional concept of 'laissez-faire' leadership. This is the 'hands-off' approach to leadership, whereby individuals are given freedom and autonomy in their work to set their own goals and drive their own success. Such a style may be useful in certain circumstances, for example where individuals are competent, motivated and trustworthy. However, some researchers such as Gill (2006) have questioned whether a laissez-faire approach is a leadership style at all.

A number of researchers (e.g. Sergiovanni, 1992) have suggested that the transformer–transactor distinction may reflect the difference between leadership and management, with the transformational style representing leadership and the transactional style being more closely aligned to management. Good management is sometimes viewed as 'doing things right', while good leadership is 'doing the right things'.

Field Marshall William Slim, the British military commander, eloquently summarised this view in 1957 (p. 7):

"There is a difference between leaders and management. Leaders represent one of the oldest, most natural and most effective of all human relationships. Managers are a later product, with neither so romantic nor so inspiring a history. Leadership is of the spirit, compounded of personality and vision; its practice is an art. Management is of the mind, more a matter of accurate calculation of statistics, methods, timetables and routine; its practice is a science. Managers are necessary; leaders are essential."

It has also been suggested that leadership is more important at the highest levels of an organisation's function, whereas management is more important at intermediate levels, although there is evidence which suggests that transformational leadership is effective at all organisational levels (Lowe & Kroeck, 1996), but simply occurs less commonly at lower levels (Tichy & Uhich, 1984). Many researchers have linked personality to transformational/transactional leadership and Judge and Bono's research (2004) showed some support for this. Their meta-analysis found positive relationships between the Big Five personality factors and ratings of transformational leadership. The strongest relationship found was for Extraversion (with an average correlation of .24). These researchers noted that "given the relative strength of extraversion in both this meta-analysis of transformational leadership and a prior meta-analysis of leadership emergence–effectiveness it seems that extraversion is a trait that shows robust relations with both leadership outcomes and rated leadership behaviours" (Judge & Bono, 2004, p. 908).

Alimo-Metcalfe and Alban-Metcalfe (2005) built on the existing transformational leadership approach by producing a model which focuses on 'nearby' rather than 'distant' approaches to leadership. This introduced concepts such as servant leadership, distributed leadership and an individual's workplace development to the transformational leadership literature. An important contribution from these researchers was to use samples including leaders who are female and/or from ethnic groups which have not been commonly (or adequately) represented in the leadership research literature.

Others, such as de Jager (2012), have equally pointed out that there is a lack of information about leadership potential across different generational samples. There has been some research into leadership and age (e.g. Kabacoff & Stoffey, 2012). Typically, younger leaders are found to have greater energy, to be more open to change and more focused on results than older leaders, who are contrastingly calmer, more considered and more focused on the development of others. However, Kabacoff and Stoffey also acknowledged that the methods typically employed in such studies are purely correlational and descriptive, rather than shedding light on causal differences between generational samples.

The concept of the transformational leader has led to research focusing in greater depth on a leader's charisma and how they develop engagement and motivation in their followers. The transformational and charismatic leadership concepts overlap in a number of ways, but perhaps the main difference is that while transformational leaders are likely to want to produce change in order to improve performance, a charismatic leader may not wish to change anything. Charismatic leaders engage their followers using such styles as charm, persuasion and self-confidence (Bryman, 1992). Some research has suggested that charismatic leadership does bring demonstrable advantages as a style of leadership – such as having a positive impact on a business's profit (Rowold & Laukamp, 2009). In the workplace, a commonly cited example of a charismatic leader is Steve Jobs. Indeed, journalist and entrepreneur Michael Wolff once described Jobs as "the last charismatic individual" (Isaacson, 2011, p. 523).

Another example showing the importance of charisma in leadership is highlighted by its lack in one of Peter Saville's experiences travelling on a transatlantic flight with a large party, including young children. Smoke began to fill the cabin of the aircraft and concerned cabin crew were soon running up and down the aisle trying to discover the cause of the smoke wafting across the rows of seats. After what seemed an eternity, the captain was heard to clear his throat over the address system and announced with more than a little hesitancy:

"Unfortunately we appear to have some malfunction causing smoke in the aircraft. I have decided therefore to try to make it to the Azores. Please keep calm in the circumstances." Then he turned the audio system off.

"Try," Peter thought, "*Try*?" Why on earth didn't he say "We are *going* to land in the Azores?" It was then that he was reminded that effective leaders sometimes have to deliver a distorted version of the truth in a charismatic and convincing way. How often must a leader reinterpret the facts to achieve an outcome? "We can do this, guys, we can do this!" a charismatic and inspiring leader may say, when they know there is little chance of doing so. Having a level of realistic pessimism is not always good in a leader, at least not openly to others at any rate. (Peter thankfully lived to tell the tale of the smoking aircraft and the flight landed with no problems!) In short, charismatic optimism can boost team morale and sometimes the apparently impossible can actually be achieved. Many a battle has been won against all the odds with such a leader at the helm.

On the other hand, there are also potential downsides of charismatic leadership. For one thing, where morale is so closely associated with the leader there is a risk that removing the leader can lead to a collapse in their troops' motivation. From the perspective of succession planning this is of course a problem; in our view, part of successful leadership is about effectively organising one's own demise.

Another potential issue with charismatic leaders is that they may be viewed by others as self-promoting, manipulative or even insincere and so charisma may not, in some circumstances, be a leadership style which is desirable. Researchers such as Veldsman (2012) have suggested that toxic leadership can occur when such strong leadership styles are sufficiently intense, frequent, far-reaching and of a lengthy duration to have a negative impact across an organisation. Veldsman speculates that there is a risk of such toxic forms of leadership becoming cloned and inadvertently recruited for when such practices become institutionalised and part of 'the way things are done around here.' One only needs to think of some apparently charismatic but deeply toxic leaders, such as Hitler or Mussolini, who were able to persuade populations to support their causes in order to appreciate the potential devastating impact of toxic leadership. The top executives at Enron are often given as a business case study of the impact of toxic leadership, in that they created and sustained a culture sanctioning systematic and organised accounting fraud that ultimately led to the bankruptcy of the corporation.

Individual Differences and Leadership Effectiveness

Leadership research has certainly come a long way since its beginnings and the recent move to focus on the impact of leadership in work-relevant contexts is an important step. However, this field of research often tends to focus on general concepts, and leadership theories are often more descriptive than explanatory. There may well be people who are great/transformational/charismatic and these people may well be effective leaders, but what are the individual differences that make one person so and another person not? In our view leadership research grinds to a halt if the influence of other individual differences such as intelligence and personality are ignored.

At the turn of the 20th century, researchers had begun to notice that leadership was in part similar across various situations. Terman (1904), for example, reported that children who emerged as leaders of their peers across different situations could be differentiated from other children in terms of individual characteristics, including speech and fluency. Thanks in part to the more recent agreement on the structure of personality and the increased accuracy in the measurement of individual differences, a number of such differences have been shown to have an impact on leadership.

Intelligence and Leadership

Various researchers have proposed a link between intelligence and leadership effectiveness. In 1920 Yoakum and Yerkes authored a book called *Army Mental Tests* which documented two intelligence tests that had recently been developed and used in World War One: the Army Alpha and the Army Beta. These were administered to over two million soldiers in order to identify those men who were suited to specific roles, including leadership positions. Links between intelligence and leadership have been shown in both classic studies (Stogdill, 1948) and more recent studies (Judge et al., 2004). Many wellknown models of intelligence (cf: Spearman, 1904; Binet & Simon, 1905; Wechsler, 1958) have been applied to research investigating leadership, with relationships found between intelligence and leadership effectiveness (Judge et al., 2004). These researchers carried out a meta-analysis of 151 independent samples of data to look at the aggregate relationship between intelligence and leadership. They found a corrected correlation of .27 between intelligence and leadership success.

It seems to us that while intelligence does have an important role to play in leadership, it is important to remember that other factors such as situation and context, as explored earlier, do too.

Personality and Leadership

A major analysis carried out by Judge et al. (2002) revealed a relatively strong relationship between the Big Five factors of personality and leadership success. This research suggested that Extroversion is the best Big Five predictor of someone's likelihood of being a successful leader. Levin and Turner (2009) argued that extroversion and conscientiousness are particularly important. They summarised the research into dispositional traits and leadership by suggesting that people who show signs of being gregarious and assertive, who demonstrate high energy and who are organised, self-disciplined and dutiful are more likely to emerge as new leaders.

Developing the 3P Leadership Model

It was with this background literature and evidence in mind that the team at Saville Consulting started developing a new leadership model. It draws and expands on the individual differences, situational and people/task concepts which are commonplace in many existing leadership theories. However, the focus in the 3P model shifts to assess the impact of leadership not only on the management of people and tasks, but also the growth of an organisation.

The 3P Leadership Model is designed to harness leadership potential, leadership styles and the situational aspects of leadership in order to provide a comprehensive picture of an individual's likely effectiveness as a workplace leader. The model features 24 leadership styles that are effective in different circumstances and, in parallel, matches each of these styles to a situation to which a given leader is most likely to be suited. The model also presents six broad leadership scales which underpin the general characteristics important for effective leadership across different situations.

Based on our extensive research the leadership scales in the 3P model are grouped under the 3Ps of leadership – Professional leaders, who are likely to be effective at leading in specialist contexts and providing professional or technical knowledge; People leaders who are likely to be effective at managing a wide range of people across teams or functions; and Pioneering leaders, who are likely to be effective at driving success, change and growth. The diagram below provides an overview of the three factors in the 3P leadership model, along with their principle sub-scales.

Figure 1: The 3P Model – Peter Saville/Tom Hopton

The development of this model has been guided by empirical data from conception to conclusion, based on international research on thousands of individuals working across hundreds of different organisations. The 3P model is powered by the Wave Professional Styles questionnaire and therefore benefits from Wave's validation-centric development method.

During the development of the 3P model we sought to clarify the empirical relationships between the six scales and a range of different workplace performance criteria. The original validation (e.g. see Hopton et al., 2014) was based on 308 individuals who completed Wave Professional Styles and for whom a set of independent performance ratings was collected concurrently from a stakeholder. We specified *a priori* which criteria each leadership construct would be expected to forecast.

The results table below presents the correlations between the six broad leadership scales in the 3P model (Logical, Expert, Adaptable, Dominant, Entrepreneurial, Revolutionary) and a range of different workplace performance criteria. We also show the correlations between the 3Ps of leadership – Professional, People and Pioneering, as well as a composite scale made of all three of the Ps called the 'Universal Leader' scale – with these same performance criteria.

The performance criteria shown in this table come from two different models. The first is Saville Consulting's three factor model of overall work performance, with the three factors being Applying Specialist Expertise, Accomplishing Objectives and Demonstrating Potential. A composite of these three factors called 'Overall Effectiveness' is also shown in the table. The second set of criteria are based on the independent Great Eight model of workplace performance (Kurz & Bartram, 2002). The criterion information for both models was collected through third-party ratings of the workplace performance of the 308 individuals.

In the tables below and on page 20 any *a priori* hypothesised relationships are highlighted in the corresponding scale colour.

Table 1.

Correlations of the Universal Leader composite scale, the 3P leadership factors and their 6 sub-scales against performance criteria (N=308)

	Overall Work Performance							
	Overall Effectiveness		Applying Specialist Expertise		Accomplishing Objectives		Demonstrating Potential	
	r	rc	r	rc	r	rc	r	rc
Universal Leader	.26	.46	.13	.28	.14	.30	.30	.49
Professional Leader	.00	.00	.06	.14	-.09	-.18	.01	.02
Logical	.00	-.01	.03	.07	-.08	-.16	.02	.03
Expert	.01	.01	.08	.17	-.07	-.15	.00	.01
People Leader	.26	.46	.12	.27	.23	.49	.25	.40
Adaptable	.11	.19	.10	.23	.12	.25	.05	.08
Dominant	.26	.47	.10	.22	.22	.47	.27	.44
Pioneering Leader	.22	.39	.07	.15	.12	.25	.29	.47
Entrepreneurial	.23	.41	.07	.16	.16	.34	.28	.45
Revolutionary	.14	.26	.04	.09	.03	.07	.22	.36

	Great Eight Competencies															
	Analysing & Interpreting		Creating & Conceptualising		Interacting & Presenting		Leading & Deciding		Supporting & Cooperating		Adapting & Coping		Organising & Executing		Enterprising & Performing	
	r	rc	r	rc	r	rc	r	rc	r	rc	r	rc	r	rc	r	rc
Universal Leader	.16	.35	.25	.74	.09	.20	.18	.33	-.09	-.19	.15	.32	.14	.34	.25	.55
Professional Leader	.15	.32	.11	.32	-.16	-.34	-.04	-.08	-.08	-.18	.09	.19	.11	.26	.02	.03
Logical	.13	.29	.04	.12	-.15	-.32	-.09	-.18	-.07	-.16	.08	.17	.08	.19	-.01	-.01
Expert	.12	.26	.15	.44	-.13	-.27	.02	.04	-.07	-.15	.08	.16	.11	.27	.03	.07
People Leader	.13	.28	.16	.49	.28	.59	.28	.52	.05	.11	.13	.27	.09	.22	.19	.42
Adaptable	.02	.05	.02	.07	.15	.32	.09	.18	.11	.24	.09	.19	.01	.03	-.03	-.06
Dominant	.15	.32	.19	.56	.27	.57	.29	.55	.01	.03	.11	.24	.11	.25	.24	.53
Pioneering Leader	.06	.12	.19	.58	.06	.14	.11	.21	-.12	-.25	.08	.16	.08	.18	.25	.54
Entrepreneurial	.07	.15	.16	.50	.10	.22	.16	.29	-.07	-.15	.12	.26	.07	.16	.29	.62
Revolutionary	.02	.05	.17	.53	.00	.00	.03	.05	-.14	-.31	.00	.01	.07	.16	.13	.29

'r' represents the uncorrected validity coefficient. 'rc' validities have been corrected for attenuation based on the reliability of the criteria (based on 263 pairs of criterion ratings). No further corrections were applied (e.g. restriction of range, predictor unreliability). Any raw correlation higher than .12 is statistically significant at the $p<.05$ level (two tailed) and any raw correlation higher than .10 is statistically significant at the $p<.05$ level (one tailed).

The results provided validity evidence supporting the 3P model. They suggest that while there are different types of leaders which can be effective in different situations, the most effective leaders tend to score high on the primary scales of the 3P model.

Conclusion

The leadership literature which we have explored here has provided a wealth of useful information that has been consolidated into the new 3P model of leadership. Our review of the existing literature has culminated in the combined approach of having both a broad 3P leadership overview in the Saville Consulting model, as well as more specific information about the styles and situations to which a specific leader may be suited. The 3P Leadership Model therefore draws extensively on established theory to help answer questions about both general leadership potential and leadership effectiveness in specific situations.

This combined approach has clear practical implications. Among other things, such a leadership model addresses the major issues of identifying which individuals possess the behavioural tendencies that increase their chances of becoming a successful leader, whose leadership style is appropriate for a given situation, and where to place chosen leaders in order to enhance organisational effectiveness. We would argue that these are critical considerations for any practitioner working in the leadership space. The 3P model provides a means to support such activities as selecting leaders, succession planning, coaching and development and assessing leader–environment fit.

The new 3P model consolidates many fascinating and useful strands of extant research to create a demonstrably valid, practical and intelligible method for assessing leadership effectiveness.

Acknowledgements

The primary development team of the 3P Leadership Model comprised Peter Saville, Rab MacIver, Rainer Kurz, Tom Hopton, Jake Smith and Sarah Chan. Thanks to these individuals and everyone else who has been involved.

References

Alimo-Metcalfe, B., & Alban-Metcalfe, J. (2005). Leadership: Time for a new direction? *Leadership, 1*(1), 51-71.

Avolio, B.J. (2007). Promoting more integrative strategies for leadership theory-building. *American Psychologist, 62*(1), 25-33.

Bass, B. M., & Avolio, B. J. (1989). *Manual for the multifactor leadership questionnaire.* Palo Alto, CA: Consulting Psychologists Press.

Binet, A. & Simon, T. (1905). Méthodes nouvelles pour le diagnostic du nouveau intellectuel des anormaux. *L'Année Psychologique, 11*, 191-244.

Blake, R., & Mouton, J. S. (1964). *The Managerial Grid: The Key to Leadership Excellence*. Houston, TX: Gulf Publishing Co.

Bolden, R. (2004). *What is Leadership?* Leadership South West, Research Report, 1-36.

Bryman, A. (1992). *Charisma and Leadership in Organisations*. London: Sage.

de Jager, W. (2012 October). The Use of Evidence Based Assessments to Predict and Manage Risk for Senior and Executive Leadership Succession. Presented at the University of Johannesburg's Annual Conference in Leadership in Emerging Countries, Johannesburg, South Africa, 2012.

Furr, R. M., & Funder, D. C. (2004). Situational similarity and behavioural consistency: Subjective, objective, variable-centred, and person-centred approaches. *Journal of Research in Personality, 38*, 421-447.

Gill, R. (2006). *Theory and Practice of Leadership*. London: SAGE Publications.

Greenleaf, R. K. (1977). *Servant leadership*. Mahwah, NJ: Paulist Press.

Hersey, P., & Blanchard, K. H. (1969). Life cycle theory of leadership. *Training & Development Journal, 23*(5), 26-34.

Hopton, T., Saville, P., MacIver, R., & Smith, J. (2014). The Universal Leader: Validating the new 3P model of leadership. Presented at the British Psychological Society Division of Occupational Psychology Annual Conference, Brighton, UK, January 2014.

Isaacson, W. (2011). *Steve Jobs*. London, UK: Little, Brown Book Group.

Judge, T. A., Bono, J. E., Ilies, R., & Gerhardt, M. W. (2002). Personality and Leadership: A Qualitative and Quantitative Review. *Journal of Applied Psychology, 87*(4), 765-780.

Judge, T. A., & Bono, J.E. (2004). Personality and Transformational and Transactional Leadership: A meta-analysis. *Journal of Applied Psychology, 89*(5), 901-910.

Judge, T. A., Colbert, A. E., & Ilies, R. (2004). Intelligence and leadership: a quantitative review and test of theoretical propositions. *Journal of Applied Psychology, 89*(3), 542-552.

Kabacoff, R. I., & Stoffey, R. W. (2012). Age Differences in Organizational Leadership. The Management Research Group, Portland, USA. Retrieved from http://www.mrg.com/uploads/PDFs/age_and_leadership_2012.pdf.

Kurz, R., & Bartram, D. (2002). Competency and individual performance: Modelling the world of work. In I. T. Robertson, M. Callinan, & D. Bartram (Eds.), *Organizational effectiveness: The role of psychology* (pp. 227-255). Chichester: Wiley.

Levin, I., & Turner, R. (2009). Can leaders really be "developed?" *The California Psychologist, 42*(1), 2.

Lowe, K. B., & Kroeck, K. G. (1996). Effectiveness correlates of transformation and transactional leadership: A meta-analytic review of the MLQ literature. *Leadership Quarterly,* 7(3), 385-425.

Mischel, W., Shoda, Y., & Mendoza-Denton, R. (2002). Situation-Behavior Profiles as a Locus of Consistency in Personality. *Current Directions in Psychological Science, 11*(2), 50-54.

Rowold, J., & Laukamp, L. (2009). Charismatic Leadership and Objective Performance Indicators. *Applied Psychology: An International Review, 58*(4), 602-621.

Saville, P., & Hopton, T. (2009). *Talent: Psychologists personality test elite people.* Jersey: Saville Consulting Group.

Schimmoeller, L. J. (2010). Leadership Styles in Competing Organizational Cultures. *Leadership Review, 10*(2), 125-141.

Sergiovanni, T. J. (1992). *Moral Leadership: Getting to the Heart of School Improvement* (1st Ed.). San Francisco, CA: Jossey-Bass.

Slim, W. (1957). Leadership in Management. *Australian Army Journal, 102*, 5-13. Retrieved from http://www.army.gov.au/~/media/Content/Our%20future/Publications/AAJ/1950s/1957/AAJ_102_Nov_1957.pdf.

Spearman, C. (1904). General intelligence objectively determined and measured. *American Journal of Psychology, 15*(2), 201-293.

Stogdill, R. (1948). Personal Factors Associated with Leadership: A Survey of the Literature. *Journal of Psychology, 25*, 35-69.

Terman, L. M. (1904). A Preliminary Study in the Psychology and Pedagogy of Leadership. *Journal of Genetic Psychology, 11*, 413-51.

Tichy, N., & Uhich, D. (1984). The leadership challenge: A call for the transformational leader. *Sloan Management Review, 26*(1), 59-68.

Veldsman, T. (2012 October). The Growing Cancer Endangering Organisations: Toxic Leadership. Presented at the University of Johannesburg's Annual Conference in Leadership in Emerging Countries, Johannesburg, South Africa, 2012.

Wechsler, D. (1958). *The Measurement and Appraisal of Adult Intelligence* (4th Ed.). Baltimore: Williams & Witkins.

Yoakum, C. S., & Yerkes, R. M. (1920). *Army Mental Tests.* New York, NY: H. Holt & Company.

Zaccaro, S. J. (2007). Trait-based perspectives of leadership. *American Psychologist, 62*(1), 6-16.

EMBODIED LEADERSHIP: A SOMATIC VIEW ON LEADERSHIP DEVELOPMENT

Peter Hamill

Think about your most embarrassing moment – okay, maybe not the *most* embarrassing moment, but something that affected you. Take a moment and really get that back into your mind.

What you'll probably notice is that remembering this moment doesn't just bring back a cognitive, rational memory as purely thought, but you feel a version of what you felt at that time. Perhaps you wanted the ground to open up and swallow you whole, or wished you could be invisible! The memory is stored with something akin to an emotional soundtrack that you re-experience on recall.

These emotional soundtracks are what neuroscientist, Antonio Damasio (2006), refers to as somatic markers. So why do we store emotional soundtracks in this way? Basically they are a means by which evolution has equipped us to deal efficiently with different situations.

Imagine yourself in a complex social situation. You don't have time to analyse everyone, their relationships with you, with each other, the political dimensions, if this is a work or organisation context, etc. Your neo-cortex doesn't have time to do all of that cognitive work, so the sub-cortical regions of the brain activate somatic markers corresponding to similar historical situations and we experience the appropriate emotional soundtrack.

So, if it's a situation which could be embarrassing, the soundtrack of your embarrassing moments will play and you will react by taking action to attempt to ensure that you are not embarrassed. This simple and elegant solution evolved for our safety walking in tribes on the savannahs, not for dealing with today's complex social situations.

But before we get into the unintended consequences of this process, it's important to understand that it is not conscious. (We use conscious processes when we analyse a situation in depth with our neo-cortex.) Instead it originates in the older regions of the brain, such as the brain-stem, amygdala and hypothalamus. It communicates directly with our bodies where it generates the feelings that we experience. So this is a pre-conscious process, which gets our attention through our feelings, rather than through our thoughts.

So what happens when we experience these feelings? Basically, we react to discomfort by making ourselves more comfortable, just like when you scratch an itch or put on a sweater when you're cold. And, it gets more interesting! Have you ever realised that you had an itch when you're already scratching it? This is reasonably common – we often react to make ourselves more comfortable without being aware we possessed the discomfort.

The same applies with somatic markers. We react to the emotional soundtrack that's playing and we make ourselves comfortable, often without being aware that we were experiencing discomfort. When we then ask people why they did something, they will either respond with an honest answer – 'it just felt like the right thing to do' – or they post-rationalise a reason as to why. Psychologists have been telling us for a long time that humans post-rationalise much of their behaviour. Through Damasio's work on understanding somatic markers we can now see the mechanism for this.

So how much control do these somatic markers have over our behaviour? This is an interesting question to consider. My argument is that our personality is basically a series of somatic markers that have a strong hold over us. Let's take the following example (a version of one in Strozzi-Heckler, 1997, pp. 19-29):

Imagine a young child coming out of nursery/kindergarten, moving towards his mother, the object of love and safety. In the next garden there's an old, grumpy dog, that the teachers/carers have warned the children to stay away from, as it might bite them. For this child, this has produced a fear of the dog.

As the child runs towards his mother, the dog starts barking. The mother has come from work and, with multiple concerns in her head, doesn't even hear the dog. The child does, and starts to cry. The mother picks him up and comforts him, trying to find out what is wrong. The child can't express what is wrong, and the dog keeps barking so the child keeps crying.

This goes on for some time and eventually the mother, reaching some level of exasperation with an upset she sees no reason for, says: 'If you don't stop crying, I'll put you down.' The child keeps crying, and eventually the mother puts him down.

In this moment the child is separated from safety in what he perceives as a moment of danger, so he learns at a deep level that he made the wrong move. He wants to reconnect with his mother, so what does he do? To stop crying, he tightens his diaphragm, brings the breathing into his upper chest, tightens the jaw, throat and eyes, which stops the expression of the emotion, and, as I will explore later, the feeling of the emotion (by changing the musculature). Now his chin will wobble a little, and he may quietly sob, but the big emotional outburst is contained.

The mother then picks up the child, consoles him again, reinforcing the message that crying was wrong, and that holding in the emotion was correct. (This is by no means an attack on mothers by the way – this is just to illustrate a point.)

This is the process of creating a somatic marker. This person will now begin to feel uncomfortable around emotional upsets – their own or others – and will respond to this discomfort in the same way, by holding in or containing emotion. If the message to contain emotions is repeated on an ongoing basis, or happens at a particularly significant (or traumatic) moment, then 40 years later you have the man who hasn't cried in 40 years. Over time this just becomes who he is.

This man will have a long term pattern of tightening the diaphragm, shallow breathing, holding the jaw tightly, and tightening the eyes, all of which are required to not feel and express that pattern of emotions. In this way a somatic marker moves from an emotional memory to the shape we take in the world. This is the shape that the person will develop. It is how he will hold himself initially when he feels emotion, but eventually practice will make this become just his normal way of being.

If this man then becomes a manager making others redundant, he will be uncomfortable seeing the emotion that others will experience. He cannot be comfortable with his own emotions and, when he is called upon to empathise with another's, he will be unable to. Empathy in this situation requires him to feel the emotion he has spent a lifetime restraining. He may then be accused of being brutal or unfeeling in the process.

All aspects of our personality can be understood in the same way. How to behave in our culture, what gets rewarded by parents and significant adults, what gets rewarded in childhood social groups, etc. All of these combine to give us our way of operating in the world – an habitual pattern of thoughts, feelings and behaviours which we call our personality.

Notice also that, as illustrated above, this personality is embodied. The personality above can be described in conversation as a repression of emotions, but it is also a shape which is created through tension in the muscles. As Nietzsche (2012, p. 314) said:

"Our most sacred convictions, the unchanging elements of our supreme values, are judgements of our muscles."

So if this is how we develop and hold our personalities, what does this mean for personal change and development, and for leadership?

Leadership

"Leadership… remains the most studied and least understood topic in all the social sciences. Like beauty, or love, we know it when we see it but cannot easily define or produce it on demand." Warren Bennis (as cited in Bennis & Nanus, 1985, p. 14)

Let us start by trying to understand the concept of leadership. However, as that quote illustrates, this is not easy. I'm not going to take on the full task of doing so here, but I will clarify an important distinction that is key to leadership from this perspective.

Leadership is not a function of a position: we've all seen people in positions of leadership who haven't led, and we've seen people lead without a position (e.g. Gandhi). Therefore speaking about leadership as a position is flawed.

Leadership is a choice, which implies risk. Leadership involves stepping up and taking responsibility for things around you that otherwise you might complain about – a step from 'why don't they (whoever they are) do something about this?' to 'why don't I do something about this?' Not everyone will like you making this move and it involves breaking solidarity with those around you who just wish to complain; it is a socially risky move.

Leadership therefore requires a purpose. What is important enough for you to take such a risk? What is it that you care about? What will your leadership create, change, make happen or build in the world? This is a radical idea for some senior executives in organisations who are used to justifying their leadership by their position. But really, when you think about it, why would you follow anyone if you do not know where they are leading you?

Leadership and control are very different things. I can control and get people to do what I want through using hierarchies, pay and bonuses. Leadership is different; with leadership people follow you because they join with you in achieving your leadership purpose, rather than because you have levers of control. This creates a paradox for senior executives who have the levers of control at their disposal and need to lead. Stepping away from control towards leadership is a step into the unknown and involves grappling with our 'control issues' and our ability to deal with ambiguity.

In this view, leadership development involves getting clear in terms of what you care about or are committed to as a leader, and then asking who you need to *be* to be able to deliver on that commitment. It becomes a focused, pragmatic process of development to ensure that the leader can be successful in achieving what they care about.

Which brings us back to where we started earlier. Do my somatic markers aid me in my leadership? And if not what can I do about this?

Developing Leadership

A traditional approach would be to do a psychometric, look at some leadership models and do some experiential activity in which we receive feedback on our performance. This combination of information and self-awareness often leads to the individual concerned leaving with a greater appreciation of what they do that doesn't work. Very often, in my experience, people with a strong inner critic have it strengthened in this process. They then have to figure out the process of change for themselves – what does it take to do something different?

Don't get me wrong, information and awareness are good, but they are not enough. I can know that I need to say 'no' more and I can want to say 'no' more yet, in the pressure of the moment, I might be completely unable to take that action. I can know (as in the emotional upset example) that I can't express my emotions or empathise. I might want to empathise because I have received feedback on the impact of my lack of empathy on others and can see business benefits in terms of my team's performance. Yet despite this I still tense up and feel incredibly awkward when someone cries or becomes emotionally upset.

This means that we need to move beyond self-awareness to self-cultivation.

Self-cultivation is the process of learning how to do something different, consistently, even when under pressure. This is also referred to as embodiment – we embody the capacity to do something different. So how do we effectively go about the process of self-cultivation?

We have to address the somatic markers, which are held in the older, more primitive parts of our brains, and which we experience in our bodies. For many reasons it makes sense to do this through the body. The body is where we feel and experience our somatic markers. It's where the behaviour that the somatic markers guide in us is expressed. It's where the shaping that we develop lives, and it's that shaping that we need to work with.

John Coates, an investment banker turned neuroscientist, gives another argument in support of this from neuroscience. The somatic markers will be processed through the older parts of the brain – brain stem, amygdala, hypothalamus etc. – known as sub-cortical regions. These regions have many neurons and connections to our neo-cortex, where we can engage in rational thought and planning, but there are much fewer running in the opposite direction (Coates, 2012, pp. 221-222). This is why it's difficult to think our way into a change, or for a model to truly change behaviour, but why these somatic markers can profoundly impact our thinking. He suggests new training programmes and states (p. 236):

"These training regimes will have to be designed in such a way that they access the primitive brain, not just the rational cortex. Since the body profoundly influences sub-cortical regions of the brain, the new training programmes may turn out to involve a lot more physical exercises than they do at present."

I would go further than Coates and say that in the field of leadership development, not including the body is a mistake. By physical exercises he and I are not referring to the gym exercises that you may do for fitness, but rather exercises that allow us to see and experience our somatic markers, how they drive our behaviours and how we can learn to do something different.

This requires a form of leadership development different from the traditional models, and is based on some fairly simple, although not necessarily easy, principles.

1. Mindfulness – in an embodied way
2. Practice – actually *deliberate embodied practices*

Mindfulness in an embodied way

We need to be able to slow down and see our somatic markers, and the actions that they drive us towards, as they occur within us. This means that we also need to learn to be with our discomforts without trying to fix them or change them; to be comfortable with being uncomfortable.

For many of us this is tough. When we are in a meeting or a social situation and someone says something which in some way diminishes our dignity, we feel it, but often don't fully realise what has happened until later. We then think of all the things we could, or would, or should have said in that moment. Of course, it's too late. Instead, we feel the discomfort in that moment, and pre-consciously respond with whatever our more normal reaction is – withdrawing, arguing, getting grumpy or passive aggressive – whatever that may be.

Mindfulness in this context relates to feeling our discomfort fully – facing it, and the somatic marker that lives inside of us. Sitting with our discomfort we can become aware of two things: one, that no discomfort is forever (that this too shall pass, all on its own without me having to do anything); and two, that we have a choice about our responses to discomfort. This is something no one can be told – we must each learn the reality of it for ourselves, through mindfulness.

In that moment we can choose something different, something other than the reactions we have developed over time to avoid and hide from our discomfort. To use the earlier example, the manager can choose a different response in dealing with emotional upsets, e.g. to relax and be with the other person in their upset, rather than tensing up with his discomfort. It will not be easy, but in sitting with his discomfort rather than reacting to it, he exercises this choice.

Mindfulness practice here refers to two things. First is a traditional process of mindfulness meditation. For our purpose, a meditation that connects with the body, such as paying attention to the breath, is more helpful than one focused on repeating mantras. This is a supporting practice in developing the greater awareness of our discomforts and somatic markers.

The second is called centring. This is a process of being mindful and present, in action, in everyday life. This is supported by the meditation process. It involves us focusing on cultivating the presence and attention of mindfulness in action. (A centring technique is given as an appendix.)

Practice – deliberate embodied practice

In order to get good at empathy, our manager will need to practise. His historical responses are practised to the degree that they are embodied – he doesn't need to think about them or consciously use effort to do them. A new response will take something else from him. It will require effort; it will not be as easy as the previous response. It will require developing an understanding of how he did the previous response and how he can do something different. It will involve practice, but not just any old sort of practice. It's embodied practice and it's deliberate practice. Let me explain what I mean by these concepts.

Deliberate practice

"First, say to yourself what you would be, and then do what you have to do." Epictetus (as cited in Carter, 2012, p. 178)

Many of the ideas that I explore here have their roots in the research and thinking of Anders Ericsson and his colleagues. Ericsson is Professor of Psychology at Florida State University, and is an editor of the Cambridge Handbook of Expertise and Expert Performance. His work has been heavily focused on understanding how expertise and high level performance are developed.

The Cambridge Handbook, mentioned above, includes contributions from more than 100 leading researchers who have studied top level performance in a range of fields, and: "Consistently and overwhelmingly, the evidence showed that experts are always made, not born." (Ericsson et al., 2007, p. 116). So if expertise in any field is made, how do we make ourselves into experts in leadership?

The research provides answers, and it turns out that practice does indeed make perfect (or at least expert). However, it is a particular type of practice, which Ericsson christened "deliberate practice", that makes the difference. Practice and experience are not the same. One can have years of experience and not have engaged in significant deliberate practice.

In a Harvard Business Review article, Ericsson and his colleagues write:

"To illustrate this point let's imagine that you are playing golf for the first time. In the early phases, you try to understand the basic strokes and focus on avoiding gross mistakes (like driving the ball into another player). You practise on the putting green, hit balls at a driving range, and play rounds with others who are most likely novices like you. In a surprisingly short time (perhaps 50 hours), you will develop better control and your game will improve. From then on, you will work on your skills by driving and putting more balls and engaging in more games, until your strokes become automatic: you'll think less about each shot and play more from intuition. Your golf game now is a social outing, in which you occasionally concentrate on your shot. From this point on, additional time on the course will not substantially improve your performance, which may remain at the same level for decades." (Ericsson et al., 2007, p. 118)

This parallels the process of learning to drive. After a period of time driving becomes automatic; we focus on where we are going, and our driving performance does not substantially improve. This parallel is seen in the medical profession, where younger doctors can at times outperform more experienced ones in diagnosing rare diseases, as they have more recently learnt about them and can more easily remember them (Ericsson, 2008).

So, say I want to improve my golf game, and I go to the driving range and spend an hour hitting a bucket of balls down the range. I know that it's important to keep my head still during the swing and to choose a target. I go through a range of clubs and hit the balls, some better than others. I then go home feeling virtuous about having practised. However, according to the research this will not substantially improve my performance – I have more experience of golf, but I have not engaged in any deliberate practice.

What this lacks are the clear structures of deliberate practice that have been outlined by Ericsson (2008) and that are understood, at least implicitly, by top performers.

These are:

- Designed activities to improve performance, usually with the benefit of teachers or coaches. Top performers work with a series of activities designed, most often by coaches or teachers, to improve their performance. The design has to take into account the pre-existing knowledge of the learner and to stretch them appropriately. Too much stretch risks disillusionment; too little and there will not be significant progress. The activities take some aspect of the person's current ability and stretch it to correct some weakness or improve performance. Some activities may not seem to relate clearly to the performance, yet may still be essential, e.g. the Olympic gold medalist Mo Farah was much more successful in long distance running after improving his upper body strength, which may not seem intuitively obvious.
- Repeated practice: this is where the famous 10,000 hours rule comes in to play. However it's not 10,000 hours of practice, but 10,000 hours of deliberate practice that makes the difference.

- Feedback on results: in leadership this requires the support of coaches, teachers and others who can give us honest feedback that helps us understand our impact.
- Concentration and mental demands: deliberate practice involves practising on the edge of our abilities. It is about constantly focusing on how we can push ourselves further and improve – a level of mental concentration above that of doing what we already know. It requires fighting off the temptations of automaticity. When we learn to drive it becomes automatic for us, and we focus on where we are going. And for many of us this is enough. However, if I want to be a Formula 1 champion, I need to go beyond this, and it turns out that running on automatic is a problem. On automatic I am no longer clear and focused on my learning. I am repeating and reinforcing what I already know – that which I do well enough to do automatically. This is having more experience, without deliberate practice, and is just as relevant in the realms of influencing at board-level, coaching team members or pitching for business. Bringing our attention and full concentration to our practice is essential for it to be worthwhile.
- Not necessarily fun: this level of practice isn't always the most fun and easiest way to practice. It's easier to do what we know how to do well, for example, playing a familiar tune. It's harder to do what we find difficult and challenging. Practising at our edge gives less short-term satisfaction, although the longer-term rewards are greater.

Embodied practice

Practising in Embodied Leadership refers to deliberate practices to forward our leadership. In the example of the manager who is unable to empathise and tenses up when others display emotion, mindfulness allows him to feel the somatic marker, and deliberate practice involves relaxing the physical tension generated in that moment and practising different moves such as empathising. Here we are focused on how someone does something, and how they can learn to do something different.

Working with Embodied Leadership

Working with Embodied Leadership involves both mindfulness and practice. Working with mindfulness builds our capacity to experience our somatic markers and avoid habitual responses. With embodied deliberate practice we develop our capacity to respond in different ways – ways which are more appropriate to achieving our commitments as leaders.

As I mentioned earlier, much of our behaviour is post-rationalised. In fact so much appears to be post-rationalised that it has caused some to challenge whether we truly have free will. My argument is that much post-rationalisation is our way of explaining our responses to our somatic markers, and that we often don't act out of free will. We do, however, have the potential to act out of free will if we cultivate that ability – it is not a given that we will ever act from free will, it requires something from us. Embodied Leadership development is the cultivation of free will in service of our ability to deliver on our commitments as leaders.

Case study

To illustrate the principles at work, I will use a case example of someone with whom I have worked (details have been altered to ensure confidentiality).

Paul is a senior manager in a global business. Paul has been very successful, partly due to his ability to get things done. He creates pressure for himself to achieve by dividing tasks up and setting tight deadlines, thereby creating tension for himself. This tension drives him forward and ensures that he is productive.

He is very concerned with being successful and being seen to be successful, and monitors the sales of houses in his area vigilantly, always wondering when he can afford the next house upgrade and the new car.

The description so far is perhaps unremarkable for many in our society

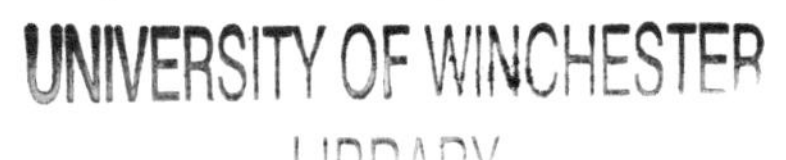

and organisations. Indeed, I have witnessed coaches encouraging people to adopt similar strategies to Paul's to be more productive.

However, for Paul, the result of this is living in a state of semi-permanent stress. His fingernails are bitten down, he holds his body taut with tension and has difficulty remaining present – skipping on to the next thing in his mind. He also leans back in his posture slightly, always distancing himself from others.

Crucially, when working with him, he identifies that he does not know what he cares about. There is no sense of something that he cares about as a leader driving him forward; it is all about meeting deadlines and a compulsive need to perform. He has substituted the intrinsic motivations with extrinsic ones, looking for those to tell him whether or not he is successful.

Our emotions tell us what we care about, and Paul has disconnected very successfully from his emotions. Life has become rather flat as a result – there are no great lows, but there are also no great highs.

His business is going through a culture change initiative, from being top-down hierarchical to being more entrepreneurial. He is being encouraged to motivate, empower and inspire those he works with, however he cannot identify what motivates him and he is not inspired himself. He is being asked to step into leadership, rather than working with the levers of control.

In exploration of his detachment from his emotions a memory comes back to him of crying as a boy and feeling judgement from his father and other men, and a sense of shame at revealing his emotions. This is the somatic marker that was established for him, and reinforced by subsequent events.

He explored somatically the way he isolated himself from his emotions and this included:

- leaning back
- a visceral feeling of withdrawing into his head and out of his body,

which accompanied the leaning back, where all of his attention left his body and entered into his thoughts – a numbing dissociation
- tension throughout his body, especially around the throat and jaw
- a collapsing at the chest

Through experimenting with different shapes and postures, Paul was able to see the shifts that he made and the internal numbness that this created for him. He was then able to practise moving between this shape and one where he was no longer numb, was more present and much more relaxed, through the process of centring.

He began to practise connecting to people. He realised that he maintained an emotional distance through this posture, so he repeatedly practised connecting with the person in front of him, in both work and social situations. This involved noticing his somatic marker reaction, becoming comfortable with his discomfort and practising a posture in which he was connected to himself and therefore able to connect to the other. This was a challenging process that he described as like running a marathon every day.

Over time he was able to connect more to his emotions and feel more joy and sadness, and part of his journey included processing unfinished grief and sadness from the past.

What this opened up for him was a greater connection to what he cared about and he found a connection to what he cared about as a leader, one which inspired and motivated him. He formulated a declaration, a statement of his commitment as a leader, and then shared this with his team. This helped him to change how he motivated himself at work, and engaged him in a different relationship with his team.

The impact of connecting with others and sharing his leadership commitment allowed his team to step up. They gave him more feedback on how he could step back and support them more effectively, rather than the monitoring and controlling he had been doing. Team meetings changed as the team moved from an unspoken agreement not to challenge each other in front of the boss, to an open conversation where they explored issues facing the business together, and openly challenged each other.

This took time. Time for Paul to see and feel his somatic markers, time for him to practise connecting with others and to build his tolerance for the intensity of real connection with others, time to get in touch with what he cared about and clarify his leadership declaration, and time to practise new behaviours. It wasn't all plain sailing, and it wasn't easy, but it worked. As well as being more effective as a leader, Paul now reports greater satisfaction and happiness from life.

Results from Embodied Leadership

Working with Embodied Leadership takes an individual through the process of gaining clarity on what they are committed to as a leader, and then working on cultivating the self that they need to be to deliver on that commitment.

I have been working for many years with the US-based Strozzi Institute on their Embodied Leadership programmes, and they have tracked the success of people in achieving their leadership commitments made on their programmes. Now this varies. Commitments are made across very different lengths of time, so some have not been achieved because of the time duration involved. However, their tracked success rate is around 88%. This is significantly high for leadership development programmes and gives a sense of the power of this way of working.

At some level, this way of working with the body in leadership development is a little weird – like Mo Farah working on his upper body strength. However, the framework I have set out here shows that it is also a pragmatic way to focus on understanding how I do what I do, and how I can do something different which will deliver the results I desire. And the results speak for themselves.

Appendix: Centring

I will take you through a basic centring process standing, as in this posture you will be able to have greater physical awareness than when seated. When you have learnt the process you will be able to apply it when seated.

Dimension 1: Length

Firstly, stand up, put your feet about shoulder-width apart, and let your arms hang down by your sides. Keep your eyes open while you do this. (It may be easier to do this with your eyes closed, but in the middle of an important meeting when you need to be centred you want to be able to practise centring in the moment without having to go away and close your eyes for a few seconds.)

Imagine that someone is pulling on a hair on the top of your head and let your spine stretch out upwards. Visualise it as allowing some air in between the vertebrae of the spinal column.

Relaxing the body

Next you will need to relax downwards – this is about aligning yourself with gravity. Start to notice where you hold yourself up, so that you can develop a sense of where exactly you need to relax in order to centre. Scan down your body from your forehead to your feet and see if you can relax each element your attention passes through: forehead, eyes, jaw, shoulders, chest, stomach, sphincters, legs and feet.

Dimension 2: Width

Next is getting balance right to left. We all have a dominant side, one side where we tend to put more of our weight, so just rock back and forth and find a point where you're putting equal weight on both feet.

Dimension 3: Depth

Then find the balance point front to back. Find the place where your weight is balanced between the balls of your feet and your heels. You're also finding a balance between the present and the future and finding that point where you are in the present.

Bringing your attention to your centre

Now that you are aligned, take some deep breaths, bringing the breath right down into your stomach and breathing out fully. Bring your attention to the body's physical centre of gravity, a point a couple of inches below the navel. Once you are centred notice what you feel from this place and stay with those feelings.

Start off by centring on a regular basis – use a trigger to remind you, such as your phone ringing, or if you have a watch which beeps every hour. Someone I know who used the phone as their trigger found they had shorter and more focused phone calls as a result. Give this a try for two weeks and notice what's different for you in your life and work.

References

Bennis, W., & Nanus, B. (1985). *Leaders: The Strategies for Taking Charge*. New York, NY: Harper & Row.

Carter, E. (2012). *The Moral Discourses of Epictetus*. London: Ulan.

Coates, J. (2012). *The Hour Between Dog and Wolf: Risk-taking, gut feelings and the biology of boom and bust*. London: Fourth Estate.

Damasio, A. (2006). *Descartes' Error*. London: Vintage.

Ericsson, K. A. (2008). Deliberate practice and acquisition of expert performance: a general overview. *Academic Emergency Medicine, 15*(11), 989-994.

Ericsson, K. A., Prietula, M. J., & Cokely, E. T. (2007). The making of an expert. *Harvard Business Review, 85*(7/8), 114-21.

Nietzsche, F. (2012). *Will to Power: Attempt at a Revaluation of All Values*. London: CreateSpace.

Strozzi-Heckler, R. (1997). *The Anatomy of Change: A way to move through life transitions*. Berkley, CA: North Atlantic Books.

LEADERSHIP FOR SUSTAINABILITY

Scott Lichtenstein & Paul Aitken

Introduction

Our greatest gift as leaders and/or developers of leadership is building resilience to face and adapt to forces often beyond our control. Our diverse personal values, the most powerful of the 'unconscious' forces influencing our willingness to change and ultimate direction of travel, are often neglected when considering human factors.

We will outline the case for leadership values and practices which create the everyday working conditions for sustaining prosperity in careers and collective enterprise. By 'leadership' we mean the social influence over others to encourage change; and by 'sustainability' we mean ongoing adaptation to change and the continuing personal–organisational–community viability this brings. We will also introduce 'leadership agility' as the critical, dynamic capability for producing this necessary adaptation.

At the 'micro' level, personal values and morality-based choices can either facilitate or prevent the emergence of sustainable behaviours, decisions and actions. Values-based communication, relationship building and knowledge exchange are vital to responding in a sustainable way to constant change.

We provide a developmental framework of the 12 research-derived leadership practices that provide the agility to remain continuously viable and demonstrate the power of role modelling through values-led leadership for realising change.

Our 'leadership for sustainability' insights have been framed as four fundamental questions for leaders, to which we offer a first response.

Question 1: Why do personal values matter as part of 'leadership for sustainability'?

Values may encourage or inhibit giving focus and priority to sustainability. We see seven ways (adapted from England & Lee, 1974) in which leaders' (often unconscious) values have impact. Values:

i. influence leaders' perceptions of situations,
ii. affect the solutions they generate,
iii. impact the quantity and quality of interpersonal relationships,
iv. influence perceptions of individual and organisational success,
v. provide a basis for determining ethical behaviour,
vi. affect the extent to which leaders accept or reject particular organisational pressures and goals,
vii. focus and shape managerial performance.

Hambrick and Mason's (1984) upper echelon theory and Finkelstein and Hambrick's (1996, p. 54) extension to it (Figure 1), provide a theoretical model illustrating leaders' personal values as a perceptual filter which ultimately shapes strategic choice, operations and performance.

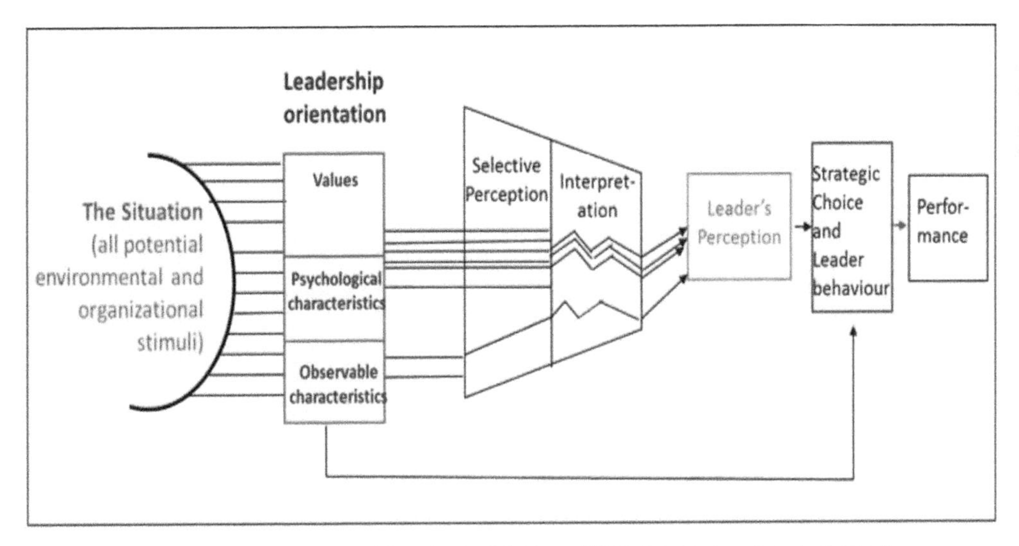

Source: Adapted from Hambrick & Mason (1984), Finkelstein and Hambrick (1996)

Figure 1: Leaders' values and their impact on performance

Our personal value systems and psychological characteristics shape and bias our perceptions. However, values-based motivations, whether in leadership roles or not, are mainly ignored, with an assumption that the power of argument alone will both create and sustain change. Business psychology and systems thinking help to transcend this and so produce more sustainable solutions. Change is difficult, often emotional, and with strong arguments from all sides. In this sense leadership is a social influencing process (Parry, 1998) affecting others as well as the natural world.

Less than 10% of the world's economically active population work for publically owned shareholding limited companies quoted on stock exchanges. There is nevertheless an implicit assumption and business media projection that profit maximisation and accountability to shareholders/owners is the only game in town (Pless, Maak & Waldman, 2012). Experience from our work with over 1000 managers and professionals in Business School and related learning environments across the world tells us it may prove difficult to get future leaders and their educators to recognise alternative perspectives. We are habitual by nature. Social conditioning, incumbent personal values and reward systems incline to the mainstream and restrict our world view.

Our leadership coaching, learning facilitation and research reveals contemporary business discourse to be predicated on a need for personal significance and esteem, primarily focused on feeding ego and maintaining control over all things, human and natural. This narrative is devoid of concern for a well-functioning community operating within its natural eco-system. Economists are increasingly calling for a more sophisticated conceptualisation of capitalism, imbued with the reciprocity and shared reward which creates sustainable prosperity for everyone, contributed to by every living thing (Porter & Cramer, 2011).

The 2014 Edelman Trust Barometer (Edelman, 2014) shows the largest ever gap of trust between business and government since the study began in 2001. From 2009 businesses had to partner with government to regain trust. Today business may be better able to lead the way towards more 'leadership for sustainability' centred solutions, which generate continuing prosperity for all those involved in the enterprise. However, in Britain at least, there is still some way to go. A survey on 'Doing the Right Thing' in business from an ethical behaviour stance (The Times; Raconteur, 17/9/2014) found:

- 38% of customers (of IT solutions) think British businesses are 'not very' or 'not at all' ethical (e.g. they capture short term sales without being entirely honest with customers on price and service level)
- 35% think ethics in business has declined over the last 10 years
- and, most critically for any professional services provider, 70% of the propensity to sustain the sales relationship is dependent on customers' perceptions of the degree to which they are ethically treated.

A values-based approach to 'leadership for sustainability'

The psychological dynamic is best explained, accessed and opened up for potential change, using a grounded personal values perspective which can then be included in leadership development processes, such as coaching.

Leadership values are not simply moral norms but rather are motivational sources of human behaviour that underpin the actions of individuals and groups (Allport, 1961; Maslow, 1970; Rokeach, 1973). As Burns (2003, p. 121) put it, "Leaders embrace values; values grip leaders", and "values play a central role in binding would be leaders and followers, broadening moral frames of reference, and serving variously as a needed unifying and dividing force", plus, "Addressing fundamental questions of human nature, values help to clarify the relations between individualism and collectivism, self-interest and altruism, liberty and equality – issues at the heart of political conflict – and in the process establish a leadership agenda for action". Bean (1993, p. 95) asserts, "Every enterprise is driven by its leaders' individual and collective values, whether those values are understood or unconsciously influential, spoken or unspoken, written or unrecorded." Moreover, the extant literature (e.g. Russell, 2001) indicates the critical importance of the leadership agility practice 'Personal Values Sensitivity', defined as "Tune into all the interests, beliefs and motivational drivers present in important communication and interaction, starting with your own" (McKenzie & Aitken, 2012).

Unfortunately, our general experience of leadership curricula across the world finds development of knowledge-based cognition as the priority, rather than deep reflection on personal values and their often unconscious impact (Aitken, 2004). Devoid of such guided personal insight, the espoused language of leadership and business may change, without actually changing any intentions, decisions, or actions. Our role as leadership developers is to bring to the surface the content, motivational force and impact of personal values.

Question 2: How do diverse personal values colour 'leadership for sustainability'?

Based on values-led leadership research (Aitken, 2004), and employing some illustrative single values items from Schwartz (1992), a typology for values-based leadership development is proposed (Table 1 opposite), using three operational domains of *Self*, *Business* and *Society* to represent the inter-connected change system within which people experience life at work and in general. This system contains six value clusters as set out in Table 1, together with their respective drivers for different forms of individual and organisational behaviour.

Table 1.
Six Leadership Values Clusters

Personal VALUES	Values examples (from Schwartz)	Motivational Direction	Engagement Focus
Needs of the Self			
Self-Approval	WEALTH (material possessions, money); SOCIAL POWER (control over others, dominance); PRESERVING MY PUBLIC IMAGE ('face' and status); RUTHLESS (drive to achieve personal ends); PERSONAL POWER (the right to exercise personal beliefs); SELF CENTRED (putting myself first); EGO DRIVEN (seeking self-esteem)	Motivated by external and self-centred measures of success	Engaged by appealing to self-interest
Fulfilment	MEANING IN LIFE (purpose for living); HUMBLE (modest, self-effacing); CHOOSING OWN PURPOSE (selecting how to live); A SPIRITUAL LIFE (emphasis on spiritual, not material matters); INNER HARMONY (at peace with myself); SELF-DISCIPLINE (self-restraint, resisting temptation); SELFLESS (others' needs before own, compassionate)	Motivated by internal and pro-social measures of success	Engaged by appealing to personal and others' growth
Needs for Business			
Stay Steady	SENSE OF BELONGING (feeling colleagues are closely connected to me); LOYAL (faithful to colleagues); RESPECT FOR TRADITION (preservation of customs, honouring those who have come before); HELPFUL (working for the well-being of others); COLLEGIALITY (accommodating others' ideas and feelings); LEGACY (building a lasting memorial)	Prefers a stable environment with reciprocal respect	Engaged by appealing to sense of belonging
Move Forward	INDEPENDENT (self-reliant, self-sufficient); SUCCESSFUL (achieving, stretching); CURIOUS (interested in everything, exploring); INNOVATION (engaging with novel, creative ideas); OPTIMISTIC (looking at life/work as opportunity); RESOURCEFUL (finding ways to make things happen)	Prefers a fast pace with opportunity for personal impact	Engaged by appealing to

Needs for Society			
World Citizen	A WORLD AT PEACE (free of war/conflict); UNITY WITH NATURE (fitting yourself into nature); DIVERSITY (tolerant of different cultures); RESPECT FOR LIFE (sanctity of human existence); ONE WORLDLINESS (interconnectivity of people); ONE PLANET (sensitive to human impact on Earth)	Connects with the world at large	Engaged by appealing to worldly responsibility
Communal Concern	SOCIAL JUSTICE (correcting injustice, care for the weak); SOCIAL ORDER (stability of society); CIVILITY (courtesy, good manners); CLEAN SURROUNDINGS (responsibility for ensuring quality environs); CIVIC PRIDE (responsibility for maintaining local reputation); NEIGHBOURLY (looking out for those living nearby)	Connects with the local community	Engaged by appealing to community spirit

Consider the link between personal values and sports performance. Research is still preliminary in this area, although it suggests that performance varies by the athlete's personal values. Elite athletes holding the intrapersonal Fulfilment values of enjoyment and personal competence prize personal best performances, essentially competing against themselves. Those with interpersonal esteem-seeking values focus on winning against opponents, i.e. 'for me to win, you have to lose'. In this sense values dictate whether playing well (intrapersonal) is more important than winning (interpersonal). The link with business performance is clear: those who are driven by Self Approval see winning at all costs in the short-term as the goal, viewing maximisation ('sweating the asset') as the means; those who prefer Fulfilment as a guiding value concentrate on building their own and others' performance capability for the long-term, preferring optimisation (win-win for sustainability).

Also, it has been suggested that different sports values vary by national culture. Athletes from Asian cultures have been found to hold more intrapersonal competence values than Australian athletes who hold interpersonal values of winning. This finding mirrors Hofstede (2001) who found national differences between 'Masculine' cultures espousing material success, being ambitious, assertive, competitive and achievement-oriented vs 'Feminine' cultures promoting quality of life, relationships, concern for weaker members and disapproval of high achievers who self-promote.

This underscores the point that members of any human enterprise focused on achieving high performance can engage in the same behaviour for very different intents, based on their personal values. Therefore, values diversity analysis can be used to promote and conduct deeper dialogue about what sits at the heart of performance at individual, organisational (club, team or company) and national cultural levels. Clearly, for those working with international teams it pays to be sensitive to the different operative values driving discretionary improvements, and the individual and collective motivation for delivering continuing outstanding performance.

We discovered the practices of leadership agility from an extensive review of the related research (see all the practice related references in Aitken & Higgs, 2010). The next question considers how these practices underpin sustainability leadership through a comprehensive values-led leadership developmental framework.

Question 3: How do communication, relationship building and knowledge generation-exchange based leadership 'agility' practices provide the bedrock of 'leadership for sustainability'?

Useable knowledge can be constantly created and utilised within and between workplaces and communities by practising the leadership agility practices.

From an analysis of over 200 change leadership research papers over 50 years (Aitken & Higgs, 2010), we have specified the 12 leadership practices which, used dynamically and contextually, create resilience (and therefore sustainable viability) in the face of continuous change at personal, team, organisational and community levels. In a study based on interviews with over 1,500 CEOs worldwide, two primary themes emerged that had not appeared in previous surveys: managing complexity and developing the creative capacity in the organisation to innovate. Both were in response to ever shifting marketplace demands, in a world of escalating turbulence. Speed, combined with flexibility of response and adaptability to change was the CEO's challenge of greatest concern (Adams, Stern & Farthing, 2010).

Since the turn of the 21st century, the pace of change has continued unabated requiring constant learning and intelligent responses by organisations to shifting and evolving employee, customer, shareholder, and stakeholder expectations. Competition for knowledge and our ability to share and co-create it in real time is essential for re-generation and re-invention. The graph in Figure 2 below illustrates that the lifespan of business is shortening. The same applies to work teams and personal careers. Consequently, leadership agility and the organisational-community agility it creates, is vital for delivering sustainable viability.

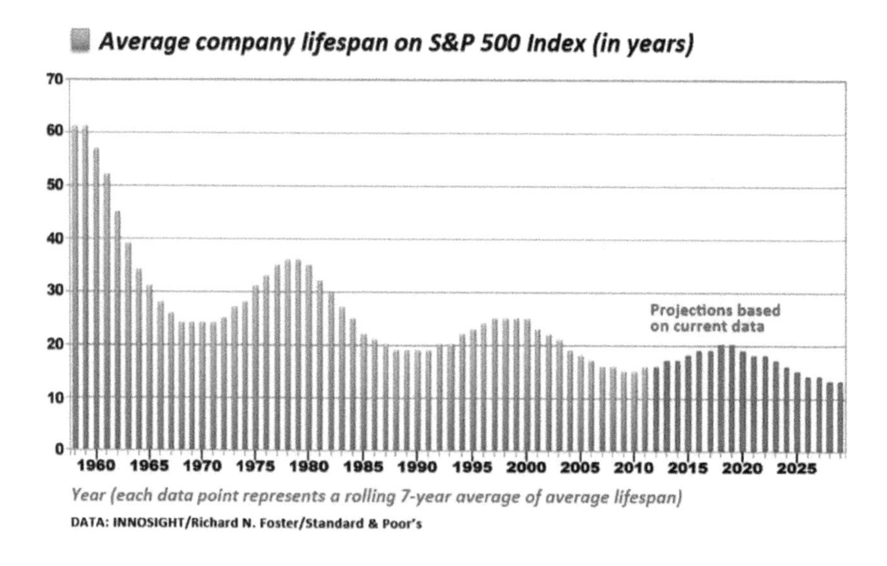

Figure 2: Corporate Longevity

The term 'leadership agility' describes the individual, team and organisational capability to access and utilise a diverse range of connected communications, relationships and knowledge exchange to avoid 'options myopia', and to achieve three things:

i. Noticing and understanding the implications for everyone of changes in the business context (internal and external),
ii. Communicating and using that understanding in a way that enables others to innovate and adapt appropriately, thereby maintaining performance levels during change, and
iii. Delivering sustainable performance improvements by embedding the capacity to change (dynamically) into a work culture and operating system where agile leadership is continuously practised.

These phases represent the natural change cycle of renewal, survival and thriving; with 'sustainability' often overlooked in change programmes, i.e. once the change programme has been completed the cultural and behaviour change reinforcement required to prevent reverting to the 'old' ways is sadly lacking.

Leadership 'agility' breaks down into 12 practices and through this framework we enable managers to examine how change is impacting their context and explore the challenges this presents. We look at each practice in turn relating to predicting, implementing and embedding organisational change. Through this process, learners get a real sense of their everyday priorities in being able to respond and adapt to ever-changing circumstances and conditions. The learning enables managers and subsequently their staff to move towards mastery of leadership agility. Indeed, one of the practices of mastering leadership agility is to support one another in increasing overall leadership capacity; so we also encourage development of collective, as well as individual, leadership. By doing so, managers grow the next generation of leaders.

Using the practices, both separately (to address the immediate change priorities) and in combination (to glue together, reinforce and review the change messages and actions), supports the cultural conditions and climate conducive to knowledge sharing, learning, engagement and collaboration. The role of leadership is to facilitate the growth of these conditions in a way which uses difference, novelty, unfamiliarity, tension between stability and change, in a positive way. Creating this stimulation, adaptation and growth prevents degeneration into the politics, conflict and uncertainty that often leaves people uncomfortable, de-motivated and resistant to change. Using the 12 leadership agility practices as an everyday dynamic, maintaining the link between development and real work will help resolve these issues. This 'in the moment' leadership agility learning is vital for individual, team and whole of organisation survival, thriving and renewal in an interconnected and chaotic world, where people often have competing values.

The 12 leadership agility practices are learned capabilities. They require extensive exposure to and practice in a broad variety of experiences where influencing others is key. This is supported by reflection and personal coaching/team facilitation to produce emotional and mental resilience to change in the learner and those they manage and coach, that develops through continued application over time. Having applied these in over 150 change leadership case studies across the world, we now know it is possible to fast track this elusive capability by focusing on the practices the leader and business need at any particular part of their change cycle.

Daily leader–follower interactions are at the heart of improving and sustaining leadership agility within its context, and by extension the organisation's continuing viability, especially through intense periods of change. Invariably, under these often trying circumstances, the purpose and values of leadership and the organisation itself come under scrutiny. Reputations can be enhanced or damaged in the process.

Using the leadership agility practices framework, sustainable leadership learners can better:

- understand the mechanisms which underpin outstandingly productive leader-follower relationships
- understand the nature, operational detail and potential impact of 12, evidence based, leadership agility practices
- understand the impact of leadership purpose and personal values on leadership practice, organisational objectives and wanted outcomes
- explore the key principles and processes of sustaining a viable business during constant change

- produce an action plan for enhancing their own contextualised leadership agility practice and related business development
- track progress towards mastery, and therefore sustainable individual, team and organisational success.

Leaders need to be personally agile to cope with different phases of change and the complexity of human behaviour, motivation and interests. Utilising values as their guiding compass and the appropriate leadership practices helps people learn and change, whilst securing and sustaining elite performance. Our coaching/facilitation approach assists managers to develop, select and combine twelve different leadership practices to suit the particular demands of the change challenge confronting them.

The three phases of change are Predicting, Implementing and Embedding transitions. The 12 practices link with leadership questions, outlined in Tables 2-4 below, which need to be continuously asked to increase the overall quality and quantity of learning and to remain sustainably viable.

Leadership agility has been de-constructed for ease of development, however, the framework should be seen as a dynamic menu. The leadership agility meta-skill is to diagnose and respond to change as it unfolds in different contexts over time. Our development process for leaders (emergent or already active) always starts with 'Personal Values Sensitivity'. Personal values always colour the communications, relationships and knowledge exchange we are involved in, and interact with our inner 'moral' compass, especially during periods of intentional change.

PHASE 1 – Predicting transitions (Strategy-Project Initiation/Development) PRACTICES 1-5

- Here the focus is on building the individual and collective (values guided) intelligence to detect shifts in the internal and external operating environment, particularly within employees, stakeholders and customers, in order to guide strategic responses.

Table 2.

'Agile Leadership' Phase 1: Predicting Transitions

LEADERSHIP FOR SUSTAINABILITY	AGILITY generating Practices and accompanying Phases of Change	Assessing current level of agility: reflective questions
PHASE 1 – Predicting transitions		
PRACTICE 1 – Personal Values Sensitivity	Tune into all the interests, beliefs and motivational drivers present in important communication and interaction, starting with your own	Can you identify the personal values which drive, motivate and guide your own work, students' learning, and colleagues' contributions?
PRACTICE 2 – Sense Make-Give	Generate the knowledge and insights which provide potential ways forward and make these understandable for others	Can you articulate the current vision, mission, strategy, and business plan? How well do you explain this in a way that makes all feel they play a key part?
PRACTICE 3 – Create Learning	Constantly learn from others and encourage others' learning so you can address problems and leverage opportunities as they arise	What do you have in place to ensure you stay abreast of all the knowledge which you need now and for the future?
PRACTICE 4 – Mindful of Impact	Engage in open, frank and reflective conversations before arriving at critical decisions	How do you make sure your ideas remain open to challenge?
PRACTICE 5 – Emotional Intelligence	Pick up, manage and use the emotions generated in interaction, including those in yourself	How tuned in are you to the feelings impacting on your own and others' work?

PHASE 2 – Implementing transitions (Strategy-Project Implementation) PRACTICES 6-8

- The emphasis shifts to building individual and collective leadership, whilst dealing openly with the positive and negative reactions to change, especially those related to values and cultural differences.

Table 3.
'Agile Leadership' Phase 2: Implementing Transitions

LEADERSHIP FOR SUSTAINABILITY	AGILITY generating Practices and accompanying Phases of Change	Assessing current level of agility: reflective questions
PHASE 2 – Implementing transitions		
PRACTICE 6 – Access Capability	Draw out and use all capabilities, in the business and elsewhere, to solve problems or innovate	What do you do to find out who can best contribute to what?
PRACTICE 7 – Cultural Competence	Tap into the different backgrounds and ways of working to enhance your view of possible approaches	How do you use the diversity around you, avoiding assumptions or stereotyping, and listen to anyone?
PRACTICE 8 – One to Many Dialogue	Communicate deeply with all relevant parties in finding shared understanding and agreeing what happens next	Rate your presentation, facilitation, action learning and chairing skills. Can you switch, depending on what happens and for different outcomes?

PHASE 3 – Embedding transitions (Strategy-Project Consolidation & Review) PRACTICES 9-12

- The intention here is to build individual and collective performance around the intended changes, sustaining them beyond the implementation phase; or, if indicated by real-time assessment of progress or new circumstances present, altering the transition goals.

Table 4.
'Agile Leadership' Phase 3: Embedding Transitions

LEADERSHIP FOR SUSTAINABILITY	AGILITY generating Practices and accompanying Phases of Change	Assessing current level of agility: reflective questions
PHASE 3 – Embedding transitions		
PRACTICE 9 – 'Total' Leadership	Role model and stay true to your main purpose, mission and values	How do you practise what you preach? How do you assess your consistency?

PRACTICE 10 – One to One Dialogue	Bring out the best in yourself and others; resolve difficulties through listening, questioning and feedback	How well do you coach/ mentor? How do you understand different needs, e.g. generations, genders, nationalities?
PRACTICE 11 – Performance Challenge	Drive and sustain innovation and improvement throughout the change transitions' twists and turns	How naturally do you say frankly what is going well or not so well? How easy do you make it for others to do likewise?
PRACTICE 12 – Agility Resilience	Learn the impact of everyday leadership practice and remove habits no longer fit for purpose	How do you make sure you and those around you remain contemporary in their ideas and working practices?

Having used this approach with many leadership learners across the world, we know it is possible to fast track development by targeting priority practices, guided learning reflection, diligent application of the practices in everyday leadership work, personal development planning, and auditing of personal/business impact. It is vital to keep practising until the practices become default. Once learnt, the relationship, communication, and knowledge exchange skills prove useful in all spheres of life.

Deeper connections are vital to learning and functioning well together when navigating change, bringing prosperity for everyone and every living thing included on the journey. Under our final question we begin to suggest some alternative ways of building, connecting to and conducting any form of enterprise, drawing on the full range of personal values available to us.

Question 4: How can we bring 'leadership for sustainability' to life for development purposes?

So, the pursuit of 'leadership for sustainability' is underpinned by everyday practices, driven by particular morals and values. Its development occurs by:

i. Continuous practice in applying the 12 practices, to suit different change challenges and contexts;

ii. Valuing the diversity of values and then seeking to understand the different drivers for change;
iii. Translating missions, goals and strategies into the operative values of those you are trying to influence.

1: Leadership agility practice

To build behaviour which promotes sustainability may require developing new behaviours or re-enforcing existing ones.

- Begin by exploring Practice 1, your Personal Values Sensitivity.

From Table 2 consider which of the practices, if strengthened, would help you deal with current organisational challenges. Use the practice related questions to help you identify these.

2: Valuing and then understanding values diversity

To influence those we wish to associate with, we first have to understand their personal values. These sometimes unconscious forces influence them already and drive and sustain all contributions.

Exercise
Identify your values. Using Table 5 allocate 100% across the 6 values systems to represent the personal values you hold most and least strongly.

Table 5.
Identify your values

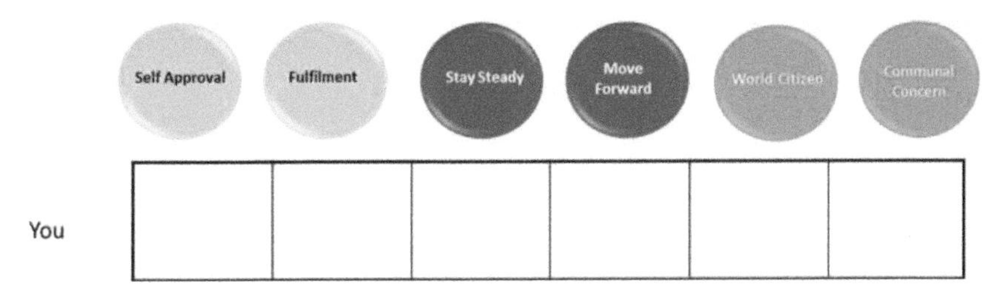

Having identified what moves you, it's often easier to identify the values you are repelled by or move away from. Maybe you love *Freedom* and *Autonomy* but avoid *Conformity* and *Tradition*; or perhaps you cherish *Security* but are repelled by *Material Wealth*?

What moves your team/colleagues to be energised and engaged for the long-term? Are there any competing values which cause unease? What about your customers and suppliers; how well acquainted are you with their drivers?

Most of us misguidedly assume what fulfils us fulfils others. Is it any wonder our record on sustaining anything (relationships, performance, profitability, peace, more equal wealth distribution, and the planet's eco-systems) is so patchy and inconsistent? You can't easily change what drives people, but you will have a chance to change their behaviour by relating to them in language which resonates with what drives them. Once they're listening, you have an opportunity to influence. This is bound to be more effective for sustaining dialogue than the all too common 'my way or the highway' school of trying to accomplish change.

3: Translate missions, goals and strategies into the operative values of those you are trying to influence

Individuals and organisations can fall into the trap of neglecting the resourcefulness of themselves and others. When people fail to achieve their goals they often blame 'money', 'time', 'technology', 'management' or some other scarce resource. What can't be achieved and sustained when you and your team remain curious, passionate, creative and determined? The leadership task, through employing the 12 practices, is to create and maintain the conditions for this to happen, not just once, but all the time.

Sustainable performance isn't a 100 metre sprint. Like the leadership agility learning journey, it's a marathon. It is therefore worth considering what resources individuals and organisations mobilise to achieve long lasting, sustainable performance. Most people can identify the *Material* and *Intellectual* resources required, yet forget the importance of *Emotional* resources driven by vision and values. Martin Luther King didn't proclaim, "I have a plan"; a plan is crucial for directing material and intellectual resources but is hardly going to get pulses racing! We need Material, Intellectual and Emotional resources to perform over the long term; miss one of these categories and performance cannot be sustained. Take for example the European Union's 'Green Policy'. There is no shortage of material or intellectual resources that can be brought to bear concerning environmental sustainability, but has it captured the imagination of European citizens? We don't think so. Understanding how a policy resonates with different value groups and what would move them to action from their values orientation would be a step forwards towards mobilising this crucial emotional resource.

We create tomorrow's organisation or project today by translating our missions, strategies and goals into the operative values based language of the people we work with to achieve our mutual ends, as depicted in Figure 3. The lynchpin of this alignment is the leader's authenticity in demonstrating their own values whilst accommodating/utilising other people's to retain flexibility for the change journey. Their leadership agility practices, comprising the various ways of communication, relationship building and knowledge exchange are then required to pull it off.

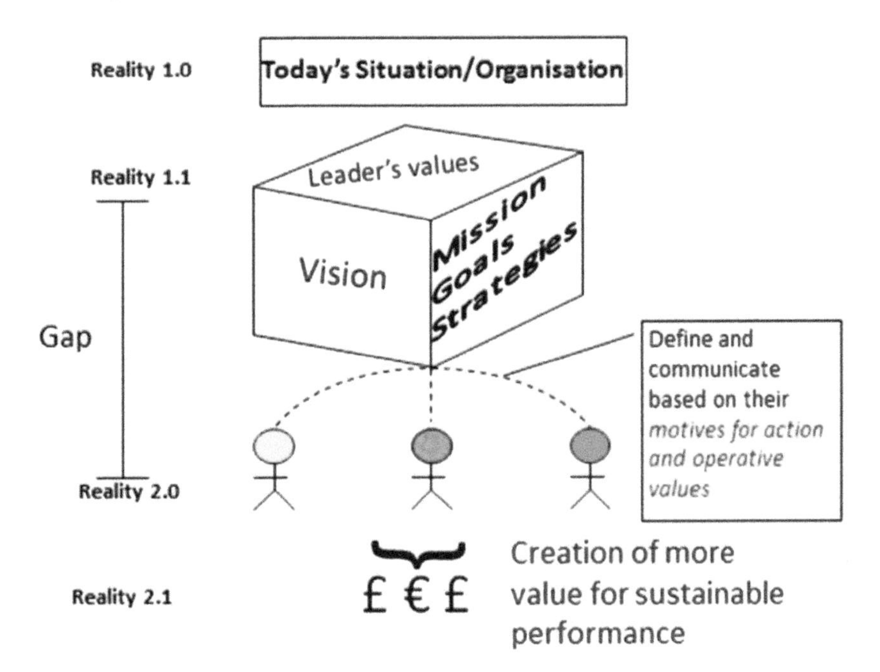

Figure 3: Creating Tomorrow Today

Concluding Remarks

There are some critical questions for leaders who are driven, or can be tempted, to embody 'leadership for sustainability' in all aspects of their lives. The new learning programme we have proposed positions people for emerging leadership careers way beyond meeting current expectations. In fact, using newly acquired personal values insights, we may innovate mutually prosperous ways of working, alongside re-discovering our humanity. In developing these programmes we must acknowledge the moral and values dynamic.

Leaders need to understand what moves them and others, how their needs and values shape their own and others' moral and ethical stances, and the consequences this has for their own brand of leadership. They also need to learn how and how much to accommodate colleagues whose needs and values differ from their own. The values of leaders create 'dis-ease' with employees and customers holding different values at an unconscious level, which can give rise to thoughts such as 'this is the wrong thing to do' or 'they are not on my wavelength'; these can lead to resistance to workplace policies/practices or, at the extreme, sabotage.

Leaders are encouraged, perhaps with the coaching assistance of Business Psychologists, to ask themselves these reflective questions:

How do I determine the values, beliefs and motivations of my own and my colleagues' leadership?

i. How can I make sure I am appealing to those values at the basic level (i.e. policies and practices that feel 'right')?
ii. How can I determine the values, beliefs and motivations of my main stakeholder groups (e.g. suppliers, communities, customers, market analysts)?
iii. How can I adapt my approach to decision making and resource allocation, keeping my treasured policies/practices, to meet a variety of needs?
iv. How can I learn to confront and navigate with others the moral dilemmas caused by personal values diversity?

We have offered a framework and techniques to encourage the deeper reflection so often missing in our short-term focused, self-serving, busy and reactive lives. The intention is to attain an interdependent, more sustainable way of conducting enterprise, built for the value creation and prosperity of all those making a contribution in a world which increasingly needs much more to renew, survive and thrive.

To find out what your main leadership agility strength and purpose is go to www.careerbirds.com and take the free 'Early Bird' assessment.

References

Adams, M., Stern, C., & Farthing, J. (2010). *Answering the CEO challenge: How quality can drive profitable growth across the organization.* Council Perspectives: Insights from the Conference Board Quality Council, Research Report number R-1461-10-RR, February, 1-8.

Aitken, P. (2004). *The Relationships between Personal Values, Leadership Behaviour and Team Functioning*. (Doctor of Business Administration Thesis, Henley Management College, Brunel University, UK).

Aitken, P., & Higgs, M. (2010). *Developing Change Leaders: the principles and practices of change leadership development*. Elsevier, Butterworth: Heinemann.

Allport, G. W. (1961). *Pattern and growth in personality*. New York, NY: Holt, Rinehart & Winston.

Bean, W. C. (1993). *Strategic Planning that makes thing happen: Getting from where you are to where you want to be.* Amherst, MA: Human Resource Development.

Burns, J. M. (2003). *Transforming Leadership*. New York, NY: Grove Press.

Edelman (2014). *The Edelman trust barometer*. In The Fourteenth Global Opinion Leaders' Study. Retrieved from www.edelman.com/trust.

England, G., & Lee, R. (1974). The relationship between managerial values and managerial success in the United States, Japan, India, and Australia. *Journal of Applied Psychology, 59*(4), 411-419.

Finkelstein, S., & Hambrick, D. (1996). *Strategic Leadership: Top Executives and Their Effects on Organisations*. St Paul, MN: West Publishing Company.

Hambrick, D.C., & Mason, P. A. (1984). Upper Echelons: The Organisation as a Reflection of its Top Managers. *Academy of Management Review, 9*, 193-206.

Hofstede, G. (2001). *Culture's Consequences: comparing values, behaviours, institutions, and organizations across nations* (2nd Ed.). Thousand Oaks, CA: Sage Publications.

Maslow, A. H. (1970). *Motivation and Personality* (3rd edition). New York, NY: Longman.

McKenzie, J., & Aitken, P. (2012). Learning to Lead the Knowledgeable Organization: Developing Leadership Agility. *Strategic HR Review, 11*(6), 329-334.

Parry, K. W. (1998). Grounded Theory and Social Process: A new Direction for Leadership Research. *The Leadership Quarterly, 9*(1), 85-105.

Pless, N. M., Maak, T., & Waldman, D. A. (2012). Different Approaches Toward Doing the Right Thing: Mapping the Responsibility Orientations of Leaders. *Academy of Management Perspectives, 26*(4), 51-65.

Porter, M. E., & Cramer, M.R. (2011). Creating Shared Value. *Harvard Business Review, Jan-Feb*, 62-77.

Raconteur (2014, 17th September). Ethical selling is key to customer loyalty. *The Times*. Retrieved from http://raconteur.net/business/doing-the-right-thing.

Rokeach, M. (1973). *The Nature of Human Values*. London: The Free Press, Collier MacMillan Publishers.

Russell, R. F. (2001). The role of values in servant leadership. *Leadership & Organizational Development Journal, 22*(2), 76-84.

Schwartz, S. (1992). Universals in the content and structure of values: Theoretical advances and empirical tests in 20 countries. In Zanna, M. P. (Ed.), *Advances in experimental social psychology*, (Vol. 25, pp. 1-65), San Diego: Academic Press.

2

SECTION

Safety and Risk

SAFETY AND RISK INTRODUCTION

Pauline Grant

There are dangers all around us, and indeed within our bodies. No activity is without risk – and of course inactivity (or indecision) carries its own problems. One of the interesting insights from studies into how people make decisions is that much of it is unconscious. We might, from time to time, impose a rational, logical process of weighing up pros and cons and assessing probabilities of different outcomes. However, that is not generally how we make decisions. Indeed, even when we apply that rational approach, it is often a justification for a more intuitive, unconsciously derived decision.

Some time ago I tried to understand why an elderly woman with dementia and her fractured arm in a plaster cast remained in hospital, though not requiring treatment. A sign above her bed said that she was not to use a zimmer frame or walking stick. The risk was that, because of her dementia, she was unlikely to follow instructions not to put weight on her fractured arm so could lengthen her recovery time. However, when she pressed down on the arm it hurt, so she would stop. A small incremental risk, but one that severely limited her mobility and had led to the judgement that it was not safe for her to return home. She was upset about not being 'allowed' to go home, and created stress for her husband by pleading with him as he left after visiting. There was no way of making her totally safe and being overly cautious was creating distress. The situation was resolved after the cautious team member, previously unwilling to agree to the patient's discharge, was persuaded to accompany her home and see how she managed. No-one could have calculated this and arguments had failed to influence; it had to be enacted in practice. This example demonstrates how the choice of which risks to focus on and the comfort individuals have with accepting known risks affects decisions and outcomes.

We start this section with Jonathan Passmore's review of coaching as a method of helping people to impart and learn safe practices. The behaviour he focuses on is driving, which is an activity that can cause injury and death, but the principles apply to other 'high risk' environments. Martin Down and David Lane take us through the natural tendencies that shape people's reactions to situations that are new or uncertain, and offer their insights from research to increase resilience and improve decision-making. We conclude with Geoff Trickey's analysis and conclusions about individuals' propensity to take risks, illuminated by the model and approach he and colleagues have devised.

SAFETY AND RISK – MEET THE AUTHORS

Jonathan Passmore is Managing Director of Embrion and professor of psychology at the University of Evora. Holding five degrees, Jonathan has written some 20 books, which have been translated into 10 languages. He has written over 100 journal papers and book chapters and has spoken at conferences across the world including in the US, South Africa, Spain, Hungary, Israel, and Kuwait. His work has been recognised with several awards including from the Association for Coaching, British Psychology Society and, most recently, the ABP as recipient of the Chair's Award for Business Excellence.

Martin Down is Managing Director at The Executive Coaching Partnership Ltd. He is an experienced executive coach, facilitator and organisational change consultant with expertise in the leadership, organisational and people side of change. He has over 20 years of management and international consulting experience with International plcs, public sector organisations, professional service firms and consultancies. Martin has a global consulting background and has also led the organisation and people change stream of major transformation programmes.

David Lane has established, and runs, work-based Masters and Doctorate degrees for coaches through the Professional Development Foundation and Middlesex University. He has coached and consulted in organisations that include multinationals, public sector and government bodies. Previously Chair of the British Psychological Society Register of Psychologists Specialising in Psychotherapy, David convened the EFPA group on Psychotherapy, and served on other professional committees. His contributions to counselling psychology gained him the BPS award for 'Outstanding Scientific Contribution'. In 2010 the BPS honoured him for his 'Distinguished Contribution to Professional Psychology'.

Geoff Trickey has been Managing Director at PCL since 1992. His career spans the three major areas of applied psychology: clinical, educational and business psychology. Geoff has worked in research (Hon Research Fellow – University College London), as a Principal Educational Psychologist in East London, as European Manager for The Psychological Corporation (the first and largest test publisher). His past has influenced and shaped PCL's direction to deliver the benefits of rigorously applied, research-based HR solutions to businesses based on sound psychological principles.

COACHING PSYCHOLOGY: APPLIED PRACTICE IN SAFETY CRITICAL ENVIRONMENTS

Dr Jonathan Passmore

Introduction

I aim to review the developing journey of coaching psychology, which has emerged over the past two decades as a distinct discipline within psychology, and its application in recent years to safety critical environments. Specifically, the areas of driver safety and offshore oil and gas safety coaching, while linking the applications in these areas to the potential for coaching psychology to contribute more widely to learning, development and change.

I start with a brief review of coaching research. My aim is to provide an understanding of the research since 2000 and how this has provided a platform for the application of coaching to new environments.

The second section will consider the application of coaching in the area of driver learning. The chapter will note how psychological research in this area has led to changes in organisational practice on how motor vehicle and HGV drivers are taught in the police forces in England and Scotland, as well as in the British Army. The implications of this are explored for other areas of learning.

The third section explores the application of coaching to safety critical environments such as the oil and gas sector, manufacturing and mining. The findings from research are discussed and the implications for wider changes in practice are considered.

Coaching has emerged onto the organisational stage and has stayed. It is now seen as an important part of human resource development strategies, as an equal with training, appraisals and similar approaches (see Passmore et al., 2014). Its emergence has been helped by the role Coaching Psychologists have played in encouraging an evidence-based approach, providing the research to underpin the claims of practitioners and meet the challenge from sceptical executives: '*so what can coaching do for us?*'

The coaching journey into the world of business started in the 1980s and became popularised by Whitmore (1992) and Whitworth et al. (1992) through their respective titles *Coaching for Performance* and *Co-active coaching*. Coaching psychology as a discipline can be tracked back to 2000 with the research work of Tony Grant, Sydney University, and the subsequent development of coaching psychology groups in the UK and Australia (see Grant et al., 2010 for an in-depth review of coaching research). These groups have now spread with some fifty national coaching psychology associations in existence from Italy to Israel and from Norway to South Africa.

The growth of interest in coaching from Business Psychologists has been matched with a growth in psychological research, first in US journals such as *Consulting Psychology*, and since 2002 in UK journals such as the *International Coaching Psychology Review* and *The Coaching Psychologist*. This research has gone through a number of phases from an initial proliferation of case studies to the more recent emergence of meta-analysis papers offering a growing body of evidence of the impact of coaching compared with other organisational interventions (see Passmore & Theeboom, in press).

Initially, we have suggested, the approach was experiential and theoretical with individuals sharing their examples of practice and debating the boundaries of an emerging domain. Then the case study and survey became popular tools for helping to explore the experience of coaching from a coach and client perspective. Later qualitative studies sought to build theoretical knowledge, while small-scale quantitative studies, often Randomised Controlled Trials (RCTs) provided interesting insights relating to specific populations. More recently we are seeing larger scale RCTs (see, for example, Grant et al., 2009 or Passmore & Rehman, 2012) and meta-studies (Jones et al., 2015; Theeboom et al., 2013) which are providing deeper insights into the efficacy of coaching practice within organisations. In simple terms these are answering the key question: 'Does coaching work?'

The first phase of case studies and surveys started around 1990 and can be seen as a thread in the literature until around 2005. Of course, prior to this there were a number of early studies of coaching. Gorby (1937) looked at the impact of coaching in a manufacturing setting where senior employees, working under a profit sharing plan, coached newer employees on how to reduce waste and increase profits. Gorby's research was quickly followed by a second study, which focused on the use of coaching to increase sales (Bigelow, 1938). However, following this early research, studies were sporadic. Between 1937 and the end of the century, a total of 93 articles, PhD theses and empirical studies were published. It was not until the 1980s that the first signs of growth can be seen and papers hinted at the potential of coaching as a tool for organisational change. Coaching started to be seen as a separate organisational intervention. An example is Holoviak (1982), in which the researcher examined a range of interventions in relation to variations in company productivity levels in coal mining. The study used a semi-structured interview method and concluded that companies that provided greater amounts of management and supervisory training, including coaching, achieved higher productivity.

By the 1990s coaching research papers were common and PsycINFO and Dissertation Abstracts International cite 41 papers published during this period. The growth continued post 2000, with an increasing focus on the distinctive nature of coaching psychology, as well as more scientifically robust methods such as RCTs and meta-analysis being used. The emergence of coaching psychology as a distinct strand of coaching led to discussion as to the nature of coaching psychology. Grant and Palmer (2002) defined coaching psychology as:

"Coaching psychology is for enhancing performance in work and personal life domains with normal, non-clinical populations, underpinned by models of coaching grounded in established therapeutic approaches."

In contrast I have suggested that the practices of experienced 'Coaches' and 'Coaching Psychologists' may be the same, but what differentiates them is the understanding of, and engagement with, research (Passmore, 2010). Alongside this position, I have offered an alternative definition of coaching psychology:

"Coaching psychology is the scientific study of behaviour, cognition and emotion within coaching practice to deepen our understanding and enhance our practice within coaching." (Passmore et al., 2014, p.5)

This definition echoes those in other areas of psychology, such as health and organisational psychology, where the focus of psychology is towards understanding research and contributing to the field as a scientific practitioner.

So what does this research tell us about the practices of coaches? The evidence suggests that coaching is both similar to, and different from, counselling and therapy (see McKenna & Davis, 2009 for a fuller discussion). The accepted view in counselling / therapy is that a number of key factors play a part, such as client readiness to engage with therapy, the behaviours of the therapist (particularly the ability to display empathy) and skills of the therapist in the use of their chosen method (Norcross, 2002). In coaching, issues such as credibility and previous experience seem to be highly prized by clients (see, for example, Hall et al., 1999). Clients are interested in knowing about the background of their coach, along with understanding how their coach can bring both challenge and an independent perspective to the conversation, while balancing this with the empathy and relational elements. Research by Hall et al. (1999) on the coach-coachee dyad identified many of the key elements that have subsequently emerged in the studies of coach behaviour since 2000 (see Table 1).

Table 1.
What works best in Coaching?

Coaches' views – what worked	Executives' views – what worked
Honest, realistic and challenging feedback	Connecting personally
Good listening	Good listening
Good action ideas	Reflecting / Checking back
Clear objectives	Caring
No personal agenda	Following up
Availability	Committing to the executive's success
Straight feedback	Demonstrating integrity & honesty
Sophistication	Openness
Coach has seen other career paths	Having good coach/executive fit
	Knowing the "unwritten rules"
	'Pushing' the executive when necessary

(Adapted from Hall et al., 1999)

The coach provides a safe and independent space for the coachee to reflect and think critically about the issues they face. For the coachee this space provides support not only while they consider, explore and develop new plans, but also while these plans are implemented. In my view, coaching stimulates intrinsic motivation through its use of open questions and reflection. It uses goal setting to enhance motivation, affirmations to build and enhance positive self-regard and feedback to encourage regular reviews. Thus it helps the coachee to maintain progress towards their goal. The ongoing supportive relationship allows the coachee to fail, while being encouraged to try again.

More interesting has been the growing application of larger RCTs and most recently, meta-analysis studies to explore the impact of coaching on individual and organisational performance. RCTs control for confounding variables that cannot be addressed by other research designs (Cook & Campbell, 1979). Especially relevant for coaching, RCT designs allow us to control for selection effects (e.g. coachees that participate in a study are strongly motivated for change), placebo effects and natural maturation (change that cannot be ascribed to the intervention). Research on related interventions such as psychotherapy consistently shows that these factors play such a significant role that they can be even stronger predictors of effectiveness than the specific intervention used (McKenna & Davis, 2009; Messer & Wampold, 2002).

The exact number of RCTs in coaching is hard to measure because it depends how the literature search categories are defined. We have recently suggested that the number may be between 50–100 RCT papers by December 2015 (Passmore & Theeboom, 2015). As Grant notes "*For some observers the small number of randomised controlled outcome studies may be considered to be the major shortcoming in the literature on coaching efficacy*" (Grant, 2012).

However, what has brought the literature forward is the publication of a number of meta-analysis studies of coaching and its impact on individuals and organisations. By July 2014, three meta-analytic studies had been published in journals (De Meuse et al., 2009; Jones et al., 2015; Theeboom et al., 2013).

De Meuse et al. (2009) used meta-analytic techniques to estimate the effects of executive coaching interventions. They identified six studies that met their four criteria for inclusion:

i. coaching was targeted at executives
ii. coaching was provided by external coaches
iii. the methodological design included pre and post coaching ratings
iv. the statistical information provided was sufficient for estimating effect sizes. The research team used a statistical technique to average the outcome variables from the six studies, which produced a weighted average impact measure (known as effect size). Furthermore, they distinguished between self-ratings by the coachee, and ratings by others (managers and/or peers).

According to the standards of Cohen (1988), effect sizes less than 0.30 can be considered to be small, an effect size between 0.31 and 0.50 would be moderate and an effect size above 0.50 would be considered large.

The results of their analysis showed that coaching can have moderate to large positive effects depending on who was responsible for the ratings. The estimated effect sizes were much larger when the outcomes were rated by the coachee rather than by others. This was in line with the results of a study by Peterson (1993) that showed that relative to the estimates of others (e.g. supervisors), coachees tend to overestimate the effectiveness of coaching interventions. Furthermore, the results showed that the effectiveness of coaching was highly inconsistent. In other words, there were major between-study differences in effect size. In addition to the small number of studies, De Meuse and his colleagues identified several factors that might have contributed to this inconsistency: differences in outcome criteria, characteristics of the coaching intervention (e.g. type of coaching) and methodological rigor of the studies.

These factors were explicitly addressed in a second meta-analysis by Theeboom et al. (2013). The research team focused on all studies investigating the effects of coaching interventions in organisational settings in which the influence of other interventions (i.e. when coaching was part of a broader leadership development programme) could be ruled out. This resulted in 18 studies being included in the final analysis.

The researchers used both a bottom-up (looking at available data) and top-down (looking at well-known outcomes in the broader psychological literature) approach to categorise the various outcomes into five clusters: performance and skills (e.g. transformational leadership behaviour), well-being (e.g. mental health), coping (e.g. ability to cope with adverse events), work attitudes (e.g. job satisfaction) and goal-directed self-regulation (e.g. goal attainment). The results showed that coaching had a positive influence on all of these outcome variables. The effect size was similar to the results presented from other meta-analysis studies that have reviewed the impact of training and other frequently used organisational interventions. The results are summarised in Table 2.

Table 2.
Summary of Effect Size

Outcome category	Effect size
Performance/skills	.60
Well-being	.46
Coping	.43
Self-regulation	.74
Work attitudes	.54

(Adapted from Theeboom, Beersma & van Vianen, 2013)

In summary, the results from the two more detailed and recent meta-analytic reviews (Theeboom et al., 2013; Jones et al., 2015) confirm that coaching can be an effective change-methodology. The effect size for coaching is broadly similar to that of training and feedback, and thus the evidence suggests that coaching does help clients to cope, learn and change.

However, this conclusion masks a number of publication biases and complexity in the literature. As Theeboom, et al. (2013) indicate, the coaching literature is susceptible to publication bias: an over-representation of published studies displaying significant, positive results, while studies with results that are not statistically significant (an associated probability value of >0.05) are subjected to the bottom draw of the filing cabinet. In other words, studies that produce statistically non-significant results are never published; this has attracted criticism from the research community (see *The Economist*, 2013 for a fuller discussion). The problem of publication bias is common across the sciences. However, given the growth in investment in coaching, estimated to be $2 billion per annum globally (International Coach Federation, 2012), there is a need for robust, empirical research that not only utilises randomised control trials but also includes the publication of both positive and negative studies in peer-reviewed research journals.

Coaching psychology: application to driver learning and impact on public policy and organisation practice

A number of studies have been conducted with formal, independent evaluation at the end of the period of coaching-learning. The participants have included advanced police learner drivers, heavy goods vehicle learner drivers and novice drivers.

A series of four studies by Passmore and his research team (Passmore & Mortimer, 2011; Passmore & Rehman, 2012; Passmore & Townsend, 2012; Passmore & Velez, 2012) explored the potential of coaching as a behavioural learning tool. The first of the four explored the use of coaching by a group of Approved Driving Instructors (ADIs) using a qualitative methodology. The study involved training the ADIs in coaching skills. The five-day course was spread over three sessions, included core coaching skills such as questioning, active listening, affirmations, reflections and summaries, as well as the application of several coaching approaches including GROW (Eldridge & Dembkowski, 2013; Whitmore, 1992) and Cognitive Behavioural Coaching (Palmer & Williams, 2013). All ADIs were then required to complete three pieces of assessed work (coaching practice, a critical essay and a reflective log), before being included in the study. The qualitative method was based on semi-structured interviews with the learner drivers and the ADIs, with each being interviewed about their experiences of the learning process using coaching. The results suggested that learners benefitted from the experience by being encouraged to more actively reflect on their learning. They felt that when the 'instructor' used a coaching approach (as opposed to instruction) learning was more centred on their personal needs (Passmore & Mortimer, 2011). The instructors reported similar experiences and they also found relationships with their learners improved. This study provided a basis for future investigation.

This and other research, such as the European Union's HERMES Novice Driver research project (Hermes, 2010) contributed towards changes in driver training. In the UK ADIs are now encouraged by the Driving & Vehicle Standards Agency to adopt a learner centred approach to their teaching and to use open questions to encourage reflection.

The hope is that this style of learning will help individuals become better, safer drivers who understand the risks associated with different situations as opposed to simply following rules. As driving related deaths form one of the largest single causes of death for young men aged 17-25 across Europe (EU, 2012), any change in practice that can reduce this figure is welcome. However, there remains a short-supply of long-term evidence on the impact of different teaching / learning methods on driver safety and accident rates. As a result it is critical that research in this field continues, if we are to make progress in understanding and reducing death rates.

The second study, using the same methodology, looked at the use of coaching with police drivers (Passmore & Townsend, 2012). The police driving instructors were taught coaching models and techniques through the same five-day programme as the ADI sample in Passmore & Rehman's HGV army study (Passmore & Rehman 2012). The police instructors were asked to apply the approach during their advanced two-week course teaching 'response driving' to police officers. In this study the police learners were already UK driving license holders and had previously undertaken basic police driver training. The results of this study echoed those identified in earlier studies with participants reporting positive experiences when using the coaching method. Instructors also judged the mixed instruction-coaching method to be faster than a traditional approach, as they could adapt their interventions based on what the learner already knew, rather than step-by-step instruction based on the syllabus (Passmore & Townsend, 2012). This paved the way for a further study into the efficiency of coaching as a learning methodology.

A third piece of research comprised two studies. The first study was a Randomised Control Trial (RCT) with a group of over 200 HGV learner drivers from the British Army. The second study used semi-structured interviews with the learners. The project aimed to compare the efficiency and effectiveness of a blended (coaching and instruction) approach with the traditional (instruction only) approach used by Army instructors prior to the coaching training. The results suggested that coaching in this context was both more efficient and more effective than the instruction only method. Learners took fewer hours to learn how to drive and achieved a higher pass rate than those taught by the instructional method (Passmore & Rehman, 2012).

The evidence from these studies reveals that the coaching process was experienced positively by both learners and instructors. Learning appeared to be enhanced in terms of the quality of driving behaviour at the point of assessment. However, research is still needed to explore the long-term effects of different training methods and the impact of coaching on driver behaviour 6 or 12 months after passing the driving test.

The fourth study (Passmore & Velez, 2012) of the series involved an insurance company and its use of specialist ADIs to observe and give feedback to fleet drivers (individuals who drive a vehicle owned by the company), referred to in this study as the 'learners'. The ADIs were taught coaching skills over a five-day period on the same course as described in the army and police studies above (Passmore & Rehman, 2012; Passmore & Townsend, 2012). The 'learners' received a one-hour session and their accident record was monitored for 12 months after the one-hour session. An RCT was used to compare the group of learners exposed to instructors using coaching methods with those who received traditional step-by-step instruction.

The results from the study revealed non-significant differences in accidents between the two groups in the 12 months following the one-hour intervention. One explanation for this is that, unlike the previous studies where most learners had 20–50 hours of instructor or coach input, the 'learners' in this study received a single one-hour session. As a result the opportunity for facilitating critical thinking was limited and there was no subsequent opportunity for observing, challenging and supporting behavioural change in driving technique or stimulating the drivers' intrinsic motivation to change.

The importance of these subtle behavioural motivators was evidenced by Newnam et al. (2008). These researchers discovered that drivers' safety motivation predicted accidents. Specifically, fleet drivers' perceptions of their fleet manager's safety commitment and values, as well as their personal attitudes and beliefs about driving and risk, predicted their motivation to drive safely. As Mathis (2009) reports from a safety culture assessment, managers don't always recognise the effect of low safety performance on the company as a whole, as their focus is often short term.

Mathis (2009) recommends a coaching model that follows three specific stages:

- First is the focus stage where supervisors analyse past accident data and then formulate safety targets to focus future behaviour.
- Second, in the feedback stage, supervisors develop their skills in delivering feedback to employees.
- Third is the facilitation stage, where the supervisor uses facilitation based on observation and feedback.

This model is one that can be replicated for use in a range of safety critical areas, from engineering and construction to offshore oil and gas exploration.

Coaching psychology: application to other safety critical environments

There have been a small number of studies looking at the application of coaching and its impact on safety in other industries.

Kines et al. (2010) found that after a 26 week coaching intervention, which focused on manager–employee communications, researchers observed a significant increase in the number of reported safety issues. They argued that the increased reporting of safety risks resulted from improved communications, which had been enhanced through the coaching intervention.

Research has also pointed to the potential benefits that safety coaching can provide in construction (Kines et al., 2010). In this study, two intervention groups of construction site foremen were coached in on-site safety communication with employees. As observed in the Kines (2010) study, conversations increased dramatically (seven-fold in one of the intervention groups), leading to employees' heightened perceptions of the level of safety on their site.

In an earlier study, Renning (2007) conducted research in the oil and gas industry and implemented a coaching programme that centred on being present, visible and accountable for safe working behaviours. Results once again highlighted the positive impact of coaching in a safety critical environment, with the coaching programme resulting in a decrease in incidents across all Norway operations. The researchers claimed that the coaching programme also helped to create a cultural shift within the organisation in that employees began to perceive safe behaviour as an expected part of the job. Specifically, workers felt practical communication helped to facilitate behaviour change towards safer working practices.

An example of the lasting impact of behaviour-based safety initiatives has been demonstrated by Al-Hemound & Al-Asfoor (2006) who introduced a safety coaching intervention for 11 employees in a research institution. Findings suggested that safety performance increased for the experimental group whilst remaining relatively unchanged for the control group. Employees continued to be observed for their level of safety performance for three months following the intervention. Findings suggested that the increases in the experimental group were maintained, suggesting that behaviour-based safety interventions can produce a lasting impact on the level of safety performance. Zhang & Fang (2012) argue that a behaviour-based safety approach combined with a behaviour-based tracking and analysis system can achieve a more cohesive safety system where standards are continually improved.

Our own work (Krauesslar, Avery & Passmore, 2015) has also shown the potential of coaching to improve safety in the offshore oil and gas sector when used over a minimum of an 8 week period. Our study employed a semi-structured interview method with both safety coaches and offshore site managers.

The findings support the findings from the wider literature (see Passmore, Krauesslar & Avery, 2015 for a fuller discussion). Our study suggested that safety coaching was viewed as a positive contribution to creating an effective, sustainable, long-term safety culture when applied skilfully by the coach and given enough time and support to make a difference. Significant skills of the coach included being able to build a relationship and to show empathy towards the coachee. These results echo earlier studies (e.g. Hall et al., 1999), showing the importance of relational aspects of coaching, including the critical nature of the coach-coachee relationship.

This research also indicated the contribution of coaching in creating a wider organisational safety culture, where safety was highly valued by all and was the primary focus, in contrast with simply getting the job done.

The single most important aspect to emerge from this research was the value of creating shared ownership of safety. Traditionally, safety advisers provided instructions, which resulted in responsibility for achieving safety being seen as their domain. After coaching, the advisers used questions instead of instructions, encouraging individuals to reflect and identify for themselves the risks they were taking.

Conclusions – Implications for practice

The research into the role of coaching within safety critical environments reveals the potential of Psychologists to contribute towards improved outcomes. Specifically, the importance of Psychologists designing and embedding evaluation studies into organisational interventions, and sharing their findings with researchers and practitioners through peer-reviewed publications. Further, I believe that evidence-informed practice is critical for improving organisational and individual performance outcomes.

The research into coaching since 2000 has shown the value of coaching in organisations generally. More recently, meta-analysis research suggests that coaching is comparable with other commonly used interventions, such as training and feedback. Psychological research, with academics partnering with practitioners, has allowed coaching to demonstrate its value as a tool to support skills transfer, learning and for career and role transition.

In the area of safety critical environments the growing body of evidence from rigorously-designed psychological studies has confirmed the impact of coaching on performance, perception and accidents. Taken together, the findings suggest that safety coaching has a role to play as part of a wider health and safety strategy contributing to the development of a generative safety culture within organisations. Specifically, safety coaching appears to be a useful intervention to support learning by reducing learning times and improving adherence to behavioural skills taught during training. Moreover, coaching as an intervention appears to be well received by employees and managers, who prefer the opportunity to think for themselves.

The research evidence over the past decade now enables us to support claims for coaching as an effective organisation intervention that supports learning and behaviour change. Further, more recent research into safety critical areas of work reveals the potential of coaching to move beyond the boardroom and training classroom into safety critical environments, from driving to offshore oil and gas exploration.

References

Al-Hemound, A., & Al-Asfoor, M. (2006). A behaviour based safety approach at a Kuwait research institution. *Journal of Safety Research, 37*(2), 201-206.

Bigelow, B. (1938). Building an effective training program for field salesmen. *Personnel, 14*, 142-150.

Cohen, J. (1988). *Statistical power analysis for the behavioral sciences* (2nd ed.). New Jersey: Lawrence Erlbaum.

Cook, T. D., & Campbell, D. T. (1979). *Quasi-experimentation: Design and analysis issues for field settings*. Boston, MA: Houghton Mifflin Company.

De Meuse, K. P., Dai, G., & Lee, R. J. (2009). Evaluating the effectiveness of executive coaching: Beyond ROI? *Coaching: An International Journal of Theory, Research and Practice, 2*(2), 117-134.

Eldridge, F., & Dembkowski, S. (2013). Behavioural coaching. In J. Passmore, D. Peterson & T. Freire (Eds.). *The Wiley Blackwell Handbook of the Psychology of Coaching & Mentoring* (pp. 298-318). Chichester: Wiley.

EU (2012). *4th European Road Safety Day Conference Report*. Retrieved from http://europa.eu/rapid/press-release_IP-12-837_en.htm on 14 June 2015.

Gorby, C. (1937). Everyone gets a share of the profits. *Factory Management & Maintenance, 95*, 82-83.

Grant, A. M., Curtayne, L., & Burton, G. (2009). Executive coaching enhances goal attainment, resilience and workplace well-being: A randomized controlled study. *The Journal of Positive Psychology, 4*(5), 396-407.

Grant, A. M., & Palmer, S. (2002). Coaching Psychology Workshop. *Annual Conference of the Division of Counselling Psychology. BPS*. Torquay, UK. 18 May.

Grant, A. M., Passmore, J., Cavanagh, M., & Parker, H. (2010). The state of play in coaching. *International Review of Industrial & Organizational Psychology, 25*, 125-168.

Grant, A. M. (2012). The Efficacy of Coaching. In J. Passmore, D. Peterson and T. Freire (Eds.) *Wiley Blackwell Handbook of the Psychology of Coaching & Mentoring* (pp.15-39). Chichester: Wiley.

Hall, D. T., Otazo, K. L., & Hollenbeck, G. P. (1999). Behind closed doors: what really happens in executive coaching. *Organizational Dynamics, 27*(3), 39-53.

HERMES (2010). *EU Coaching Project Final Report*. Retrieved from http://ec.europa.eu/transport/road_safety/pdf/projects/hermes_final_report_en.pdf on 23 May 2015.

Holoviak, S. J. (1982). The impact of training on company productivity levels. *Performance & Instruction, 21*(5), 6-8.

International Coach Federation (2012). Retrieved from http://www.coachfederation.org/files/FileDownloads/2012GlobalCoachingStudy.pdf?_ga=1.154453816.124482212.1424978859 on 19 October 2015.

Jones, R., Wood, S., & Guillemeau, F. (2014). *Meta-Analysis of Coaching*. A paper presented to the BPS DOP Conference, January, Brighton, UK.

Jones, R. J., Woods, S. A., & Guillaume, Y. R. F. (2015). The effectiveness of workplace coaching: A meta-analysis of learning and performance outcomes from coaching. *Journal of Occupational and Organizational Psychology*. doi: 10.1111/joop.12119.

Krauesslar, V., Avery, R., & Passmore, J. (2015). Taking ownership of safety. What are the active ingredients of safety coaching and how do they impact safety outcomes in critical offshore working environments? *Journal of Occupational Safety and Ergonomics*, *21*(1), 39-46.

Kines, P., Anderson, L., Spangenberg, S., Mikkelsen, K., Dyreborg, J., & Zohar, D. (2010). Improving construction site safety through leader-based verbal safety communication. *Journal of Safety Research, 41*(5), 399-406.

Mathis, T. L. (2009). Supervisory Safety Coaching: Growing a Safety Culture from the Middle Out. *EHS Today,* (pp. 20-22). Retrieved from: http://ehstoday.com/safety/supervisory-safety-coaching-culture-5634 on 25 June 2014.

McKenna, D. D., & Davis, S. L. (2009). Hidden in plain sight: The active ingredients of executive coaching. *Industrial and Organizational Psychology, 2*(3), 244-260.

Messer, S. B., & Wampold, B. E. (2002). Let's face facts: Common factors are more potent than specific therapy ingredients. *Clinical Psychology: Science and Practice, 9*(1), 21-25.

Newnam, S., Griffin, M., & Mason, C. (2008). Safety in Work Vehicles: A Multilevel Study Linking Safety Values and Individual Predictors to Work-Related Driving Crashes. *Journal of Applied Psychology, 9*(3), 632-644.

Norcross, J. C. (2002). Empirically supported therapy relationships. In J. C. Norcross (Ed.), *Psychotherapy relationships that work: Therapist contributions and responsiveness of patients*. New York, NY: Oxford University Press.

Palmer, S., & Williams, H. (2013). Cognitive behavioural coaching. In J. Passmore, D. Peterson and T. Freire (Eds.), *The Wiley Blackwell Handbook of the Psychology of Coaching & Mentoring* (pp. 319-339). Chichester: Wiley.

Passmore, J. (2010). Leadership Coaching. *International Coaching Psychology Congress*. City University: London. 15 December.

Passmore, J. (2013). Coaching in safety critical environments. *The Coaching Psychologist, 9*(1), 27-30.

Passmore, J., Krauesslar, V., & Avery, R. (2015). Safety Coaching: A Critical Literature Review of coaching in high hazard industries. *Industrial & Commercial Training*, 47(4), 195-200.

Passmore, J., May, T., Badger, L., Dodd, L., & Lyness, E. (2014). Coaching for success: The key ingredients for coaching delivery and coach recruitment. London: ILM.

Passmore, J., & Mortimer, L. (2011). The experience of using coaching as a learning technique in learner driver development: An IPA study of adult learning. *International Coaching Psychology Review*. *6*(1), 33-45.

Passmore, J., Peterson, D., & Freire, T. (2014). The Psychology of Coaching and Mentoring. In J. Passmore, D. Peterson and T. Freire (Eds.), *The Wiley Blackwell Handbook of the Psychology of Coaching & Mentoring* (pp.1-11). Chichester: Wiley.

Passmore, J., & Rehman, H. (2012). Coaching as a learning methodology – a mixed methods study in driver development – a Randomised Controlled Trial and thematic analysis. *International Coaching Psychology Review*, 7(2), 166-184.

Passmore, J., & Theeboom, T. (In Press). Coaching Psychology: A journey of development in research. In L. van Zyl (Ed). *Coaching Psychology: Meta-theoretical perspectives and applications in multi-cultural contexts.* London: Springer.

Passmore, J., & Townsend, C. (2012). The role of coaching in police driver training – An IPA study of coaching in a blue light environment. *An International Journal of Police Strategies, 35*(4), 785-800.

Passmore, J., & Velez, M. J. (2012). Coaching Fleet drivers – a randomized controlled trial (RCT) of 'short coaching' interventions to improve driver safety in fleet drivers. *The Coaching Psychologist, 8*(1), 20-26.

Peterson, D. B. (1993). Measuring change: A psychometric approach to evaluating individual coaching outcomes. Presented at the annual conference of the Society for Industrial and Organizational Psychology, San Francisco.

Renning, S. (2007). Innovative coaching program enhances safety culture. *Offshore, 67,* 80-81.

The Economist (2013). *Unreliable research: Trouble at lab*. Retrieved from http://www.economist.com/news/briefing/21588057-scientists-think-science-self-correcting-alarming-degree-it-not-trouble on 14 October 2014.

Theeboom, T., Beersma, B., & van Vianen, A. E. (2013). Does coaching work? A meta-analysis on the effects of coaching on individual level outcomes in an organizational context. *The Journal of Positive Psychology, 9*(1), 1-18.

Whitmore, J (1992). *Coaching for performance*. London: Nicholas Brealey Publishing.

Whitworth, L., Kimsey-House, H., Kimsey-House, K., & Sandahl, P. (1992) *Co-active coaching*. Boston: Nicholas Brealey Publishing.

Zhang, M., & Fang, D. (2012). A continuous Behaviour-Based Safety strategy for persistent safety improvement in construction industry. *Automation in Construction, 32,* 1-7.

LEADERSHIP FOR RESILIENT ORGANISATIONS: THE CHANGING CONTEXT OF ORGANISATIONAL RESILIENCE AND LEADERSHIP

Martin Down & David Lane

Like quicksand, the economic environment has the illusion of stability. However, hidden instabilities lie just beneath the surface and prevailing assumptions continue to blind people's perceptions of systemic risks in a world that is increasingly interconnected.

The recent financial crisis provides a good example. Some did foresee the crisis and expressed concerns about imbalances in the global economy creating a 'global savings glut' leading to some investors offering high returns at the expense of risk. Some warned about the risk of house price increases. Others tried to challenge prevailing assumptions and were labelled as whistle-blowers and their warnings fell on deaf ears. However, the minority voice was not heard and acted upon by the majority as prevailing assumptions blinded them to the risks. For example, the assumption was that easy credit and rising prices would cover the cost of borrowing. This led to an accumulation of unsustainable levels of debt, inappropriate mortgage terms for sub-primes and growth in asset based securities (possession of assets e.g. houses, cars, etc.). Instead rising interest rates contributed to defaults and spiralling debts.

The assumption that risks could be minimised by offloading defaults (thereby hiding the size of the risk), led to defaults being exported into the financial system through the packaging of debts into securitised loans. It is known that people in groups can make riskier decisions than individuals (Stoner, 1961) although this is not always the case (Moscovici & Zavalloni, 1969).

Instead, a slagheap of toxic assets toppled global financial stability. The speed and intensity of the downturn took people by surprise. Many found it difficult to see risks to the system as a whole. People trusted Banks (based on historic legacies of '*My word is my bond*') and their boards with globally recruited talent and records of public life. Financial/economic models, good at predicting short-term risks, were inadequate for the complexity emerging. Lenders were tempted to over-lend, the complexity of structures made it unclear where the real value was and politicians were charmed by the market – the 'end of boom and bust'. The pursuit of shareholder value as an end in itself and the prevailing assumption 'let the party continue' created a short-term mindset. The futility of the blame game that has since ensued has not helped to capture learnings that have implications for the journey ahead.

Her Majesty the Queen visited the London School of Economics in November 2008 and asked why nobody had noticed the credit crunch was on its way. The British Academy convened a forum on June 17, 2009 to debate the question with contributions from business, the City, its regulators, academia and government. In their letter to Her Majesty the Queen they stated:

"One of our major banks reputedly had 4000 risk managers. But the difficulty was seeing the risk to the system as a whole rather than to any specific financial instrument or loan... Everyone seemed to be doing their own job properly on its own merit... the failure was to see how collectively this added up to a series of interconnected imbalances over which no single authority has jurisdiction. This, combined with the psychology of herding and the mantra of political and financial gurus, led to a dangerous recipe. Individual risks may rightly have been viewed as small, but the risks to the system as a whole were vast" (T. Besley & P. Hennessy letter from British Academy, July 22, 2009).

We can see a number of psychological processes at work. These include group polarisation – (Myers, 2005) and shift to majority position to gain group approval (Isenberg, 1986). Group think (Janis, 1972) may also have occurred where consensus reached too quickly resulted in poor decision-making.

Awareness of such processes to help leaders become alert to the dangers of decision short cuts and thereby mitigate them is one area where business psychology can play a role.

The context of organisational resilience is changing

This has major implications for the leadership of resilient organisations, which requires leaders to take a more systemic perspective of potential risks. Developing an understanding of the changes ahead and implications for the economy, people, markets and organisations is key to creating the knowledge that executives need to manage for tomorrow rather than yesterday. It is interesting that amongst the volumes of literature on leadership and the many models there is not much reference to the context of leadership. Our perspective is that leadership is all about context and the skill of leadership is about defining what approach best fits different contexts. Thinking about leadership as context based rather than in terms of the characteristics of great leaders is perhaps a direction in which we can help to steer the debate.

Lessons learned from the recent financial crisis have important implications for dealing with greater uncertainties that lie ahead with the combined impact of climate change, peak oil, insurgency and other risks to our way of life.

However, as the green shoots of economic recovery emerge the focus can quickly shift away from discussions about learning to 'business as usual'. The financial crisis is discarded as yesterday's news when yesterday's learning is critical if we are to avoid history repeating itself. Amy Fraher in her book *The Next Crash – How Short Term Profit Seeking Trumps Airline Safety* (Fraher, 2014) provides a shocking perspective on the state of the aviation industry. She draws parallels between the 2008 Financial Crisis and post 9/11 airline industry to make the case that America is entering a period of unprecedented aviation risk.

We are in the middle of a historic economic transition

The old economic environment was protected by boundaries of territory, culture, accessibility of knowledge etc. The transition is to a boundary-less global economy where everything is connected and everything is at risk. The UK is emerging from a period of financial turbulence unprecedented since the 1929 crash. Turbulence, which defines a state of change that was not foreseen, is not new. The late Peter Drucker stated:

"The executive world has been turbulent for as long as I can remember – I started work two years before the 1929 crash." (Drucker, 1992, p. 8)

However, what is new is the advancing impact of globalisation, increasing complexity, speed of communication and exchange of knowledge, insurgency and market volatility amongst other factors. These are creating a new reality that is almost unrecognisable to previous generations. What is clear is that our understanding has failed to keep up with the pace. Peter Drucker refers to transitional periods in history, which challenge prevailing assumptions and require a new approach. He describes these transitional periods as 'Great Divides'

"At some point between 1965 and 1973 we passed 'a great divide' into the next century leaving behind the creeds, commitments and alignments that had shaped politics for a century or two. At the most profound level, The Enlightenment faith in progress through collective action 'salvation by society' which had been the dominant force of politics since the eighteenth century – was thoroughly dashed. This was not the first such divide… the last such divide was crossed a century earlier in 1873. That liberal century, in which the dominant political creed was laissez faire, began in 1776 with Adam Smith's The Wealth of Nations *and ended with the Vienna stock market crash and short lived panics in Paris, London, Frankfurt and New York in 1873."* (Drucker, 1992, pp. 1-2)

The evidence of the recent economic crisis suggests that we are in the middle of another 'Great Divide' as the economic environment shifts to one where there is greater inter-connectedness and consequently higher levels of unpredictability. The dynamic of this lies in many more factors impacting on outcomes and with cause and effect widely separated in space and time. This limits the ability to make rational judgements since they assume a linear cause/effect relationship.

It has now become almost commonplace for people to say that we are living in a period of unprecedented turbulence, socially, economically and environmentally, yet defining how best to respond to this is rarely voiced coherently. Instead, solutions are based on prevailing assumptions, which do not address the lessons learnt or the leadership that will promote resilient organisations.

Many traditional management tools used for forecasting, planning, measuring, assessing risk and financial modelling are insufficient for the purpose because they assume there is an ordered and objective reality that can be uncovered with increasingly sophisticated techniques based on linear cause and effect.

"As we advance deeper in the knowledge economy, the basic assumptions underlying much of what is taught and practiced in the name of management are hopelessly out of date. Most of the assumptions about business, technology and organization are at least 50 years old. They have outlived their time." (Drucker, 1998, p. 162)

The human reaction to changing contexts

The human reaction in quicksand is to grab onto the familiar. When dealing with an economic environment characterised by uncertainty and unpredictability the reaction is to focus on the tried and trusted. But what if the old ways prove to be insufficient as evidenced by the causes of the financial crisis? For example, traditional approaches to risk management ignored the systemic risks that were building up and financial models focused on short-term shareholder value and risks. Therefore leadership for organisational resilience requires leaders to assess whether the old ways are sufficient in dealing with the changing context.

A second human reaction is to assume that the future will continue to be a projection of the past or that step by step management procedures and processes will be sufficient in addressing increasing complexity and uncertainty. As with past 'Divides' prevailing assumptions dominate people's thinking about what is about to unfold. Such assumptions exclude thinking systemically and considering other possibilities outside our immediate frame of reference. Organisational resilience therefore requires leadership that challenges prevailing assumptions and considers whether they are fit for purpose in addressing the changing context.

The British Academy wrote a second letter to Her Majesty the Queen dated February 8, 2010 after hosting a seminar. This was to examine the 'never again' question in response to their earlier commitment to determining how Crown servants might develop a new horizon scanning capability. In their response they state:

"There is a need to develop a culture of questioning in which no assumption is accepted without scepticism and a sufficiently broad array of outcomes is considered." (T. Besley & P. Hennessy letter from British Academy, February 10, 2010)

The profitability of many global plcs far exceeds the GDP of many countries so, although this letter refers to Crown servants, it needs to apply even more to organisations. Leadership plays a key role in creating this culture.

A third human reaction is to exclude other possibilities and counter-perspectives that do not fit with the prevailing dominant narrative; for example 'let the party continue', 'the end of boom and bust', 'the focus on performance and growth' etc. In the lead up to the current financial crisis some claimed that they foresaw the risks but were not able to get their voice heard when the dominant thinking was so absorbed with the needs of the present moment, focusing on performance and growth. The impact of ideology, as Foucault describes (Foucault, 1980), is perhaps at work here.

Paul Moore, the former Head of Group Regulatory Risk at HBOS, claimed in his submission to the UK Treasury sub-committee on the Banking Crisis that the Bank had "a cultural indisposition to challenge". Michael Skapinker's article (2007) 'Silencing the dissenters can end your career' in the Financial Times on 6 November 2007 reported that "*Stan*

O'Neal Head of Merrill Lynch and Chuck Prince, Head of Citigroup were both renowned for removing those executives that disagreed with them". Likewise, similar comments have been made about Sir Fred Goodwin, the former CEO of RBS. Of course there are two sides to any story but there appears to be a broader issue, which is not confined to the Banking sector.

Martin Bromiley (2011), an aviation pilot, describes in a YouTube Video titled 'Just a Routine Operation' how his wife died due to complications in a routine operation. He described how a team of clinicians, all technically skilled, had failed to respond appropriately to an unanticipated emergency by focusing on certain remedial actions to the exclusion of other options. At the same time the nursing staff knew what was needed but did not know how to broach the subject. He attributes this to human factors, which include failure of leadership, situational awareness, prioritisation, decision making, communication and assertiveness, rather than technical ability. He draws parallels with the aviation industry, where such 'human factors' are present in 75% of accidents, and shows how the industry addresses this through training and safety checks which might provide lessons for the provision of clinical care. Following his wife's death he set up the Clinical Factors Group to promote awareness of human factors in healthcare from board to ward.

The BBC reported on their website on 11 February 2015 under the caption *'NHS Staff afraid to speak out'*. The head of a review into the treatment of whistle-blowers in England, Sir Robert Francis QC, tells the BBC he has heard "shocking accounts of suffering by staff who raised concerns". The Public Enquiry report (Francis, 2012) referred to: "a culture focused on doing the system's business – not that of the patients"; "A serious failure of the Trust Board it did not listen sufficiently to its patients and staff"; "A culture of fear in which staff did not feel able to report concerns" and the fact that "Management thinking was dominated by financial pressures and achieving Foundation Trust status to the detriment of care".

In an operating environment characterised by increasing uncertainty and unpredictability of outcomes the leadership of resilient organisations requires leaders to create a safe space for constructive challenge. They need to actively seek different and contrary perspectives, including the whistle-blowers, to better anticipate what is unforeseen. In this changing context scenario planning is not an optional extra but a key tool for strategic planning. As human beings easily get locked into their own frames of reference, which shut down other possibilities, the constructive use of conflict can enrich the whole and lead to better commercial outcomes (Lane & Corrie, 2012).

Kayes (2006) has provided a number of examples of this, most notably in the Everest climbing disaster. He identified critical decision errors where leaders continued to pursue the goal of reaching the summit against mounting evidence that this could not be achieved. Where goals become the exclusive drivers for action (what Kayes calls goalodicity) they provide a justification for action and a means to ignore alternative perspectives. Rather than accept conflicting views as evidence for decision making, the goal drives out alternatives, resulting in risky and potentially unethical behaviours. The reality for leaders is that, although many agree constructive conflict can improve the quality of decision-making, achieving this can be a task for which they feel ill prepared. Many find it really difficult not to be seduced into defensive discussions with someone who holds the opposite point of view. Therefore avoiding defensive reactions and personality attacks is an important ground rule for making the most effective use of constructive challenge.

Equally many find it difficult to share their different perspectives, particularly if it is the opposite point of view to the CEO! Anxieties flood their mind and they might struggle to find the right words to express themselves. Therefore creating a safe environment for people to share their contrary perspectives is a highly skilled art. It requires an appreciative and enquiring mind-set, which some describe as 'a beginners mind', avoiding defensive reactions and actively seeking the wisdom of the person's counter-perspective that will enrich the whole. The coaching skills of active listening, reflective summarising and open questioning help the person articulate their views. Reflecting and summarising the main themes briefly in two or three words keeps the focus on the person sharing. It also makes it easy to ask open questions which follow from what they have just said. This avoids the pitfall of using questions to drive them in the direction of your solution, which defeats the whole purpose. For the person who holds a contrary perspective, the challenge is how to get their voice heard when the dominant narrative is going in a different direction.

There are 3 things that can help, based on Myrna Lewis's (2015) 'Deep Democracy' method (www.deep-democracy.net) derived from Process Oriented Psychology. Firstly 'Prepositioning' to create a desire to be heard by stating *"I have a different perspective which I think has some benefits – can I share this with you?"* Secondly 'Share your perspective' with particular focus on communicating the benefits. Thirdly 'Follow up' by asking *"What elements of what I have just shared would you like to build on/discard"* and/or *"Is there anyone else here, like me, with a different perspective that they would like to share?"* The sharing of a different perspective and the invitation of others to share their different perspectives helps to create a safe environment.

"The presence of diverse viewpoints has been shown to significantly increase a team's creativity" (Hackman et al., 2007, p. 83). Although many agree with the potential benefits of recruiting and building diverse teams *"Too many leaders make the mistake of using a highly diverse mix of players as their core decision making team, without preparing either the team or the members to use their differences effectively."* (Hackman et al., 2007, p. 83)

People in an organisation have different levels of access to and understanding of the evolving external context, of which they are part. Not all have equal access to sharing their perspective with senior decision makers. A key role of leadership is to create common access for sharing these different perspectives that results in a better-shared understanding of the whole.

A fourth human reaction is anxiety and fear. The ability of leaders to manage their internal anxieties is critical to how they respond to the anxieties of others. They need to balance empathy with positivity, hope and a focus on what we can do to engage people's creative versus defensive reaction. Self awareness and understanding of instinctive human reactions is really important here. Personality questionnaires help executives create self awareness and the understanding that leads to more informed and effective choices that counter their instinctive human reactions.

Dealing with extreme stress or experience well beyond the normal is an important area of research in psychology. Insights from trauma psychology, resilience theory, and narrative restructuring provide ways in which psychology can help organisations and leaders to deal with anxiety and fear.

Trauma studies since the 1990s, which include people involved in natural and created disasters, hostage taking etc., mostly report recovery. Many report that people have learned something beneficial which has changed their lives for the better. For example following the 9/11 attack on the Twin Towers in New York some 58% of people reported benefits (Joseph, 2012). (Clearly those involved would rather the event had never happened; but once it had they learned something beneficial from it.)

An important factor in post-traumatic growth appears to be the existential wake up call – people cannot avoid the realisation that life is unpredictable and vulnerable. People who report growth may be deeply distressed by the event and suffer Post Traumatic Stress (PTS). It seems some degree of PTS is a necessary pre-cursor to psychological change following adversity. However, if the stress remains overwhelming it stifles growth. An inverted U graph seems to represent it. Over time those who report growth also report less stress (Joseph, 2012). The American Psychological Association, in looking at resilience, reported on a number of factors, which are helpful:

- Making connections with others
- Avoiding seeing crises as insurmountable
- Accepting that change is part of life
- Moving towards goals
- Taking decisive actions
- Looking for opportunities for self-discovery
- Nurturing a positive view of oneself

- Learning from the past
- Maintaining a hopeful outlook
- Self-care.

Of particular value is reconstructing the narrative of events (Corrie & Lane, 2010), moving from a narrative of ourselves (or our organisation) as victim to survivor to thriver. Joseph (2012) identifies six 'signposts' or steps:

i. **Take stock**: Check you are physically safe, getting help, eating and sleeping well and keeping physically active. Focus on what you can do. Be compassionate with yourself, observe reactions without judgement, confront traumatic memories, tune into emotions and how they influence you and reflect on what you learnt from past challenges that will help you manage the current situation. At the same time actively seek to connect with others not withdraw.
ii. **Harvest hope**: Use others' positive stories of how they have got through similar difficult situations. Take a step by step approach to defining what you could do. Use the miracle question (if you woke up tomorrow and the problem no longer existed – what would now be possible?). Build relationships that build hope. Create a picture of a future that is better.
iii. **Re-author:** Re-author or re-frame the negative stories you might be telling yourself about being a victim to being a survivor or thriver. Develop a mindset of *'everything is possible.'*
iv. **Identify change:** Keep a daily diary of what goes well and write down the things you feel grateful for.
v. **Value change:** Notice and value the changes you have been able to make. Remember and value what you have not lost.
vi. **Express change by action:** Think about what you have done and develop objectives to build on these actions.

Actively practising these six steps helps to address self-limiting beliefs of the mind that reinforce anxiety and fear in order to liberate hope and inspire actions that can positively help the transition from being a victim to a thriver.

Organisational resilience is elusive in an operating environment of high levels of unpredictability and uncertainty. The existing and new perspectives on leadership that are most relevant to this changing context are:

1) Adaptive (or Generative) Leadership

Uhl-Bien et al., (2007) in their paper on Complexity Leadership Theory make the distinction between *"Administrative Leadership"*, grounded in traditional notions of hierarchy, alignment and control; *"Enabling Leadership"*, creating the right conditions to optimise learning, explore different perspectives and solve problems; and *"Adaptive (or Generative) Leadership"*, an emergent and interactive dynamic that actively seeks different perspectives to deliver adaptive outcomes.

The cases quoted above: "*CEOs that removed executives that disagreed with them*" and "*cultures indisposed to challenge*" suggest a dominance of *Administrative Leadership* at the expense of an *Enabling* and *Adaptive* Leadership style. This increased risk exposure in a context of volatility and change.

2) Leadership as story telling

The stories that are told in organisations and in society, reinforced by the authority that people give to those in positions of power and influence, can have a dominating psychological effect in people's thinking and assumptions.

One such story is the way in which the numbers, 'the bottom line' or other such fallacies, come to dominate thinking.

The Mid Staffordshire Public Enquiry (Francis, 2012) states "Management thinking was dominated by financial pressures and achieving Foundation Trust Status to the detriment of care" and also refers to "Inadequate risk assessment of staff reductions". In the run up to the Financial crisis CEOs rejected warnings that all might not be well with the cry that "the numbers speak for themselves". This is well illustrated by the reported comment Chuck Prince, Citigroup's CEO, made to the FT in Japan (Nakamoto, 2007) "When the music stops, in terms of liquidity, things will get complicated. But as long as the music is playing you have got to get up and dance. We're still dancing."

Numbers can give us very useful information, but they can also provide an illusory sense of control resulting in a failure to examine our perspectives on numerical data with sufficient clarity (Lane & Corrie, 2006). There are many examples of companies who look at their own figures and congratulate themselves while failing to see emerging trends. A classic example is Smiths Crisps, at one time the brand leader. They continued to see sales grow for their crisps yet found themselves well behind the market in this area. Even more damaging was their failure to see the potential of the savoury snack category. Non-potato vegetable proteins could be produced more cheaply and were better suited to esoteric flavours. Comfort in their own numbers blinded them to these other possibilities (Berry & Norman, 2014).

Tversky and Kahnemann (1980) refer to the illusory correlation in which we assume that events are causally related where no such relationship exists. This short-cuts decision-making. The basic human need for control may be the dominant driver of this behavioural response. Emerging research from neuroscience may provide greater insights on how uncertainty triggers the control mechanism of the brain.

The way in which certain stories come to dominate is important if we are going to manage complexity. Foucault (1980) named the way priority is given to the dominant position as a regime of truth, which drives out alternative perspectives. Lane and Corrie (2006) suggested too much of our thinking and actions are reactions to what has been defined by others because we have internalised these regimes of truth. More recently they have extended this debate to look at the 'totalising' effect that dominant stories have in excluding alternatives (Corrie & Lane, 2010). In this the dominant story becomes the way in which all information has to be interpreted – that which fits the story is included, that which does not is excluded.

The 'totalising' effect of dominant stories is not confined to the private ('for-profit') sector but also applies in the public ('not-for-profit') sector. However, the different focus of the private and public sectors on 'shareholder value' and 'the public interest' plays out in different ways. In the case of the private sector dominant stories focus on delivery of shareholder value. This is often at the expense of meeting the wider needs of society and can have disastrous consequences e.g. destruction of rain forests and the proposed dumping of the Brent Spa Oil Platform in the North Sea by Shell, who misjudged the strength of public feeling. In the case of the public sector the focus on 'the public interest' can lead to policies that are narrowly defined on a country basis (e.g. 'light touch' Financial Regulation) and fail to take account of the need for global collaboration in an increasingly interconnected global economy.

3) Anticipating the unforeseen – the Black Swan factor

The critical challenge for leadership is to become better prepared to anticipate the unpredictability and vulnerability of unforeseen risks and overcome the blindness that comes when our dominant focus is absorbed by the immediacy of the moment. Focus often narrows in times of stress and this can exclude other possibilities. Taleb (2007) uses the term "the Black Swan factor" to describe improbable occurrences that are impossible to predict, have a major impact and create reactions of shock because people could never conceive of such an event happening. Within the training of military personnel this is well known. Concepts such as "operational pause" (Vego, 2010) to allow for a wider vision to occur have been proposed as a way to help. An operational pause is a pause in operations after an intermediate military objective has been achieved to consider the next phase, while retaining the initiative in other ways.

4) Complexity theory

Complexity theory provides a means to explore volatility. It is concerned with appreciating how sudden and unpredictable changes occur after a period of stability. It proposes that there are no pre-fixed destinations, but rather there are potentials (Wheatley, 1999). A classic example of decision failure was the attempt by the Rand Corporation to apply learning from the success of putting a man on the moon to solving problems in the education and health systems. It was assumed that the same systems thinking that solved the complicated task of a moon landing could improve our schools and hospitals. According to Checkland (1989) the moon landing was an instance where everyone agreed the purpose, the mission was clear and the science was understood. This was not the case for schools or hospitals where there were multiple competing objectives, issues that were dimly understood and multiple events that could not be predetermined. In other words, the problems were complex rather than complicated.

Problems can be tough because they are complex in three ways:

*"They are **dynamically complex**, which means that cause and effect are far apart in space and time… they are **generatively complex** which means they are unfolding in unfamiliar and unpredictable ways… they are **socially complex** which means that the people involved see things very differently and so problems become polarised and stuck."* (Kahane, 2007, pp. 1-2)

Kahane argues that as a result we cannot work from fixed positions of "telling" but rather have to embrace values of transparency, creativity and collaborative dialogue.

Stacey's complexity theory and his agreement/certainty matrix (Stacey, 1996), which we have adapted as detailed in Figure 1 below, provides a useful starting point. However, Stacey warns against this model being used as if it were possible to select in advance which tools to use, which misrepresents complexity. Indeed, he thinks the danger so great that he has stopped referring to this model. Hence we are not suggesting that you can predict and select in complex situations as if they were linear.

Cavanagh and Lane (2012) provide the illustration of a car driver: filling the car with fuel is simple, fixing a fault might be complicated, driving is always complex and getting caught up in another's road rage is chaotic. We never know when one might become the other.

i. **The level of certainty**
   - A **high level of certainty** of outcomes associated with driving

the short term agenda/strategy typically requires the traditional tools of planning and performance management

- **A low level of certainty** associated with increasing complexity and systemic risk requires leadership to take a systemic and consultative approach in mapping out different scenarios

ii. **The level of agreement on outcomes**

- A **high level of agreement** on outcomes is typically associated with the short term agenda
- A **low level of agreement** on outcomes is typically associated with complexity

Stacey's matrix provides a framework for defining the leadership approach dependant on the level of 'Certainty' and 'Agreement'

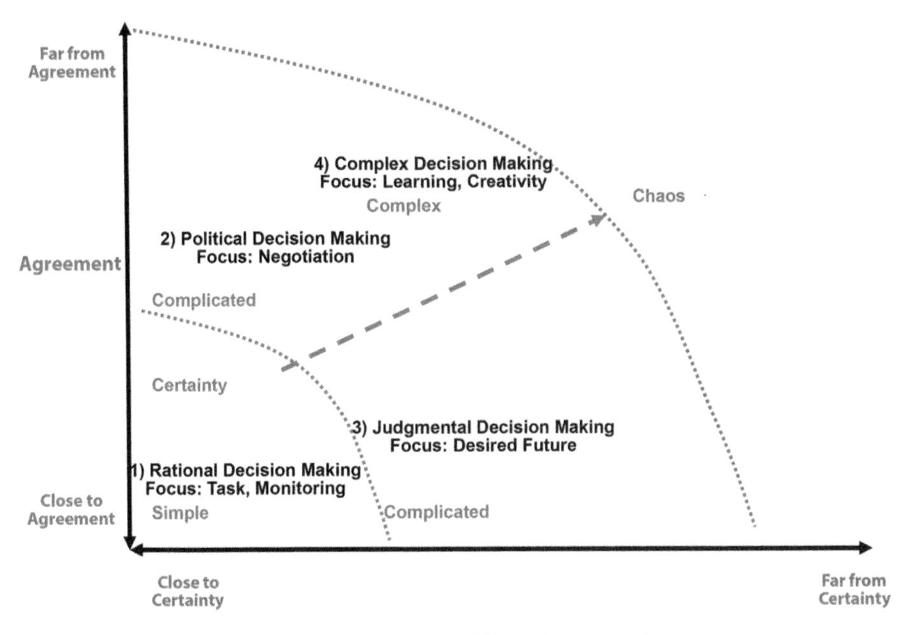

Figure 1: Agreement/Certainty matrix
(Adapted from R. Stacey)

This is rarely an either/or choice. Executives need to be good at managing both the short term agenda, typically characterised by higher levels of agreement and certainty, with the ability to manage situations where there is a low level of agreement and low levels of predictability. But you cannot predict and select in advance what state will exist. The complex cannot be divided up.

The following table lists examples of tools and thinking styles that might be appropriate to these different contexts – but keep in mind the warning above.

Table 1.
Tools & Thinking Styles

High level of agreement and certainty	**Low level of agreement and certainty**
Examples of tools • Strategic planning • Goal setting • Performance management • Measurement and progress evaluation • Plan Do Review • GROW performance coaching model based on agreed goals	**Examples of tools** • Scenario Planning • Facilitation • Dialogue • Conflict Management • Learning • Mindfulness • Transformative coaching – to challenge prevailing assumptions and generate new awareness and thinking
Dominant thinking style • Functional thinking – delivery of growth targets, alignment and control • Linear thinking – cause and effect	**Dominant thinking style** • Systemic & integrative thinking seeing the connections between the parts

"Most developmental psychologists agree what differentiates leaders is not so much their philosophy of leadership, their personality, or their style of management. Rather it's their internal 'action logic' – how they interpret their surroundings and react when power or safety is challenged." (Rooke & Torbert, 2005, p. 1*)*

Power and safety are often challenged when closer to chaos, where conventional wisdom no longer applies. Torbert's Action Inquiry Model (Torbert, 2004) provides a developmental framework to learn different action logics. The framework defines seven developmental action logics: Opportunist, Diplomat, Expert, Achiever, Individualist, Strategist, and Alchemist. Traditionally most management development has focused on the first four action logics, which fit well with conventional approaches to leadership. In the future it will be increasingly important to develop leaders in the last three action logics, which are a better fit with the management of uncertainty.

A number of emerging management tools and techniques enable systemic thinking and transformative dialogue, and support the leadership of uncertainty. For example Appreciative Enquiry, World Café, Open Space Technology, Scenario Planning, Deep Democracy (Bojer et al., 2008).

The Agreement/Certainty Matrix helps us to recognise different decision approaches we adopt. In the events leading up to the current financial crisis leadership was primarily engaged with the delivery of growth targets, alignment and control. It was less focused on identifying systemic and emergent risks to delivering a robust, stable global financial system in an increasingly interconnected global economy.

Case Study – Leadership in contexts of low agreement/low certainty

South Africa – The Transition from Apartheid

Adam Kahane (2007) describes how leaders from different national constituencies participated in workshops at the Mont Fleur Conference Centre near Capetown to explore the birth of the new South Africa. The Mont Fleur process engaged participants in a process of dialogue, which involved mapping scenarios based on what might happen. He describes how *"simple problems, with low complexity, can be solved perfectly well – efficiently and effectively – using processes that are piecemeal, backward looking and authoritarian. By contrast highly complex problems can only be solved using processes that are systemic, emergent and participatory"* (Kahane, 2007, p. 32). This echoes Stacey's model, which defines complex problems in terms of low agreement and certainty. The Mont Fleur process was *"unusual because it was well suited to solving highly complex problems – to enacting profound social innovations. … it was* systemic *building scenarios for South Africa as whole, taking account of social, political, economic and international dynamics. It was* emergent, *because it recognized that precedents and grand plans would be of limited use but instead used creative teamwork to identify and influence the country's critical choices. And it was* participatory *involving leaders from most of the key national constituencies."* (Kahane, 2007, p. 32)

Complex problems require a different way of listening and engaging with others to shift the entrenched positions that lead to problems getting stuck. This means listening openly and reflectively to different perspectives in order to be open to new possibilities and the emergence of an agreed purpose. Kahane describes how Mont Fleur *"helped to shift the economic thinking and acting of the ANC and other left-wing parties and to avert an economic disaster."* (Kahane, 2007, p. 25)

Conclusion

If we see the future as essentially predictable then we may infer that leadership is about 'command and control' in driving the organisation and people to a predefined goal. If the future is seen as being unpredictable then we may infer that leadership is about dialogue and learning. Seeing the future as a combination of both, with the short term being more predictable and the medium to longer term more unpredictable, raises a further question about the leadership that is required to achieve a balance.

We have argued that existing, linear models of management can be used if there is a high level of agreement and predictability of outcome but are inadequate in addressing a world that is becoming less predictable and more turbulent. Resilient organisations require leadership to be adaptive, selecting the approach that best fits with the context and actively seeking different perspectives to map out alternative scenarios of the future. At the same time it requires the leader to be skilful in handling issues associated with power, conflict and blame as people struggle with their own ability to deal with ambiguity. How leaders contend with uncertainty in the external world is partly a function of how they deal with uncertainty within themselves. Leaders make better choices based on self-awareness and understanding of personality than when they just follow their impulsive reactions.

References

Berry, S., & Norman, P. (2014). *A Brief History of Crisps*. London: Harper Collins.

Besley, T., & Hennessy, P. (2009, July 22) Letter to Her Majesty the Queen. London: British Academy.

Besley, T., & Hennessy, P. (2010, February 10) Letter to Her Majesty the Queen, London: British Academy.

Bojer, M. M., Roehl, H., Knuth, M., & Magner, C. (2008). *Mapping dialogue essential tools for social change*. Chagrin Falls, OH: Taos Institute.

Bromiley, M. (2011). *Just a routine operation 2011*. Retrieved from https://www.youtube.com.

Cavanagh, M., & Lane, D. (2012). Coaching psychology coming of age: The challenges we face in the messy world of complexity. *International Coaching Psychology Review,* 7(1), 75-90.

Checkland, P. (1989). An application of Soft Systems Methodology. In S. Rosenhead (Ed.), *Rational Analysis for a Problematic World* (pp. 71-100). Chichester: Wiley.

Corrie, S., & Lane, D. A. (2010). *Constructing stories, telling tales: A guide to formulation in applied psychology*. London: Karnac Books.

Drucker, P. F. (1992). *Managing for the future*. Oxford: Butterworth-Heinemann.

Drucker, P. F. (1998). Management's new paradigms. *Forbes, 162*(7), 152-170.

Foucault, M. (1980). *Power/knowledge: Selected interview and other writings.* New York, NY: Pantheon.

Fraher, A. L. (2014). *The next crash: How short term profit seeking trumps airline safety.* Ithaca: Cornell University Press.

Francis, R. (2012). *Report of the Mid Staffordshire NHS Foundation Trust Public Enquiry, Executive Summary*. London: The Stationary Office.

Francis, R. (2015). *NHS Staff afraid to speak out.* Retrieved from http://www.bbc.co.uk/news/health-31362196.

Hackman, J. R., Wageman, R., Nunes, D. A., & Burruss, J. A. (2007). *Senior leadership teams.* Boston, MA: Harvard Business School Press.

Isenberg, D. G. (1986). Group polarization: A critical review. *Journal of Personality and Social Psychology, 50*, 1041-1051.

Janis, I. L. (1972). *Victims of group think*. Boston: Houghton Mifflin.

Joseph, S. (2012). *What doesn't kill us: The new psychology of post-traumatic growth.* London: Piatkus Little Brown.

Kahane, A. (2007). *Solving tough problems: An open way of listening and creating new realities.* San Francisco, CA: Berrett-Koehler.

Kay, J. (2003). *The truth about Markets: their genius, their limits, their follies*. London: Penguin.

Kayes, D. C. (2006). *Destructive goal pursuit: The Mount Everest disaster*. Basingstoke: Palgrave.

Lane, D. A., & Corrie, S. (2006). *The modern scientist practitioner: A guide to practice in psychology*. Hove: Routledge.

Lane, D. A., & Corrie, S. (2012). *Making successful decisions in counselling and psychotherapy*. Maidenhead: Open University Press.

Lewis, M. (2015). *Inside the no: Five steps to decisions that last.* Retrieved from http://www.deep-democracy.net.

Myers, D. G. (2005). *Social psychology.* (8th ed.). New York, NY: McGraw Hill.

Moscovici, S., & Zavalloni, M. (1969). The group as a polarizer of attitudes. *Journal of Personality and Social Psychology, 12*, 125-135.

Nakamoto, M. (2007). *Citigroup chief stays bullish on buy-outs.* Retrieved from http://www.ft.com/cms/s/0/80e2987a-2e50-11dc-821c-0000779fd2ac.html #axzz3YRMGb9Ax.

Rooke, D., & Torbert, W. (2005). Seven transformations of leadership. *Harvard Business Review, April*, 1-12.

Skapinker, M. (2007, November 6). Silencing the dissenters can end your career, *Financial Times*, p. 15.

Stacey, R. D. (1996). *Strategic Management & Organisational Dynamics.* London: Pitman.

Stoner, J. A. F. (1961). *A comparison of individual and group decisions including risk.* (Master's thesis, Massachusetts Institute of Technology. Boston).

Taleb, N. N. (2007). *The black swan – The impact of the highly improbable.* London: Penguin.

The American Psychological Association. (n.d.). *Facilitating post trauma growth – APA guide the road to resilience.* Retrieved from www.apa.org/helpcenter/resilience.aspx.

Torbert, W. (2004). *Action inquiry: the secret of timely and transforming leadership.* San Francisco, CA: Berrett-Koehler.

Tversky, A., & Kahnemann, D. (1980). Judgment under uncertainty: heuristics and biases. *Science, 185*, 1124-1131.

Uhl-Bien, M., Marion, R., & McKelvey, W. (2007). Complexity leadership theory: Shifting leadership from the industrial age to the knowledge era. *The Leadership Quarterly*, *18*(4), 298-318.

Vego, M, M. (2010). *Operational warfare at sea: theory and practice*. New York, NY: Routledge.

Wheatley, M. (1999). *Leadership and the new science: Discovering order in a chaotic world*. San Francisco, CA: Berrett-Koehler.

RISK, OPPORTUNITY AND PERSONAL RESPONSIBILITY

Geoff Trickey

In everyday life there is a tacit recognition that people vary considerably in their risk taking behaviour. Dangerous incidents, accidents and even major disasters can almost always be accounted for by the behaviour of individuals, but this perspective is barely considered in risk management strategy or professional practice.

Risk within organisations has largely been addressed through 'blanket' procedures, processes and systems designed to contain them, approaches that have been enforced by regulation and legislation. This exclusive focus on the risk without consideration of the characteristics of the perpetrator has significant limitations.

Firstly, it encourages the simplistic view that risk is necessarily a bad thing, something to be eliminated. It restricts the risk agenda, it restricts the national debate and, more subtly, but perhaps of greater consequence ultimately, it also understates the role of personal responsibility.

People vary considerably in their disposition towards risk, differences that are very significant in terms of personality, behaviour and survival. Since psychology has a great deal to say about individual differences and about risk related behaviour, business psychology has an important contribution to make to this discussion. A time when risk taking within financial institutions brought us close to global catastrophe is a good moment to get involved.

It would seem that, to all intents and purposes, the human factor has generally been assigned to the 'too hard basket', just too vague and complex to deal with. The pre-eminence of a systems approach that is mostly concerned with procedures, rules and regulations has sometimes resisted the idea of individual differences as something that might be used to excuse undesirable risk behaviour. There is a worry that, once we recognise that some people are by nature more impulsive than others, for example, they may somehow 'get away with it'.

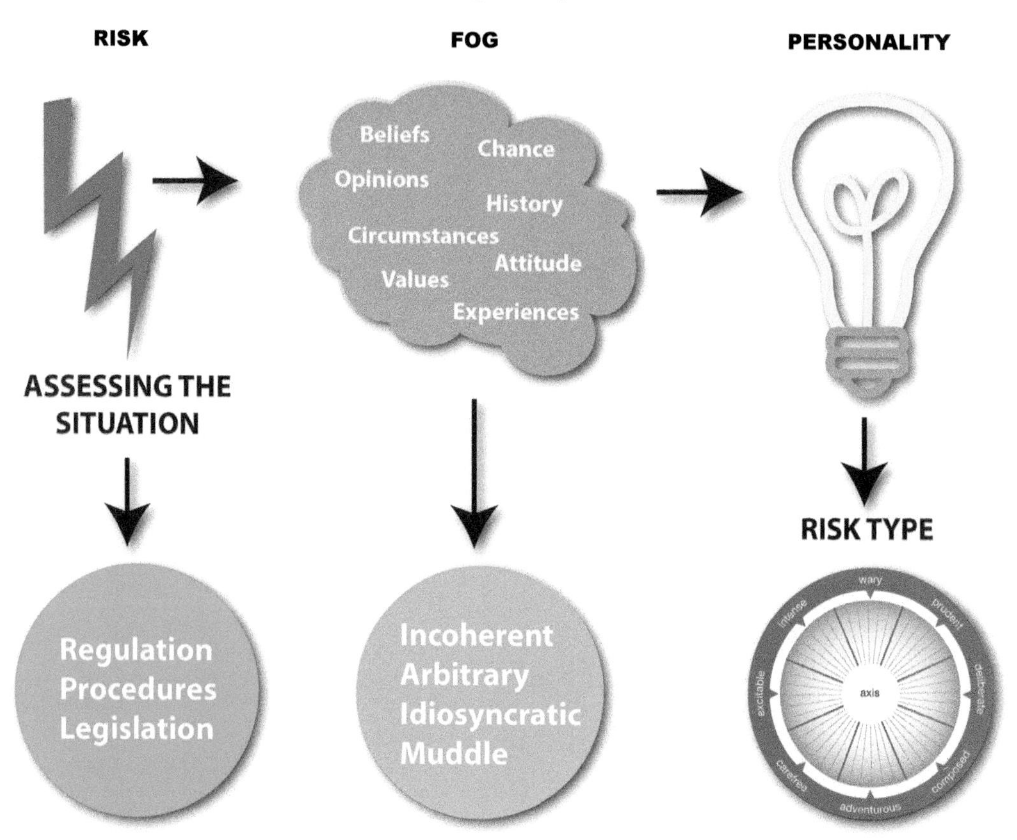

Figure 1: Risk, Fog and Personality

The conceptual confusion surrounding risk and behaviour provides some justification for this attitude. The determinants of behaviour are rarely simple or obvious and the terminology that surrounds this subject is anything but clear, raising more questions than answers. Figure 1 signposts our journey through the 'FOG'.

It's hard to think of any person, subject, situation, object, or profession that is untouched by risk. Our dreams, our relationships and our very existence are all both exposed to risk and potentially pose risk to others.

Risk is in attendance from the point of conception. We experience it in the processes of nurturance and upbringing, and grapple with it in learning to walk. Like the air we breathe, we take its presence for granted, dealing with it intuitively and taking it in our stride until we run into difficulties. The omnipresence of risk, the depth of our familiarity with it and the subconscious nature of our awareness of it, all sit uncomfortably beside efforts to define, formalise, and quantify it.

Risk isn't a prescribed subject, like History or Geography or Science, because risk operates within those subjects – indeed within *any* subject. Although we may talk about it as if it were something tangible, 'risk' is actually a highly abstract concept. It's an over-arching term, a way of classifying things according to their current condition or circumstances. Rather than being something that exists independently as a discrete entity, 'risk' actually means very different things across a universe of situations. Without a context, the term 'risk' is virtually meaningless and indefinable beyond its passive connotations of 'vulnerability and loss' or its active connotations of 'danger'.

This is not merely a matter of semantics. The main strategies of risk management have focused on the risk itself and matters of definition and measurement are critical for that approach. If risk isn't defined, then it certainly cannot be measured. If risk depends on context for its definition and measurement, this imposes considerable limitations on the development of any body of generalisable risk management methods and techniques. What applies to financial risk may have no parallel in health risk or recreational risk. Within the risk domain, measurement has to be defined as is appropriate to the situation, in terms of incidents, frequencies or impact and there can be no single metric that is common to all risk.

Addressing risk through the procedures and processes of Health and Safety regulations has had a lot of success, but the statistics confirm that there is still an awfully long way to go. Approaching risk from the 'people' angle at the level of individual differences, teams and organisational culture opens up exciting new frontiers and a lot of possibilities for the application of scientific psychology.

FOG

Recent efforts to assess individual differences in propensity for risk were given impetus by the Financial Conduct Authority (FCA – previously Financial Services Authority), one of the main regulators within the world of banking and finance. In the wake of various mis-selling scandals, they required financial advisors to assess each client's appetite for risk as a guide to suitable recommendations about financial products. The difficulty was that there was no very convincing way to do it. Not surprising really, since at that time this was hardly a prominent topic in the academic literature on psychometrics or individual differences. However, there was prolific activity in the financial world as a result of this ruling and no shortage of questionnaires, many described as 'psychometric' and some with as few as four items! To anyone with any kind of psychometric background, this looked suspect. Even for many financial advisors, it was difficult to muster any conviction about the utility of the exercise. The issue, for wealth managers, was how to prevent this becoming a mere box-ticking chore driven by the insistence of regulators rather than something that really worked for a service provider or for their clients.

Many of these assessments were thoughtful and ingenious but, understandably, they were technically very limited. In most cases, the declared aim of assessment was to assess 'risk attitude'. Attitude is a term that is used in a variety of ways, but it is usually considered to be something that can change. Government agencies have been successful in changing attitudes to drink-driving and smoking for example. Surveys suggest that attitudes to disability were influenced by the Paralympics. Changes in attitudes to financial risk, or 'sentiment' are monitored closely as a reflection of market activity. Since markets change continually, the intended purpose of the FCA surely required assessment of something more stable than attitudes.

This example highlights the conceptual minefield existing around the fringes of personality. When terms like attitude, values or temperament are used as explanatory concepts, they need to be defined. The danger otherwise is that they contribute to the semantic confusion rather than providing answers. As suggested in Figure 1, ill-defined concepts contribute to the muddle.

PERSONALITY

The surprising thing is that the importance of personality had been overlooked as a key influence on risk behaviour. Paradoxically, the success of personality assessment as an almost routine HR tool may have contributed to this oversight. Over recent years the predictive utility of personality has undoubtedly been 'oversold' and sometimes viewed as having an almost mechanical relationship with performance. Figure 2 is suggested as a more realistic view.

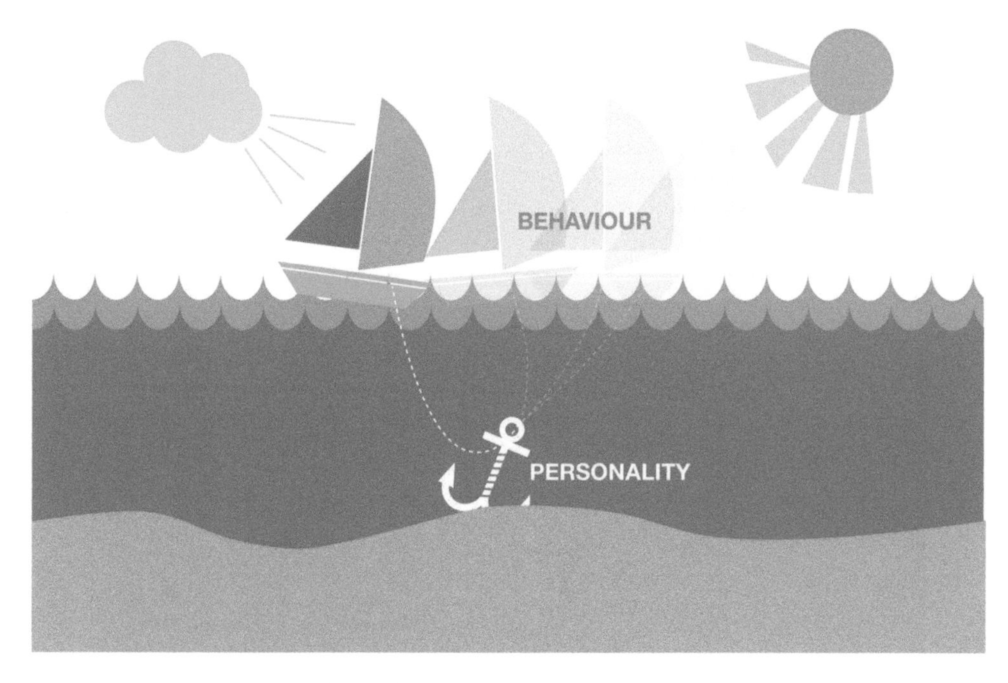

Figure 2: Personality and Behaviour

Since personality characteristics are, to some extent, heritable, the genetic element is likely to have a consistent and persistent influence. Whatever the other influences on behaviour may be, they will be intermittent and will vary. Personality is about dispositions and inclinations and, rather than tightly controlling behaviour, its influence on risk taking is likely to be in establishing thresholds and setting boundaries. As sentient beings, of course we have the capability to act in many ways, pushing the limits and stretching our comfort zones. We have goals and aspirations of the moment and we have free will in dealing with an infinite variety of situations, but our risk taking is anchored by dispositions that underpin distinct personal preferences and limits.

At the beginning of our research into Risk Type, there had been some success in exploring the relationships between personality and risk taking. The surprising thing was that, even though results had looked promising and although personality was referenced in many texts as being relevant to risk issues (e.g. Elvin, 2004 and Fenton-O'Creevy et al., 2005), 'risk personality' has never achieved any degree of prominence. The lines had already been drawn for the big debate in risk and that did not include the human factor. In the financial world it was all about regulation vs. unrestrained market forces. Health and safety had also committed to a rules and regulations approach which brooked no variation or personal discretion and in which personal responsibility was reduced to obedience.

Following the early work of Hogan at Johns Hopkins University on the Five Factor Model (FFM) in the early 1970s, there was a steadily growing consensus about the measurement of personality. Subsequent meta-analyses (Costa & McCray, 1992 and Barrick & Mount 1991) and an extensive and growing global literature gave us a lot of risk related material to draw from. For example, high scorers on Neuroticism interpret ambiguous stimuli as more threatening (MacLeod & Cohen, 1993). The sensation seeking aspect of Extraversion is associated with higher risk tolerance (Pan & Statman, 2012). Higher scorers on Openness search for new experiences and actively seek out risk (Kowert & Herman, 1997). High Conscientiousness is significantly associated with being intolerant of uncertainty, change and innovation (Nicholson et al., 2005), and with a need for conformity and control (Hogan & Ones, 1997). These and numerous other observations provided convincing evidence that what was already known about risk and personality provided a solid foundation for further research.

THE PCL STUDY

We found many studies that illustrated the relationship between risk behaviour and four of the five FFM factors (Emotional Stability, Conscientiousness, Open-to-experience and Extraversion). Evidence for the fifth (Agreeability) was difficult to interpret with any confidence. Clearly, the common assumption that a propensity for risk was simply a linear scale from reckless at one end and risk-aversion at the other was not going to reflect this complexity. However, FFM assessments tap into aspects of personality far beyond the focus on risk and, from a practical point of view, the FFM questionnaires are too lengthy and complex for the purposes of financial advisors and risk managers. Merely shortening the FFM questionnaire would compromise on measurement quality and still lack focus. For these reasons we set out to extract the personality themes of FFM that were risk related, leaving behind what might, for this purpose, just be noise in the system.

22 subthemes were identified as potentially relevant in some way to risk taking or risk aversion and selected for inclusion in the research. In a process involving data collection, factor analysis and classical methods of item analysis and scale construction we developed two bi-polar scales. In effect we reorganised the FFM content relating to risk to create coherent and meaningful dimensions of risk disposition: the perception of risk, emotional reaction to risk and the propensity to take or avoid risk. An understanding of these two scales is the key to the Risk Type Compass®.

The first bi-polar scale looks very much like a version of FFM Neuroticism, although its content is entirely risk related. One pole defines a disposition that is extremely alert to risk and emotionally aroused to action by it. The threshold for risk perception for those at this end of the scale will be very low. Their predisposition is anxious, apprehensive and fundamentally pessimistic so that anything unfamiliar or ambiguous will be perceived as a threat until proved otherwise. Their reaction to risk is visceral, strong, passionate and expressed physically and vocally, more tuned for flight than for fight. Those falling at this extreme have very sensitive risk antennae. They are the early warning system for our species: vigilant, anxious, apprehensive and emotional with a passionate concern about security and loss.

People falling at the other pole of this first scale would have opposite characteristics: an unusually high threshold for the perception of risk, an unemotional response to it and a greater readiness to take risks. Such people will view unfamiliar or ambiguous events with interest rather than apprehension. Their optimism leads to anticipation of positive outcomes, new possibilities and opportunities. They will resist the perception of risk until certain that it is worth worrying about, hanging on to their positive expectation as long as possible. As a consequence, they may be the last to appreciate the danger and may be forced to take last minute action. Being calm and unemotional, they are well equipped to deal with such situations and to bounce back from failures. Tuned for fight rather than flight, disappointments, upsets, or failures arouse little emotion, no regrets, disparagement or remorse; such set-backs can easily be taken in their stride. Their willingness to take it down to the wire before bailing out will open doors to opportunities that would otherwise have been missed.

The second of our two bi-polar scales is concerned broadly with restraint and impulsivity, and the priority given to planning and detailed preparation. In personality terms, this is a more complex scale that draws something from three FFM factors: Extraversion, Conscientiousness and Openness to Experience.

The first pole is characterised by the need to understand, to make sense of things and to prepare appropriate and suitable actions, carefully and in detail. At this extreme people will not do anything until they see good reason to do so and unless they have a clear and well-prepared plan of action. Preparation of a response for such people draws heavily on accumulated knowledge, established practices and approval of the elders. In this sense they are conservative, conventional and respectful of tradition. Rather than presume that they are sufficiently qualified to act, they seek approval or permission. The assumption seems to be that there will be a correct way of doing things. Their ideal is to organise risk out of the equation. In their need to comprehend, they seek to displace uncertainty and ambiguity through understanding. These characteristics are the antithesis of spontaneity. This disposition makes them thorough, but also makes it difficult to innovate.

The opposite pole of this second scale is concerned with excitement seeking and impulsivity. Those who score at this extreme will be easily bored, preferring the new to the familiar and the unconventional to the traditional. Because they enjoy and embrace uncertainty they are more comfortable about doing things 'on the fly' than planning events carefully or in plenty of time. They are imaginative and experimental but will struggle with vigilance and routine, repetitive tasks that they will find irksome. Restless and easily bored, they seek action, welcome change and may be frustrated by traditions and conventions that stand in their way. They are prone to challenge the *status quo*, have little respect for rulebooks and will do little to restrain their impulses. Curious, questioning, and stimulated by novelty and innovation, they broaden any debate and bring enthusiasm and fresh ideas to the table.

The important caveat to these four cameo descriptions is that these one dimensional perspectives will always be elaborated and embellished by all the themes of personality not addressed by this assessment, but which will all interact with and qualify these risk characteristics in one way or another.

Everyone falls somewhere on both of these scales. It's not difficult to suggest which extreme might be preferred in accounts, in sales, in bomb disposal or in caring for young children on a railway platform.

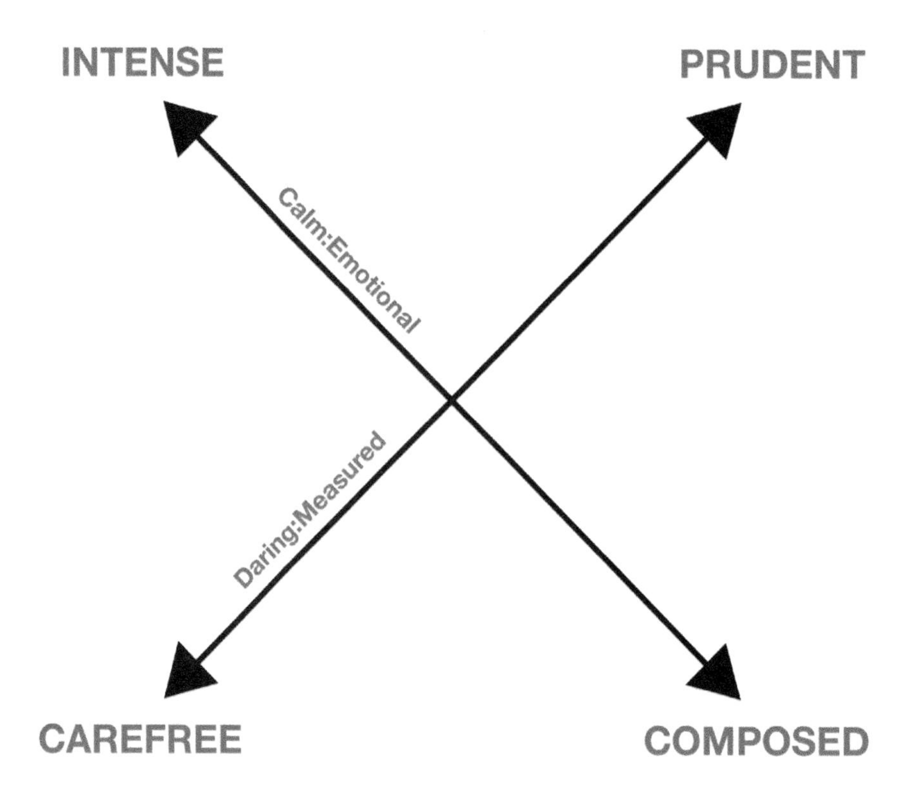

Figure 3: Four Factors – two bi-polar scales

The basic differentiating outcome would be an individual scoring towards the extreme of one of the scales (Prudent, Carefree, Intense *or* Composed). However, every individual will actually score somewhere along both of these scales, creating the possibility of scoring at one or other extreme on both. To address this inevitability, four intermediate radii were required to describe those achieving high scores on two neighbouring compass points, creating the following model:

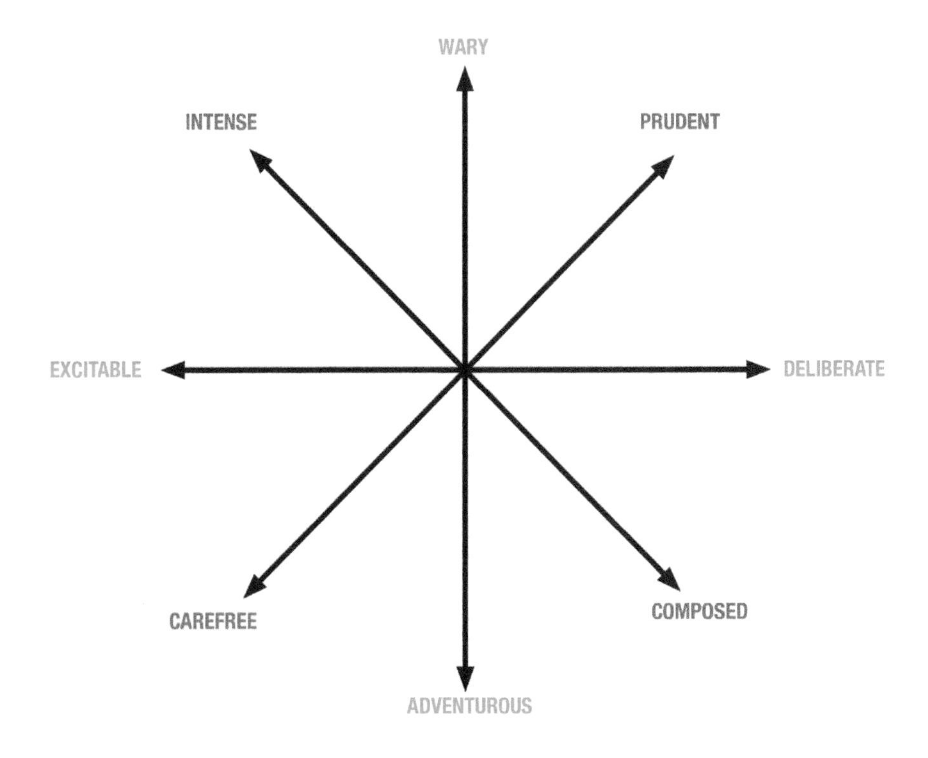

Figure 4: Eight Risk Types

The original four compass points were described as 'pure Risk Types' and the additions, which involved interaction between two high scores, were described as 'complex Risk Types'. In reality, this is a continuous 360° spectrum in which neighbouring Risk Types blend into each other and this is reflected on the positioning of the candidate's 'dot' radially and in terms of distance from the axis.

The final task was to design algorithms that would accurately place individuals within the compass space according to their scores on the two underlying scales. The compass space illustrated below allowed for 25 different locations within each segment after having designated a central 'axial' group that achieved scores close to the mean on both scales.

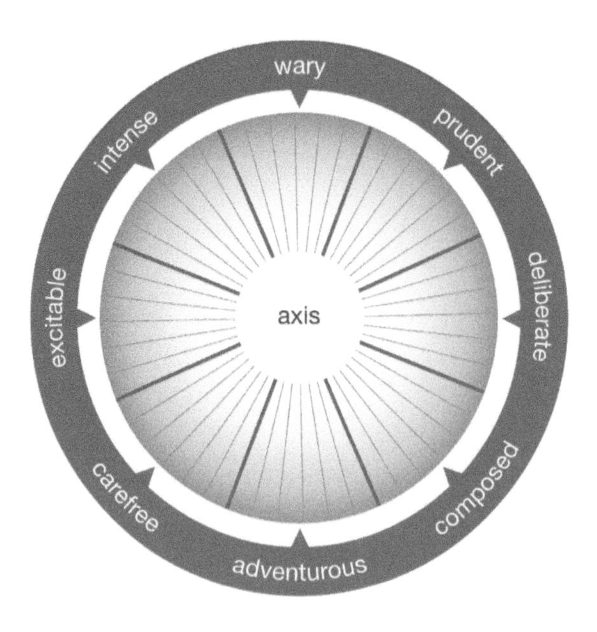

Figure 5: The Risk Type Compass®

The incidence of the eight Risk Types defined by the process described above, using data from 4200 individuals from a variety of industries and sectors, is illustrated in Figure 6.

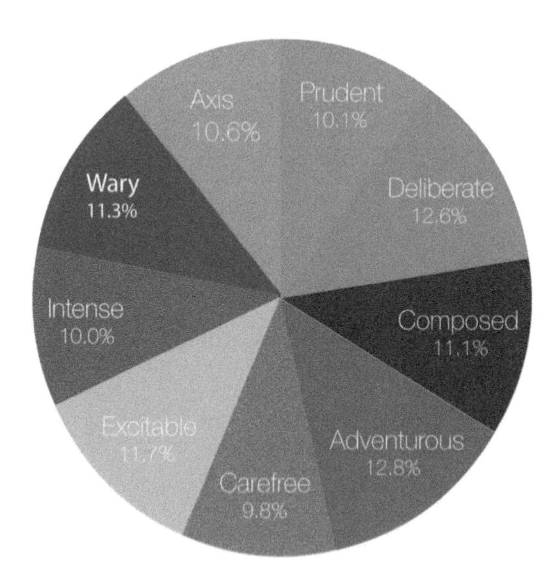

Figure 6: Incidence of Risk Types

This equality of incidence of Risk Types in this data clearly reflected the symmetry of the distribution of the two underlying scales.

THE RISK TYPE TAXONOMY

Excitable

Uninhibited and unconventional, they are attracted to the spontaneity and excitement of unplanned decisions like moths to a flame. Risk taking appeals because of their impulsivity but, because of their passion and emotionality, they are likely to be distraught when things go wrong.

Intense

Extreme examples are highly strung, pessimistic and anxious. Alert to any threat, they are cautious and defensive in relationships and in decision-making. The passion and intensity they invest when they commit to something leaves them vulnerable and the scars of failure take a long time to heal.

Wary

Organised, highly vigilant and fervent in their concerns about security, they are pro-active in their desire to enlist others to their cause and seek to control people and situations. Difficult to reassure, and defensive in their decision-making, they are wary of innovation and are procedural and regulatory in their approach to risk.

Prudent

This type is troubled by ambiguity and uncertainty and will rely on conformity and convention. These preferences reflect a need for understanding and certainty which may make them cautious, inflexible and slow to change. They are self-disciplined and most comfortable with continuity and familiarity.

Deliberate

Reliable and compliant, this Risk Type likes to 'do things by the book'. They tend to be calm, even-tempered and self-confident. They experience little anxiety and tackle risk and uncertainty in a purposeful and business-like way. They never walk into anything unprepared.

Composed

The Composed Type is consistently cool-headed, confident and optimistic. They seem to take everything in their stride and manage stress well. Even in conflict situations that would be disturbing to most they will keep their heads. At the extreme they seem almost oblivious to risk and unaware of its effect on others.

Adventurous

Both impulsive and fearless, the Adventurous Risk Type has two risk taking impulses. They combine a deeply constitutional calmness with high impulsivity and a willingness to challenge tradition and convention. Their need for excitement makes them enthusiastic, open to new ideas, and intrepid.

Carefree

Spontaneous and unconventional, they are excitement seeking and at times reckless. With no time for detail or careful planning, their imprudence can lead to hasty and unwise decisions. Their enjoyment of unpredictability and willingness to test the limits can add an original and exciting perspective to the debate.

The Axial Group

About 10 to 12% of people fall close to the axis of the Risk Type Compass® and cannot be assigned to one particular Risk Type. This group is well placed to appreciate the various Risk Type viewpoints and any biases resulting from those dispositions. This is a vantage point for mediation and conflict resolution.

Two important points to bear in mind are: firstly, that the Risk Type Compass® actually presents a continuous 360° spectrum of risk dispositions. The risk typology above simply provides framework of reference; secondly, there are no good or bad Risk Types. As with all personality characteristics, each has potential benefits and disadvantages in different circumstances and situations. Although there may be particular attractions in some occupations for particular Risk Types (and the evidence strongly suggests that this is the case), every organisation and profession will still have some positions that buck any such general trend; an argument in favour of Risk Type diversity.

The more risk averse professions will need some risk takers in, for example, business development roles, R&D, marketing, PR and promotion. The professions that necessarily take more risks will need to balance this with people who are more cautious and attentive to detail, particularly in their financial, risk management, compliance and legal functions. Whatever an individual's role, they need to be aware of the particular behavioural biases implied by their Risk Type. There will be both benefits and potential pitfalls that define a personal agenda for each individual. An appreciation of these strengths and limitations enables them to take personal responsibility for their behaviour and improve their performance.

The Risk Type Compass® developments described above were designed to achieve the benefits of a risk typology within a compass format that could readily be understood. It defines a human risk factor vocabulary that adds to utility of the model for risk managers and could generally be beneficial in the wide range of industries where it might have application.

RISK TYPE IN CONTEXT

Having decided on personality as the exclusive focus of the Risk Type Compass®, many other influences fell logically into place. We had decided on personality as our starting point because of the broadly consensual taxonomy provided by FFM and all the associated research. However, other terminologies abound in the risk literature and some stand out as making important and complementary contributions to our understanding of risk behaviour. The following glossary of terms makes some important distinctions and provides an introduction to the conceptual framework within which Risk Type plays its part. These are terms that go with the territory.

Risk Attitude: attitudes are changeable. They may not be of any long term significance but they are likely to contribute to current behaviour (the movement of the boat in Figure 2). Attitudes are influenced by training, exposure, circumstances and experience. As a result, we may seem more risk tolerant in areas that we have become familiar with, where we have learned to navigate the risks particular to that domain. Any apparent increase in risk taking may be due to domain knowledge, familiarity and the reduction of uncertainty, rather than to any change in risk tolerance or Risk Type.

Risk Intelligence: (Apgar 2006; Evans 2012) this is the capacity to learn about the nature of risk from experience and to understand its probabilistic nature – its statistical likelihood. It relates to the development of strategies for estimating risk rationally rather than emotionally. Fear of flying, for example, does not reflect the statistical data demonstrating the relatively higher risk of travelling by car.

Risk Savvy: (Gigerenzer, 2014) this term addresses similar territory to Risk Intelligence. It focuses on the prevalent lack of understanding about risk and its impact on decision-making, on the dangers (paradoxically) of defensive decision-making by doctors, on interpreting research and on the distortions created by sensational journalism quoting the relative health risk (of, for example, a particular diet) without specifying risk baseline. Doubling the risk may be acceptable if previously rated as 1:10,000,000 but not if previously rated as a 1:10 probability.

Risk Tolerance: this is generally understood to be about emotional resilience and the absence of fear, anxiety or apprehensiveness. The more risk tolerant you are, the more risk you can cope with. But it is clear from the Risk Type model that high risk tolerance may be expressed through impulsivity or lack of prudence as well as lack of emotion.

Risk Appetite: this term can be defined as the combined effects of Risk Type and Risk Attitude on current behaviour. In terms of the metrics of the Risk Type Compass®, it is helpful in describing the Risk Attitude 'pizza' graphic, the differently sized segments representing current relative 'appetite' while the Risk Type determines the overall size of the pizza.

Risk Comfort Zone: this is broadly synonymous with Risk Appetite, another holistic term that has contextual and narrative utility, but be careful about what is being implied!

Risk Type: this is concerned with deeply rooted aspects of temperament that are, to a significant degree heritable (as are all aspects of personality). The term 'constitutional' may be appropriate because if they are not genetic, they are likely to have been established in early infancy. Risk Type exerts a persistent and pervasive influence on the management of risk and risk behaviour.

APPLICATIONS OF RISK TYPE

Assessment of Risk Type has proved valuable at the level of the individual, the team and the organisation as a whole.

Individual Level of Application

There are two distinct applications at this level. The first is personal self-awareness and insights into the implications of Risk Type to the individual.

Three measures are reported by the Risk Type Compass®, together with explanatory narrative: Risk Type, Risk Attitude and the Risk Tolerance Index. The individual assessed is able to consider to what extent the definition of Risk Type, and the statements about the likely benefits and challenges of that Risk Type, concur with their expectations. Self-reflection will be assisted by expert feedback or through discussion with close associates. Considering the accuracy of self-awareness and whether new insights create a more realistic and balanced understanding can plant the seeds for personal development and increased self-awareness. Having been alerted, future experiences will either reinforce or negate those views and, ultimately, will determine whether they influence self-perceptions. The aim is to achieve a better appreciation of any Risk Type behavioural bias that impacts decision-making. This is an important corrective for anyone whose responsibilities in any way cover risk and uncertainty.

The second application at the individual level concerns developing an understanding of others: the characteristics, prevalence and variation of Risk Types. Since the incidence of the eight Risk Types is quite evenly distributed, most people will work with others of a different risk disposition. The extent to which they see eye-to-eye on risk related issues will be affected by such differences. These differences may be emphasised by departmental functions or because those functions attract people of a particular risk disposition e.g. Sales and Marketing may tend to attract the more risk tolerant types, while Accounts might have a greater prevalence of the more risk averse. This could have implications for departmental relationships and dynamics and the effectiveness of communication strategies.

Team Level of Application

Research has consistently shown that people react differently to risk when in groups compared to when they make decisions individually. The 'Risky Shift' phenomenon refers to the 'risk polarisation' that occurs when high risk takers predominate. In this situation risk taking escalates and the individuals involved sanction greater levels of risk than any would normally if they were acting alone. Wallach et al. (1964), suggest that this is due to diffusion of responsibility; social bonds decrease decision-making anxiety as responsibility for the outcome is perceived to be shared. Similarly, a group of risk-averse individuals within a team can behave in an overly cautious manner as each person encourages the next to make increasingly wary or defensive choices. This is sometimes known as 'Cautious Shift'. In both scenarios, teams can unknowingly fall victim to these biases, resulting in group decisions that have become either too risk averse or too risk tolerant.

The Risk Type Compass® can be used to audit groups and teams to increase understanding of a team's strengths, limitations, dynamics and overall propensity for risk taking. This may highlight the need to develop or for a more suitable balance in the risk taking tendencies of the team.

Organisational Level: Risk Culture

Risk culture is inevitably influenced by the individuals who comprise that culture. Schneider's 'attraction, selection, attrition' hypothesis is the clearest exposition of this (Schneider & Brent Smith, 2004). In this two-way dynamic relationship, people make an important contribution to culture and culture influences the people. Culture influences who is *attracted* to the organisation and influences the approach and the criteria for *selection* of new recruits. *Attrition* influences who is drawn (or pushed) towards the exit. Schneider's assertion is that, 'the people make the place'. Clearly, without people there can be no culture, so there is some merit in the model. From a cultural development perspective, surveying the propensity for risk of individuals provides a reliable, objective and deliverable strategy for the elucidation of the wider Risk Culture.

The risk culture of an organisation reflects the values, style and behaviours prominent amongst current staff (particularly of senior staff), but it will also reflect the legacy of their predecessors. Considering this perspective, the Risk Type Compass® assessment provides objective measures and the vocabulary for the debate through which to identify shortcomings and set goals, shape, foster and monitor the risk culture and manage change across an organisation.

The Risk Onion graphic (Figure 7) suggests the relationship between Risk Type, Risk Attitude, Risk Behaviour and Risk Culture. Risk Type is seen as the core of risk culture.

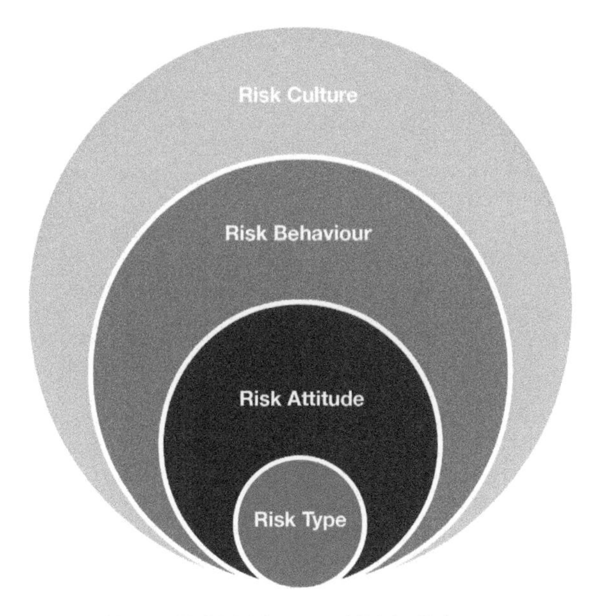

Figure 7: Risk Type and Risk Culture

CONCLUSIONS

There is a job to do in shifting entrenched views and expectations established over many years with little influence from applied psychology. Business psychology has a lot to offer within the wide and varied world of risk and risk management. The risk management strategies that are currently most prevalent are unable to embrace many opportunities for influencing risk behaviour because they fail to address the variability in individual risk dispositions. Perhaps most worryingly, the stricter rules and regulations approaches reduce personal responsibility to a matter of obedience, often establishing an intolerance of discretion and the exercise of intelligence or common sense.

The debate has also narrowed by the reluctance of risk management professions to recognise that failure to take risks in order to pursue the opportunities available can be as disastrous as taking too much risk. Organisations have gone out of business through failure to take risks: failure to innovate, to market their wares effectively or to see and act on the opportunities that exist. All these options involve risk taking and sometimes doing nothing, taking no risk, will be the riskiest option of all.

Risk managers often feel that the executive and the board fail to give their programmes adequate support, or to involve them in major decisions. Maybe the problem is that they both have very different agendas. The board has to balance risk against opportunity and that, of course, is different from risk management that is wary and hopes to eliminate risk.

While the objective of risk elimination may be understandable for Health and Safety, the culture of control and regulation that accompanies it is counterproductive in most other contexts. Recognition of the importance and positive impact of risk-taking would also contribute to a healthy widening of the risk agenda. It should encourage 'buy in' from those who want to concentrate more on enterprise and innovation than on the risks involved and lead to a more fruitful dialogue that addresses both sides of the risk/opportunity coin.

Generally, recognition of individual differences is appreciated by employees, potentially having motivational and attitudinal benefits that impact on co-operation and compliance. Individuals of each Risk Type face very different personal challenges in dealing with different regulatory regimes. This needs to be reflected in more people-centric approaches, not to excuse unacceptable risk behaviour, but to gain greater compliance as well as to exploit the advantages that are associated with all Risk Types. New opportunities would arise by monitoring human factor risk at individual, team and organisational levels.

Risk pervades every aspect of our lives and it is important to recognise the impossibility of micro-managing it out of existence. The majority of risk management is a matter of personal responsibility. We are free to decide how we cross roads, what we eat, whether we fly, how we exercise, what we do with our money, how much we engage with others, and so on. Legislation and regulation, backed by the power of the justice system and sanctions, are necessary ways to curb the extremes in all societies, and different societies have drawn this line in different places.

Regulations cannot sensibly be scripted to cover all eventualities. Most risk can be influenced broadly and with a light touch, by the establishment of basic principles and the development of public attitudes that support them. In this scenario, personal responsibility plays a very significant role in a regimen that is flexible enough to allow discretion at the edges rather than slavish obedience to the rulebook. Overly strict adherence and the lack of sensible personal discretion have created both amusing and tragic headlines.

Risk psychology, with its detailed focus on individuals, addresses the full risk agenda and counterbalances the emphasis on blanket processes and regulation. At a very practical level, there is an opportunity to direct professional support towards self-awareness, personal development and personal responsibility around risk disposition. There are great advantages in achieving risk management goals through personal responsibility, rather than through more directive methods. The benefits play out in terms of personal dignity, self-fulfilment, career satisfaction, and enhanced engagement. Together with a proper respect for the opportunities side of the equation, this creates new and exciting opportunities across the entire risk agenda.

References

Apgar, D. (2006). *Risk Intelligence: Learning to live with what we don't know.* Cambridge, MA.: Harvard Business School Press.

Barrick, M. R., & Mount, M. K. (1991). The Big Five Personality Dimensions And Job Performance: A Meta-Analysis. *Personnel Psychology, 44(*1), 1-26.

Costa, P. T., & McCray, R. R. (1992). *The NEO-PI-R Manual.* Odessa, FL: Psychological Assessment Resources.

Elvin, P. (2004). *Financial Risk Trading: an introduction to the Psychology of Trading and Behavioural Finance.* Chichester: John Wiley & Sons Limited.

Evans, D. (2012). *Risk Intelligence: How to live with uncertainty.* London: Atlantic Books.

Fenton-O'Creevy, M., Nicholson, N., Soane E., & Willman, P. (2005). *Traders: risks, decisions, and management in financial markets.* Oxford: Oxford University Press.

Hogan, J., & Ones, D. S. (1997). Conscientiousness and integrity at work. In Johnson, J., Hogan, R., & Briggs, S. (Eds.), *Handbook of Personality Psychology* (pp. 849-870). London: Academic Press.

Gigerenzer, G. (2014). *Risk Savvy; How to make good decisions.* London: Allen Lane an imprint of Penguin Books.

Kowert, P. A., & Hermann, M. G. (1997). Who takes risks? Daring and caution in foreign policy making. *Journal of Conflict Resolution, 41*(5), 611-37.

MacLeod, C., & Cohen, I. L. (1993). Anxiety and the interpretation of ambiguity: A text comprehension study. *Journal of Abnormal Psychology, 102*(2), 238-247.

Nicholson, N., Soane, E., Fenton-O'Creevy, M., & Willman, P. (2005). Personality and domain-specific risk taking. *Journal of Risk Research, 8*, 157-176.

Pan, C. H., & Statman, M. (2012). Investor Personality in Investor Questionnaires. *Journal of Investment Consulting, 14*(1), 48-56.

Schneider, B., & Brent Smith, D. (2004). Personality and Organizational Culture. In Benjamin Schneider and D. Brent Smith (Eds.) *Personality and Organizations* (pp. 347-370). Mahawah, New Jersey: Lawrence Erlbaum Associates.

Wallach, M. A., Kogan, N., & Bem, D. J. (1964). Diffusion of responsibility and level of risk taking in groups. *Journal of Abnormal and Social Psychology, 68*, 263-274.

3 SECTION

Seeing Things Differently

SEEING THINGS DIFFERENTLY INTRODUCTION

Pauline Grant

Our personal reality is in part a product of our history, expectations and preferences which sit alongside the data and sensory inputs we experience in the moment. Individuals form their own interpretations as to what is happening and why, which inform their predictions about what is likely to happen next. Much of this happens unconsciously, and the rationalisations we give for our assumptions and actions are also constructs from our inner world rather than a reflection of immutable logic. The diversity we encounter between different groups and individuals is not surprising; perhaps the marvel is that we find so much common ground. Listing the roots of difference – which would include genes and pre-natal environment as well as social/cultural experience – could be interesting. However, it inevitably takes us down a road of classifying and generalising, and none of us fits neatly into any given box. That the word 'diversity' has come to be associated with specific categorisations is unfortunate, but understandable – even predictable – as it reflects our tendency to categorise and impose order.

The writers in this section present us with different lenses to observe and interact with our fellow human beings. Sebastian Salicru helps us to take the learning from studies of cultural difference and apply it to leadership. Sylvana Storey presents a smorgasbord of psychology-based models and interventions in frequent use and demonstrates how they can be selected and applied to support a diversity and inclusion agenda. In doing so she sets out what many Business Psychologists carry in their heads. Whilst these techniques and models are not a replacement for 'doing Business Psychology' (see Consulting), it is useful to acknowledge the range and scope available.

Where we choose to notice 'difference' determines the questions we ask and the data we collect. Sally Moore invites us to look at people with specific talents that often accompany patterns of social interaction and motivation that make them stand out. Getting the best out of diversity takes more than a liberal attitude, although this can be a good starting point, and Sally provides some useful practical pointers. Another lens to observe difference takes us into the culture that arises within an organisation. Gillian Hyde uses the Hogan 'dark side' descriptors to highlight the implications of people gravitating to different types of work and environment, and recruiting people who 'fit' with the prevailing approach. Finally, we acknowledge that with such a range of different ways of interpreting and thinking it is unsurprising that disagreement and conflict arise. Stephen Benton and Anna Sommers give an overview of the literature and research, demonstrating how applying this understanding can assist with resolution.

SEEING THINGS DIFFERENTLY – MEET THE AUTHORS

Sebastian Salicru works with senior executives, building the leadership capability required to succeed in the increasingly demanding global economy, where hyper-complexity is the new normal. Working in Australia, USA, Europe, UAE, China and Singapore, he assists global and domestic leaders to minimise the business risks, enhance their intercultural effectiveness, drive innovation and deliver business results when working across cultures and with people from diverse cultural backgrounds. Sebastian regularly presents at industry events and conferences, and his forthcoming book is entitled *Ultimate Personal Leadership Branding*.

Sylvana Storey is a Business Psychologist and Founder of Global Organizational Integrators. This boutique consultancy provides strategic advice to organisations on how they can best change, align and integrate strategic objectives with performance through inclusive leadership and people capability. Sylvana's interests and expertise are firmly set within global leadership, diversity, inclusion and organisational culture. She is author of *The Impact of Diversity on Global Leadership Performance – LEAD™*.

Sally Moore is Director and Chartered Psychologist at Top Stream Coaching and Consulting with over 15,000 hours experience. She cuts through the mumbo jumbo so people perform, flourish and succeed in their working lives. With a deep science and experience-based understanding of what makes people tick and how they relate to each other, she focuses on strengths and positives. Working from the highly specialised evidence-based perspective of neurodiversity, Sally serves the highest value experts who relate well to their work and find the people side more challenging.

Gillian Hyde is Director at Psychological Consultancy Ltd (PCL) and a Chartered Occupational Psychologist with 20 years' Business Psychology experience. A graduate of UCL, Cambridge and Birkbeck College, Gillian's specialties are within personality assessment, career derailers and researching tailor-made assessment solutions for organisations. An expert trainer for the Hogan Development Survey, providing in-depth assessments and feedback, Gillian is fascinated by the link between leaders' strengths and blind spots and the potentially negative consequences of the relative lack of feedback available to, or accepted by, people in senior positions.

Stephen Benton created the first postgraduate MSc in Business Psychology in 1997 and is course leader, Professor of Business Psychology and Director of the Business Psychology Centre at the University of Westminster, UK. He has researched and lectured, in the UK and beyond, in visual and auditory psychophysics, psychometrics, cognitive psychology, human factors and Business Psychology. The continuing theme is the identification of processes underlying performance and the subsequent development of applied interventions to augment and support individuals' quality of life as well as performance.

Anna Sommers, after working in the tourism industry in London, is now applying her Business Psychology knowledge as a Consultant at Obermann in Cologne, Germany, specialising in Assessment Centres, management audit, development and HR processes. She holds a double-degree in Hospitality Management / International Business and an MSc Business Psychology degree. Anna's dissertation at the University of Westminster was about Conflict Management in Organisations, which is how the collaboration with Prof. Stephen Benton came into being.

GLOBAL LEADERSHIP DEVELOPMENT

Sebastian Salicru

In the current global economy, organisations with international interests need to operate successfully across geographic markets characterised by increasing competitiveness, complexity, uncertainty, ambiguity and inherent cultural differences. Many strive to achieve (or consolidate) 'world-class' status by providing the highest possible quality of goods or services in a commercially competitive manner while being timely, ethical, socially responsible and – naturally – highly profitable.

Within this context, the ability to attract and develop leaders that not only operate effectively but also influence and motivate people at a global level provides a key competitive advantage (Caligiuri & Tarique, 2009).

Global leadership that delivers high performance requires the competencies, potential and talents of a diverse set of people. Holt & Seki (2012) note the lack of convergence of global leadership definitions in the literature and conclude that it is not intrinsically hierarchical: a global leader is "anyone who operates in a context of multicultural, paradoxical complexity to achieve results in our world" (p. 199). Mendenhall et al. (2012) provide a more comprehensive definition stating that global leaders are "individuals who effect significant positive change in organizations by building communities through the development of trust and the arrangement of organizational structures and processes in a context involving multiple stakeholders, multiple sources of external authority, and multiple cultures under conditions of temporal, geographical and cultural complexity" (p. 17).

Global leadership development comprises activities that assist leaders of global organisations to develop the critical competencies required to ensure business success. The many models available differ according to four theoretical perspectives adopted by researchers and practitioners:

i. Focus on acquiring a 'global mindset' (Javidan & Teagarden, 2011);
ii. Derived from the intercultural sensitivity literature and developmental theory rather than competencies (Hammer et al., 2003);
iii. Models based on constructive development theory (McCauley et al., 2006);
iv. Approaches using a positive psychological capital (PsyCap) perspective (Vogelgesang et al., 2014).

Holt & Seki (2012) summarise the eight most common methods of developing global leaders:

i. Experience – trial and error;
ii. Assignments – international, team, early career and stretch assignments, rotations and exchange programs;
iii. Projects – global virtual teams, task forces, action learning groups and long-term project work;
iv. Training – intercultural communication, language, negotiation and conflict resolution, target skills, interactive cases and using videotapes;
v. Coaching – executive coaching, mentoring, feedback and cultural guides;
vi. Assessment – 360 degree feedback using global leadership assessment, cross-cultural assessments, assessment centres, cultural simulations and role plays;
vii. Networking – multicultural associations, annual global leadership conferences, staying connected via Skype, social learning;
viii. Personal development plans.

Cross-cultural competencies are more relevant to global leaders than those with traditional/domestic roles (Mendenhall et al., 2013). They are, however, relevant to leaders working within a multicultural environment in their own society. In modern economies this is now the norm and has resulted in an increasing number of workplace initiatives aimed at managing and leveraging cultural diversity. This, coupled with demographic shifts towards a diverse, multigenerational workforce, has elevated global leadership development to being the top strategic challenge faced by organisations around the world.

House et al. (2014) report that to maintain fluency and flexibility leaders facing complex global challenges must develop the capacity to innovate and inspire others. In addition, they must be sufficiently agile to familiarise themselves with rapidly changing technologies and disciplines. According to Lane & Maznevski (2014), the main challenge faced by global leaders is not dealing with the 'global' context *per se* but the added complexity this represents for them. This includes influencing individuals and groups (who represent diverse cultural/political/institutional systems) to help achieve their corporation's global ambitions. Osland et al. (2012) emphasise that the most effective global leaders can manage multiplicities, tackle huge challenges, grapple with instability and navigate ambiguity.

Mendenhall et al. (2013) provide a comprehensive review of the six main categories of global leadership constructs and competencies, a summary of the main global leadership development models available, and a detailed comparison of the 12 most researched intercultural global leadership assessment instruments.

I will substantiate the need to consider leadership and leadership development from this global perspective and outline the implications – challenges, opportunities and benefits – for business psychology practitioners and our clients. I will also propose a global leadership model supported by the experiences and research that have informed my thinking.

The Future

Foresight analysis, with globalisation identified as the major megatrend that will dramatically impact organisations in the future, indicates that Asia is expected to dominate the global economy (National Intelligence Council, 2012). Predictions for 2014 included a new and urgent focus on growth and building global leadership as organisations struggle with leadership gaps at all levels (Bersin & Deloitte, 2013), and the need for leadership development programs from a global perspective worldwide (Deloitte & Bersin, 2014).

As predicted by Heifetz et al. (2009), leaders across sectors and industries around the globe face increasing adaptive challenges. To successfully address these Petrie (2014) identifies four relevant trends:

i. More focus on 'vertical' development as opposed to the mere acquisition of competencies;
ii. Transfer of greater developmental ownership to the individual;
iii. Increased focus on collective rather than individual leadership;
iv. Greater focus on innovation in the design and delivery of leadership development methods.

The stages of 'vertical' development mentioned above are based on Kegan's (1980, 1994) seminal work on constructive-developmental theory which has been adopted by various leadership frameworks (McCauley et al., 2006). Kegan's (1980) theory refers to a stream of psychological work that focused on the development process of meaning and meaning-making throughout an individual's life. This stage theory of adult development proposes that, to understand the self and the world, individuals advance through five sequential and hierarchical stages or orders of mind:

i. Impulsive mind;
ii. Instrumental mind;
iii. Socialised mind;
iv. Self-authoring mind;
v. Self-transforming mind.

According to Kegan (1994), approximately 58% of the adult population is below the Self-authoring mind level and only 3–6% of adults between 19–55 years make the transition between the fourth and fifth stages.

Senior leaders' confident expectations of corporate growth (PriceWaterhouseCoopers, 2014) are framed by a growing demand for transparency in an increasingly global, cross-cultural, interdependent, networked and unpredictable environment (Accenture, 2014). Global companies often outsource leadership development because of a lack of internal expertise and the need for timely initiatives. This is where Business Psychologists can take a leading role.

Challenges and Opportunities

A global survey of CEOs reported that 76% believed their organisations needed to develop global leadership capability, but only 7% believed they were doing so effectively (Ashridge Business School, 2008). More recently, survey responses from 13,124 global leaders and 1,528 human resource executives within 2,031 organisations representing multinationals and local corporations, 32 major industries, and 48 countries (Sinar et al., 2014) revealed that only one in five organisations emphasised global leadership development. Only one-third of the leaders reported being effective in leading across countries and cultures – the lowest single skill effectiveness rating in the survey.

Other authors (Gentry & Eckert, 2012; Holt & Seki, 2012) argue that effective development of global leaders requires four fundamental shifts:

i. Developing multicultural effectiveness;
ii. Becoming adept at managing paradoxes;
iii. Cultivating the 'being' dimensions of human experience;
iv. Appreciating individual uniqueness in the context of cultural differences.

Cultivating the 'being' dimension of human experience means assisting global leaders to deal with their busy schedules and their resistance to alternative ways of working. Holt & Seki (2012) contend that current assessment instruments used for global leadership development are outdated and inadequate, and advocate approaches such as Maslow's (1999) work on the psychology of being and Nagata's (2009) intercultural work on body mindfulness.

Lessons from the Field

These examples illustrate some pervasive business risks of not appreciating cultural differences. They are drawn from actual field work with names and locations changed to protect anonymity.

Universal Expectations but Different Behaviours

In 2013, I delivered a one week intensive training program to a group of highly educated executives (most holding PhDs) in the United Arab Emirates. During the first two days, I announced the material and activities planned for the next day thus: "Tomorrow we are going to cover…" To my surprise, on the third day a participant took me aside and confided that I was coming across as arrogant and disrespectful. "We in the Arab world," he said, "use the expression *Insha'Allah* which translates as 'God willing'. This term is commonly used in the Islamic world, and also in some Christian groups in the Middle East, when speaking about plans or future events. The phrase acknowledges submission to God, with the speaker putting him or herself into God's hands. Muslims believe that everything is *'maktub'* (it is written) and that therefore whatever one plans will only occur if it is God's will. Being culturally educated in this way was a very humbling experience. During the rest of the week I made sure I used the expressions I had been taught, and received smiles of acknowledgement and gratitude from my audience.

Showing respect to others is a universal expectation that I unknowingly failed to meet until the gap in my cultural knowledge was bridged. While universal leadership characteristics and expectations are equally important across cultures, their expression differs according to the cultural and social context. Hence, leaders require high levels of cultural intelligence (CQ) to function effectively in today's global and multicultural world (Ng et al., 2012). CQ reflects an individual's capability to deal effectively with people from different cultural backgrounds and includes concepts such as global mindset and cross-cultural competence. The personal example provided above reinforces the need to learn from experience in intercultural contexts.

Power Distance – Leadership and Hierarchy

Jan Rotmensen, a senior manager of a global company, was transferred to Italy. He noticed that his egalitarian style, appreciated in the Netherlands, was perceived as a lack of leadership by his new team; they complained that he was weak, indecisive and ineffective. Jan would have benefitted from intercultural coaching to make him aware of his unconscious cultural programming and ethnocentric assumptions to avoid the negative impact of his behaviour on the performance of his team.

Jan's situation, however, is not surprising considering that Italy and the Netherlands are 12 points apart in Hofstede's Power Distance Index (PDI) (Hofstede et al., 2010, p. 59). The PDI compares the extent to which a culture values respect for authority and hierarchical relationships. In cultures with high PDI scores (e.g. Russia, India and China) leaders are not treated as equals by subordinates. In contrast, in cultures with low PDI scores (e.g. USA, UK, Netherlands) the hierarchical difference between leaders and their subordinates is much less noticeable.

Jan's experience is in line with Laurent's (1986) research. When European managers were asked to agree with the statement "It is important for a manager to have at hand precise answers to most of the questions that his subordinates may raise about their work" (p. 94), the difference between countries was pronounced and explains the misunderstandings between Jan and his team.

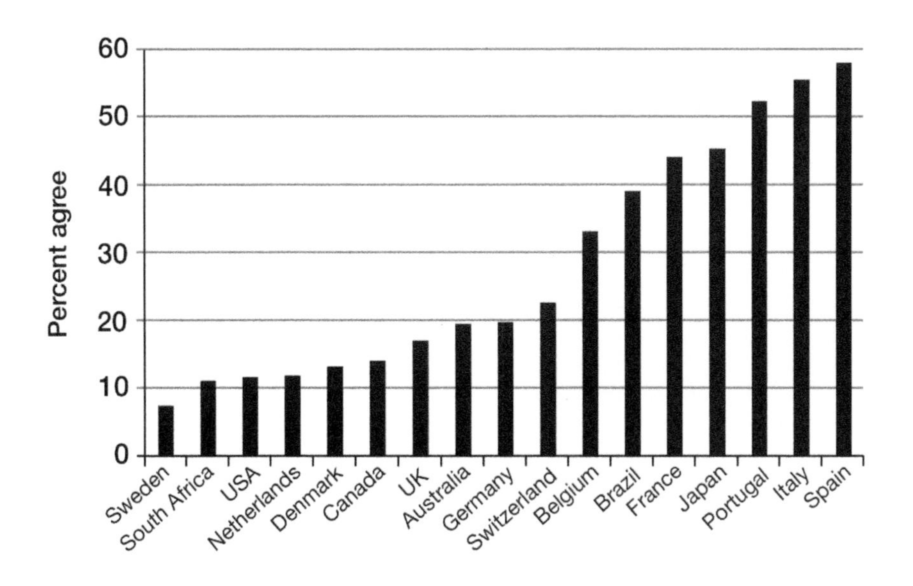

Figure 1: Differences among European managers.
Reprinted with permission © John Wiley & Sons, Inc.

Persuasion and Reasoning Styles

Bruce Morris is a leading Australian engineer with extensive experience in presenting solutions persuasively to his American and British colleagues. Prior to his first trip to Saint Petersburg to present to a group of Russian decision makers he prepared thoroughly and, as usual, rehearsed his case by practising potential questions and objections.

Bruce began his presentation by getting directly to the point, summarised his key recommendations and highlighted the practical benefits of his proposed approach. Within five minutes, one person in the audience had abruptly interrupted him: "How did you arrive at these recommendations? You are providing solutions but you have not explained to us how you got to this point". Immediately, someone else joined in: "What methodology did you use to arrive at your conclusions? Who did you interview? What did you ask them?" Bruce reacted badly to the emotional tone of the questions; he felt mistrusted and under attack and he became defensive. Ultimately, his proposal was rejected.

The ability to persuade is a key business skill rooted in cultural, philosophical, educational and even religious beliefs. Russians (like Germans, French, Spanish and Italians) favour deductive reasoning (principles-first) seeking to understand the 'why' prior to moving into action. Conversely, Americans, Canadians, British and Australians, to whom Bruce was used to presenting, favour inductive reasoning (application-first) and focus more on the 'how' rather than the 'why' (Nisbett, 2003). Most people are able to use both deductive and inductive reasoning, but their habitual style will have been reinforced by their cultural education. Bruce's Russian audience felt that they were expected to 'swallow' whatever he told them without explanation. Like Jan Rotmensen, Bruce would have benefitted from understanding his ethnocentric assumptions.

High vs. Low Context Communication Styles

A major global insurer with over 15,000 employees in 50 countries decided to establish a new call centre service hub in the Philippines, outsourcing hundreds of jobs to generate sustainable savings. However, the forecasted savings were jeopardised by underestimating the cultural impact.

Filipinos use a 'high-context' communication style which tends to be indirect and formal, combining verbal and non-verbal messages to convey meaning. The listener must 'read between the lines' and take into account non-verbal nuances to fully comprehend the message. Individuals from 'high-context' cultures find it extremely difficult to say 'no', as it can be construed as confrontational, unfriendly and disrespectful, causing loss of face and embarrassment. For the Filipinos, maintaining harmony – a Confucian value shared across Asia – is far more important than being informative. As an example, remaining silent and not questioning customers' understanding of the policies would be preferred over checking to confirm comprehension.

In contrast, 'low context' cultures (such as the USA, Canada, the UK and Australia), where most of the insurer's customers reside, and with whom the Filipinos in the call centre have to deal, use a direct communication style. This style relies on literal and precise meaning with preference for explicit conversations in which words convey the entire message, or at least most of it. Not surprisingly, these marked contrasts in communication styles caused havoc during the early days at the new call centre. The lesson for the insurer was that ignoring cultural differences and assuming that English fluency equates to effective communication can be very risky.

The confusion in customer communication was only part of the story. Internal communications were also compromised. Requests commonly used by people from the insurer's head office such as "Would you mind sending the latest figures?" were indecipherable to the Filipinos. A more direct request such as "Please, send me the latest figures as soon as possible" would have been far more effective.

Further, it is important to be mindful that the Filipino culture uses holistic thinking (understanding the system by sensing its large-scale patterns and reacting to them) as opposed to an analytic style (understanding the system by thinking about its parts and how they work together to produce larger-scale effects). Business Psychologists assist clients to identify and understand the implications of their culturally programmed thinking style when communicating with individuals from different cultures. Needless to say, this would have been beneficial in preventing the issues in the call centre.

Eventually, the insurer invested heavily in comprehensive intercultural training, both for key head office employees and call centre employees in the Philippines. The outcomes of the training included increased mutual understanding and appreciation of cultural differences and improved communication between the call centre and head office.

Insights From a Global Champion

Company X is a global leader in engineering solutions. It enjoyed net sales of around €5 billion in the previous financial year, employs around 17,000 people of 120 nationalities, and operates in 150 locations in 50 countries. The company's strategy is to develop a high performance, agile culture that fosters quick decision making and strengthens accountability. The intended outcome is to capture growth opportunities within the organisation's end markets while maintaining solid profitability.

Over the last three years, I have had the privilege of being involved in the global delivery of Company X's leadership development initiative attended by leaders from nations in North America, Northern and Southern Europe, the Middle East (UAE) and the Asia Pacific Region.

To adapt effectively to local cultures and market needs, a shift to decentralised and collaborative decision making is underway. A major challenge is to maintain a pipeline of leaders capable of working in any location, with global business acumen, nous and intercultural competence. To do this, the company has positioned culture as a business risk and embedded intercultural competencies in its global leadership development using the following criteria:

- Reflect customers' cultural diversity in the top leadership of the company;
- Ensure global leaders effectively align employees with the company's mission and values, empowering people to lead and collaborate horizontally, often using matrix structures, rather than managing vertically;
- Develop hundreds of leaders worldwide who are comfortable operating in a variety of cultures, as opposed to, for example, only concentrating on the development of the top 50 or 100 leaders;
- Attract, develop and retain executives from emerging markets; and
- Ensure the development of global leaders includes the acquisition of knowledge and skills related to country differences, cultural sensitivities and their implications, and collaboration. This emphasises the focus on competencies such as: learning agility, curiosity and inquisitiveness; engagement in personal transformation; emotional, social and cultural intelligence; and the ability to coach and empower others. It also includes the placement and rotation of executives in various geographical locations in which the company operates.

The following key elements were embedded in the design of this global initiative:

i. Simplicity of competencies by using meta-competencies, a personality assessment, and an integrated 360 degree feedback process;
ii. Experiential approach incorporating action learning;
iii. Strategic scope – placing strong emphasis on the long-term aspirations of the organisation and the required leadership capability to achieve these successfully;
iv. Peer coaching and reflective learning, including journaling; and
v. Mentoring program.

The main goal of this program is to turn technical expert contributors (predominantly engineers) into leaders of teams and strategy implementers (middle/senior managers) into strategic thinkers. The program assists participants to acquire the repertoire of skills to operate effectively cross-culturally; to contribute to creating the company's culture in developing a common understanding of the group values, vision, strategy and ways of working; to develop their leadership abilities; and to become more aware of the influence of their actions and decisions on the group results.

The overwhelmingly positive feedback received from hundreds of participants has made this program the most acclaimed leadership development initiative in the company's history. So, what makes it so successful?

Participants complete four key preliminary components which provide them with the basis for drafting their initial personal action plan (PAP):

i. Online assessment which includes a personality profile and 360 degree feedback survey based on the competencies mentioned above. Comparative ratings on how participants, their boss and others perceive their work environment are also reviewed.
ii. Discussion with their immediate superior to define learning objectives.
iii. Preparation of team project presentations on strategic topics defined by the company based on strategic business priorities.
iv. One-to-one feedback discussion session with an external facilitator/ coach on their personality test and the 360 survey results.

They then attend a one-week intensive residential workshop based on action learning methods. Unlike more formal education training programs, participants learn from their experience while working collaboratively on issues of strategic importance to the organisation. The issues increase in complexity during the week. New knowledge and perspectives are created inductively. This includes how experiences, including environmental factors, cognitions and emotions influence their learning process. Kolb's (1984) four modes of the experiential learning cycle (concrete experience, abstract conceptualisation, reflective observation and active experimentation) are facilitated throughout the program.

Each participant is assigned to a project team with a specified strategic topic and to a peer coach to work on their PAP. The composition of each team is carefully selected by mixing individuals from different business divisions, functions, management levels and geographical/cultural regions. This ensures they gain direct exposure to the range of issues and challenges they can expect to encounter as leaders. Teams present their findings to their peers and one member of the Executive and, during a highly interactive strategy session, face questions and receive feedback. Throughout the program, participants work in pairs coaching their counterparts. In order to consolidate and anchor their learning experiences, they also keep a daily learning journal as an additional reflective learning aid.

On completion of the week, participants are encouraged to use the company's global mentoring program, initially as mentees, and subsequently as mentors. Post-workshop assignments include: a discussion with their superior to review how the PAP will be implemented and the support and resources needed; the changes that will be demonstrated in their leadership behaviour; and the completion of 3 one-hour e-learning modules ('Engaging their Team', 'Communicating Vision' and 'Executing Strategy'). Finally, a follow-up discussion with the participants takes place two to three months after the program to measure the quality of implementation of their PAP and provide additional support, if required.

Imperatives in Moving Forward

In addressing gaps in the literature on global leadership two key imperatives must be taken into account. Firstly, we need to discontinue strong reliance on historical leadership development approaches that are not applicable to current times. Doing more of the same is unlikely to yield different outcomes. A case in point is the competency movement in leadership development which has been astutely referred to as "a repeating refrain that continues to offer an illusory promise to rationalise and simplify the processes of selecting, measuring and developing leaders, yet only reflects a fragment of the complexity that is leadership" (Bolden & Gosling, 2006, p. 148). While competencies still matter (Hernez-Broome & Hughes, 2004), they are just part of the way forward. The current view is that contemporary leadership assessment and development is out of sync with the actual demands faced by global leaders (Gentry & Eckert, 2012; Holt & Seki, 2012). As a result, a new way of thinking combined with an understanding of how we have reached the current situation is required (Harman & Horman, 1993). This includes paying greater attention to the leader's character and integrity (Hernez-Broome & Hughes, 2004). It is precisely this point that leads to the next premise.

The second imperative, a strong recurring theme in the literature, is that leadership is a relational phenomenon – a psychological process based on relationships between people. Hence, its effectiveness depends, above all, on the quality of relationships and the leader's ethical behaviour, integrity and ability to build trust. The 'lone-ranger', superhero or alpha male leader stereotype is no longer relevant for either current or future times.

The relationship between these two imperatives clearly points to the need to develop more meaningful relational and integrated outcome measures of leadership. This has been recently highlighted by Salicru & Chelliah (2014) using psychological contracts (PCs) as a theoretical framework. The promotion of PCs through leadership has been identified as the missing link between successful execution of HR strategy and performance (McDermott et al., 2013). PCs assist leaders to:

i. focus on their stakeholders' specific sets of expectations;
ii. align their behaviours with strategies across organisational levels in ways that are consistent with the various HR configurations of the organisation; and
iii. add missing relational dimensions of competencies by focusing on outcomes as opposed to behaviours.

Global Leadership Psychological Contracts

The leadership psychological contract (LPC) sets the dynamics and measures for the leader-follower relationship by taking into account the set of unexpressed and unwritten beliefs, expectations, promises and perceived responsibilities or obligations followers have of their leaders (Salicru & Chelliah, 2014). The global leadership psychological contract (GLPC) is a predictive model that incorporates four key elements to address the emerging context of global leadership:

i. Results of GLOBE – 'Global Leadership and Organizational Behavior Effectiveness', the largest leadership research program ever conducted (House et al., 2014). The GLOBE project covers an 11-year period (still in progress), involving 160 social scientists and management scholars from 62 cultures representing the major regions of the world. These results include the identification of the 22 most universally desired effective leadership attributes across cultures;
ii. Measures of leader integrity and credibility (trust, fairness and fulfilment of expectations);
iii. Measures of leader impact (follower emotional and behavioural outcomes); and
iv. Final results, which refer to specific business outcomes.

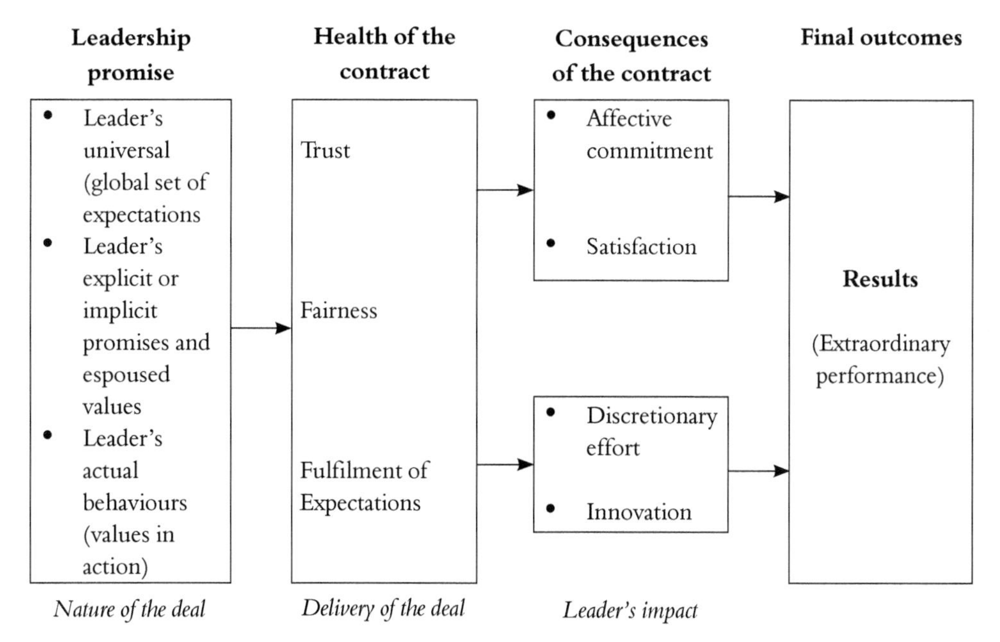

Figure 2: Global Leadership Psychological Contract (GLPC)

These four components of the GLPC model (Figure 2) are labelled in language that is consistent with the promissory nature of PCs initially introduced by Guest (1998): the leader's promise or nature of the deal, the delivery of the deal or health of the contract, the leader's impact or consequences of the contact, and results.

Leadership Promise

The first component of the model comprises three elements:

i. The universal set of expectations of leaders;
ii. The leader's explicit or implicit promises, principles and espoused values;
iii. The leader's actual behaviours or values in action.

These three elements are sometimes referred to as the contract makers.

This component constitutes the 'nature of the deal' that leaders offer to their followers, team members, stakeholders or constituents. For instance, Jan Rotmensen's arrival in Italy inevitably generated a set of expectations from his new team. The agents of the insurer's new call centre in the Philippines would have formed their own expectations about the changes, shaped by multiple sources including official announcements, speeches at inaugural meetings, previous similar experiences and rumours. The promise becomes the criteria by which followers judge the health of the contract (i.e. the leader's integrity and credibility) – the second component of the model.

Health of the Contract

The health of the contract (or delivery of the deal) reflects the extent to which the leadership promise has been fulfilled. Followers assess (a cognitive response) the leader's behaviour compared to their expectations. The extent to which expectations of their leader have been fulfilled constitutes the leader's level of credibility or integrity and hence the followers' levels of trust.

Contracts are said to be fulfilled or intact when individuals perceive their leader(s) to have honoured or upheld their promises and/or obligations. Contracts are breached (inadvertently) or violated when expectations are unmet. My example of training a group of executives in the UAE was an inadvertent breach of contract as opposed to a refusal to comply with a cultural norm and was addressed by my subsequent corrective action. Violation is more severe, and followers' reactions can range from frustration to resentment, anger and distrust, ultimately resulting in termination of the relationship (e.g. leaving the team or organisation).

Consequence of the Contract

The third component of the model relates to the leader's impact and refers to followers' emotional and behavioural responses to the delivery of the deal. The followers' emotional response includes their levels of affective commitment and satisfaction. Their behavioural response is seen in discretionary effort and innovation. The latter refers to creative thinking and innovative behaviour which results from the individuals' orientation towards change and likelihood to generate or adopt new ideas/practices, as well as perseverance in engaging in higher levels of thinking and implementing new and promising ideas. Leading across countries and cultures and fostering employee creativity and innovation have been identified as the two most critical skills insufficiently addressed by existing global leadership development programs (Sinar et al., 2014).

Results

The final component of the model refers to results that take the form of extraordinary (as opposed to mediocre or expected) performance. Such results are also referred to as 'game-changing' or 'breakthrough' and relate to the accomplishments that are unprecedented. Indicators include objective team and organisational performance.

Summary

Unmet expectations represent a breach or violation of the leader's contract. This, in turn, translates to low levels of trust, commitment, satisfaction, effort, innovation and performance. In Jan Rotmensen's case, the health of his contract moved through the whole chain of the model. To begin, his team's expectations of their new leader were grossly unmet and as a result he lost credibility. They felt unengaged and unmotivated and their levels of performance dropped.

In Bruce Morris' case, instead of putting effort into restoring his contract by re-aligning with his audience's expectations, his energy went into defending himself. This suggests a lack of emotional and social intelligence (e.g. self-awareness, ability to regulate his emotions and control his behaviour), components of cultural intelligence (CQ). Not surprisingly, his contract violation went beyond repair and he neither persuaded his audience nor closed his deal.

In the case of the insurance company, the breaches of PCs spilled over to the customers, who expected direct and concise communication. This not only jeopardised the short-term delivery of the company's customer policies, but also the longer-term reputation of the brand. This risk could have been mitigated, and customer casualties prevented, by incorporating an inter-cultural assessment component into the strategic planning for their new call centre in the Philippines.

In contrast, Company X, more experienced with a track record of multiple mergers and acquisitions, strategically planned their future by building a robust global leadership pipeline. The company closely monitors the feedback provided by participants, facilitators/trainers and customers and progressively adjusts the program. At a time when many companies cut their training budgets, Company X retained this important initiative and in doing so made its commitment to employees, customers and other stakeholders explicit.

Conclusion

The current context of post-GFC recovery and globalisation presents new and exciting opportunities for Business Psychologists to support organisations' strategic HR management agendas of growth with a strong focus on global leadership development. As Business Psychologists we need to:

- Understand that the consequences of the rapidly changing global economic landscape include the need for developing multicultural effectiveness and managing complexity and paradoxes;
- Understand and articulate key distinctions related to global leadership development (e.g. domestic vs. global leadership, global mindsets, cultural competence and cultural intelligence) and have access to relevant assessment instruments and strategies;
- Position culture as a business risk to our clients, i.e. the need to maximise the advantage of cultural strengths and mitigate the risk of cultural weakness; and
- Understand and articulate the most pervasive dimensions of culture and associated risk in business.

Business Psychologists competent in the areas outlined above will be equipped to focus on specific interventions to assist their clients to:

- Gain strategic insight and clarity around culture and the global leadership capabilities and skills they need to develop;
- Identify and develop the pipeline they require to create an abundant supply of effective global leaders by generating a pool of high-potential candidates for future global leadership roles;
- Select the inter-cultural competencies and behaviours needed to achieve their business goals;
- Create selection criteria – using an appropriate framework – to assess candidates' suitability and potential;
- Roll out, evaluate and enhance company-specific coaching programs, with emphasis on cross-culture issues, to accelerate on-the-job development; and
- Design and deliver customised global leadership development programs that integrate cutting-edge research and best practice.

In conducting any of the above interventions the overarching goal should be to assist clients to unite strategy formulation, implementation, long-term performance and financial success.

References

Accenture (2014). *CEO Briefing 2014. The global agenda: Competing in a digital world*. Retrieved from http://www.accenture.com/SiteCollectionDocuments/PDF/Accenture-Global-Agenda-CEO-Briefing-2014-Competing-Digital-World.pdf.

Ashridge Business School (2008). *United Nations Global Compact Principles for Responsible Management Education (PRME). Developing the global leader of tomorrow – a joint project*. Retrieved from http://www.unprme.org/resource-docs/developingthegloballeaderoftomorrowreport.pdf.

Bersin & Deloitte (2013). *Predictions for 2014: Building a strong talent pipeline for the global economic recovery – Time for innovative and integrated talent and HR strategies*. Deloitte Consulting LLP. Retrieved from http://www.cdmn.ca/wp-content/uploads/2014/02/C-inetpub-wwwroot-Prod-uploadedFiles-122013PSGP.pdf.

Bolden, R., & Gosling, J. (2006). Leadership competencies: Time to change the tune? *Leadership, 2*(2), 147-163.

Caligiuri, P., & Tarique, I. (2009). Predicting effectiveness in global leadership activities. *Journal of World Business, 44*(3), 336-346.

Deloitte Consulting LLP & Bersin (2014). *Global human capital trends 2014: Engaging the 21st-century workforce*. Retrieved from http://www2.deloitte.com/global/en/pages/human-capital/articles/human-capital-trends-2014.html.

Gentry, W. A., & Eckert, R. H. (2012). Integrating implicit leadership theories and fit into the development of global leaders: A 360-degree approach. *Industrial and Organizational Psychology, 5*(2), 224-227.

Guest, D. E. (1998). Is the psychological contract worth taking seriously? *Journal of Organizational Behavior, 19*(S1), 649-664.

Hammer, M. R, Bennett, M. J., & Wiseman, R. (2003). Measuring intercultural sensitivity: The intercultural development inventory. *International Journal of Intercultural Relations, 27*(4), 421-443.

Harman, W., & Horman, J. (1993). The breakdown of the old paradigm. In M. Ray & A. Rinzler (Eds.), *The new paradigm in business: Emerging strategies for Leadership and organizational change* (pp. 16-27). New York, NY: Jeremy P. Tarcher/ Pedigree Books.

Heifetz, R. A., Linsky, M., & Grashow, A. (2009). *The practice of adaptive leadership: Tools and tactics for changing your organization and the world*. Boston, MA: Harvard Business Press.

Hernez-Broome, G., & Hughes, R. L. (2004). Leadership development: Past, present, and future. *Human Resource Planning, 27*(1), 24–32.

Hofstede, G., Hofstede, G. J., & Minkov, M. (2010). *Cultures and organizations: Software of the mind* (3rd Ed.). New York, NY: McGraw-Hill.

Holt, K., & Seki, K. (2012). Global leadership: A developmental shift for everyone. *Industrial and Organizational Psychology, 5*(2), 196–215. doi:1754-9426/12.

House, R. J., Dorfman, P. W., Javidan, M., Hanges, P. J., & Sully de Luque, M. F. (2014). *Strategic leadership across cultures: GLOBE study of CEO leadership behavior and effectiveness in 24 countries*. Thousand Oaks, CA: Sage.

Javidan, M., & Teagarden, M. B. (2011). Conceptualizing and measuring global mindset. In M. H. Mobley & M. L. Ying Wang (Eds.), *Advances in global leadership* (pp. 13-39). Bingley, UK: Emerald Group Publishing.

Kegan, R. (1980). Making meaning: The constructive-developmental approach to persons and practice. *The Personnel and Guidance Journal, 58*(5), 373–380.

Kegan, R. (1994). *In over our heads: The mental demands of modern life*. Cambridge, MA: Harvard University Press.

Kolb, D. A. (1984). *Experiential learning: Experience as the source of learning and development* (Vol. 1). Englewood Cliffs, NJ: Prentice-Hall.

Lane, H. W., & Maznevski, M. (2014). *International management behavior: Global and sustainable leadership*. New York, NY: John Wiley & Sons.

Laurent, A. (1986). The cross-cultural puzzle of international human resource management. *Human Resource Management, 25*(1), 91-102. © John Wiley & Sons, Inc.

Maslow, H. (1999). *Toward a psychology of being*. New York, NY: John Wiley & Sons.

McCauley, C. D., Drath, W. H., Palus, C. J., O'Connor, P. M. G., & Baker, B. A. (2006). The use of constructive-developmental theory to advance the understanding of leadership. *The Leadership Quarterly, 17*(6), 634-653.

McDermott, A. M., Conway, E., Rousseau, D. M., & Flood, P. C. (2013). Promoting effective psychological contracts through leadership: The missing link between HR strategy and performance. *Human Resource Management, 52*(2), 289-310.

Mendenhall, M. E., Osland, J. S., Bird, A., Oddou, G. R., Maznevski, M., Stevens, M., & Stahl, G. K. (2013). *Global leadership: Research, practice and development* (2nd Ed.). New York, NY: Routledge.

Mendenhall, M. E., Reiche, B. S., Bird, A., & Osland, J. S. (2012). Defining the 'global' in global leadership. *Journal of World Business*, 47(4), 493-503.

Nagata, A. L. (2009). Bodymindfulness for skillful use of self. In B. Fisher-Yoshida, K. D. Geller & S. A. Schapiro (Eds.), *Innovations in transformative Learning: Space, culture, and the arts* (pp. 223-243). New York, NY: Peter Lang.

National Intelligence Council (2012). *Global Trends 2030: Alternative Worlds*. Washington, DC: US Government Printing Office. Retrieved from http://publicintelligence.net/global-trends-2030/.

Ng, K. Y., Dyne, L. V., & Ang, S. (2012). Cultural intelligence: A review, reflections, and recommendations for future research. In A. M. Ryan, F. T. L. Leong, & F. L. Oswald (Eds.), *Conducting multinational research: Applying organizational Psychology in the workplace* (pp. 29-58). Washington, DC: American Psychological Association.

Nisbett, R. E. (2003). *The geography of thought: How Asians and Westerners think differently…and why*. New York, NY: The Free Press.

Osland, J., Bird, A., & Oddou, G. (2012). The context of expert global leadership. In W. H. Mobley, Y. Wang, & M. Li (Eds.), *Advances in Global Leadership*, vol.7 (pp. 107-124). Oxford, MA: Elsevier.

Petrie, N. (2014). *Future trends in leadership development: The Center for Creative Leadership CCL*. Retrieved from http://www.ccl.org/leadership/pdf/research/futuretrends.pdf.

PriceWaterhouseCooper (2014). *17th Annual Global CEO Survey: Fit for the future – Capitalising on global trends*. Retrieved from http://www.pwc.com/gx/en/ceo-survey/2014/download.jhtml.

Salicru, S., & Chelliah, J. (2014). Messing with corporate heads? Psychological contracts and leadership integrity. *Journal of Business Strategy, 35*(3), 38-46.

Sinar, E., Wellins, R., Ray, R. L., Abel, A. L., & Neal, S. (2014). *Ready-Now Leaders: Meeting Tomorrow's Business Challenges. Global Leadership Forecast 2014 | 2015*. The Conference Board & DDI. Retrieved from http://www.ddiworld.com/DDI/media/trend-research/global-leadership-forecast-2014-2015_tr_ddi.pdf?ext=.pdf.

Vogelgesang, G., Clapp-Smith, R., & Osland, J. (2014). The relationship between positive psychological capital and global mindset in the context of global leadership. *Journal of Leadership & Organizational Studies, 21*(2), 165-178.

HOW BUSINESS PSYCHOLOGY ENABLES GLOBAL LEADERS TO DRIVE DIVERSITY AND INCLUSION

Sylvana Storey

Introduction

This article is based on a five year global study examining the impact that diversity has on a global leader's performance. Seven multinationals representing seven different sectors across twenty-two countries/five continents participated in the research. Eighty senior leaders were interviewed and their insights provide the central tenet for the discussion in this article. That is, leadership and diversity have to be updated and reframed for working in our global village in the 21st century.

My research was based on the unprecedented challenges faced by leaders of global organisations in terms of scale, pace, complexity and variety. These challenges come from both external and internal forces. External challenges range from the threat of cyber attacks to social unrest and from employment and financial volatility to environmental issues. Internal challenges range from inter-generational issues and talent management to culture, and from the impact of social platforms and 'big data' to performance metrics.

Aside from these challenges are the paradoxes that prevail: globalisation vs. localisation; cost-cutting vs. investment; short-term vs. long-term; control vs. chaos; competition vs. cooperation; compliance vs. choice; creativity vs. logic; stability vs. change; transparency vs. opaqueness; and diversity vs. meritocracy and so on.

In addition, current topical concepts such as 'shared value', 'sense of purpose', 'sustainability', 'inclusive capitalism', 'stakeholder health', 'resilience', and 'innovation' encourage leaders to embrace ideologies that widen and deepen their thought leadership. These concepts demand both agility and adaptability that takes leaders outside their own comfort levels and compels them to question whether the very architecture of their leadership is fit for the future.

How are leaders to respond to these challenges, paradoxes and emerging concepts? How can they manage their performance in relation to their capability to best deal with the cultural, political, financial and environmental volatility and complexity? How can they integrate and embrace new ideologies?

The common denominator across these challenges, paradoxes and new ideologies is globalisation, and a central component of globalisation is diversity. Diversity is acknowledged as pivotal to continued growth, sustainability and competitive advantage in our increasingly globalised world. With this in mind, it was viewed that leaders will need to broaden their organisation's approach to accessing, positioning and facilitating diversity in their organisations.

Leadership and diversity programmes can no longer focus solely on identity (e.g. gender specific programmes and affinity groups etc.). An organisation has to consider an integrated diversity agenda that brings together three different dimensions. The first dimension examines organisational structures, systems and processes. These enable employees to practise autonomy, to develop in-depth skills in the areas that align with and endorse their purpose as well as feeling valued and heard. The second dimension considers the different ways that people think. For example, how they innovate, make decisions and solve problems. Third, the different ways people behave in differing contexts need to be examined and understood (e.g. organisational & country cultures; communication break-down across subsidiaries, divisions and functions).

The Business Need

Given my central tenet that leadership and diversity need to be reframed and updated, the critical question remains – 'is there a business need for a positive relationship between diversity and global leadership performance?' The research definitively identified the business need in two domains: strategy and organisation, and cognition and behaviour.

Strategy and Organisation:

In the first domain, the business need pointed to the importance of alignment between strategic performance and organisational performance. Strategic performance takes into account how the organisation's strategic objectives translate into actual outcomes that secure competitive advantage for the firm whilst addressing stakeholder benefits. Organisational performance focuses on how the systems, processes and behaviours across various business units (e.g. finance, HR, operations, sales and marketing, R&D etc.) work with each other to achieve the strategic goals of the organisation. Therefore, it is essential for an organisation to understand how the strategic and organisational performance indicators calibrate, impact and support each other.

It was acknowledged that given the shifting dynamics of the marketplace there is a pressing need for strategy within an organisation to present a joined-up and integrated approach with an acute focus on resources and measures. It was stated that better environmental scanning and governance is required to reduce financial risk across operations. Also, in order to build competitive advantage, the inherent tension between cross-border integration and local adaptation has to be exploited.

Added to this, given the shift in economic power from West to East, there is an increasingly common strategic aim to penetrate new markets so as to augment market share. Underpinning this aim, customer centricity was seen as vital. 'Customers' is an umbrella term for employees, consumers, clients, shareholders, vendors, suppliers, government bodies, and regulatory agencies. This diverse array of customers both contextually and culturally plays a significant part in diversity and inclusion.

With regard to people, a coherent and integrated diversity strategy was linked to reduced labour costs associated with recruitment, retention of talent and training and development. It was also deemed necessary for organisations to enhance their brand reputation so that prospective employees would regard the organisation as an employer of choice. An organisation that values *all* people and reflects the demography of the regions in which it operates was seen as maximising and exploiting the benefits of a 'global/local' talent pool.

Behaviour and Cognition:

In the second domain the business need focused on how the organisation as a system thinks and behaves, in other words, the underpinnings of the organisation's culture, ethos and ways of working. Engagement was seen as key as it helped to build relationships, foster collaboration and gauge the emotional temperature for all stakeholders. Tied to this, the value of interdependence and interconnectedness was consistently stressed, with a focus on collective ways of working and collaboration as opposed to operating from an individualistic platform. To develop these ways of working, opinions voiced suggest that it was necessary to attend to the organisation's structure and how this impacted on communications, power and conflict across borders.

Within this sphere, leaders advocated that transparency, equality, fairness and conflict resolution are central to good leadership and diversity practice. Therefore it was viewed that leadership capability fit for 21st century global leaders needed to attend to cognitive ability so that problem solving, decision making and innovation are enhanced and maximised. Also, social and behavioural skills have to be agile enough to flex in differing contexts, environments and cultures. That is, the global literacy of leaders is key.

The interplay between the new leadership development and the diversity and inclusion agenda

To address these identified business needs, it became necessary to update and broaden the scope of both 'leadership' and 'diversity' to provide an explicit focus on the interplay between these two concepts. To this end a multi-level perspective in the form of the LEAD³ analytical tool was developed. LEAD³ presents an integrated change management process that utilises business psychology methodologies for building global leadership and diversity capability.

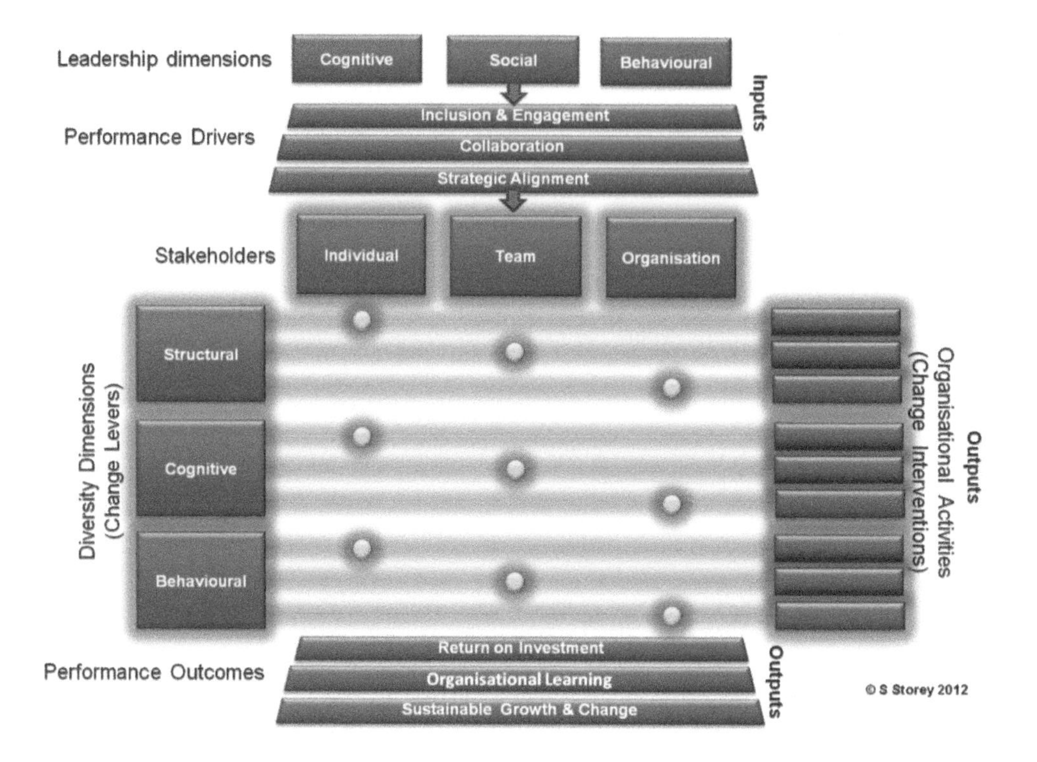

Figure 1: LEAD³

Leadership Capability:

The starting point for LEAD³ is that leaders are the architects of their organisations' culture and climate, and the key connectors to their workforce. Therefore it is imperative that they are equipped with the necessary skills to be this guiding force. The research captured several skills that 21st century global leaders need to have within their capability portfolio. How these capabilities can be applied to drive a diversity agenda in their organisations was also ascertained.

Six skills were identified. The three foundation skills sitting at the top of the model are at a cognitive level (how to process and analyse often competing information), a social level (the ability to appropriately apply interpersonal skills) and a behavioural level (adapting behaviours, not just with followers, but also with diverse multiple stakeholder groupings). Three further leadership skills that sit within the model are strategic, business and global skills. 'Strategic' refers to leaders' ability to see the 'big picture'. 'Business' is a leader's capability to demonstrate their technical competence. 'Global' is the ability to be agile and adapt their approaches, thinking styles and behaviours across differing cultural contexts, and was seen as an essential competence.

Quotes from my research that exemplify these skills include "as a leader you focus on the future and focus on the message and not do it at the expense of anyone's dignity" and "a global leader cannot just look at financial targets. You have to be aware of sub issues. That is, you have to have a vision of how these issues are moulding the world in terms of the environment, human rights issues, human development etc. Therefore you have to take account of global issues."

Performance Drivers:

A tree cannot grow and flourish without its roots. Applying this metaphor, when you equip leaders with the appropriate skills to manage the dynamics of a diversity and inclusion agenda, they have to be accompanied by a solid foundation of performance drivers. These performance drivers were identified as Inclusion and Engagement, Collaboration and Strategic Alignment. They serve as a compass to enable leaders to 'walk the talk' and embed a robust culture that is sustainable through growth and change.

Inclusion and Engagement are often used interchangeably, but there is a subtle difference. Inclusion is how we value others' differences. Inclusivity demonstrates a genuine openness to valuing and hearing all voices. Engagement is involving and integrating others. It embraces working with differing identities and different ways of thinking and behaving when working with diverse peoples. The holy grail of high performing organisations is integrating all facets of organisational life so that the whole is greater than the sum of its parts.

So for instance, companies may have achieved their target of employing a woman to their Board, but how are the Board behaviours manifested so that she feels valued and involved? Are her opinions or recommendations listened to and respected so that she feels an integral part of the board? A quote from my research illustrates this aptly: "it is not a question of just bringing different people in...people we bring in need to slip into the culture..." That is, they have to adapt to us, and not the culture has to adjust for them! From another stance a further quote that amplifies this is "it is one thing to advocate for a diverse workforce and another to accept the differences that the diverse workforce will bring to the table."

The second performance driver, collaboration, is seen as a key way of working in our globalised world. Being collaborative is about helping each other and sharing knowledge, resources and practices. It is fundamental to breaking down silos – silos that stem from a perceived threat to role security, status, power and reward. Collaboration as a way of working moves the organisational structure from one that is hierarchical and bureaucratic to one of 'communities at work'.

The last performance driver is strategic alignment. It is about finding that equilibrium that enables us to focus and align our purpose and objectives with our practice. Strategy consists of five elements: knowing where we are at (present) and where we need to go (future) so as to grow and develop; what we need to do; how we are to get there; who is involved; and when it is to happen.

Strategy is pertinent to both leadership and diversity. At the leadership level, leaders have the responsibility for mapping out the direction of their organisation. They have followers and stakeholders alike who appreciate being led both artfully and with courage, and it is they who define the future of a diverse, inclusive and sustainable working environment. Diversity itself is a strategic goal. It is not a bolted-on / 'nice-to-do' activity, but rather is a measurable business objective that adds financial value to the bottom line.

Strategic alignment is achieved when elements of the organisation's overarching strategy translate to, and marry with, its diversity strategy.

Strategic alignment enables diversity and inclusion to become 'how we do things around here'. So, how does this play out on a day-to-day basis? How often have you heard leaders cry out for the need for ever-increasing innovative products only to close down creative problem solving and empowered decision making because they do not fall within the boundaries of 'how we do things around here' and/or conflict with bureaucratic structures and processes? How often have you been part of a performance management system that measures your individual contribution rather than the collective efforts of the team despite collaboration being one of the values that the organisation purports to hold? Strategic alignment helps us to focus on all elements of the system and how they come together to support and achieve the organisation's goals.

The next three groupings – stakeholders, diversity dimensions and organisational activities – represent the operational element of LEAD³. It enables the diversity dimensions (change levers) to be mapped to the different stakeholder groups so that organisational activities (change interventions) can be tailored to address diversity concerns through focused initiatives and solutions.

Stakeholders:

Three sets of stakeholders are considered for their unique characteristics towards harnessing diversity efforts. LEAD³ recognises individual, team and organisational needs so that diversity efforts and initiatives are both focused and tailored, and collective impact is achieved. For example: at an individual level, where capability is developed and retained; at a team level where opportunity for creating and sharing knowledge enables collaboration; and, at an organisational level where behaviours, structures, systems, processes and policies are integrated for multiple stakeholders.

Diversity Dimensions (change levers):

In our global village, the leader's performance is magnified and complicated by the diversity of stakeholders that global leaders need to engage with and the diverse workforce that they need to connect to. However, the relationship between leaders and diversity can be a contentious one – not least because of the negative and often emotional connotations that the term diversity continues to evoke. For instance, persistent discussions circulate with regard to the viability of targets for gender that place gender ahead of merit and, at the same time, devalue a man's contribution. A quote that exemplifies this point is "at present, diversity training is simply a tick in the box exercise…one of the problems we struggle with is…don't get yourself in trouble over sex or race discrimination; so it is a legally driven agenda". For white males, the fear of losing status or feeling redundant is often a reaction to diversity, with one executive referring to white males as 'the threatened species'.

The three diversity dimensions advocated in LEAD^3 – structural, cognitive and behavioural – aim to move the conversation from a negative one-to-one that is dynamic and embraces the organisation as a whole system. The research exposed that diversity and inclusion cannot be facilitated and implemented solely from a platform of identity. Therefore, in addition to 'Structural Diversity' (which incorporates demographic and process differences), it advances the conversation on diversity to include two further dimensions: 'Cognitive Diversity' which emphasises different ways of thinking and 'Behavioural Diversity' that encompasses the different ways in which we behave. These three diversity change levers can be mapped to a range of activities that can be systemically operationalised into organisational programmes that effectively target the needs of stakeholders.

One quote from my research that serves to illustrate the above is: "it is all about meeting the customer's needs. The advantage of a diverse workforce is that it celebrates differences and affords a broad input of experience. As a result you tend to get better decisions because you are casting your net wider and decisions are based on a more representative sample of your customers."

Organisational Activities:

These activities (change interventions) are explicitly aligned with the organisation's strategy. They take into account the differing stakeholder groupings and diversity dimensions and marry them to a wide range of approaches, methods and tools. These activities will be further expanded on in the next section, LEAD³ in Action, where we examine how business psychology contributes to leadership and diversity.

Performance Outcomes:

Performance outcomes are the outputs that are realised from a comprehensive and integrated leadership and diversity programme and correspond with the traits of high performing organisations. They were identified through the research as return on investment, organisational learning and sustainable growth and change.

Return on investment is the measure of financial results that have been realised by implementing a programme. Organisational learning is the outcome that demonstrates how the organisation is learning as it collaborates and how that learning is leveraged and embedded. Lastly, sustainable growth and change is the overarching aim that shows how the strategy and its corresponding change efforts continue to evolve, motivate and transform in spite of changing contexts and circumstances. As these diversity and leadership practices and attributes become embedded they will undeniably promote the long-term health and viability of the organisation by providing the resilience to adapt to continuous change.

Quotes that aptly reflect this emphasis on performance outcomes are: "changing behaviour and culture is difficult and it is a long process. Take the time and persevere. Celebrate the small steps, but be aware of the long haul!" And, "you need to declare a future and get the senior team on a common platform. You need to realise how you want to change your culture. See it as a priority and take it away from minimum compliance to essentially changing people's behaviour."

LEAD³ in Action

Given the accounts of the business need the question arises as to how LEAD³ can be translated and applied. That is, how does it move from the theoretical to the practical so as to embed the relevant culture, mindset, behaviours and skills for leaders as their organisations pursue their strategic diversity intentions? And how do those intentions foster engagement through inclusive ways of working with an array of diverse stakeholders?

It is at this juncture that the principles and practices of business psychology can offer a distinctive contribution. Its theories, methodologies and tools serve as key components for an integrated approach to leadership and diversity. LEAD^3 involves, for example, business psychology practices relating to diagnostics, psychometrics and evidence-based evaluation. It also presents a broader approach whereby all elements of the whole organisational system can be interrogated by applying business psychology principles and practices.

The components of LEAD^3 are aligned to an array of psychological theories, tools, and practices. It goes without saying that not every psychological theory and methodology will be covered here, nor will those mentioned be discussed in any depth. The examples that follow serve to illustrate how business psychology contributes to the interplay between leadership and diversity. These examples reflect conversations with clients and show how LEAD^3 is used in action both as a diagnostic and an operational tool, better integrating leadership and diversity to take account of the organisation as a whole system.

Beginning with the leadership dimension, an organisation wanted to understand how to become more effective at retaining female senior management talent. We looked at the various interventions that fall within the 'Structural/Individual' level through both the development and talent management lenses and identified two interventions that would get to the root of understanding how senior female management can be better retained. These were reverse mentoring and a returnship programme.

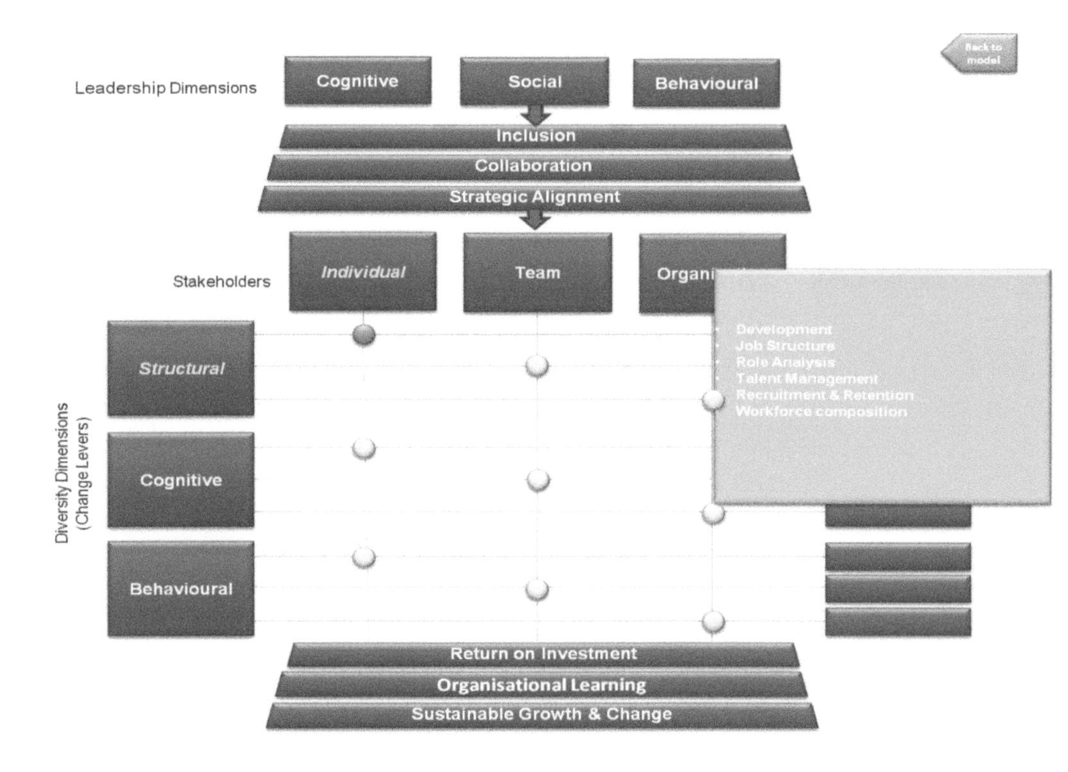

Figure 2: LEAD³: Structural/Individual

Additional business psychology applications for the leadership dimension that can deepen a client's understanding include:

- Cognitive processes:- decision making, problem solving, cognitive complexity, cognitive capacity, cognitive neuropsychology, cognitive dissonance, and strategic thinking.
- Behavioural change:- self awareness, interpersonal skills, influence, relationships; attitude & mindset, mindfulness, and attribution theory. (e.g. Fogg's (2009) Behavioural Model, and Nadler & Tushman's (2011) Congruence Model).
- Social skills:- social intelligence and non-verbal communications, agility and adaptability. An example of a tool is 'The Johari Window' by Luft & Ingham (2009).
- Development:- coaching, well-being, leadership and management development programmes and emotional intelligence. Amongst

numerous models are the well known Heron Model (2001) and the GROW model (Alexander, 2006).

- Leadership styles:- understanding and interrogating a range of styles such as transactional, transformational, authentic, situational etc.
- Competency:- psychometric tools, profiling, capability analysis, skill gap analysis, and assessment & development.
- Performance:- reviews, 360° feedback, job design and role analysis.

With regard to the performance drivers' dimension, a client wished to ascertain how teams could be more innovative in their decision making and collaborate more effectively across divisions. By assessing the interventions that fall within the 'Cognitive/Team' level we delved into the cognitive neuroscience arena to isolate interventions from both cognitive and behavioural psychology that would foster greater innovation. To encourage greater collaboration, we pin-pointed 'Groupthink' practices that were hindering collaboration and ways to overcome these practices, and also assessed motivation factors linked to engagement and rewards.

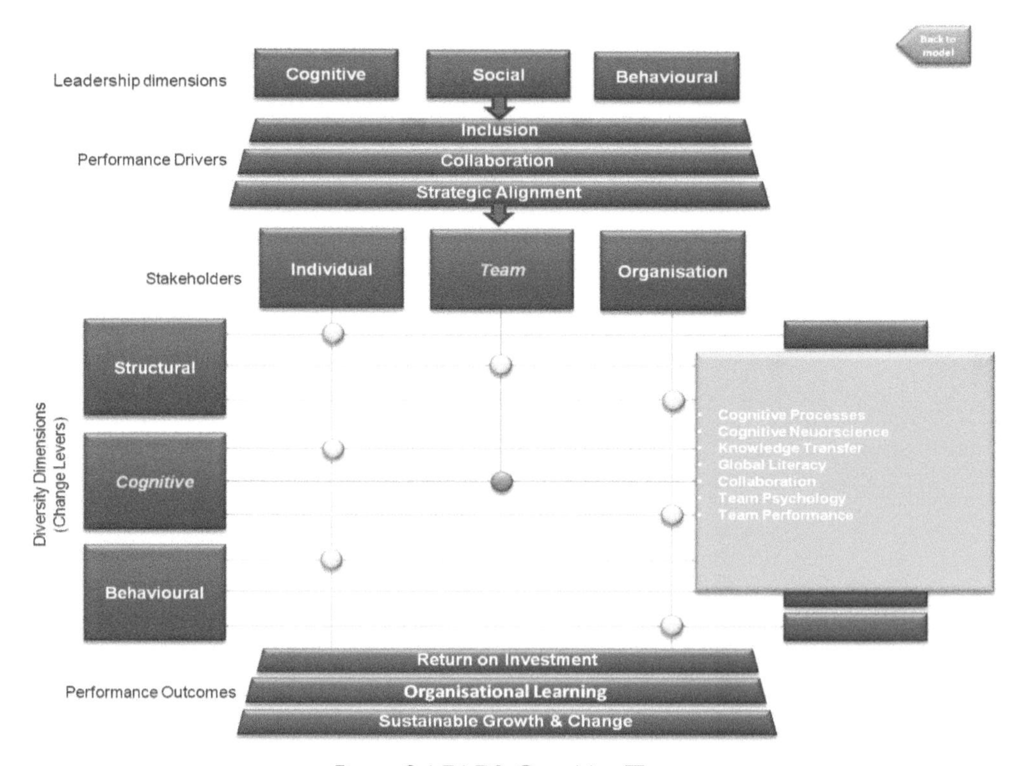

Figure 3: LEAD³: Cognitive/Team

Further business psychology theories/methodologies for the performance driver dimension that can be employed include:

- Engagement:- motivation e.g. intrinsic and extrinsic motivators, content theories such as Maslow's (1954) hierarchy of needs, Hertzberg's two factor theory (Hertzberg, et al., 1959), and Alderfer's (1972) Existence, Relatedness, Growth theory (ERG); cognitive theories such as Goal-Setting and expectancy theories, behavioural economics, psychological flexibility, psychological contracts and job satisfaction.
- Inclusion:- identifying organisational culture and analysis of values, purpose, and ways of working; innovation and creativity, employee value proposition, and organisational design. Examples of models include Johnson & Scholes's (Johnson, 1992) Cultural Web, Deal & Kennedy's (1982) Cultural Model and Barrett's (1997) 7 levels of Organisational Consciousness.
- Collaboration:- creating avenues for dialogue through appreciative inquiry; social network analysis for connecting, designing structures that break down silos and enables knowledge transfer, and role-modelling collaborative behaviour. Relevant approaches include Axelrod's (2010) Engagement Principles and Gebauer and Lowman's (2008) Engagement Gap.
- Strategic alignment:- values mapping, organisational design and job design.

The LEAD^3 dimensions consisting of stakeholders, diversity (change levers) and organisational activities (change interventions) demonstrate where a plethora of business psychology applications and practices can be utilised. An example is where a client wanted to develop more effective ways of managing communication and conflict management across cultural boundaries. At the 'Behavioural/Organisation' level we conducted a deep dive by assessing the dynamic of intercultural communications and its impact on communication breakdowns and also examined the part that power and politics played in ongoing organisational conflict.

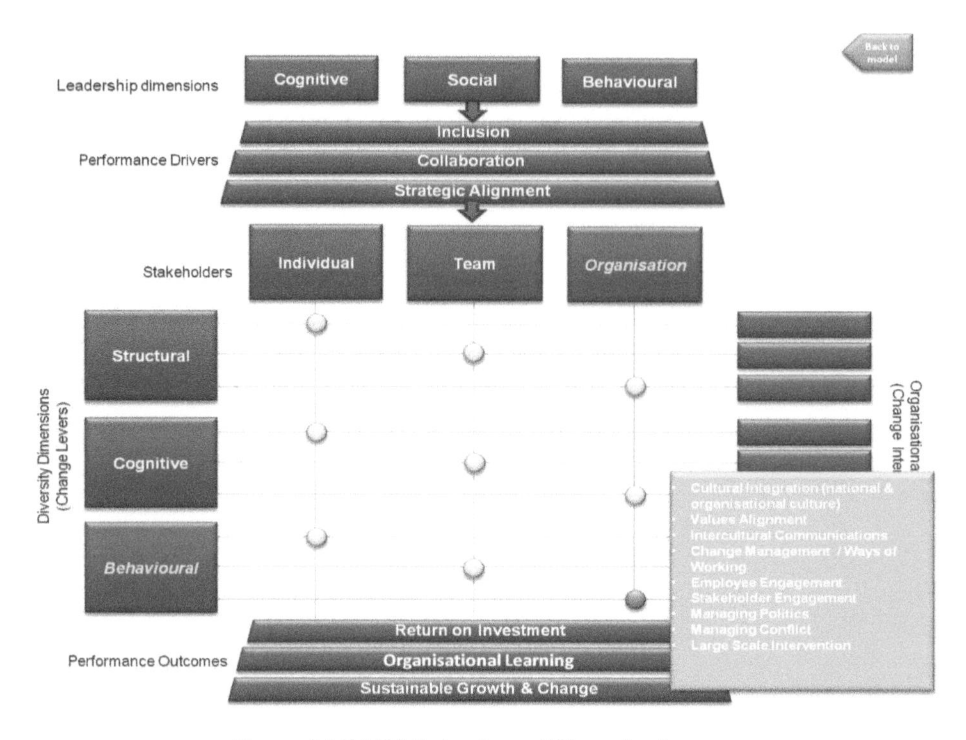

Figure 4: LEAD³: Behavioural/Organisation

Other business psychology approaches and tools that can be utilised for this element of the model are:

- Global literacy:- involves an understanding of cultural integration and an identification of organisational cultural types & dimensions (e.g. Denison's (1990) Company Performance Index).
- Change management:- complexity theories (e.g. Snowden & Boon's (2007) Cynefin complexity model), resistance and acceptance (e.g. Elisabeth Kubler-Ross's (2005) *The Change Curve* and *The Change Equation* by Beckhard & Harris (1987)), transformational change (e.g. *Theory U* by C. Otto Scharmer (2009)).
- Diversity:- exploring cognitive biases & errors (e.g. Kahneman's (2011) Systems 1 and 2), implicit bias testing, social identity theory, cognitive behavioural therapy, and microinequities.
- Processes:- analysis of talent management processes; recruitment processes (e.g. hiring and exit interviews), retention strategy,

skills strategy, gap analysis, performance reviews, role analysis and competency assessment.

- Conflict:- the management of silos, difficult conversations, appreciative inquiry, organisational justice, power and politics. Models include Bell & Hart's (2008) Betaris Box, the Thomas-Kilmann (1977) Conflict Model Instrument and Baddely & James's (1990) Model of Political Skills.
- Communications:- including non-verbal communication, dialogue, active listening, cross-cultural communication, and openness and transparency.
- Stakeholders:- exploring engagement and connection, utilising stakeholder analysis and mapping, and social network theory.
- Group dynamics:- including analysis of team composition & roles (e.g. Belbin, 1981), team formation and performance (e.g. McGregor's (1960) Theory X and Theory Y; Tuckman's (1965) group development), Janis's (1971) Groupthink, and the dysfunctions of teams (e.g. Lencioni's (2002) 5 Dysfunctions of Teams).

Lastly, in performance outcomes, relevant business psychology practices employed can include:

- Measuring the impact and outcomes of interventions through data collection from surveys, statistical analysis and evidence-based practice.
- Understanding how individuals, teams and the organisation as a system learn through methodologies such as training needs analysis, double-loop learning, learning cycles, learning styles, social learning, development programmes, role playing and action learning.
- Embedding sustainable change and growth programmes by analysing organisational readiness for change, resilience & resistance; systems thinking, ergonomics and large-scale interventions (e.g. World Café/ Open Space/Future Search).

Conclusion

Business psychology appreciates that organisations are complex adaptive systems that embody human processes: the humanness and quality of our relationships that ultimately drive an organisation's success lie at the heart of diversity as well as at the heart of successful change.

It is this humanness that is common to current topical concepts referred to in the introduction. These concepts are both advocated and operationalised in LEAD[3]. For instance: leadership skills fit for an increasingly globalised world; performance drivers that place a premium on stakeholder health by demonstrating inclusivity and collaboration to form the backbone of a high performing culture; cultures where a sense of purpose drives and activates the strategy; and, diversity dimensions, stakeholder needs and change activities that are aligned with the strategy so that organisational learning is cultivated, growth is sustained and resilience is built into the system.

Business psychology contributes in two ways to this humanness. First, the philosophy, ethos and guiding principles of business psychology ensure that activities are rooted in practices that are both scientific and evidence-based. Secondly, business psychology helps us to appreciate and understand the value of context, taking a long-term view above short-termism. For example: to understand why it is important for stakeholder health to be prized above shareholder value; to understand why it is important that the behaviour of inclusion is nurtured and the notion of in-group and out-groups is devalued; to appreciate the benefits of investing in strategic alignment so that the whole is greater than the sum of parts as opposed to simply practising corporate compliance.

So, what is the significance of this and how can we realise these practices? Put simply, significance can be attributed to acknowledging and viewing human beings as essential components of the whole system. Once we take a view that people lie at the core of business, that human capital drives financial capital, then the value of business psychology insight can be realised and applied to organisations.

Further, Business Psychologists' understanding of the business environment as well as the business need enables us to tailor advice and solutions to organisational communities. Within these communities we acknowledge the often competing and diverse dynamics central to organisations such as globalisation and diversity, cultures and sub-cultures, leadership, performance management, customer relationships, technology, risks, innovation, talent, operations, value and supply chains, vision and values, and learning and development.

Business Psychologists understand the interplay between these internal and external organisational factors and the resulting impact on the human being. We are able to take a systemic view of the organisation and address the challenges and paradoxes that leaders face as they endeavour to position, facilitate and implement more diverse and inclusive structures and practices in their organisations. LEAD^3 provides a lens through which we can access this psychological insight and practice.

References

Alderfer, C. P. (1972). *Existence, Relatedness, and Growth; Human needs in organizational settings.* New York, NY: Free Press.

Alexander, G. (2006). Behavioural coaching: The GROW model. In J. Passmore (Ed). *Excellence in Coaching*. (pp. 83-94). London: Kogan Page.

Axelrod, R. H. (2010). *Terms of Engagement*. San Francisco, CA: Berrett-Koehler Publishers.

Baddely, S., & James, K. (1990). Political Management: Developing the management portfolio. *Journal of Management Development*, *9*(3), 42-59.

Barrett, R. (1997). *The 7 Levels of Organisational Consciousness*. Retrieved from https://www.valuescentre.com.

Beckhard, R., & Harris, R. T. (1987). *Organizational transitions: Managing complex change* (2nd ed.). Reading, MA: Addison-Wesley Publishing.

Belbin, R. (1981). *Management Teams: Why they succeed or fail*. London: Elsevier.

Bell, A., & Hart, B. (2008). Betaris Box. In P. Clements & J. Jones (Eds.), *The Diversity Training Handbook: A practical guide to understanding and changing attitudes* (3rd Ed) (pp. 216-217). London: Kogan Page.

Deal, T. E., & Kennedy, A. A. (1982). *Corporate Cultures: The rites and rituals of corporate life*. Reading, MA: Addison-Wesley.

Denison, D. R. (1990). *Corporate Culture and Organisational Effectiveness*. New York, NY: Wiley.

Fogg, B. J. (2009). A Behavioural Model for Persuasive Design. *Proceeding of the 4th International Conference on Persuasive Technology*. Article No. 40. New York, NY, USA: ACM.

Gebauer, J., & Lowman, D. (2008). *Closing the engagement gap*. New York, NY: The Penguin Group.

Heron, J. (2001). *Helping the Client: A creative practical guide*. London: SAGE Publications.

Herzberg, F., Mausner, B., & Snyderman, B. B. (1959). *The Motivation to Work* (2nd ed.). New York, NY: John Wiley.

Janis, I. L. (1971, November). Groupthink. *Psychology Today*, 442-7

Johnson, G. (1992). Managing Strategic Change – Strategy, culture and action. *Long Range Planning, 25*(1), 28-36.

Kahneman, D. (2011). *Thinking, fast and slow*. London: Allen Lane.

Kilmann, R., & Thomas, K. W. (1977). Developing a Forced-Choice Measure of Conflict-Handling Behavior: The "MODE" Instrument. *Educational and Psychological Measurement, 37*(2), 309-325.

Kübler-Ross, E. (2005). *On Grief and Grieving: Finding the Meaning of Grief Through the Five Stages of Loss*. New York, NY: Simon & Schuster Inc.

Lencioni, P. (2002). *The Five Dysfunctions of a Team: A leadership fable*. San Francisco, CA: Jossey Bass.

Luft, J., & Ingham, H. (2009). The Johari Window. In P. Clements & J. Jones (Eds.), *The Diversity Training Handbook: A practical guide to understanding and changing attitudes* (3rd Ed) (pp. 218-219). London: Kogan Page.

Maslow. A. H. (1954). *Motivation and Personality*. New York, NY: Harper & Brothers.

McGregor, D. (1960). *The Human Side of Enterprise*. New York, NY: McGraw-Hill.

Nadler, D. A., & Tushman, M. L. (2011). Integrated Models for Understanding Organizations and for Leading and Managing Change. In W. Warner Burke (Ed.), *Organization Change: Theory and Practice.* (pp. 198-203). California: SAGE Publications.

Scharmer, C. O. (2009). *Theory U*. San Francisco, CA: Berrett-Koehler Publishers.

Snowden, D., & Boon, M. E. (2007, November). A leader's framework for decision making. *Harvard Business Review*, 69-76.

Storey, S. (2014). *The Impact of Diversity on Global Leadership Performance: LEAD^3*. London: Palgrave Macmillan.

Tuckman, B. W. (1965). Developmental sequence in small groups. *Psychological Bulletin, 63*(6), 384-399.

GETTING THE BEST FROM THE BRIGHTEST: INSIGHTS FROM NEURODIVERSITY

Sally Moore

"In a world changing faster than ever, honoring and nurturing neurodiversity is civilization's best chance to thrive in an uncertain future."

Steve Silberman, 2013

Those applying psychology in the classroom, the clinic or the workplace have long been interested in understanding how different people think, feel and behave. In business, individual differences that are widely understood and measured include ability, personality, learning style, social style and emotional intelligence. Neurodiversity is a relatively new area of neuroscience and applied psychology that offers deeper, more precise explanations of how different people experience the world and their working lives.

I became curious about this after talking with coaches, psychologists and consultants about their work with people they referred to as being "High IQ, Low EQ", "supergeeks" or Myers Brigg type "ISTJ". I was struck by the qualitative similarities in the issues described with those presented by some of the young people with Asperger's Syndrome (AS) I encountered in my career as an NHS Clinical Psychologist. These teenagers often did exceptionally well academically, but found the social demands of school very challenging to cope with. In the last 20 years there have been rapid developments in identifying, understanding and working with those who have neurodevelopmental differences such as AS. As a result we have better ways of understanding how they experience the world. Strategies for good practice have developed and better outcomes in health and education have been achieved.

The young people I worked with often went on to university and then into employment. I have often wondered what their experience of working life might be like in terms of fitting in and if they were able to use their undoubted talents to their full potential.

Can neurodiversity, particularly what is known about AS, potentially provide insights for managers, leaders, psychologists and coaches to engage different kinds of clever minds in business? I could see what difference it had made to the young people I had worked with, their families and their schools. Could this help inform ways to optimise outcomes in business?

After considering neurodiversity and its meaning in broad terms, I will discuss research relevant to the people and contexts where it can add value in business. We will then dig deeper into the area of High Functioning Autism (HFA) or Asperger's Syndrome (AS) with a focus on both clinical and sub-clinical manifestations observable in the workplace. Recent developments in the theoretical understanding of autistic thinking will be covered by way of shedding light on what might be happening beneath the surface of observed behaviours. We will then explore implications for practice in business psychology.

What is Neurodiversity?

The term "neurodiversity" was first coined in the late 1990s by Australian sociologist Judith Singer (as cited in Corker & French, 1999). Referring to life-long, largely heritable differences in brain structure and function, neurodiversity arose out of campaigning by those in the autism community who regarded themselves as different rather than disordered.

While initially referring to HFA or AS, the term has expanded to include other differences including IQ, dyslexia and handedness. When we explore neurodiversity a little further, it becomes obvious that the human brain is not easily categorised and these variations are best understood as continua or spectrum differences.

Neurodiversity is an important concept because it challenges the assumption that any difference has to mean a disability or something to be cured. Some differences such as exceptional mathematical or musical ability are highly valued while others, such as global learning disability are not.

How do we decide whether we are looking at a disability, a normal variation or a valuable difference? Until it was essential for everyone to read, dyslexia wasn't even identified. In relatively recent times, being left-handed was seen as problematic. These examples demonstrate the role of environment – culture, time, values, norms and demands – in determining whether someone might be judged to be 'normal', a genius or a liability.

When I use the term 'neurodiversity', I am considering difference not disability. I am concentrating specifically on Asperger's Syndrome (AS) or characteristics and traits that have qualitative similarities. I use the term synonymously with 'High IQ, Low EQ', 'geek', 'supergeek' or, to go back into the clinical arena 'broad autistic phenotype' (BAP). There is not yet a single accepted term within applied psychology that accurately reflects the complexity and diversity within this group of people.

Neurodiversity in Business Psychology

Neurodiversity exists in many businesses and a wide range of occupational groups. However, there are businesses and occupations where Business Psychologists may be more likely to find it relevant to their practice.

In our increasingly knowledge-based economy, businesses need original gifted thinkers who thrive on solving complex problems. In a world where not all brilliant minds are the same and one good idea can make or save millions, a business can gain a competitive edge by better understanding, attracting and getting the best from the brightest minds.

The strengths and challenges that neurodiversity brings to business are those identified in line with the cognitive profile of AS and include: focus on detail; exceptional memory; intense concentration; a clear preference for rationality; impeccable dependability; extraordinary capacity for difficult technical challenges; highly expert knowledge in areas of keen interest and conscientious persistence. At their core is a style of thinking described by Baron-Cohen (2009) as "systemizing" which is the drive to analyse how systems work in a precise and exact way and then to predict and control those systems or create new ones. This way of thinking is required in occupations such as engineering, science, computing, technology, mathematics and other highly specialist professions. People are often employed because of their capability to think in this way.

However, a highly systemising mind that processes information in a way that can be of such high value to business can have difficulties with understanding other people. Baron-Cohen (2009) calls this low "empathising" and it is important to note that this is very different from the lack of empathy demonstrated by those with psychopathic traits who have received considerable attention from business psychology. People like Daniel and James, described below, are quite capable of caring, but have poor understanding of others' thoughts, feelings and intentions that looks much more like social awkwardness, introversion or a lack of emotional intelligence.

Daniel is a brilliant metallurgist in his 30s. He is a loner and a colleague describes him as having no sense of proportion or ability to compromise. However, the MD of the business recognised that the most troublesome of his staff tended to be the most effective. Daniel left to take an elevated position in another company, but was fired after only a few weeks as they found his 'quirks' difficult to manage.

James, 26, despite his excellent software development skills, has had problems in several jobs because he caused offence to others by, in his mind, just telling the truth. If he thinks a customer has had a terrible idea, he tells them exactly that. When faced with a situation requiring diplomacy and sensitivity, he has persisted forcefully with his point of view because he is convinced he is right. He cannot read the nuances of different social situations and modify his responses to fit.

Other challenges associated with neurodiversity can include: a lack of commercial awareness because of over-attention to detail; pedantic use of language; rigid thinking; excessive perfectionism; resistance to change; indifference to authority, arrogance, higher likelihood of stress and poor communication (Attwood, 2007; Moore et al., 2013). These can impact on performance and working relationships to the extent that businesses see people as either too high maintenance to retain or too challenging to develop.

Businesses today place high value on both technical and social competencies. They are keen for their brilliant thinkers to be able to deal with customers, work in a team, collaborate with or lead others. However, exceptional technical and social skills do not always reside in the same person. What if a technical genius struggles to work in a team? How often do businesses face challenges with people who are hugely able from a technical point of view, but find the people side of working life mystifying? How do they make sense of what is happening and what do they do about it? How can they maximise the strengths and manage the challenges presented by this exceptional talent?

Before we look at some research from business, what evidence is there for AS traits in the general population and particular occupational groups?

Evidence from research

"It seems that for success in science or art, a dash of autism is essential...an ability to turn away from the everyday world...to rethink a subject with originality, and create new untrodden ways... "

Hans Asperger (1944)

Hans Asperger clearly saw the strengths and talents of the young people he originally described in the 1940s as having fluent language, a lack of empathy, little ability to form friendships, one-sided conversation and intense absorption in special interests.

Most research in neurodiversity has been carried out in health and educational settings where neurodevelopmental differences are still most likely to be identified. There are now more research efforts geared to adults with AS. Simon Baron-Cohen and his team at the Autism Research Centre in Cambridge have developed a standardised questionnaire measuring AS traits in the general adult population, the Autism Quotient (AQ) (Baron-Cohen et al., 2001).

The Cambridge team have also developed measures of systemising (SQ) and empathising (EQ). They have demonstrated that people with AS score significantly higher on the SQ and significantly lower on the EQ compared to the general population (Baron-Cohen, 2009).

In a 2001 study, the AQ questionnaire was administered to over 1,000 adults in Cambridge. Of these, 58 had AS, 840 were Cambridge undergraduates, 174 were randomly selected controls and 16 were Maths Olympiad winners. As expected, those with AS scored significantly higher than controls. Within the control group, men scored slightly, but significantly, higher than women with twice as many men (40%) as women (21%) having at least moderate levels of AS traits. Students did not score significantly higher than the control group, but those studying science and maths scored significantly higher than humanities and social science students. This finding was replicated with the Maths Olympiad winners.

This suggests there may be more likelihood of AS traits at sub-clinical levels in some occupational groups, replicating the finding of a 1998 (Baron-Cohen et al.) study by the same team that autism occurs more often in families of physicists, engineers and mathematicians. Cognitive style in the form of systemising has been shown to be a better predictor than gender for those entering STEM (Science, Technology, Engineering and Maths) occupations (Billington et al., 2007).

Genetic and twin studies demonstrate that autism and autistic traits in the general population are highly heritable (Ronald et al., 2005).

Autistic Spectrum Conditions are also more likely to be diagnosed among children in regions that attract businesses in IT and technology where talented systemisers live and work (Roelfsama et al., 2011).

Evidence from business

What does this look like from a business point of view? To investigate this, I teamed up with colleagues from Business Psychology firm Nicholson McBride to conduct a commercially focused piece of qualitative, exploratory research. As research outlined above had identified STEM occupations as more likely to demonstrate neurodiversity in the form of AS traits, we interviewed 21 leaders of organisations employing STEM in the following sectors: universities; pharmaceutical; data analytics; science and biotechnology.

Our semi-structured interview explored how businesses address the issues of STEM highly technical and less social minds. Why do businesses employ STEM? How are STEM different from other employees? How can businesses get best performance from STEM and what are the benefits of doing this better than a competitor? How can increasing expectations for collaboration be met? What do businesses consider in managing and leading STEM? What are the optimum ways of maximising engagement?

Strengths

STEM were clearly identified as indispensable to the businesses that relied on scientific and technical innovation to create new products. STEM were seen as the "powerhouse of innovation", "critical to business success" and "employed for how they think". STEM were described as a diverse and often quirky group who thrive on logic, data and rationality. This often meant interpersonal issues are dealt with unemotionally.

Culture and Environment

Where business success relies on STEM talent, efforts were made to ensure this talent was motivated, developed and retained. This required an environment tolerant of risk and accepting that failure was part of longer-term success. Peer-assessment and external review were highly valued and effective for managing performance in STEM.

Challenges

A common theme identified by participants was that STEM were less able than other employees to see the business relevance of their work, tending to favour technical purity over commercial need. Over-attention to detail could compromise deadlines and mean others could not always plan ahead. STEM were also reported as finding change more challenging than others, tending to demonstrate a lack of flexibility and adaptability.

Another common challenge was communication. This could mean presentations being too long or detailed "losing themselves in the minutiae"; difficulties in breaking communication down effectively; frustration for others with "getting ideas out of their heads in a timely way" and a lack of subtlety being "too direct with others" or "showing off". Influencing skills, team-working, giving feedback and sharing a common vision were also seen as more challenging areas compared to non-STEM employees. Managers considered that STEM took up more of their time and one-to-one attention by needing more detailed explanations, more careful feedback and more repetition of information. This reflected their limited generalisation to different situations.

Responses to Challenges

Businesses managed the challenges in a number of ways. Some excluded 'extreme STEM' from recruitment or promotion while others relied on outsourcing. Bigger firms with extensive experience of engineering talent had created dual-track career paths so STEM could gain seniority through their technical capabilities rather than management or leadership. There was an underlying sense of businesses managing the more challenging or extreme characteristics by avoidance.

Is neurodiversity acceptable in business?

We took opportunities to gauge the acceptability of the notion of neurodiversity in business. We found our interviewees to have a high level of interest in this idea with several speaking about individuals personally known to them with AS. There was recognition that some of the strengths and challenges they identified in STEM had very similar qualities. There was strong interest in the idea that neurodiversity might help explain some the behaviours observed and offer new ways to integrate STEM into organisational life.

The quantity and quality of research into AS over the past 20 years adds credibility and rigour to the practical application of neurodiversity in business, something that will appeal to those who favour facts, logic and rationality. I will now summarise relevant issues arising from research in AS, then review the main psychological theories about how these minds work before moving onto implications for best practice.

AS – a brief overview

Asperger's work was not translated into English until 1981 (Wing, 1981) and until then, it was thought that 75% of those with autism had IQ less than 70 whereas now it is believed that 75% have average IQ or higher (Rajendran & Mitchell, 2007). AS was recognised as a separate diagnostic category in 1994 (DSM-IV) prompting a surge of research into this fascinating group of people. Those identified as having AS have themselves become much more vocal, providing powerful insights into their experiences in all aspects of life.

The boundaries between clinical and sub-clinical manifestations are blurred and often subjective with diagnosis based on behavioural observations rather than objective biological means. Core features are life-long differences in: sensory sensitivity; understanding and social use of language; communication and social interaction; thinking patterns favouring rules, logic and rationality; and detailed knowledge in areas of interest to the individual. These interests strongly influence career choice.

It is important to emphasise that what AS looks like in any particular individual is hugely variable. Contrary to popular belief, people with AS can be introvert or extrovert. For some, social communication may be particularly challenging, while for others rigid thinking or sensory issues may be the most prominent characteristic. AS can also co-exist with other neurodevelopmental differences such as ADHD or dyslexia.

Autism in all its forms, including AS, is currently thought to occur in around 1% of the adult population (Brugha et al., 2009) and the vast majority remain unidentified. The male to female ratio for those with AS is reported at 5:1 with much ongoing debate on the recognition of AS in women (Gould & Ashton-Smith, 2011). This is roughly in line with the STEM gender gap (Ceci & Williams, 2010).

How people with AS experience working life

Of adults who have a formal diagnosis of AS, only 15% are in employment and 79% of those out of work want to work (Redman, 2009). This is not because people with AS are unable to perform on the job, but because businesses generally provide workplaces designed for the 'neurotypical' – those who can manage change and have well developed social competencies.

People with AS have described existing in a neurotypical world like being on another planet or like having a different 'operating system'. Tony Attwood (2007) describes four ways in which people might cope. These are:

A retreat into a personal world of creativity and imagination: *"I have the ability to be blissfully ignorant of the annoyance I'm causing other people."*

Heroic and often failed attempts to fit in: *"I'm a puzzle piece and I don't quite fit. I want to approach some sort of normal but it's not easy. It takes effort, like I have to load an app. When it doesn't work, I get stressed. It feels risky to keep trying."*

Arrogance and a view that others are at fault: *"These rules don't make any sense so I'm going to ignore them. They don't apply to me."*

Observing and copying others: *"Meetings are like some weird game and I have no idea what the rules are. I'll copy what John says and does."*

Activity: What does neurodiversity feel like in a neurotypical environment?

Have a 5-minute conversation with another person about a simple topic e.g. the last time you visited a supermarket or your journey to work. In this conversation, follow some different rules – do not use your hands for gesture (put them on your knees) and look only at the other person's left shoulder.

What does it feel like to do this? Was it difficult or easy? What impact did following these rules have on the conversation?

How would you manage in a difficult conversation?

What if there were hundreds or thousands of these rules to learn and follow? What if they kept changing and you had to think about them constantly?

What would be the impact of trying to follow these rules all day, every day? How would it feel to be judged based on your ability to follow them? What would you need from others to make it easier? What difference would it make to have more understanding and less judgement?

The challenges of coping can leave people with AS or associated characteristics at higher risk for stress, anxiety and mental health problems (Attwood, 2007). They may, therefore, present to practitioners with an unusual profile of experiencing stress in situations that others appear to take in their stride.

A great deal of work has focused on developing ways to help people with AS 'fit' in neurotypical environments. Research into psychological theories seeks to inform practice and improve outcomes by precisely characterising the cognitive style of people with AS and what distinguishes them from others. This is complemented by practice-based evidence from practitioners developing and shaping interventions in education, health and employment settings. Links between theory and practice continue to grow and these will now be briefly summarised.

Psychological theories of autism

Autism and AS are now amongst the most studied disorders in the world. This hard scientific graft has resulted in three main cognitive theories – Weak Central Coherence, Theory of Mind and Executive

Functioning. Leading researchers in this area are Uta Frith, Lorna Wing, Francesca Happe, Simon Baron-Cohen and Peter Vermeulen. I will only be touching on the vast research on each of these theories. Please see below for sources of further reading.

Weak Central Coherence

The Weak Central Coherence (WCC) theory arose out of work by Frith & Happe (1994) and argues that people with AS process details at the expense of global meaning. They do not construct a centrally coherent theme from the information available to them.

Their research found that children with AS have a narrower cognitive perspective, allocate their attention in unusual ways and may focus on details others consider to be trivial. WCC is argued to become most apparent in processing social and emotional information.

While there are results that show AS individuals have a tendency for fragmented perception, there are also studies that suggest that people with AS are able to process globally when they are instructed to do so (van Lang et al., 2006). Some people with AS have also questioned the existence of one universally recognised 'big picture' and argue that a contextual understanding held by someone with AS can be equally valid.

Interventions based on WCC recognise, accept and value a distinctive thinking style rather than try to change it. They include: clear communication of expectations; managing perfectionism; giving unambiguous information about which aspects of a task requires attention; and increased use of written and visual communication (Attwood, 2007).

Theory of Mind

Theory of Mind (ToM) is a high-order cognitive process and refers to the ability to understand the thoughts, beliefs, feelings and intentions of other people. This theory argues that people with AS are drawn to different cues, often relating to objects or patterns, which means they have not had the social learning experiences by which most of us learn ToM automatically.

Research into ToM has involved the very creative use of stories and tasks such as the 'false belief' test that assesses ability to infer another person's mental representation of a situation; animated geometric shapes that are moved in a way that represents social interaction; and the 'Eyes test' where participants are asked to infer mental state from looking at eyes. These different tasks were designed to cover all aspects of language and IQ within the autistic spectrum. ToM typically develops by around 5 years of age while those with autism, regardless of age or IQ, are much more likely to find ToM tasks more challenging than their peers. ToM very much looks like a core cognitive difference specific to autism (Baron-Cohen, 2009). A study has also demonstrated lower than normal levels of ToM in relatives of those with autism who are considered to demonstrate a Broad Autistic Phenotype (BAP) (Gocken et al., 2009).

It could be argued that ToM reflects a difference in social understanding rather than a deficit and this may be a more compassionate starting point for intervention. When I talk with people who have AS, they are often puzzled by the neurotypical experience of the social world while seeing their own perspective as rational and sensible. They also recognise the tensions and, on occasions, the comedy of two versions of reality coming together.

Interventions have been developed to teach mind-reading skills e.g. Golan & Baron-Cohen (2006). These have included: ways to read verbal and non-verbal signals to infer other's mental states; teaching interaction and conversational skills; improving social cognition and social skills. People with AS make good use of computer based instruction, which is less pressured and more focused than a classroom environment. In a recent review of ToM based interventions, Fletcher-Watson et al. (2014) found that while there is evidence that theory of mind, or related skills, can be taught to people with AS, these skills are not well maintained or generalised to other settings. This suggests that learning and development opportunities need to go beyond a 'classroom' setting to ensure effective application of new skills.

Executive Functioning

Executive Functioning (EF) is an umbrella term for cognitive functions such as working memory, planning, sequencing, prioritising, organisation and flexibility of thinking. EF typically develops fully in adolescence and early adulthood along with the brain's frontal and pre-frontal cortices. There is considerable research using neuropsychological tests that confirms adults with AS and BAP demonstrate differences in EF (Hill, 2004). In the workplace, this presents as differences in attention and concentration, resistance to change or feedback, a lack of social 'filter', preference for working on one task at a time and perceived issues with time management and organisation.

Interventions based on EF support people in engaging with goal-directed activity by: using unambiguous language; providing clear structure and routine; time management strategies; and developing flexibility in thinking through problem-solving. In supporting EF skills, many parents of young people with AS find themselves acting as 'executive secretary' for their child well into adulthood. In the workplace, this may need to be done by a mentor, manager or indeed an Executive Secretary.

Context Blindness

Research into WCC, ToM and EF have yielded a great deal of insight into how autistic minds work right across the spectrum, from classic autism, to AS and the Broad Autistic Phenotype or systemisers. However, they tend to explain parts of the AS cognitive profile rather than all of it. In his recent book, Peter Vermeulen (2012) builds on these cognitive theories with the idea of autism being a form of context blindness.

Vermeulen focuses on how the brain processes information on context often at a pre-conscious level i.e. what happens within the first milliseconds of perception and information processing. Context is what is going on in the environment and inside our brain that guides our way of giving meaning to things. Vermeulen describes 'context sensitivity' as our ability to select, use or ignore this information to generate meaning. He argues that the neurotypical human brain is inherently context sensitive whereas the autistic brain is 'context blind'.

Activity: How do you use context?

Context takes many forms and its use is automatic for many of us.

How did you decide what to wear today? What is the best gift for someone you know? What is the correct meaning of the word 'right'? What do the words 'friend' and 'like' mean?

What information did you use to answer these questions? Where did it come from? If you couldn't have access to this information, what difference would that have made to your answers?

Context sensitivity is crucial for social and emotional intelligence in the workplace. It is also needed for technical performance by explaining the task that needs to be completed, how feedback processes work, how decisions get made and communication required.

One strategy to develop context sensitivity that could be used in business was developed by Carol Gray (2003), a teacher and consultant who works with children who have autism. Gray developed the use of social narratives in the form of Social Stories™, articles and visual representations that use specific criteria for structure, content, language, development and implementation. These narratives provide individually tailored information to build context sensitivity and have also been used in interventions relating to ToM, WCC and EF. There is a clear emphasis on the generalisation and maintenance of learning and, while the development of Gray's approach largely pre-dates Vermeulen's work, there is promising potential here for linking practice and theory. There is growing evidence of the effectiveness of social narratives (Test et al., 2010) that can be adapted for use across the autistic spectrum.

Implications for Practice in Business Psychology

Business Psychologists are in a good position to make use of insights provided by neurodiversity in their work. These can be useful in any aspect of working with highly specialist talent from recruitment through to performance management, career progression, training or leadership development. They are likely to be particularly valuable when: an organisation wants to improve selection and retention of specialist talent; demands for team working, collaboration or relationships with customers increase; support is needed to manage change; tensions exist between technical detail and business priorities or there are concerns about levels of occupational stress.

It is not unusual for managers to become exasperated with someone who, although brilliant, does not respond to feedback, performance management strategies or learning in the same way as others. An essential individual might be brought in at a senior leadership level to resolve a technical crisis, but their relatively poor communication skills can impact negatively across the whole organisation. In both these scenarios, ongoing frustration can lead to deterioration in relationships and a climate increasingly characterised by negativity, blame, stress and perceived failure. The result can be loss of employment for the individual concerned and loss to the business of their unique talents.

An understanding of neurodiversity can enhance and complement existing skills of Business Psychologists to generate better ways of getting the best from people whose minds work in different ways. It may be one of several issues that practitioners need to take into account or it may clearly be the most useful way of understanding what is happening for any particular individual in a specific context at a point in time. Neurodiversity provides ways of responding that work for the individuals rather than simply expecting them to fit in. Interventions focus on work with the individual, but also include educating those around them in the workplace. It can make a huge difference to working relationships if behaviours on the surface perceived as rudeness, poor timekeeping or a lack of commercial awareness can be understood as a different, but equally valid way of experiencing the world.

There are some general principles for working with neurodiversity that provide a setting for the specific strategies that I will describe.

General Principles

- Improve your own awareness and understanding of neurodiversity as a way of engaging and understanding different kinds of minds rather than a representation of disability and impairment. Consider learning more about AS and strategies effective for this population.
- Develop ways of identifying when a neurodiversity perspective is likely to be of value e.g. change in work role, an increase in social or communication demands, unusual stress profile or awkward working relationships.
- Promote understanding of neurodiversity in client organisations so strengths can be maximised and challenges can be anticipated before they become problems. Challenge stereotypical views of AS, neurodiversity or 'geeks'. The characteristics I have described are generally well recognised so developing a language around engaging different kinds of minds can be very helpful.
- Reframe additional time and effort required to manage neurodiversity as an investment.

Specific Strategies

The following are examples of strategies that might be used directly by Business Psychologists or developed within client organisations.

- Make no assumptions about how people experience the world and their working life. Accepting their perspective as equally valid, but different, provides an optimal starting point for solutions based on mutual respect and understanding.
- Be prepared to explain structure and boundaries with information on expectations, sequencing, prioritising, communication and social context. Where people are good on details, micro-management is unhelpful.
- Use plain language. Say what you mean, avoid jargon and make the abstract concrete. Providing information visually and in writing minimises the need for repetition.
- Leverage social competencies of others in the organisation. This

might involve line managers, PAs, team colleagues or workplace mentors.

- Challenge assumptions that social competencies can't be learned. Ensure Learning and Development opportunities are designed with neurodiversity in mind. Position them as having an equal or prestigious status. Pay attention to developing understanding of context as well as skill development.
- Focus only on essential social competencies. Pay attention to developing skills, but also understanding the contexts in which they need to be used. In this way, better maintenance and generalisation of learning will occur.
- Use evidence-based methods to promote Emotional Intelligence e.g. modified Cognitive Behavioural approaches.
- Differentiate coaching by: awareness of strengths and challenges consistent with AS cognitive profile; less reliance on person-centred assumptions for coachees who may have missed opportunities for learning social context; more closed questions; using a more directive than facilitative approach; allow more time for building trust and setting up for success; use of the coaching relationship to promote social understanding in real-time; and a structured problem-solving focus.
- Pay attention to the physical environment and its potential impact on sensory issues, for example light, noise and smell.

There is increasing anecdotal evidence, from both education and business, that strategies characterised by clearer structure, uncluttered communication, better explanations and fewer assumptions are effective and popular with students and employees other than those identified as having AS. They also give teachers and managers a sound sense of competence and satisfaction in their abilities to work with different kinds of people.

Case Study

Bob was a software developer who had been with his employer for 6 years. Generally well liked, he was quite extrovert, but at times clumsy in his interaction with others which had led to complaints. More of an issue though was concern over his performance. Bob had been placed on a Performance Improvement Plan (PIP) on a number of occasions, which gave much clearer direction on what he was required to do. With a PIP in place, Bob's performance improved dramatically, but these gains were immediately lost when the PIP was withdrawn. This precipitated anxiety for Bob and frustration for his employer. As the performance management process progressed, a team colleague identified the possibility of unidentified AS. Following consultation with this author, it was confirmed that an understanding based on neurodiversity was indeed appropriate. Bob did not wish to pursue a formal diagnosis and intervention took the form of: awareness training for those working with Bob; ways for his manager to give the structure needed without a PIP; neurodiversity-based workplace mentoring and social narratives for managing meetings and communication. The outcome has been that Bob has received his first positive appraisal in 6 years and his manager is pleased that his skills in managing different people have improved.

In Conclusion

Neurodiversity provides a way of joining understanding from neuroscience, the autistic spectrum and individual differences at a time when 21st century businesses demand more systemising minds. Businesses look to Psychologists for help in maximising the strengths, while managing the challenges, of this high value talent. Employers who develop a reputation for understanding and supporting these individuals will become the employers of choice and may be well placed to gain a competitive edge over other businesses.

Therefore, it is timely for Business Psychologists to develop their knowledge of neurodiversity and make use of the insights in combination with their other skills to get the best outcomes for the individuals concerned and the businesses they work for. Psychologists are also well placed to facilitate research into neurodiversity and its applications in business.

References

American Psychiatric Association (1994). *Diagnostic and Statistical Manual of mental disorders* (4th ed.). Washington, DC: American Psychiatric Association.

Asperger, H. (1944). Die 'Autistischen Psychopathen' im Kindesalter ['Autistic psychopaths' in childhood]. *Archiv für Psychiatrie und Nervenkrankheiten* (in German), *117*, 76-136.

Attwood, T. (2007). *The Complete Guide to Asperger's Syndrome.* London and Philadelphia: JKP.

Baron-Cohen, S., Bolton, P., Wheelwright, S., Scahill, V., Short, L., Mead, G., & Smith, A. (1998). Autism occurs more often in the families of physicists, engineers and mathematicians. *Autism, 2*, 296-301.

Baron-Cohen, S., Wheelwright, S., Skinner, R., Martin, J., & Clubley, E. (2001). The Autistic Spectrum Quotient (AQ): Evidence from Asperger's Syndrome/ High Functioning Autism, Males and Females, Scientists and Mathematicians. *Journal of Autism and Developmental Disorders, 31*(1), 5-17.

Baron-Cohen, S. (2009). Autism: The Empathizing-Systemizing (E-S) Theory. *Annals of the New York Academy of Sciences, 1156*, 68-80.

Billington, J., Baron-Cohen, S., & Wheelwright, S. (2007). Cognitive style predicts entry into physical sciences and humanities: Questionnaire and performance tests of empathy and systemizing. *Learning and Individual Differences, 17*, 260-268.

Brugha, T., McManus, S., Meltzer, H., Smith, J., Scott, F. J., & Purdon, S. (2009). *Autism spectrum disorders in adults living in households throughout England: report from the Adult Psychiatric Morbidity Survey, 2007*. Leeds: NHS Information Centre for Health and Social Care. Retrieved from: http://www.hscic.gov.uk/ catalogue/PUB01131.

Ceci, S. J., & Williams, W. M. (2010). Sex Differences in Math-Intensive fields. *Current Directions in Psychological Science, 19*(5), 275-279.

Fletcher-Watson, S., McConnell, F., Manola, E., & McConachie, H. (2014). Interventions based on the Theory of Mind cognitive model for autism spectrum disorder (ASD). *Cochrane Database of Systematic Reviews*, Issue 3. Art. No.: CD008785. DOI: 10.1002/14651858.CD008785.pub2.

Frith, U., & Happe, F. (1994). Autism: Beyond Theory of Mind. *Cognition, 50*, 115-132.

Gocken, S. Bora, E., Erermis, S., Kesiikci, H., & Aydin, C. (2009). Theory of Mind and verbal working memory deficits in parents of autistic children. *Psychiatry Research, 166*(1), 46-53.

Golan, O., & Baron-Cohen, S. (2006). Systemizing empathy: Teaching adults with Asperger syndrome or high-functioning autism to recognize complex emotions using interactive multimedia. *Development and Psychopathology*, *2*, 591-617.

Gould, J., & Ashton-Smith, J. (2011). Missed diagnosis or misdiagnosis? Girls and women on the autism spectrum. *Good Autism Practice, 12*(1), 34-41.

Gray, C. (2003). *Social Stories 10.0*. Arlington, TX: Future Horizons.

Hill, E. (2004). Evaluating the theory of executive function in Autism. *Developmental Review, 24*(2), 189-233.

Moore, S., Kambitsis, N., & Seward, E. (2013). *Neurodiversity: Getting the Best from Scientists, Technologists, Engineers and Mathematicians.* Available from sallymoore@top-stream.co.uk.

Rajendran, G., & Mitchell, P. (2007). Cognitive theories of autism. *Developmental Review, 27*, 224-260.

Redman, S. (2009). *Don't Write Me Off: Make the system fair for people with autism.* London: The National Autistic Society.

Roelfsama, M. T., Hoekstra, R. A., Allison, C., Wheelwright, S., Brayne, C., Matthews, F. E., & Baron-Cohen, S. (2011). Are autism spectrum conditions more prevalent in an information technology region? A school-based study of three regions in the Netherlands. *Journal of Autism and Developmental Disorders, 42*(5), 734-739.

Ronald, A., Happe, F., & Plomin, R. (2005). The genetic relationship between individual differences in social and nonsocial behaviours characteristic of autism. *Developmental Science, 8*(5), 444-458.

Silberman, S. (2013, April). Neurodiversity rewires conventional thinking about brains. *Wired Magazine*. Retrieved from http://www.wired.com/2013/04/neurodiversity/.

Singer, J. (1999). Why Can't You Be Normal for Once in Your Life? in M. Corker & S. French (Eds.), *Disability Discourse* (pp. 59-67). Buckingham, England: Open University Press.

Test, D. W., Richter, S., Knight, V., & Spooner, F. (2010). A Comprehensive Review and meta-analysis of the Social Stories literature. *Focus on Autism and Other Developmental Disabilities, 26*(1), 49-62.

van Lang, N., Bouma, A., Sytema, S., Kraijer, D., & Minderaa, R. (2006). A comparison of central coherence skills between adolescents and an intellectual disability with and without comorbid autism spectrum disorder. *Research in Developmental Disabilities: A Multidisciplinary Journal, 27*(2), 217-266.

Vermeulen, P. (2012). *Autism as Context Blindness*. Kansas: AAPCP publishing.

Wing, L. (1981). Asperger's Syndrome: a clinical account. *Psychological Medicine, 11*(1), 115–129.

THE RELATIONSHIP BETWEEN ORGANISATIONAL CULTURE AND DERAILERS

Gillian Hyde

Introduction

This article discusses the interplay between extreme personality characteristics of individuals and the culture of the organisation they work in.

Can derailers shape and define the culture?

Research findings from a survey of the incidence of derailers, or 'dark side' characteristics in various industry sectors, illustrate clear differences suggesting a link between organisational culture and the relative prevalence of 'dark side' characteristics. Business Psychologists need to have an awareness of this issue as it could have a bearing on coaching outcomes. For instance, an individual might prove resistant to changing a quality that has been positively reinforced in the prevailing culture. Equally, the organisation's structures and reward systems may actively encourage such behaviours.

Derailers

What are derailers?

Derailers, or 'dark side' personality characteristics, are flawed interpersonal strategies with their roots in successful styles of interaction that, at their extreme, become counterproductive overplayed strengths. They reflect an individual's imprecise and, often, inaccurate beliefs about the way their behaviour impacts on others. They undermine loyalty and commitment and they negatively influence careers. These dysfunctional tendencies emerge during novel, stressful, or heavy workloads, as well as in situations that encourage successful leaders at the pinnacle of their careers to relax previously tightly controlled impulses and where there is no restraint. So the tipping point for these behaviours can be down to both stress and success.

How can we assess derailers?

In 1997, Bob and Joyce Hogan first published the Hogan Development Survey (HDS), a personality questionnaire with an important difference (Hogan & Hogan, 1997; 2009). Rather than focusing on leadership talents, the HDS is based on research into management derailment and the reasons why leaders frequently self-destruct (Bentz, 1985; McCall & Lombardo, 1983). It identifies eleven patterns of dysfunctional interpersonal behaviour. These 'dark side' tendencies erode trust, loyalty and enthusiasm. They are of particular concern in relation to managerial and leadership roles where they can seriously hinder career progression and negatively impact on employee relationships, team effectiveness and organisational productivity.

The HDS eleven styles of counterproductive behaviour fall into three clusters or higher-order factors that characterise the underlying insecurity or anxiety for any particular scale. These three clusters closely resemble the three self-defeating styles that Horney (1950) identified for managing anxiety in relationships. According to Hogan, each cluster is based on a particular interpersonal strategy (Kaiser & Hogan, 2007):

- **Moving Away or Intimidation** – gaining security by unnerving people or discouraging involvement. This cluster relates to the first five scales of the HDS, from *Excitable* to *Leisurely*.
- **Moving Against or Flirtation and Seduction** – winning recognition with self-promotion and charm. This cluster relates to the next four scales of the HDS – *Bold* through to *Imaginative*.
- **Moving Towards or Ingratiation** – obtaining approval by being loyal and indispensable. This cluster comprises the final two HDS scales *Diligent* and *Dependent*.

It is important to remember that while the HDS assesses potential derailers, these extreme characteristics can be strengths up to a certain point. The table below describes the behaviours associated with each scale both at the Effective Functioning level and when it tips over into an Overplayed Strength.

Table 1.

HDS Scales: Behaviours at the Effective Functioning and Overplayed Strength Levels

HDS SCALE	EFFECTIVE FUNCTIONING	OVERPLAYING THE STRENGTH
Excitable	Spirited and interested, but easily disappointed.	Swing from enthusiasm for people, projects and organisations to disappointment or disaffection with them.
Sceptical	Astute, seldom caught off guard. Detect problems before others.	Mistrust others' motives. Take criticism personally and prone to retaliate when they feel they have been wronged.
Cautious	Careful to avoid mistakes. Self-critical and conscious of risk.	Concerned about being embarrassed or criticised. Reluctant to take initiative/ express controversial opinions.
Reserved	Unemotional and detached when analysing situations.	Self-sufficient and indifferent to social feedback or the moods and feelings of others.
Leisurely	Independent, free thinking and socially skilled.	Inflexible, stubbornly sticks to own timetable/ standards. Procrastinates and reluctant to be part of a team.

Bold	Confidence and energy to get things done. Strong first impression. Adversity strengthens their resolve.	Overestimate own talents/ accomplishments; ignore shortcomings; a strong sense of entitlement. Opinionated, self-absorbed, and unwilling to learn from their mistakes.
Mischievous	Charming, spontaneous, fun loving and exciting. They adapt quickly to change, even embrace it, and are fun to be with.	Impulsive, excitement seeking, and manipulative. Take risks and ignore their mistakes. Hard to advise and don't fully evaluate consequences of their decisions.
Colourful	Interesting and entertaining. Active and energetic and can do several things at the same time.	Expect to be seen as interesting and worthwhile. Self-centred, impulsive, overcommitted, quick to take credit and unwilling to listen – especially to negative feedback.
Imaginative	Playful and creative; bring a sense of fun and imagination to projects/ relationships.	Think/act in unusual/odd ways. Impulsive, eccentric and unaware of how socially inappropriate their ideas may be.
Diligent	Meticulous, attentive to detail and follow through on commitments. High standards.	Indiscriminate about when to be attentive to detail. Unable to delegate. Fussy and critical.
Dependent	Co-operative, congenial team-players. Often able to 'smooth over' problems.	Eager to gain approval and to please superiors. Defers to others to maintain amicable relationships. Indecisive.

Why do we assess derailers?

Assessing derailers can have significant implications for the individual, for their colleagues and also for the organisation. An individual's counterproductive behaviours can interfere with the achievement of work and personal goals, because they result in failure to gain the support of their team. Self-awareness of one's dark-side profile gained through coaching or feedback can be the first step to reining in some of these more extreme tendencies and establishing more positive relationships with colleagues at work.

Coaching around derailers can also have significant benefits for colleagues. Organisational climate surveys often show that about 75% of working adults report the most stressful aspect of their job is their immediate boss (Hogan, 2007).

Finally, for the organisation, there can be a significant impact on the bottom line. For example, Fleenor (2003), at the Center for Creative Leadership, found that derailers can interfere with a leader's capacity to shape a coherent and positive organisational culture. Specifically, he found that more skilled leaders are more likely to have a corporate culture that supported long-term success. Such leaders were therefore better at leading a company through periods of transition such as downsizing. This is a strong argument for addressing and developing a leader's weaknesses, and not just focusing on their strengths.

Another study providing support for the impact of derailers at the organisational level was carried out by Harter et al. (2002) at Gallup, using a sample of more than 20,000 managers from over 5,000 organisations across all industry sectors. Their research had three main findings: firstly, a manager's personality affects staff morale; secondly, when morale is up, good business results follow and vice versa; finally, the link between a manager's personality and the business unit performance is mediated by staff morale.

The Link Between Personality and Organsational Culture

Before presenting the results from our study I want to consider previous research linking personality with organisational culture. The research falls into three main groups: links between normal personality and organisational culture; links between dark-side personality characteristics and organisational culture; and examples of extreme personality characteristics actually being of benefit within particular professions.

Normal personality and organisational culture

Research by Schneider (1987) asserted that "the people make the place"; that people are attracted to and recruited into organisations where they think they will fit. Over time, in ways that are outside of individual awareness, organisations maintain the characteristics of the high-status people within them. As a more distinct culture emerges, the organisation tends to attract and retain people of a similar personality, thus reinforcing the culture.

Schneider adopted Holland's (1985) theory that the organisational culture reflects the personalities of the dominant people in it. This was a critical new perspective; Holland defined environments in terms of the personal characteristics of the high-status people in them, rather than by more tangible aspects such as office locations, industry sectors, or organisational charts, which can be more easily measured. Miller et al. (1982) carried out research that supports Holland's notion; they found that the behaviour "in and around organisations is a function of the personalities and capacities of specific individuals". They also reviewed evidence showing that individual differences in CEOs' scores on locus of control (a measure of self-confidence) predicted a number of organisational outcomes, such as the degree of innovation, risk-taking, proactiveness, future orientation, dynamism, and heterogeneity of the environment.

Schneider (1987) described the development of organisational culture in five stages:

i. the personality of the CEO shapes or creates organisational culture;
ii. the longer a CEO is in place, the more impact he or she will have on defining the culture;
iii. people whose personalities fit with an organisation's culture will be attracted to that organisation;
iv. people whose personalities don't fit with an organisation's culture will tend to leave;

v. ultimately, organisations become more homogeneous over time in relation to the personality characteristics of the employees.

This forms the basis of Schneider's Attraction Selection Attrition model and provides strong evidence for the link between individual personality characteristics having an impact on organisational culture.

Derailers and organisational culture

Kets de Vries and Miller (1984), in their publication "The neurotic organization", provide evidence of links between extreme dark-side personality characteristics and the culture of organisations. Specifically, they found a link between the dysfunctional personalities of senior management and dysfunctions of the organisation.

Using a taxonomy created from their analysis of the most widely discussed neurotic styles among individuals, they identified five 'pathological organisational types' and related each of these to the ideas, fantasies and dysfunctional personality styles of their senior executives. These five types are called paranoid, compulsive, histrionic, depressive and schizoid. The Paranoid type has fantasies of persecution and is most closely related to the Sceptical scale on the HDS. The Compulsive type is driven by control and aligns with the Diligent scale of the HDS. The Dramatic type has fantasies related to grandiosity and is a blend of Bold and Colourful at the individual level. The Depressive type has fears of helplessness and combines the Excitable and Dependent scales of the HDS. The Schizoid type is driven by themes of detachment and relates to the Excitable and Reserved scales of the HDS.

A Paranoid organisation will have strict controls of information. Its power base and decision making will be centralised, strategies will tend to be reactive rather than proactive and it will tend to be conservative.

A Compulsive organisation will have standardised rules, policies and procedures. It will be hierarchical and focus on reducing uncertainty rather than taking risks. There will be an emphasis on detail, careful planning and checking, and change may prove difficult.

A Dramatic organisation will be impulsive, venturesome, risk-taking, but there may be too much power vested in the founder of the organisation. Strategy may not be well thought through and actions may be taken for dramatic effect, rather than for a clear business purpose.

A Depressive organisation may have been established for a long time and now lacks purpose and an aim. Jobs are completed simply as a matter of routine with no vision or guidance from a leader. It will be a passive organisation, lacking confidence.

Finally, a Schizoid organisation will suffer from a leadership vacuum. With senior executives fearful of engaging with colleagues, the next level of management may try to compensate, possibly leading to political in-fighting and jostling for power. Having no clear sense of direction, strategy may come from individuals and not be integrated, so the organisation will probably become divisive.

Clearly, each of these organisational types has structural, functional and strategic elements that strongly relate to and, Kets de Vries and Miller (1984) would argue, are probably caused by, the dysfunctional personality style of the senior management.

Can the dark side be a benefit if it fits with the organisational culture?

Two other studies worth mentioning focus on the benefits of certain derailers for some occupations and organisational cultures.

Firstly, Furnham (2010), in his book *The Elephant in the Boardroom* suggested that there were optimal levels of characteristics we see as being potential derailers, and indeed that some of these tendencies are in fact useful in specific sectors. Those who are sceptical and mistrusting may fit in well in R&D departments or security. Imaginative and idiosyncratic people may actually be encouraged to think up ever more unusual ideas in more creative and innovative cultures. Attention seeking, flamboyant types may suit careers in advertising, the media, perhaps fashion or the dramatic arts. A final example would be the fussy, picky, diligent types who fit in organisations that emphasise ritual, plan every detail in advance, are thorough, conforming, hierarchical, and have elaborate rules, policies and procedures.

Secondly, Harms et al. (2011) studied 900 officer cadets at West Point, and found that four scales on the HDS – Cautious, Bold, Colourful and Diligent – were all positively associated with cadets' leadership development. While personality characteristics such as conscientiousness and emotional stability have been found to be predictive of positive performance in many jobs, usually the focus for dark-side characteristics has been on negative performance outcomes. This study turns this around.

"Mae West told us that when she's good, she's good. But when she's bad, she's even better. We chose to investigate so-called subclinical or 'dark side' traits because we really didn't know much about how and to what degree they affected performance or development," said Peter Harms, assistant professor of management at University of Nebraska-Lincoln and the study's lead author. "Was it possible that they might be beneficial in some contexts? For some of them, it turns out that the answer was yes."

So while some characteristics assessed by the HDS were associated with negative outcomes in this study – being too sceptical and cynical for one – others, such as being cautious, compliant and rule following, or confident and making a strong social impact, were associated with positive performance and leadership skills. However, it was the combined effect of these four characteristics – Cautious, Diligent, Bold and Colourful – that had the significant impact on the development of leadership skills; on their own each characteristic had only a small effect. The authors caution that these results might only be applicable in a military context. Clearly the four dark-side characteristics combine to form a pattern of behaviour that is very particular and perhaps quite unusual. This profile suggests an ability to take charge, to be optimistic, to have a can-do attitude, to inspire confidence in others. At the same time the profile indicates checking for facts and relevant knowledge leading to making sound decisions, whilst adhering strictly to the required policies, procedure and protocol. To me, this describes a leader who acts, who is bold and decisive, but who will stick rigidly to the rules and to the facts. These qualities are clearly relevant to a military context where sticking to rules and following protocol is of the utmost importance, but where there is also a need for dynamic and inspiring leadership. This study demonstrates a direct link between the culture of a military organisation and the extreme personality characteristics that are required to succeed as a leader within it.

Findings from PCL's Research

Many have wondered, but few have researched, whether those who choose to work in different sectors have differences in personality; in particular, are there differences between private and public sector workers?

Research focusing on 'dark side' characteristics originally carried out at PCL was replicated and extended in the paper "Do your Dark Side Traits Fit? Dysfunctional Personalities in Different Work Sectors" (Furnham et al., 2014). This looked at possible differences between adults working in different sectors and industries. Previous research looking for sector differences has tended to focus on the relationship either between values and job satisfaction or ability and career success rather than personality. If particular dark-side characteristics are associated with specific industry sectors, this will have implications for patterns of leader and managerial derailment in those sectors, as well as for the future development of these key staff.

Study 1: Public vs. Private sector

In Study 1 we compared the 'dark side' profiles of 2840 public sector employees with 2866 private sector employees taken from our database of online HDS completions.

Public sector:

The overall picture of the public sector sample is that, on average, they are more cautious and socially anxious than their private sector counterparts. Public sector employees are less likely to display the levels of persuasive, influential, self-confident and innovative behaviour found in the private sector. Being more self-conscious and concerned about the embarrassment of failure may inhibit managers in voicing their opinions or making the independent contribution of which they may be capable. They may also tend to become more inward looking and uncommunicative when under pressure and find it hard to ask for help or advice. The data also indicated that senior public sector staff are more inclined to take people as they find them and not to be preoccupied by their ulterior motives.

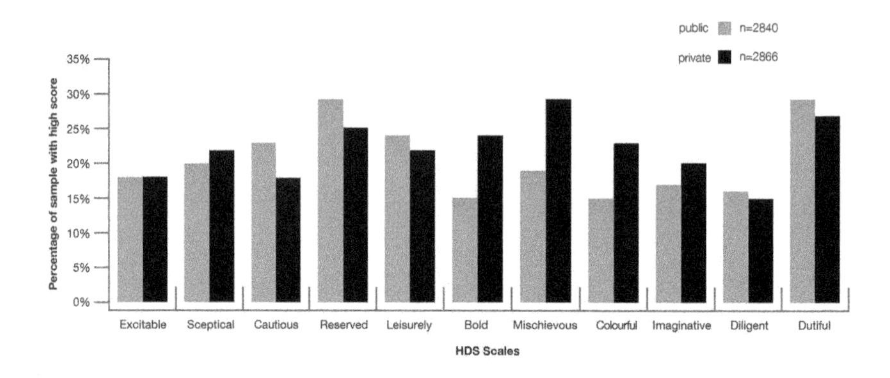

Figure 1: Public sector versus private sector employees

The public sector is less exposed to managerial excesses expressed in terms of arrogance, bullying, dogmatism or flamboyant behaviour and poorly thought-through innovation. The prevalence of excessively mistrustful leadership styles is also lower in this sector. The risk in the public sector is of avoiding or delaying decisions, associated with being worried about 'rocking the boat' or being held responsible for mistakes.

Private sector:

The four scales in the Moving Against cluster of the HDS are significantly higher on average for those working in the private sector. This category possesses a deeply rooted optimism and certainty. Compared to the public sector there are, on average, more private sector individuals with enhanced communication skills that are more likely to involve others in their work. They will be more outgoing and talkative and less socially anxious or remorseful, often using their charm to influence colleagues and clients. They are also more likely to have fresh ideas and suggest innovative solutions to problems than their public sector counterparts. On the other hand, the data suggests a greater tendency to be cynical about others' motives and to suspect others of organisational politicking and machination.

The risk exposure of the private sector concerns the potential for managerial styles to become arrogant and overbearing where senior staff overestimate their own talents and become unwilling to listen to restraint or advice. People who are more outgoing and talkative carry the associated risk of perhaps becoming superficial in their dealings with others, preferring the sound of their own voice to listening. Being highly imaginative exposes this sector to risk associated with vague, impractical, time wasting ideas or changing things just for the sake of change. In excess, greater cynicism can produce a suspicious, paranoid, 'low trust' leadership style.

Study 2: Comparing industry sectors

As well as looking generically at the differences between public and private sector employees we also wanted to analyse specific differences between companies or industries. To highlight some extreme differences we looked at groups from the Emergency Services, the Finance and Insurance sectors and a small number of Entrepreneurs. The Entrepreneurs had started their own businesses, persevered and been successful.

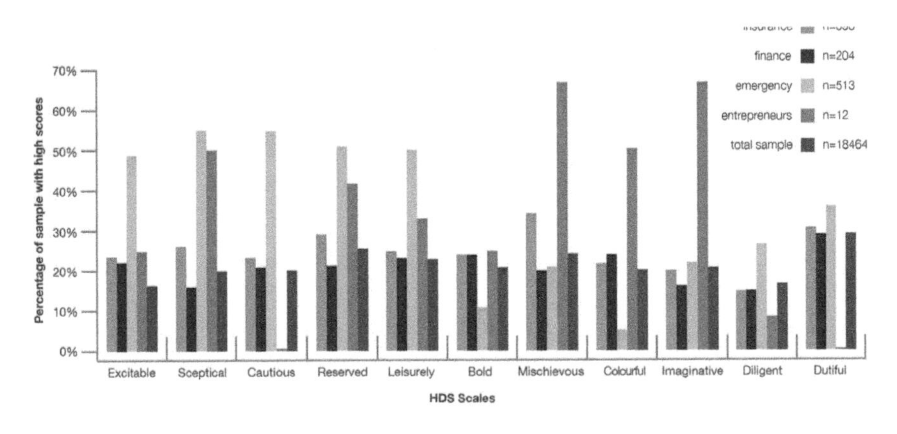

Figure 2: Dark-side profiles in different sectors

Finance & Insurance:

The results from over 500 employees in the Finance and Insurance sectors show that there are no significant extremes of dark-side tendencies and, on the whole, their spread of dark-side profiles is unexceptional. In the main, these two sectors are similar to each other and their exposure to risk reflects that of the total sample/general population.

Around 10% to 20% of this sample score in the high-risk range across all the HDS scales suggesting that the personality characteristics that distinguish individuals in this sector will be diverse.

There are, however, risks associated with such a diversity of dark sides; firstly, the culture may be less distinctive with fewer cues to expected behaviour; secondly, there may be increased potential for misunderstanding and conflict between people in these diverse cultures where dark sides are very varied and therefore each type is infrequently displayed. In contrast, those organisations or industry sectors that have fewer dark side characteristics and hence a more coherent culture are likely to provide greater familiarity with the patterns of behaviour associated with the narrower range of prevailing dark sides.

Entrepreneurs:

The Entrepreneurs are characterised by high scores on *Mischievous* and *Imaginative* and low scores on *Cautious* and *Dependent* (zero incidence).

Our small sample of Entrepreneurs exhibits very different tendencies and much spikier profiles than the more evenly spread profiles of those working in large corporations. They are on average exceptionally high on all the HDS scales that contribute to social performance. They will often be self-confident, charming and interesting. A high percentage demonstrates particularly well developed persuasive skills, innovation, and a lack of self-consciousness, social anxiety or remorse. Equally, the numbers indicate that they are not anxious to make decisions on the basis of pleasing people. In short, they are risk-taking, creative and don't tend to give a damn what anyone else thinks!

Our sample of Entrepreneurs seem to share with the Emergency

Services group a general tendency to mistrust others and to be detached and hard to know. It appears that both may deal with these tendencies by seeking certainty in dealing with others, although reaching very different solutions. While the Entrepreneurs are more likely to overwhelm, the Emergency Services appear to accept a more dutiful and dependent role than other groups.

The highest risks for Entrepreneurs are that only some of their imaginative ideas will ever prove both feasible and effective. Indeed many of these ideas will prove so abstract or nebulous that they cannot be translated into action, while others will just be impractical. Other risks are associated with their social skills. When not taking care of their performance, they may appear shallow or manipulative and undermine trust or commitment as a result.

Emergency Services:

We also wanted to look at another group whose working environment was different from large organisations. Over 500 people in the Emergency Services have completed the HDS over the last 10 years.

For all the Moving Away HDS scales (Excitable, Sceptical, Cautious, Reserved and Leisurely), around 50% of this group achieve high scores. This is also the group with the highest scores in the Dependent and Diligent scales. This group shows an extreme version of the public sector pattern described previously. On the whole they have lower self-esteem and lower self-confidence and tend to withdraw from others at times of stress or when feeling insecure. They are much lower on the HDS *Moving Against* characteristics where an individual's social skills come into play to charm and manipulate people around to their way of thinking, yet they are potentially more eager to please than those working in large corporations. They are also far more likely than any other group in this analysis to be passionate and to show their emotions. This raises issues about the resilience of almost 50% of the group given the nature of their work.

The greatest risks for this group are associated with their tendency to be detached, cautious, mistrustful and volatile, all characteristics that may impede ease of relationships and teamwork. Given the very high level of incidence, these characteristics must often combine within the same individual, amplifying this risk. The other potential risk area relates to the incidence of high ratings for Dependence. This raises doubts about their ability to make independent decisions or take confident independent action, particularly under stress.

Implications for Coaching

This interplay between extreme personality characteristics of leaders, individuals and the culture of an organisation has a number of implications for coaching.

Three things worth considering in the individual coaching context are:

i. **Is an individual coachee's dark side profile a misfit with the prevailing culture of their organisation?** Is there a way this could be used to the individual's advantage? Exploiting the strengths side of their derailer profile might give them an edge and an insight into how they could make a unique contribution to an organisation. At the same time awareness of the potential downside of these characteristics, if taken to their extreme, should be addressed. Given that their particular dark side is a misfit with the culture, the counterproductive behaviours associated with their profile may be particularly detrimental to their working relationships and career advancement.
ii. **Is the coachee's dark-side profile a fit with the organisational culture?** And if it is, what does this mean for coaching? If these extreme tendencies are condoned and possibly positively encouraged in such a culture, the individual may find it hard to acknowledge the potential downside of such behaviours and to break through the protective cocoon. The coachee, with the coach's help, needs to build strategic self-awareness, to know when to play their dark side and when to rein it in.
iii. **Is the coachee's dark side now a misfit with the demands of their job?** Perhaps their profile once fitted with the prevailing culture

of the profession or the organisational goals but, now in a senior position, those tendencies are clearly a disadvantage. An example of this would be an individual whose profession demands a precise, meticulous and diligent approach to their work, but who is now hyper-critical of others and reluctant to delegate even though this is incompatible with their position in the organisational hierarchy.

So workplace coaching needs to take the organisational context into account. The individual needs to come to terms with their own nature AND the nature of the organisation, to see where the potential fit or misfit is, and to understand how to best deploy their particular characteristics to advance the organisational goals. I am not advocating that organisations and the individuals within them should necessarily seek to become more homogenous in relation to their derailers. Instead, I believe that an appreciation of how a derailer culture may be formed by the senior people within an organisation, and an insight into whether one's own profile aligns with this or not, can provide individuals with a route map to effective deployment of their particular skills. The coachee could be encouraged to find a way to maximise the positive impact of their dark side and to play their dark-side profile appropriately by taking into account their fit or misfit with the organisational culture.

Implications for coaching the leadership team:

Clearly, though, the leadership in an organisation may also play its part in determining whether dark-side characteristics are restrained within their positive aspect, or whether they foster a climate that encourages the counterproductive aspect to find expression. The following case study illustrates the link between a leadership team's derailer profile and their perceived strengths and weaknesses.

Case Study

A global firm of consulting engineers commissioned a program to identify talent within the shareholder and director group to help with succession planning at the most senior levels.

The organisation had grown significantly in a short period of time, but was under-performing in some divisions and regions. Early promotion for some key figures had resulted in a partner group with an unusually large age range. Individual performance is stringently reviewed by their director colleagues as it has a direct impact on share price and bonuses. For under-performers, this scrutiny can add another layer of pressure. 15 directors took part in a process that included assessment of potential derailers as well as of cognitive ability, personality, values and a 360-degrees feedback process.

Focusing on the derailer profile of these 15 directors there was one area of congruence for this group that diverged from other leader and engineer groups. This was a tendency to score high on the Mischievous scale of the HDS. This suggests a culture of pushing boundaries and tolerance of a higher degree of risk in their decision-making than most other people. It also indicates, at an individual level, a degree of restlessness and impulsivity, impatience with rules and the minutiae of organisational life, along with a more relaxed attitude to commitments and procedures. Finally, a third facet of this scale relates to an ability to appear charming, especially when they think they may derive a benefit from persuading or manipulating others.

The question is what impact did this shared style of behaviour have on the group and the organisation? Is it positive or negative? Is it context specific? Has it pervaded the culture? Looking at the 360-degree feedback comments from 199 peers and direct reports, the Mischievous style of behaviour clearly links to both the top strength and the top opportunity to improve. The top strength is given as "client focused and good with clients" and the top opportunity to improve is to "challenge poor performance". There seems to be a gap between their client-focused skills and their internal interpersonal skills. They can turn on the charm when needed (i.e. to win and maintain business and perhaps to increase their own status), but sidestep the more mundane, less rewarding everyday workings of the organisation and the people within it. Tackling poor performance and holding people accountable both within the director team and in the rest of the organisation is cited time and time again as an area for improvement.

Perhaps the Mischievous profile of the senior team places focus on the more glamorous side of the business, which this director team are good at. When it comes to internal relationships, policies and procedures, no one is interested in taking on this responsibility. Also, Mischievous people can be skilled at playing situations to their advantage and wriggling out of situations they find uncomfortable. These characteristics could well be at the root of the rallying cry from their peers and reports to "call poor performance to account".

In this case study it seems there is little counterbalancing influence to rein in the more impulsive tendencies of this leadership team, resulting in concerns from colleagues about their lack of rigour and discipline when managing both themselves and others. However, dark-side tendencies can undoubtedly be shaped and actively managed by the goals, the policies, procedures and reward systems created by the senior management. Coaching of leaders could address this issue by assessing the potential derailers of the senior management team, then characterising the organisation by predominant derailer patterns, and describing the potential pitfalls associated with such a culture as illustrated in the work of Kets de Vries and Miller (1984) on the Neurotic Organization.

Conclusion

The data show a trend for people with different dark-side personality characteristics to be attracted to different types of employment. There is a very marked difference, for example, between the derailers found to be most prevalent in public and private sector employment. This is reflected in the culture of these two sectors, both as a cause and as a consequence. Attitudes to risk and security are very different and the recruitment aims of the two sectors need to be different too. The private sector needs to take greater risks and needs people who can thrive on this. The public sector has to be more prudent and conservative to ensure that it manages taxpayers' money responsibly. However, in order to be successful across a wide range of functions, each has to find the most effective balance of personality and talent for them.

The associated risk for the private sector is that leadership and managerial styles may become excessively arrogant, manipulative, risk-taking and unproductively imaginative. The recent downfall of the worldwide banking sector speaks to this high level of arrogance and extreme risk-taking. Conversely, the public sector should be concerned with the possibility of leadership and managerial styles becoming more indecisive, angst-ridden and uncommunicative.

Analysing dark-side profiles in this broad range of industries demonstrates that there are specific character traits on display within different types of organisations. There are statistically significant differences in the character traits of public and private sector employees and between other industry sectors. The 'attraction-selection-attrition hypothesis' (Schneider, 1987; 1995) describes a systemic link between organisational culture and the predominant characteristics of its population and would predict the existence of the kinds of differences we have observed.

Derailers may have cultural biases so, for example, being withdrawn, hard to reach and quietly intimidating is more acceptable in a public sector culture simply because it is more usual. This embedding of derailer types in different organisational cultures obviously has implications for coaching. Coaching around derailers needs to take into account the organisational culture that the individual is working in and the extent to which it is 'accepted' behaviour or is a particularly unusual characteristic for that type of organisation.

References

Bentz, V. J. (1985, August). *A view from the top: A thirty-year perspective on research devoted to discovery, description, and prediction of executive behavior.* Paper presented at the 93rd Annual Convention of the American Psychological Association, Los Angeles.

Fleenor, J. (2003, April). *Creative Leadership, Tough Times: Soft Skills Make the Difference.* Center for Creative Leadership, 36-37. Retrieved from http://www.ccl.org/leadership/pdf/research/cclCreative.pdf

Furnham, A. (2010). *The elephant in the boardroom: The causes of leadership derailment*. Basingstoke: Palgrave Macmillan.

Furnham, A., Hyde, G., & Trickey, G. (2014). Do your dark side traits fit? Dysfunctional personalities in different work sectors. *Applied Psychology, 63*(4), 589-606.

Harms, P. D., Spain, S. M., & Hannah, S. T. (2011). Leader development and the dark side of personality. *The Leadership Quarterly*, *22*(3), 495-509.

Harter, J. K., Schmidt, F. L., & Hayes, T. L. (2002) *Well-being in the workplace and its relationship to business outcomes*: A review of the Gallup Studies. In C. L. Keyes & J. Haidt (Eds.), *Flourishing: The Positive Person and the Good Life* (pp. 205-244). Washington, D.C.: American Psychological Association.

Hogan, R. (2007). *Personality and the fate of organizations*. Mahwah, NJ: Lawrence Erlbaum.

Hogan, R., & Hogan, J. (1997, 2009). *Hogan Development Survey Manual*. Tulsa, OK: Hogan Press.

Holland, J. (1985). *Making vocational choices: A theory of vocational personalities and work environments*. Englewood Cliffs, NJ: Prentice Hall.

Horney, K. (1950). *Neurosis and human growth*. New York, NY: Norton.

Kaiser, R. B., & Hogan, R. (2007). The dark side of discretion: Leader personality and organizational decline. In R. Hooijberg, J. Hunt, J. Antonakis, K. Boal, & N. Lane (Eds.), *Being there even when you are not: Leading through strategy, systems and structures*. (Vol. 4, pp. 177-197). London: Elsevier Science.

Kets de Vries, M., & Miller, D. (1984) *The Neurotic Organization*. San Francisco, CA: Jossey-Bass.

McCall, M. W. Jr., & Lombardo, M. M. (1983). *Off the track: Why and how successful executives get derailed.* Greenboro, NC: Center for Creative Leadership.

Miller, D., Kets de Vries, M., & Toulouse, J. (1982). Top Executive Locus of Control and its Relationship to Strategy-making, Structure and Environment. *Academy of Management Journal*, *25*, 237-253.

Schneider, B. (1987). The people make the place. *Personnel Psychology*, *40*, 437-453.

Schneider, B., Goldstein, H. W., & Smith, D. B. (1995). The ASA framework: An update. *Personnel Psychology, 40*, 747-773.

ORGANISATIONAL CONFLICT AND CONFLICT RESOLUTION – A CRITICAL REVIEW

Stephen Benton & Anna Sommers

Introduction

While conflict has long been viewed as an intrinsic part of organisational life (Falconer & Bagshaw, 2004; Kolb, 2008) it is arguably the case that the acceleration toward global free market practices has added behavioural pressures that can foster workplace conflict, and that this has been escalating with the associated changing Global Business Signature (GBS). For example, only 10 of the current biggest 100 companies remain from 1960, and over a quarter of the companies are new since the last ranking in 2007 (Engel & Weigel, 2012). GBS is a term used here to denote the global shift in competitiveness experienced by economies as they have moved, largely since the 1960s, towards free-market and deregulated business practices. In short, sustained competitiveness requires an operational capacity to maintain fitness for stability as well as fitness for maximising opportunities. This changing business context has intensified the volatility in the working environment. The term 'VUCA' reflects increasingly **v**olatile, **u**ncertain, **c**omplex and **a**mbiguous (Lawrence, 2013) working environments, where workplace conflict has consequently become even more ingrained into organisational life (De Dreu & Gelfand, 2008).

Luttwak's (1999) view is that huge and dynamic market forces have been released by deregulation and the adoption of free market 'fundamentalism'. This provides an overarching framework within which to identify the economic drivers behind VUCA, socio-political and organisational environments. Luttwak thinks that this form of deregulated capitalism, termed Turbo-Capitalism, has undermined a stabilising balance between economic policies and social values. He argues that Post World War II mixed economies acted as a moderating influence, reflecting their host societies' national values and political priorities. However, this influence has now largely been stripped. The result is increased direct pressure on organisational performance as demanded by raw global, free-market parameters rather than national indices. For example, the past decades have seen the reduction and elimination of subsidies to staple food and fuel, at the same time as the International Monetary Fund continues to state that "subsidy *reform* can lead to a more efficient allocation of resources, which will help spur higher economic growth over the longer term." (IMF, 2013).

Overall, the convergence of views points to the strong likelihood that pressure on individual performance and organisations' competitiveness will continue to increase. This will intensify as economic and technological influences interact to both create and sate market opportunities within the context of politically endorsed 'free-market' consumerism. In this highly competitive environment, organisations have acknowledged it is not only the type, depth and quality of people's skills that are valued, but also an ability to work effectively and creatively through cycles of intense change (Luthans et al., 2006). Accordingly, organisations have implemented policies and procedures designed to make best use of the talent and potential for creativity of their increasingly dynamic and diverse workforces (Liddell, 2004b).

All of which needs to occur within 'real-time' organisational environments that Maravalas (2005) argues have become more "terrifying and less predictable". As organisations restructure, refocus and rethink they have tended towards the creation of flatter hierarchies and employed a highly diverse, empowered workforce (De Dreu & Gelfand, 2008). Today's workforce is better educated, more sophisticated and more demanding than a decade ago (Law Reform Commission, 2010). Meanwhile, decline in manufacturing means that organisational growth is associated with the expansion of services. In 2011, 9% of the workforce in England and Wales worked in manufacturing (declining from 38% in 1961) and 81% worked in services (an increase from 45% in 1961). At the same time, dramatic technological innovations and organisational restructurings are replacing previously indispensable human skills, prompting fundamental changes in work practice and the composition of work-roles across all sectors. For example, Witschge & Nygren in their 2009 review, highlight the impact of new media technologies on both functional competences and on the very nature of 'reportage'. The overarching impact on work-roles is expressed by the speed in which organisations now access, share and exploit information.

Established role-based governance protocols and work-role boundaries are undermined in new job and performance expectations. In these flatter organisations, with intensive networking and pragmatic democracy, conflict is no longer suppressed by a strict hierarchy. Employees, encouraged to challenge the process and 'add value' to their roles, increasingly refuse to simply accept decisions that affect them (Fisher et al., 1991). These factors converge to drastically increase the potential for workplace conflict (De Dreu & Gelfand, 2008). Arguably as a consequence, recent years have witnessed a steady increase in the cost of conflict, with an estimated annual loss of 370 million working days in the UK (Saundry, 2014). Moreover, evidence from the 2012 Skills and Employment Survey (Gaille et al., 2013) suggests that failed resolution and costly disciplinary and conflict practices have produced increasingly toxic work relations characterised by fear of dismissal and discrimination. An estimate of the overall cost of such environments, the combined cost of workplace bullying, absenteeism and staff turnover, was £13.75 billion for 2007 (Giga et al., 2008).

Definition of Workplace Conflict

Conflict has broadly been defined as "a process that begins when an individual or group perceives differences and opposition between itself and another individual or group about interests and resources, beliefs, values, or practices that matter to them" (cited in De Dreu & Gelfand, 2008, p. 6). Conflict in the workplace has also been defined as "an interactive process manifested in incompatibility, disagreement, or dissonance within or between social entities (i.e. individual, group, organisation, etc.)" (Rahim, 2002, p. 207). It has been acknowledged that organisational conflict is a common occurrence "because people always have divergent views on various issues, interests, ideologies, goals, and aspirations" (Deutsch, 1990 as cited in Salami, 2009, p. 44).

There are two, well reviewed and fundamental, dimensions of conflict: **relationship conflict** (also labelled *affective* or *emotional conflict*) and **task conflict (**also called *substantive* or *cognitive conflict*)**.** The first refers to disagreements caused by emotional or interpersonal issues, whereas the second one describes disagreements relating to task issues (Rahim, 2002).

Even though conflict is an acknowledged intrinsic component within organisational life (Kolb, 2008), its perceived role has changed drastically over the past decade (Robbins & Judge, 2012). The *traditional* view represents conflict as something entirely negative that needs to be avoided and that its occurrence indicated malfunctioning behaviour. Later research, however, acknowledged that conflict not only has positive effects, but is a necessary part of healthy organisations (Robbins & Judge, 2012) that can lead to change, creativity, innovation and high performance (Falconer & Bagshaw, 2004). This *interactionist* perspective of conflict states that a minimal level of conflict is essential to groups being self-critical, viable and creative (Robbins & Judge, 2012). This view stresses the importance of distinguishing between *functional* conflict, which supports group goals, and *dysfunctional* conflict, which hinders group performance. These perspectives tend to polarise ways of viewing conflict as either entirely positive or completely negative.

Recent research into organisational conflict has examined the potential for building a third approach. This is a *resolution focused* view of conflict. It acknowledges the need to manage the stress, reduced respect and mistrust that can result from encouraging conflict. It focusses on *constructive* conflict resolution that stimulates behaviours which promote robust exchanges of views, critical and focused use of information, and that generate innovative solutions. Arguably, increased resolution skills translate into robust and high quality information exchange rather than degenerating into personal attacks. It's argued that positive conflict resolution behaviours, such as building shared commitment, are worth the risk (Falconer & Bagshaw, 2004; Tjosvold, 2008). Both camps acknowledge that positive outcomes are linked with the quality of conflict-handling behaviours and processes.

Causes of Organisational Conflict

Organisational conflict can have many different causes, which can be classified into six different categories, as outlined in Figure 1 and discussed in more detail below.

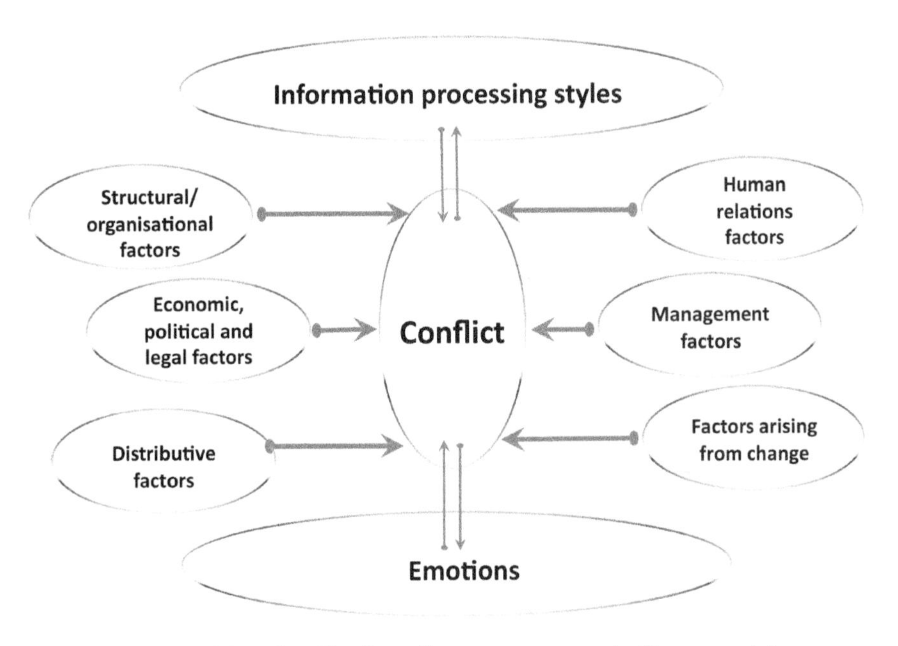

Figure 1: The Conflict Paradigm – causes and effects model
Adapted from Liddell, 2004a, p. 17.

External (Economic, Political, Legal and Technological) Factors

Organisations are open systems embedded in their global and local community, and institutional and cultural contexts. These elements are potential sources of conflict in organisations (De Dreu & Gelfand, 2008), because of the rapid and high impact of change. Fluctuating employment levels, inflation rates and scarcity or inequality of access to resources are factors that strongly affect organisations' ability to conduct business successfully (Liddell, 2004a). Those responsible for making far reaching strategic decisions and planned programmes of change require tactical agility to manage unexpected consequences and unforeseen events (Balogun & Johnson, 2005). Insecurity, generated by unpredictable events and behaviours, is a key cause of conflict and especially destructive conflict (Falconer & Bagshaw, 2004). This appears to be an increasingly significant feature in organisations with tight budgets, increased workloads and job insecurities (Podro, 2010). Research by the CIPD (2011) showed that the average number of grievance cases per organisation surveyed in the UK had risen since the recession from a mean of 8 per organisation in 2007 to 22.3 in 2011, (Higginbottom, 2011, p.1). The number of employment tribunal cases increased by 13% from 2009 to 2010.

Sources of Conflict: Internal Factors

Conflict can represent a disparity between people's needs, objectives, expectations and perceptions (Falconer & Bagshaw, 2004). Conflicts that are not recognised and managed effectively early can become ingrained and destructive, as negative behaviours and attitudes accumulate, distorting or displacing positive perceptions and expectations.

Change can be threatening and challenging to employees especially when implemented too quickly. It can induce a sense of bewilderment and cynicism that makes them uncertain about their own identity and career (Stensaker & Meyer, 2012). The other four types of internal sources are summarised below.

Distributive Factors

Distributive conflict, or conflict of interests, results from resources within organisations being scarce and finite (De Dreu & Gelfand, 2008). Conflict can occur when resources or rewards are perceived to be distributed unequally across the workforce (Liddell, 2004a) and/or when the demand for resources exceeds the resources available (Pondy, 1967) resulting in competition, for instance for staff time or investment in development. Resource-based conflicts can exist between individuals within the same unit or between different departments and can generate frustration and behaviours such as failure to acknowledge others' input, harassing, complaining, ignoring directives, and slow working. At a group level, resource conflicts may manifest as failure to share a vision, polarisation of views, social loafing and group-think. At the organisational level conflict can escalate into partner schisms such as union-management disputes.

Structural/Organisational Factors

Structural features can create tensions between departments and individuals. For example, the inherent ambiguity in job roles and responsibilities can create tensions between marketing and sales or design and production, which undermine interdepartmental as well as individuals' and teams' capacity to establish workable common ground. Moreover, rigid and inflexible structures that are slow to respond to changes and emerging role demands can create or perpetuate conflict amongst the workforce (Liddell, 2004a). Any professional intervention would benefit from a diagnosis of the perceptions held by staff of how well they believe their manager/organisation has understood their functional needs in adapting to new practices.

Human Relation Factors

The way an individual deals with conflict reflects their skill-set, personal preference for managing anxiety-provoking behaviours and perceptions of the relative value and need for a particular outcome. The term 'personality' is frequently used to explain or cover-up the causes of conflict in the workplace. Clashes between individuals may result from differences in expressed emotionality and thinking styles, responses to perceived threats or ways of processing information (e.g. the type of questions asked; divergent or convergent) under stress. For example, Extraversion has a positive relationship with a 'dominating' style (low concern for others), while Agreeableness and Neuroticism have negative relationships with dominating and a positive relationship with 'integrating' style (high concern for others). One of the earliest theoretical contributions, which still has worldwide influence in organisational life, comes from C.G. Jung and his work *Psychological Types* (1921; 1971). Jung's classification of people into *extraverted* and *introverted* types with combinations of four psychological functions, namely *sensation*, *intuition, thinking* and *feeling* is familiar to many in organisations through applications such as the Myers Briggs Type Indicator (MBTI) and the Insights Discovery Profile. Such tools have been used to guide the development of robust interpersonal conflict behaviour by locating behavioural change within the individual's 'authentic' preferences as identified by their psychological type profile.

It has been reported that different 'types' behave differently in conflict situations with, for example, introverted people tending to avoid conflict more than extraverts and "feelers" being more cooperative and less assertive than "thinkers" (Kilmann & Thomas, 1975). The Thomas-Kilmann Instrument (TKI) provides an accessible way to identify the style of behaviour used by someone during conflict. According to this approach, a person's chosen conflict style reflects how they balance two competing demands of Assertiveness (Task Focused) and Cooperativeness (Relationship Focused). In principle any style is available to an individual, although it is suggested that different types of personality are more likely to be predisposed to a particular style. Interaction of the two fundamental axes produces five styles: Competing (or forcing), Accommodating, Avoiding, Collaborating and Compromising (Thomas and Kilmann, 1974). An illustration of Thomas and Kilmann's model is shown below.

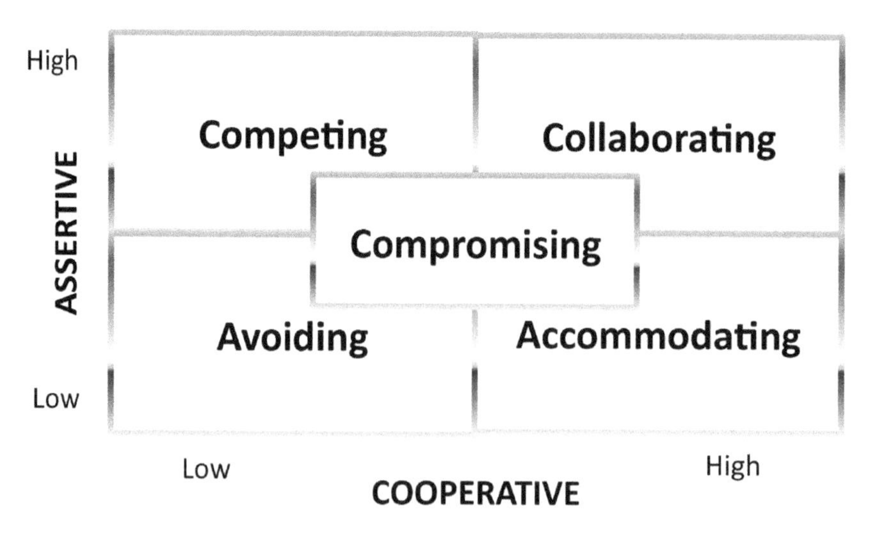

Figure 2: A Summary of the Thomas and Kilmann Conflict Modes

These conflict styles, often described as 'modes' or a 'habitual way of handling conflict' are relatively stable across different conflict situations. Failed conflict resolution can be attributed to the mis-reading of 'type and/or style' or a breakdown of communication, the misunderstanding of the dynamics at play between individuals leading to mistrust and defensiveness. Incomprehension of others' behaviour can trigger anxiety which impels individuals towards defensive and ingrained behaviours associated with 'perceived threat'. Models, such as those cited above, can help people to notice those behaviours which prompt misunderstandings by identifying the areas of mis-match between the style(s) they are facing. Having identified the style they can adapt and align their behaviour in accordance with their needs and preferences rather than respond with habitual emotionality. For example, having identified a person as Analytical, you may recognise their tendency (if not need) to focus on facts and see their communication style and pace of interaction as consistent with a preference for reflection on facts.

Many approaches to helping people to respond to conflict positively rest on the view that during conflict most people will default to one conflict-handling style, and that this is likely to be from habit rather than an optimal choice. Effective negotiation therefore depends on an individual's ability to identify the styles of their counterparts and to judge the relative value assigned by the counterpart to the relationship and substantive issues.

While personality is a major contributory construct when diagnosing conflict behaviour, individuals bring other influences to the conflict context. The generic model below, Figure 3, highlights factors that shape an individual's behaviour. Their perceptions of past experiences (e.g. Beliefs), interactions with work-colleagues (e.g. Roles) and view of the future (e.g. Expectations) provide a framework for scanning the context within which a conflict occurs.

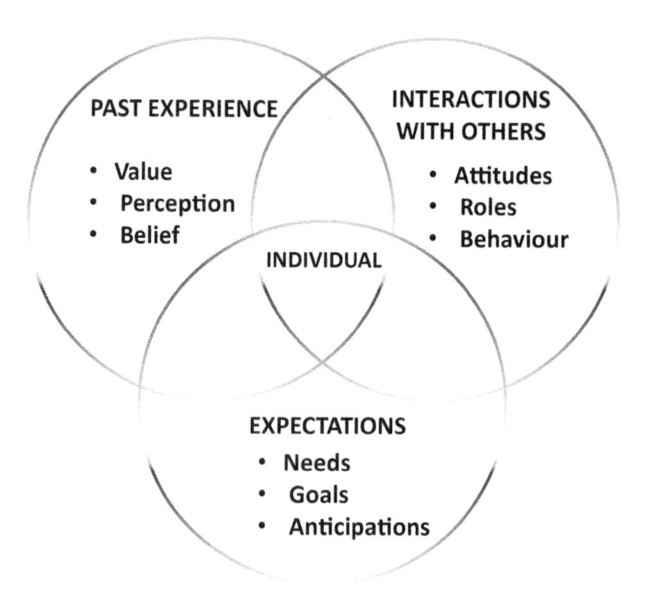

Figure 3: Individual Conflict-Influencing Factors

Management Factors

Perceived intolerant or over-tolerant behaviour (unfairness) can undermine shared values within a working environment and trigger resentment. For example, an overly authoritarian leadership style can lead to frustration, especially since many workers find it difficult to address these issues with their bosses (ACAS, 2009). Ongoing, truthful communication from managers to employees is vital to demonstrate the viability of an organisation's declared set of values. For example, organisations may develop appropriate policy guidelines on equal opportunity, health and safety and performance rewards, yet if related decisions, especially unpopular ones, are not communicated effectively staff resentment can result in negative stereotyping of management.

Unwanted Consequences of Conflict

The consequences of dysfunctional conflict can be considered in terms of their impact on people's working lives, within the individual, group and organisational contexts.

Psychological Impact of Conflict: The Individual

Destructive conflict yields negative results for everybody affected and is generally driven by deep emotional reactions to threatening situations (Falconer & Bagshaw, 2004). Like our primeval ancestors, we often respond to threats with "*emotional arousal*", i.e. either "fight" (fighting the other party so that they freeze or flee), "flight" (withdrawing or fleeing from the conflict), "freeze" (doing nothing and waiting to see what happens) or "fall" (submitting and yielding to the other person) (Liddell, 2004a, p. 16). Emotional arousal not only has deep psychological effects, such as fear, anger, shock and aggression, but also physical ones, like sweating, adrenaline rushes or nausea (Falconer & Bagshaw, 2004). Dysfunctional conflict can trigger habitual defensive behaviour which narrows cognitive processing and strengthens emotional responses, making an individual seem irrational, impulsive and uncontrolled. Disputants who focus on a narrow range of information and transactions, are predisposed to escalate into hostility.

In these situations, the emotional consequence of a disagreement can take over and replace the original cause or substantive issue. Individuals may find themselves locked in an emotional situation without really understanding how it happened. It can block communication and negotiation skills, empathy and objectivity (Liddell, 2004b). As the parties' positions harden, conflict can continue to escalate leading to blame and the adoption of dogmatic positions (Higginbottom, 2011). It shifts people's focus away from finding a solution to 'beating' the other party. This leads to withholding information and creates an environment of blame and negativity, where egos are more important than issues (Falconer & Bagshaw, 2004). It often distorts perception, and thus leads to biases, such as stereotyping, zero-sum thinking (my gain will be from your loss) or egocentric judgement, i.e. distorting the estimate of others' interests and priorities by an overreliance on their own interests and priorities (Thompson et al., 2006).

Defensive behaviour that prevents organisational members from spotting and correcting errors hinders them from engaging in problem-solving. These bouts of conflict often result in greater absenteeism, lower productivity, tardiness, retaliation and aggressive behaviour (Maravalas,

2005). This does not only affect employees at their workplaces as it can easily spill over into their private lives, leading to self-directed harm, e.g. suicide or drug abuse, or outer-directed reactions such as domestic violence or threatening behaviour (Government of Newfoundland and Labrador, 2013, p. 4). Negative behaviours that spill over into individuals' home lives can then influence behaviour and performance back in the organisation. An unresolved argument may produce displaced anger on return to the office. Business Psychologists may need to explore the overall 'well-being' of individuals to identify sources of stress and conflict separate from their organisational life.

The Group

At the interpersonal, *group level*, dysfunctional conflict can decrease performance by damaging the trust required to communicate effectively or by impeding coordination (De Dreu & Gelfand, 2008). Unresolved conflict in a group can undermine the core functional and process attributes associated with effective teamwork. The functional aims and needs of people working together revolve around sharing information, ideas, emotional and cognitive support and a focus on mutual objectives (Tjosvold, 2008). Failure of communication may be presented to the Business Psychologist called in to help the team's performance, when in reality underlying unresolved conflicts can be shaping the team's conduct. Clues to this underlying dynamic may be failing collaboration, poor supportive and participative behaviour and limited exploration of others' views. Other indicators include distortion of information, negative speculation, malicious conversations, poor critical analyses and ineffective problem-solving. In broad summary, unresolved conflict can create a climate of fear, cynicism and mistrust amongst the workforce, eliminating commitment, spontaneity, enthusiasm and creativity (Firth-Cozens, 2001).

Organisational Level

The impact of unresolved conflict cascades through the organisation as distortions of individual performance undermine team and group transactions. In a survey jointly conducted by CPP Inc. and OPP Ltd. (2008) of 5,000 full time employees spanning the Americas and Europe it was found that 33% of employees felt that managers needed be more effective when dealing with 'toxic' individuals, 40% wanted the manager to take an earlier lead in mediation at the onset of a conflict and 40% wanted managers to role-model appropriate conflict resolution behaviours. It is perhaps not surprising that as the relationships and helping mechanisms that support individuals (Weisbord, 1976) are compromised that costly problems emerge and accumulate in other parts of the organisation.

The costs easiest to quantify are the financial and legal costs, e.g. litigation or mediation, including time spent on paperwork, going to court and staff replacement (McCrindle, 2004). The costs of trying to solve conflict between two employees can involve the salaries of four – those in conflict, their manager(s) and perhaps an HR manager. What are sometimes described as 'hidden costs' also escalate as conflict leads to increased stress, absenteeism and staff turnover, all extremely expensive for organisations.

In 2002, measures of sickness absence rates showed an estimated cost to British industry of £11.6 billion, with recent figures pointing to an increase rising to £24 billion (CIPD, 2011). Studies have shown that employees who believe they are being bullied take, on average, seven days per year more sick leave than others as well as the withdrawal of engagement and breach of trust which results in lower innovation and creativity (Podro, 2010).

Conflict Resolution

There are various forms of resolving workplace conflict. Formal processes, such as employment tribunal litigation, provide forums for determining disputes between employers and employees (Gilhooley, 2009). These are usually either a grievance from an employee or a disciplinary action taken by the employer against an employee (Saundry & Wibberley, 2012) and disputes are about, e.g. unfair dismissal, redundancy payments or discrimination (Ministry of Justice, 2013). As employment tribunals cost up to £20,000 (CIPD, 2011), organisations are increasingly turning away from judicial towards informal, voluntary forms of conflict resolution which tend to be cheaper, faster and more flexible (Brown, 2004). Effective informal resolution processes require professionals with expertise in listening, understanding of interpersonal dynamics and emotionally charged behaviour as well as a capacity to build rapport between the parties, all aspects of the Business Psychologist's portfolio.

Distributive Bargaining

This approach is characterised by extremes with tactics designed to support the originally stated position, to concede as little as possible before fixing on a deal. Each party is likely to adopt an inflated or extreme initial position, and to expect that it will be unacceptable to the other and likely lead to rejection. Response tactics would include obfuscation, guile, bluffing, brinkmanship and outright misleading comments about objectives. Distributive negotiators (often described as confrontational) play out negotiation as a process of distributing a fixed amount of value. Such approaches involve the presupposition that negotiations are *zero-sum* transactions such that one person's gain is another person's loss. Negotiators focusing on a *fixed* amount of some good or benefit will measure success in terms of how much the other side had to concede.

Characteristic aspects of distributive bargaining (adapted from Saner, 2012):

i. Coercion: using force, or the threat of force to wrestle concessions from an opponent.
ii. Opening strong: starting out with a position that is higher than what you realistically estimate you can achieve.
iii. Salami tactics: prolonging a negotiation to a painstakingly slow pace, only giving a very small concession to the other side when it can no longer be avoided in order to placate the other side for a little while longer.

Relationship focused Negotiation

Negotiation is probably the most important set of skills associated with conflicts (Falconer & Bagshaw, 2004) and is a form of dispute resolution that does not involve a third party, but only the opponents concerned. It aims to find common ground where there are different perspectives and mutual interests. A key prerequisite for negotiation is that the "allocation of gains among participants to an agreement is subject to their own choice rather than predetermined by their circumstances" (as cited in Spears & Parker, 2009, p. 56).

Principled Negotiation

One of the most prominent negotiation methods is termed *'principled negotiation'*. Fisher et al. (1991) stress the positive potential of conflict and argue that the aim is not to eliminate conflict, but to deal with it in a productive, problem-solving manner.

In practice this approach starts from the perspective that positional bargaining promotes stubborn resistance, raises the emotional stakes and tends to override or ignore underlying interests. Consequently, we need a 'way of seeing' what is going on that is not distorted by the emotional noise. This approach consists of four basic elements each elaborated below:

i. *Focus on interests, not positions*, i.e. finding out what the underlying interests of the conflicting parties are instead of over-focussing on their stated positions.
ii. *Separate the people from the problem*, i.e. attacking the problem, not each other. Avoiding common habitual emotional and psychological traps.
iii. *Invent options for mutual gain*, i.e. adopt multiple perspectives in developing multiple options to work with.
iv. *Insist on using objective criteria*, such as market value or benchmarked practice instead of a 'strength of view' to judge outcomes.

These strategies are underpinned by a BATNA – the individuals' Best Alternative to a Negotiated Agreement. This seeks to prevent individuals making a knee-jerk agreement after seeing their preferred option fail. There are steps that can be taken to develop your BATNA:

i. If you cannot reach an agreement, begin to explore the alternatives and consequences of failure.
ii. Convert the most promising of the alternatives into concrete options (build around real examples).
iii. The single best option becomes your BATNA.
iv. Check your BATNA against any of the proposals generated during negotiations.

v. If there is an offer better than your BATNA, work to improve it, while considering accepting it.
vi. Any offer worse than your BATNA is a candidate for rejection.
vii. If an attempt at full resolution fails, deploy your BATNA or reject.

Fisher and Ury (1981) argued that if negotiators can find ways to follow these basic principles the rewards for the resolution process are greater creativity, mutual understanding and buy-in for outcomes. These benefits result from better quality of information being shared and the manner in which it is explored and analysed, and are supported by questioning and rapport. The fundamental premise is that underlying concerns and interests will remain hidden and likely subvert communications if these methods, which seek to avoid habitual reactions to position taking, are not adopted. Unlike position statements, which are commonly rehearsed prior to the meeting and frequently repeated, interests may remain ill-defined and obscure.

Focus on interests, not positions

Principled negotiation does not focus on the parties' positions, but on their interests. It acknowledges the interest of the opponents in both the outcome and the relationship. It is neither *hard,* i.e. competing against the other party in order to 'win', nor *soft*, i.e. giving in to the other party in order to preserve the relationship, but aims at reaching mutually satisfying agreements, thus creating wiser outcomes. According to Fisher and Ury (1981), the first practical step in principled negotiations is to identify the *interests which may underlie stated positions* as otherwise an early focus on stated positions can frame positions as being diametrically opposed. Interests may be unspoken or even hidden behind a party's stated demand or position and so harder to identify than positions.

Example of Positional Bias:

Two departments, Technical Support and Marketing, both need an extra member of staff. There is budget for one only. Both departments refuse to explore options and instead both resort to part-time posts which do not offer the depth of skills they need. An exploration of interests may have found that Marketing needed someone with technical knowledge of an online marketing application and the Technical support department needed someone to drive the development of an online strategy.

Separate the people from the problem

Another aspect of this approach requires the negotiator to focus on the *People* dimension during a dispute. Parties in a dispute often forget that others are just as prone as they themselves to unwanted emotions (e.g. anger, fear), potential for misunderstandings and mistaken assumptions and stereotype judgements of trust. Hence a guiding rule for the 'principled' negotiator is to 'separate the people from the problem'. This refers to keeping the relationship issues (e.g. perceptions, personalities, emotions, communication style and quality) from contaminating the substantive issues. If successful, this focus supports people in working on the merits of the issues without the need to shift focus in order to deal with 'negative emotions' and the shifting merits of the relationship. The better the relationship, the more likely that information and views will be shared, listened to and questioned. In practice Fisher and Ury recommend the use of tactics that help negotiators to get to know the other party. For example, meeting informally, arriving early to talk or making time to talk after formal negotiations end.

Invent options for mutual gain

After parties start to build relationships and exchange information, from which a clearer understanding of interests can emerge, they should move on to generating *options*. In negotiations, "options are possible solutions to a problem shared by two or more parties" (Alfredson & Cungu, 2008). In principled (integrative) negotiating, options represent feasible ways of meeting as many of all parties' interests as is practical. When two people (or organisations) get locked into pursuing narrow solutions or are governed by habitual patterns of thinking in response to conflict, they become blinded to the possibilities that a little creative thinking might uncover. Various techniques can facilitate the generation of options and one of the most popular is brainstorming. This technique often has strong practical value as it creates a space for lowering the 'quality control' dimension initially to prompt and support the participation and different perspectives. For example, the technique can involve asking parties to list ideas that come to mind in a positive and non-judgemental environment without criticism. All ideas would be noted and accepted at this stage, helping to prompt spontaneity. This frequently helps to re-set the climate within which the parties had been 'blocked' and encourages 'out of the box' thinking about a problem while also fostering shared problem solving.

Insist on using objective criteria

Even after a settlement has been reached a position-based process can leave significant bitterness, resentment and distrust between the parties. When distrust is ingrained between the parties, where will the criteria for evaluating the outcomes come from? Clearly, the selected criteria should be demonstrably independent from either parties' influence. One method is to appeal to *fair standards* relevant to the dispute. Examples would include precedents, scientific judgment, professional standards, efficiency, costs, moral standards, equality and tradition. Such standards allow decisions taken and agreements made to be measured against relevant 'objective' criteria. By framing negotiations around such objective criteria it becomes possible to inhibit the impact of distrust. Negotiators free themselves and the other side from digging into a position stubbornly in order not to appear (or feel) weak or disingenuous.

In the absence of standards the burden of fairness may fall on the fairness of procedure. "The process of shared decision-making increases the perceived fairness of the process, improves satisfaction with outcomes, promotes positive relations between parties, enhances the legitimacy with which agreements are viewed and helps to create a willingness to abide by the commitments made" (Alfredson & Cungu, 2008, p.23). Whether fair standards or fair procedures, the essential need, according to the theory of principled negotiation, is to frame the basis for logical decision making such that both parties perceive the negotiated solution as legitimate. In this way, disputants may spend less time and energy attacking one another's positions, and instead focus their energies on analysis and problem solving.

For the principled approach to deliver these added value outcomes there needs to be a building of commitment, within the process, to high quality communication. Without this commitment and capacity to share information, countering common communicational errors, it would be impossible to uncover underlying interests or engage in effective problem solving. A key error of most negotiators is a tendency to focus predominantly on their own responses, rehearsing their comments and failing to listen to what the other side is actually saying. Effective listening should yield essential information for the listener, and also demonstrate that you are attentive to the other side's thoughts and respectful of their concerns. One practical technique for improving communication skills is *active listening*. In broad terms good listening is directed by four guiding principles:

i. Listen actively to both verbal and non-verbal cues.
ii. Get beneath the surface – ask questions to learn.
iii. Describe your 'Data'.
iv. Inquire, don't try to persuade. (Mercy Corps, 2006)

This technique emphasises "not to phrase a response, but to understand [the other party] as they see themselves" (Fisher and Ury, 1981). Competence in active listening is indicated by asking different types of questions (e.g. open, closed and elaborative), paraphrasing without necessarily agreeing, and acknowledging what is or is not said (Wondwosen, 2006).

Negotiation outcomes are more likely to produce a rational, value-adding solution when they have been crafted around mutually acceptable principles and criteria. Moreover, such negotiated agreements are more likely to be durable, and perceived to be legitimate to the constituencies of both sides, as solutions can be evaluated against objective and fair criteria as time goes on.

Conclusion

Organisations now seem not only to have a better understanding of conflict, but also to increasingly accept conflict as an inevitable part of organisational life. We know that competition can bring the best and the worse out of people. It is expected that competition within and between organisations, across all sectors, will continue to increase. Intelligent investment in personal and organisational conflict resolution skills will support the positive behaviours associated with competition. Individuals, teams and organisations will increasingly seek the input of trained Business Psychologists to build resilient behaviour at all levels and fundamental conflict handling skills will be a central part of this process.

The positive effects of constructive conflict can be a major source for change, creativity and innovation and lead to higher performance, greater resilience and better decision making. We have identified the process and benefits of Principled Negotiation as a route to capitalising on these potential benefits.

References

ACAS Report (2009). *Managing Conflict at Work Booklet*. London, UK: ACAS. Retrieved (19/2/2015) from http://www.acas.org. uk/media/pdf/h/5/Managing_Conflict_at_Work_December_2009.pdf.

Alfredson,T., & Cungu, A. (2008). *Negotiation Theory and Practice: A review of the literature. EasyPOL Online resource materials for policy making*.FAO Policy Learning Program. Retrieved from http://www.fao.org/docs/up/easypol/550/4-5_negotiation_background_paper_179en.pdf.

Balogun, J., & Johnson, G. (2005). From Intended Strategies to Unintended Outcomes: The Impact of Change: Recipient Sense making. *Organization Studies, 26*(11), 1573-1601. doi:10.1177/0170840605054624.

Brown, W. (2004). Third party intervention reconsidered: an international perspective. *The Journal of Industrial Relations, 46*(4), 448-458.

Chartered Institute of Personnel and Development Report (2011). *Conflict management – Survey Report*. London, UK: CIPD.

CPP Human Capital Report (2008). Workplace Conflict and How Businesses can Harness it to Thrive. Retrieved from: https://www.cpp.com/pdfs/CPP_Global_Human_Capital_Report_Workplace_Conflict.pdf.

De Dreu, C. K. W., & Gelfand, M. J. (2008). Conflict in the workplace: Sources, functions, and dynamics across multiple levels of analysis. In C. De Dreu & M. Gelfand (Eds.), *The Psychology of Conflict and Conflict Management in Organizations* (pp. 3-54). New York, NY: Taylor & Francis Group.

Engel, A., & Weigel, E. (2012, April 4). S&P 500's 100 Largest Companies Ranked by Market Cap. *Perception Express*. Retrieved (3/2/2015) from http://www.globaleconomicandinvestmentanalytics.com/archiveslist/articles/287-sp-500-100-largest-companies-ranked-by-market-cap.html.

Falconer, H., & Bagshaw, M. (2004). Conflict in the workplace. In H. Falconer (Ed.), *IRS Managing Conflict in the Workplace* (pp. 1-9). London, UK: Reed Elsevier.

Firth-Cozens, J. (2001). Multidisciplinary teamwork: the good, bad and everything in between. *Quality in Health Care, 10,* 65-66. doi:10.1136/qhc.10.2.65.

Fisher, R., & Ury, W. (1981). *Getting to Yes: Negotiating Agreement Without Giving in.* (1st ed.). New York, NY: Penguin.

Fisher, R., Ury, W., & Patton, B. (1991). *Getting to Yes: Negotiating an Agreement Without Giving in.* (2nd ed.). London, UK: Random House Business Books.

Gaille, D., Felstead, A., Green F., & Inanc, H. (2013). Fear at Work in Britain – First Findings from the Skills and Employment Survey, 2012. Retrieved (10/11/2014) from http://www.cardiff.ac..uk/socsi/ses2012.

Giga, S. I., Hoel, H., & Lewis, D. (2008). *The cost of workplace bullying*. London: Unite the Union/Department for Business, Enterprise and Regulatory Reform.

Gilhooley, D. (2009, February 11). Judicial Mediation – a different approach to alternative resolution? *The Times Higher Education Supplement*. Retrieved (8/3/2015) from http://www.timeshighereducation.co.uk/405349.article.

Government of Newfoundland and Labrador (2013, May). *The cost of conflict*. Retrieved (10/12/2014) from http://www.psc.gov.nl.ca/psc/rwp/costofconflict.html.

Higginbottom, K. (2011, July). *Recession drives increase in workplace conflict.* Retrieved (12/1/2015) from http://www.thetcmgroup.com /news/ 286-conflict-in-the-workplace-sees-rise-with-recession.

IMF (2013, March 27). Calls for Global Reform of Energy Subsidies: Sees Major Gains for Economic Growth and the Environment. Press Release No. 13/93. *International Monetary Fund*. Retrieved from http://www.imf.org/external/np/sec/pr/2013/pr1393.htm.

Jung, C. G. (1971). *Psychological Types.* (6th ed.) London, UK: Routledge.

Kilmann, R. H., & Thomas, K. W. (1975). Interpersonal conflict-handling behavior as reflections of Jungian personality dimensions. *Psychological Reports, 37*, 971-980.

Kolb, D. M. (2008). Making sense of an elusive phenomenon. In C. De Dreu & M. Gelfand (Eds.), *The Psychology of Conflict and Conflict Management in Organizations* (pp. 425-434). New York, NY: Taylor & Francis Group.

Law Reform Commission (2010, November). *Alternative Dispute Resolution: Mediation and Conciliation. Law Reform Commission report.* ISSN 1393-3132. Dublin, Ireland: White, N.

Lawrence, K. (2013). *Developing Leaders in a VUCA Environment.* Chapel Hill, NC: UNC Executive Development 2013. Retrieved (15/12/2014) from http://www.kenan-flagler.unc.edu/~/media/Files/documents/executive-development/developing-leaders-in-a-vuca-environment.pdf.

Liddell, D. (2004a). The causes of workplace conflict. In H. Falconer (Ed.), *IRS Managing Conflict in the Workplace* (pp. 11-35). London, UK: Reed Elsevier.

Liddell, D. (2004b). Reaching agreement in cases of conflict: the role of mediation. In H. Falconer (Ed.), *IRS Managing Conflict in the Workplace* (pp. 133-160). London, UK: Reed Elsevier.

Luthans, F, Vogelgesang, G. R., & Lester, P. B. (2006). Developing the psychological capital of resiliency. *Human Resource Development Review*, *5*(1), 25-44.

Luttwak, E. (1999). *Turbo-Capitalism: Winners and Losers in the Global Economy*. New York, NY: Harper Perennial.

Maravalas, A. (2005). *How to Reduce Workplace Conflict and Stress*. Franklin Lakes, NJ: The Career Press.

McCrindle, M. (2004). The costs of conflict. In H. Falconer (Ed.), *IRS Managing Conflict in the Workplace* (pp. 37-59). London, UK: Reed Elsevier.

Mercy Corps (2006, June). *A Mercy Corps Negotiation Skills Workshop: Building on the Ideas of Roger Fisher and his Colleagues*. Mercy Corps Civil Society and Conflict Management Group. FAO, Rome, Italy.

Ministry of Justice (2013). *Employment Tribunal Guidance.* Retrieved (1/8/2014) from http://www.justice.gov.uk/tribunals/employment.

Podro, S. (2010, March). *Riding Out the Storm: Managing Conflict in a Recession and Beyond: Acas Policy Discussion Papers*. London, UK: Acas. Retrieved from (25/3/2015) http://www.acas.org.uk/CHttpHandler.ashx?id=2694&p=0.

Pondy, L. R. (1967). Organizational conflict: Concepts and models. *Administrative Science Quarterly, 12*(2), 296-320.

Rahim, M. A. (2002). Toward a theory of managing organizational conflict. *The International Journal of Conflict Management, 13*(3), 206-235.

Robbins, S. P., & Judge, T. A. (2012). *Essentials of Organizational Behavior.* (11th ed.) Harlow, UK: Pearson Education.

Salami, S. O. (2009). Conflict resolution strategies and organisational citizenship behaviour: The moderating role of trait emotional intelligence. *Europe's Journal of Psychology, 2*, 41-63.

Saner, R. (2012). *The Expert Negotiator*. (4th ed.) Leiden, Netherlands: Martinus Nijhoff.

Saundry, R. (2014). *Putting conflict management at the heart of organisational strategy*. Retrieved (10/3/2015) from http://www.ipa-involve.com/news/conflict-management-and-organisational-strategy/.

Saundry, R., & Wibberley, G. (2012). *Mediation and Early Resolution. A Case Study in Conflict Management*. ACAS Research Paper. Retrieved from http://www.acas.org.uk/media/pdf/5/c/Mediation-and-Early-Resolution-A-Case-Study-in-Conflict-Management-accessible-version.pdf.

Spears, M. C., & Parker, D. F. (2009). Negotiation recognition and the process of decision making. *Journal of Organizational Culture, Communications and Conflict, 13(*1), 55-64.

Stensaker, I. G., & Meyer, C. B. (2012). Change Experience and Employee Reactions: Developing Capabilities for Change. *Personnel Review, 41*(1), 106-124.

Thomas, K. W., & Kilmann, R. H. (1974). Thomas-Kilmann conflict mode instrument. Mountain View, CA: CPP, Inc.

Thompson, L., Nadler, J., & Lount, Jr., R. B. (2006). Judgmental biases in conflict resolution and how to overcome them. In M. Deutsch, P. T. Coleman & E. C. Marcus (Eds.), *The Handbook of Conflict Resolution: Theory and Practice* (2nd ed.) (pp. 243-267). San Francisco, CA: John Wiley & Sons.

Tjosvold, D. (2008). The conflict-positive organization: it depends upon us. *Journal of Organizational Behavior, 29*, 19-28.

Weisbord, M. R. (1976). Organizational Diagnosis: Six Places to Look for Trouble with or without a Theory. *Group and Organization Studies, 1*(4), 430-447.

Witschge, T., & Nygren, G. (2009). Journalism: a profession under pressure? *Journal of Media Business Studies, 6*(1), 37-59.

Wondwosen, M. (2006, August). *Negotiation: A Concept Note*. Retrieved (21/11/2014) from http://www.mondodigitale.org/files/Negotiation-concept.pdf.

4 SECTION

Consulting

CONSULTING INTRODUCTION

Pauline Grant

Business Psychologists work as both professional advisers and specialist contractors, in either case generally in partnership with their clients. There are some parallels with other specialists that businesses typically employ, legal or tax advisers for example, where the professional view is valued and taken into account when making decisions. However, sometimes there is a more iterative conversation, as with an architect for instance, to clarify the desired outcome and suggest ways of achieving it. Just as a good architect will take time to understand the purpose of a new building and how it will work in practice, a Business Psychologist will start by working with their client to understand the required result of any intervention they might make before they start to construct it.

The writers in this section outline some of the background to being a good consultant and offer their experience (together with the outcomes) of designing powerful interventions based on sound theory and solid evidence. David Biggs provides an overview of the research on consulting that has formed the basis of his teaching to new entrants to Business Psychology, which is of course also relevant for experienced practitioners. For clients, this serves as a guide as to what they should expect from their professional partners. Colleen Addicott offers reflections and insights from her research, a personal view that has informed her consulting practice. In doing so she exemplifies the importance of taking time to question and explore rather than taking a brief and assuming that everyone means the same thing when they make what might appear to be a straightforward statement.

Both client and contractor benefit from taking the time to understand the real issue, the root cause, the underlying problem, before deciding what should be done about it. Nigel Harrison and Steve Whiddett both have wisdom to offer around that theme that should give confidence to practitioners and clients alike when embarking on a path that contains inevitable uncertainty. Nigel has adapted a particular methodology and presents it as a framework that, in addition to being useful for professional practitioners, can also become a way of working within a corporate setting. Steve gives his view of what it means to be a Business Psychologist. He points out that using the tools and techniques that have arisen from Business Psychology, for instance instruments that non-psychologists can be trained to apply, is different from 'doing' Business Psychology. Clients that understand this distinction will decide when they need the special expertise that goes beyond application of established techniques.

CONSULTING – MEET THE AUTHORS

David Biggs is programme director and lecturer at the University of Gloucester. He is responsible for postgraduate Occupational and Business Psychology and also provides training, recruitment and research services. He has previously held consultancy and project management positions. He has also taught at other universities, been involved in validating other programmes and is a Distinguished Speaker at Goldsmiths College, London. In 2010, David was recognised in *Who's Who in the World*. David's research interests lie in non-traditional employment, the use of technology at work and in consulting.

Colleen Addicott, a Chartered Occupational Psychologist and founder and Director at Totem Ltd, has worked in the Business Psychology arena for 13 years and was previously in the financial sector. Her passion for working with people to ensure they are at their best not only led to her research, but also means she gets involved in leadership, management and team development and assessment. Focused on the robust application of the principles of psychology to deliver behaviour change, she has worked with a wide range of organisations across sectors.

Nigel Harrison is a Performance Consultant and Chartered Business Psychologist. Nigel was trained in Instructional Design and Performance Technology while working as a Training Analyst for the Control Data Corporation then went on to complete a Masters in Occupational Psychology at Birkbeck College. Since then Nigel has been working as an Independent consultant and is a Fellow of the Learning and Performance Institute. He wrote *Improving Employee Performance*, *How to be a True Business Partner by Performance Consulting* and *How to Deal with Power and Manipulation by Performance Consulting*.

Steve Whiddett is MD and Chief Business Psychologist at WHE UK Ltd. A former Chair of the ABP, he is passionate about helping individuals and organisations develop sustainable high performance. He does this by helping them understand that people are more often not the problem but the channel through which problems become apparent. Steve prides himself on working with his clients to identify interventions needed to address the symptoms of performance issues (unwanted outcomes and behaviours) and remove their causes (the bit that usually gets missed).

CONSULTING

David Biggs

Introduction

There are many different sayings when it comes to consulting, such as "a consultant uses your watch to tell you the time", coined by Townsend (1970). Others are probably more known in the management consulting industry; "those that can, do; those that can do better, consult". As an academic, I don't want to rely too much on the popular literature and/or thought leadership articles that influence consulting. However, leading commentators such as Fiona Czerniawska, Don Leslie and Calvert Markham greatly aid our understanding of what consulting is and what consultants do along with academic enquiry. Since the start of the 21st century the management consulting industry has embraced business psychology and as a result many students in work psychology have become consultants. The Management Consultancies Association promotes the principle that consulting adds value to an organisation (MCA, 2012) and it is both an industry and a practice (Biggs, 2010).

I wish to explore three aspects of consulting. Firstly, consulting as an industry, this will give context in terms of the type of employment that is available and where consulting operates. The second is about the processes of consulting. These processes are recognisable and many reading this will identify with their importance. Indeed, Masters degree programmes – MBAs and MScs in Business and Occupational Psychology – have at last seen this. While these programmes won't produce seasoned consultants, they can at least inform the student in the processes of consulting. In this manner, students can know what they don't know – why client consultant relations are important, etc. The third aspect revolves around the types of behaviours that are necessary to be a good consultant. A competency framework was developed out of two leading firms and this is used to demonstrate the skills and behaviours noted as being essential for good performance in consulting.

Consulting as an industry

Management consulting as an industry has been segmented in many different ways. Many of these divisions are by the type of consulting that a firm does. The Institute of Consulting for instance divides the industry into: business strategy; manufacturing and business services; financial and management controls; human resources; marketing; environmental management; quality management; and information technology (Inside Careers, 2013). Business psychology can inform all of these areas. It may therefore be seen as distinct as it can contribute towards effective human resource policy or even strategy of a company. Given this, it is probably more helpful if instead we adopt the framework based on size of the consulting firm, large versus boutique/niche, linked in with their particular specialisms (Biggs, 2010).

Large firms

Many will have heard of the Big Four: Deloitte; PwC; Ernst & Young; and KPMG. These are the four largest international firms which offer a range of professional services (actuarial, audit, consulting, etc.) and employ in the region of 150,000 to 200,000 employees. Obviously not all of these employees are in consultancy; however, it does give a sense of scale of their operations. In addition to the Big Four are other firms equally prominent coming from the engineering and computer based industries (McKenna, 2006).

On the global market there are US engineering firms that dominate such as AECOM and URS Corporation. The largest UK engineering based consultancy is Atkins with over 17,400 employees worldwide. Our students of business psychology have worked for Atkins in areas such as nuclear, defence and consulting in general. Arup is similar to Atkins and also provides engineering, design, project management and consulting services.

In terms of computing based industry, IBM and Capgemini are familiar names that provide consultancy services. IBM is probably the largest of the IT based firms with over 430,000 employees worldwide reported in their 2013 end of year accounts. Capgemini is also a big player with more than 130,000 people in over 40 countries. These firms acknowledge their traditional link with technology but in addition provide consulting and outsourcing services.

So is bigger better? Gerstner (2003) former CEO at IBM believes it is. The advantage with size is that everything a business needs to be effective is under the same roof. Gerstner argues that there are three essential areas that need to be clarified: grabbing hold, strategy and culture. 'Grabbing hold' is dealing with all the issues within and outside of the organisation. This may mean removing duplication and streamlining. Strategy is also vital. This is versed within the history of the firm but at the same time can be changed. Culture is essential to get right and can be changed through business psychology.

Once a large firm has grappled with these three big areas, then it benefits by being quickly able to respond to a client need. An example of this is from a £124m project to widen and renovate a motorway and bridges in an archaeologically rich site in Kent. The project involved individuals from different organisations, with different areas of expertise: archaeologists to excavate the site, geo-technical engineers to ensure the suitability of the ground, bridge engineers to renovate and build new bridges and road engineers to construct the actual road. Prevention and reduction of hostilities and pent-up emotions is essential when different experts work together. In previous projects emotions had flared as individuals, teams or organisations came into conflict. This tended not to be a problem when the emotions could be sorted by open communication. Consultancy could facilitate this open communication either by using specific tools such as emotional intelligence in conjunction with workshops, or by encouraging firms to contribute to group endeavours such as newsletters. Increasing the collaboration between experts adds value to the client organisation. Not only can you bring different experts from different fields in larger firms but this size does give the client reassurance (Biggs, 2010).

Boutique firms

So if size matters what about the smaller, boutique concerns, sometimes referred to as 'niche'? These firms don't need to employ tens or hundreds of thousands of employees. What they do well is to occupy a niche corner of the market extremely well. Areas such as psychometrics, assessment centres, management development and coaching are dominated by these niche firms. If a larger consulting firm needs a psychometric test provider or executive coach it is easier to employ a boutique firm to do this specialist work. For instance, recently I teamed together with a former employer and psychometric test provider to provide specialist testing on resilience in an undergraduate population.

Boutique firms can have a large impact even though they may only employ a handful of consultants. In Cheltenham, UK, for instance, JCA Ltd has really developed the emotional intelligence arena. Their specific measures of emotional intelligence for the individual and the team provide unique insights and approaches on fulfilling potential, working effectively with emotions and achieving performance improvement.

External versus Internal consulting

Much of the early literature in consulting concerned the difference between operating internally in an organisation and coming into an organisation from outside. There are definite advantages and disadvantages for each. The internal consultancy will have the richness of context as they are based within the client firm. They are also a fixed resource within an organisation that can be used internally within the company. For instance, my second job as a Business Psychologist was in MFI, which at the time was the largest furniture manufacturer in the UK. Here an internal consultancy team comprised three Business Psychologists along with supporting staff. This team ran recruitment and selection across the whole of the UK as well as the management development programmes within the company. This internal consultancy reduced costs for the organisation by providing a valuable service within the company and avoiding the use of external consultants.

Internal consultancies working within the organisation might run recruitment, training, development etc. However, they might have to compete for such work against external consultancies (Sturdy, Wylie & Wright 2013) which might appear more 'slick' or credible to the commissioning client. Interestingly, Vosburgh (2007) sees HR departments becoming more like an internal consultancy, like my MFI example, but incorporating the whole HR function. If this is the case they will need to address the credibility challenge.

External consultants are employed by a particular consulting firm which brings its demands but also benefits. Consultants need to be looking for new projects in order to be successful. The role is almost like a fixed term contractor going from contract to contract but on a permanent basis of employment. Working externally from the client means the consultant can remain impartial, removed from the client's politics.

Characteristics in consulting

Markham (2004) describes the 'top' consultant as having three characteristics as shown in Figure 1. The first characteristic is subject knowledge, in the case of a Business Psychologist this would be our subject knowledge in psychology. The second feature is applying that subject knowledge to the real world. This is consulting. The third characteristic is business acumen and experience. This is accumulated over time but can be taught via case studies. It is essential that practitioners understand these three characteristics as Nikita Mikhailov, a former student, states below. The subject knowledge area should be in a solid academic area, which is why so many consultants are still recruited from MBAs or specialist degrees such as MSc Business Psychology which have all three of Markham's (2004) characteristics covered leading to employability.

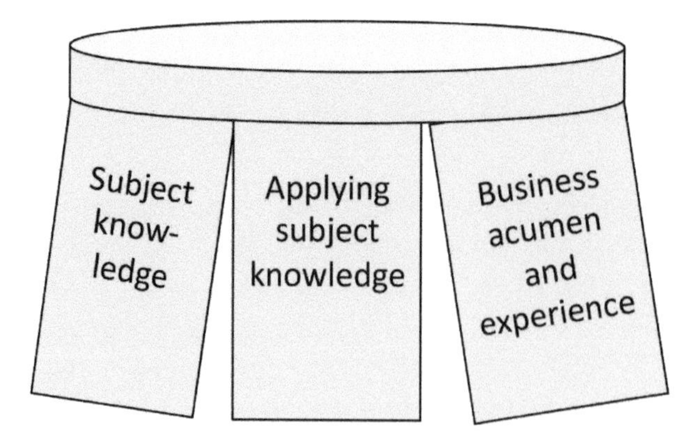

Figure 1: A 'top' consultant has three characteristics

Nikita Mikhailov, Duty Psychologist at Hogrefe Ltd:
To me being a consultant is being versed in a number of tools (i.e. psychometrics) and having the expertise of identifying when and how to use them to help the client achieve their goals. Therefore, before going in to consulting I feel it is crucial to have a firm understanding of the area which should include the principles that it works on and the language that it uses to describe the tools and the client needs, otherwise how can we ever match the two?

Trotter (2012) argues that there are important processes in consulting. These directly relate to Markham's (2004) second area listed above and include aspects such as: client relationship management; rapid implementation and continuous improvement; ability to anticipate future needs; strategy execution; coaching and advisory services.

Client relationship management is crucial in consulting (Davenport & Early, 2010; Nikolova et al., 2009). This involves the behaviours of communication, influencing others, organising and planning. Appelbaum (2004) states that, to be successful, consultants: have to be competent and skilled at what they offer; have an emphasis on client results; have clear outcomes and expectations; have visible executive support from a senior member of the consultancy firm; adapt readily to the client's needs; invest in learning about the client's environment; and include themselves in the implementation of any solutions. Again, this supports the idea of three key characteristics that a consultant should have as these refer to applying the subject knowledge business psychology.

Starting a client relationship can be thought of as a process of matching, between what the client wants and what the consultant can provide (Karantinou, & Hogg, 2001). Entry into a client relationship often involves identifying three players: those who know, care and can (Biggs & Watt, 2013). 'Those who know' are aware of the problems faced. 'Those that care' suffer from the issues in the organisation and 'those that can' are the sponsors of the project with the authority to give the work the go ahead. All three groups are vital to engage.

Indeed, the reason for many failed prospective projects was that often 'those who know' and 'those that care' are engaged but 'those that can' are not, thus no budget for work was available. After entry into a client relationship, this then leads to a number of different phases which Mulligan & Barber (2001) summarise as:

- Preparing for contact – this initial preparation can be facilitated by examining the client's website, annual accounts, etc. Obviously, the best source of information is what the client has given to the consultancy either in an expression of interest, tender document or just the assistance they are asking for. The focus should be on what is valuable to the client (Sobel, 2006).
- Orientation – the first meeting between client and consultant in the spring of the relationship (Mulligan & Barber, 2001). As neither party knows the other well orientation is about sounding each other out, building rapport and sharing experiences.
- Identification – when trust between the two parties is developed. Clients are not just passive receivers of wisdom but integral to the process of finding out any failings (Fincham, 1999). The client knows what the issues are and the consultant relates their experience to identify what needs to be addressed. This is an important point and is illustrated in Figure 2, whereby Luft and Ingram's (1955) Johari window is applied to organisations. This illustrates how the consultant can often see issues that the client cannot, even though they may be obvious to the consultant.
- Exploration – the actual work commences, although relationships need to be further strengthened. Exploration regards the increasing awareness of the client's needs by the consultant and their socialisation into the client's culture.

- Resolution – when the work has been delivered successfully and the project or programme is closed usually with a report or a service delivered that finishes the project. Nevertheless, this may not be the end of the relationship.

Resolution is the most interesting of these phases as some of the criticism levied at consultancy is that management consultants try to get the client to rely on them (Clegg, Kornberger & Rhodes, 2004). The resolution process can prevent this by finishing the project or programme. However, in terms of client–consultant relations consultants often keep in touch with their clients. For instance, I have written practitioner articles with clients after a project has been resolved and this then led to further work through the identification stage listed above.

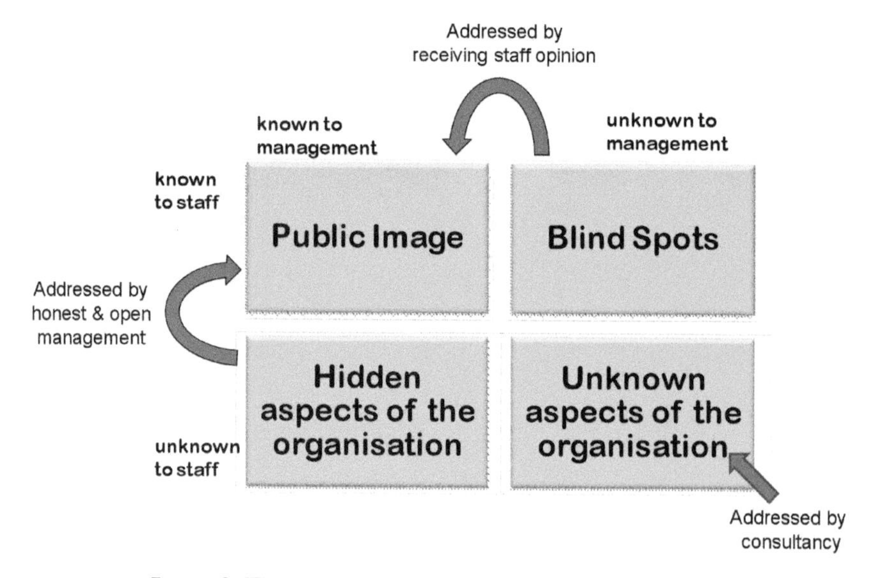

Figure 2: The Johari window applied to organisations (reprinted with permission from Biggs, 2010)

Trotter (2012) said that rapid implementation, continuous improvement, ability to anticipate and strategy execution were also necessary skills. These, in the practitioner literature, come under the term project/ programme management. Project management concerns the cost, time and quality of a venture. Projects can be huge multi-million pound concerns or involve the production of, say, an academic article. So projects range enormously and systems such as PRINCE2 are scaleable as relevant. Costs are maintained by using project accounting and are well known in advance. Time is typically planned so it is seen as a limited resource. Quality involves the scope of the project and what it seeks to achieve (Biggs, 2010).

The word 'rapid' involving the speed of the project is also important here. It can take time for the eventual business benefits to be realised. Clients want to see progress and results. Most business psychology projects, and indeed projects in general, do not produce these immediately. A systematic project management system gives comfort to the client by making visible the organisation of the work and the milestones that have been achieved (as shown in Figure 3). Obviously, the work needs to be carried out effectively; good project management reveals when this fails and identifies the stages that need to be addressed.

	EA04 Humble Manager Book chapter	DB05 Perms and temps	DB06: LFS & law	EA07: Doaa's article	Major events
04/05/2015					EA04 Intro, Industry, Skills and Competencies.
11/05/2015					EA04 Case study additional writing, DB05 Complete review of ST changes
18/05/2015					EA04: Complete chapter send for review, DB05: Complete and send to publisher
25/05/2015					DB06: Start LFS analysis. Check with Simon regarding longitudinal qualitative data
01/06/2015					Finish DB06: Send to relevant law journals
08/06/2015					Start on EA07: Doaa's article – reduce and submit to accountancy journals

Figure 3: Plan for four consecutive projects

It is important that clients feel they can trust the advice that the consultancy provides. Consultancies often have consultants on a client site who are to provide advice and cost up potential projects. Business Psychologists are less likely to be on site, but rather aim to be a trusted partner.

Consulting processes represents a huge area. Luckily for us this knowledge is often published as consultancies will bring in further revenues by championing a particular method or way (Biggs, 2010). Before leaving this subject, research skills are also vital for a consultant in business psychology. Some believe there is a dumbing down of research skills in psychology, as universities see statistics as an unpopular subject. The research methods employed along with our knowledge of psychology really distinguishes the Business Psychologist from a management consultant.

Knowledge of how to gain data about real world issues, using quantitative and qualitative methods, is vital even if you employ statisticians to do the maths. In our case study example, Bob was interested in the rise of consultancy as a revenue source within UK universities. Considerable revenue, approximately £400 million, was earned through consulting activity in 2012/13 (HEFCE, 2014). Discourse analysis was used very effectively to ascertain if individuals from consultancies and academics believed universities could ever replace consultancies.

Case Study 1:
Can universities replace consultancies? Bob Lloyd-Smith

This qualitative research investigates the changing relationship between university academics and commercial management consultants. Academics are increasingly venturing into management consultancy in search of extra funding. Management consultants are starting to recover after suffering at the hands of the recession. Discourse analysis identified how participants from each corner of the issue really feel about their individual contributions. These included on the university side a current senior academic who used to work in commercial management consultancy and a university business manager who has to inspire academics to take on consultancy work. It also included a commercial management consultant and a director of a global consultancy firm who dismissed any commercial threat from academics. The research reveals an insight into remarkably different worlds. The emerging conclusion is that for universities to survive stringent government cutbacks, and for commercial firms to access up to date research, there is a tangible need for the two sides to bond and deliver. This research found little evidence of any real competition between universities and consultancies, but rather a symbiotic relationship.

Behaviours in consulting

Behaviours are observable. Behaviour in this context is what an individual 'says' or 'does' or 'does not say' or 'fails to do' when something is expected of them. At work, these behaviours are brought out in job analysis and arranged in terms of competencies. A competency can be defined as a collection of behaviours associated with effective or superior performance (Ballantyne & Povah, 2004). Single competencies can then be collected into a competency framework. The competency framework should then, through the single competencies within, contain all of the behaviours necessary for effective performance in a particular job role (Bowler & Woehr, 2006).

In 2008 I was approached to write a book about consulting to aid students at postgraduate level. I wanted to systematically analyse behaviours seen as essential in consulting. Job analysis (using critical incident and job incumbent methods) was conducted within two firms, an international management consultancy and a boutique firm, to capture any differences between the large or small firms. This generated information that led to a competency framework being developed that could be used by both students and seasoned consultants (Biggs, 2010). The 'eight consultancy competency framework' specifically detailed the behaviours necessary for good performance in consulting. Since it was created, postgraduate students in business, occupational and forensic psychology at Gloucestershire have used it to create a personal plan of development that improves their employability. The competency framework is also used as the basis of assessment centre exercises, such as renegotiating a client contract with a Human Resources Director, that help students to understand what is required as a consultant.

The eight consultancy competency framework was listed in Biggs (2010) as:

- Communication,
- Influencing others,
- Organising and planning,
- Problem solving,
- Teamwork and consideration of others,
- Leadership,
- Drive,
- Tolerance for stress/uncertainty.

Communication was defined as the extent to which an individual conveys oral and written information and responds to questions and challenges. Interestingly, this was distinct from influencing others, as sometimes documents and reports are purely for dissemination rather than to persuade others to take a particular course of action.

Communication in consulting may involve face to face presentations ranging from conferences to face to face business meetings. As communication is so key, I have had a lot of, sometimes uncomfortable, training in the area, drawing attention to my lack of detail or how many 'OKs' I said in a five minute presentation. Written communication – reports, tenders or expressions of interest – is also vital. Again practice is key and all writing needs to be proof read.

Influencing is the extent to which an individual persuades others to do something or adopt a point of view in order to produce desired results. It takes place when one's own convictions are dominant rather than others' opinions. The consultant might need to persuade the CEO, Director or manager to adopt a certain course of action. This may be unpleasant for the person to hear but can be vital for their business's continued existence as seen in Case Study 2.

Case Study 2:
Saving a Birmingham manufacturing plant: David Biggs

When a business has had a long history it is difficult for staff and front line management to see that the company may be going through a rough patch. However, with this particular client, established in the late 19th century, that was exactly what was happening. The MD had re-mortgaged his house twice to provide finances, though most staff were not aware of this. Consequently they were adding to the hard times of the company, for instance by overtime and even sabotage of the machines. The MD had to tell his workers that the company faced a serious crisis, which was quite difficult for him as he saw it as his own failing.

Nevertheless, he listened to the consulting advice he was given. He met with all the staff on a Saturday to tell them the news. Overtime had to be banned and machines needed additional maintenance to operate effectively. If staff worked on a particular machine that broke, rather than heading to the café for a bacon sandwich, they had to work on other machines. The news was a shock. However, staff who risked losing their jobs bore the weight of the changes so that the firm could survive.

Organising and planning is the extent to which an individual systematically arranges his/her own work and resources as well as that of others for efficient task accomplishment. It is also the extent to which an individual anticipates and prepares for the future. Some of this can be taught in terms of skills and project management.

Problem solving involves three steps: data gathering, judgement and then decision. Data gathering includes understanding relevant technical and professional information. However, there comes a point where judgement is needed. Consultancies often use terms like 'analysis paralysis' or 'don't boil the ocean' to describe when data gathering starts to hinder the problem solving. The consultant should, before analysis paralysis, generate viable options, ideas and solutions. The data gathering skills used by Business Psychologists are rooted in the research methods that we employ. The focus is on the question rather than the solution or statistics to be used. So qualitative and quantitative methods can be used to gather the relevant data. This then leads to the decision process whereby the consultant selects supportable courses of action for problems and situations, using the available resources to produce imaginative solutions.

Teamwork and consideration of others also involves participating as a member of a group and being aware of the impact and implications of decisions on others. Teamwork is essential in consulting as often experts in different fields will come together for the good of a project. Project management helps by defining clearly what the roles and responsibilities are in a project team.

Leadership was also seen as a competency leading to success as a consultant as there are often situations where the project team needs leadership and motivating. The competency is defined as the extent to which an individual takes on the responsibility for providing focus to a team and develops members of that team. This can also involve leading a client. Indeed, at times when delivering bad news, leadership can be exhibited and demonstrate a way forward for those who are concerned about their futures. This may take the form of development for those concerned or it just may be about reassuring them about an outcome.

Drive is the extent to which an individual originates and maintains a high activity level, sets high performance standards and persists in their achievement. It is in essence the desire to advance and move forward. Drive is essential in consulting as with drive comes the motivation to succeed.

Tolerance for stress/uncertainty was the final competency found to relate to performance in consulting: the extent to which an individual maintains effectiveness in diverse situations under varying degrees of pressure, opposition, and disappointment. It therefore encompasses the concept of resilience. The job analysis found that alongside many successes there were also disappointments. This could range from a consultancy contract not being awarded to failed projects. Consultants with this competency could evaluate the disappointment in an objective manner, learn lessons from the failure and then move on.

Conclusion

The consulting industry is far from homogeneous, providing bewildering choice for clients as well as new entrants. The pressure to drive revenues and contain costs is yielding new collaborations between academia and practitioners, between internal and external providers and between different consulting firms. In parallel we see the increasing professionalisation of consulting through the greater emphasis in post-graduate programmes on defining and teaching consulting skills. Indeed, most MSc courses in Business Psychology now detail extensive consultancy knowledge. These skills will be expected by those who employ consultants. Some of it seems straightforward; have an open and honest relationship with your client, don't boil the ocean, etc. Others are more nuanced as revealed in the eight competency framework. Clients rightly demand results, and consultants need to respond by demonstrating their competence to deliver successful assignments. It is necessary, but not sufficient, to have the requisite subject knowledge. Building consulting competences into ongoing professional development is therefore an imperative, and this can be accomplished using the framework offered.

References

Appelbaum, S. H. (2004), Critical Success Factors in the Client-Consulting Relationship. *Journal of American Academy of Business*, *4*(1/2), 184-191.

Ballantyne, I., & Povah, N. (2004). *Assessment & Development Centres*. Hants: Gower Publishing Ltd.

Biggs, D. M. (2010). *Management Consulting: A guide for students*. London: Cengage Learning.

Biggs, D. M., & Watt, D. (2013, January). *The right ones? Identifying, engaging and building rapport with new clients*. Paper presented at the BPS DOP Conference, Chester, UK.

Bowler, M. C., & Woehr, D. J. (2006). A Meta-Analytic Evaluation of the Impact of Dimension and Exercise Factors on Assessment Center Ratings. *Journal of Applied Psychology, 91*(5), 1114-1124.

Clegg, S. R., Kornberger, M., & Rhodes, C. (2004). Noise, Parasites and Translation. *Management Learning, 35*(1), 31-44.

Davenport, J., & Early, J. (2010). The Power-Influence Dynamics in a Consultant/Client Relationship. *Journal of Financial Service Professionals, 64*(1), 72-75.

Fincham, R. (1999). The consultant-client relationship: critical perspectives on the management of organisational change. *Journal of Management Studies, 36*(3), 335-351.

Gerstner, L. (2003). *Who Says Elephants Can't Dance?: How I Turned Around IBM*. New York, NY: HarperCollins.

Hargie, O. (2006). *The handbook of communication skills* (3rd Ed.) London: Routledge.

HEFCE (2014). *Higher Education – Business and Community Interaction survey 2012-13*. Retrieved on 30/4/14 from: http://www.hefce.ac.uk/pubs/year/2013/201311/name,81914,en.html.

Inside Careers. (2013). *The official graduate career guide to Management Consultancy 2013/14*. London: Cambridge Market Intelligence Ltd.

Karantinou, K. M., & Hogg, M. K. (2001). Exploring Relationship Management in Professional Services: A Study of Management Consultancy. *Journal of Marketing Management*, 17(3-4), 263-286.

Luft, J., & Ingram, H. (1955). *The Johari Window: A graphic model of interpersonal awareness.* Proceedings of the Western Training Laboratory in Group Development. Los Angeles: University of California Extension Office.

MCA (2012). *Generating value: making a difference. An analysis of the value that management consultancies are adding to British businesses*. Retrieved on 25/09/14 from: http://www.mca.org.

WHAT DOES IT REALLY MEAN TO BE AT YOUR BEST IN WORK?

Colleen Addicott

As a Consultant Business Psychologist I like to keep up with the latest research in order to understand what might benefit my clients. One of the areas that we have seen to have great impact is the notion of working to strengths – first understanding them and then working out how to make the most of them. As my company, Totem, has developed from being essentially just me on my own to what is now a growing team, it is certain that understanding what each of us does well and gets a kick out of doing has really helped us allocate work more effectively and be more productive. Yet there are still days when I am not necessarily at my best – we all have those days, when we are distracted or just 'not in the zone'. So it would seem that being at your best is more than just working to our strengths.

That word 'best' also comes up in coaching and in initial conversations with clients. I often ask coachees, "When are you at your best?" or I ask clients "What do you mean?" when they say they want to "get the best from their people". Somehow those are questions that people just 'get' – they are able to answer them easily. What I began to notice was that there seemed to be some consistency in those responses. There were elements of what people are feeling and what they are doing that came through in most of the individuals' responses. They were talking about their internal conversations and their positive feelings about themselves, their work and their colleagues. They were also talking about getting things done, even when challenged, and how they were working with others to do that. So it struck me that perhaps we have a shared understanding about what 'being at your best in work' really means – it is certainly a more accessible term to discuss than concepts such as engagement or potential. That thought led me to some interesting discoveries in the course of my PhD research.

Unpicking what we mean by 'being at our best', will help us to quickly remedy distractions or other limitations. This will be useful on an individual basis, in coaching and management conversations or in designing development interventions for clients that will allow for speedier behavioural change.

'Best' in existing literature and research

Initially I was quite overwhelmed by the range of subject matter that appears to link to the question of when people are at their best in work. Similar to my conversations around being at your best, the academic research also makes reference to internal characteristics (feelings) alongside behaviours (actions). I chose to keep my focus on the literature that relates to positive psychology. Being at one's best falls very naturally into positive psychology; after all, the founding father of positive psychology notes, "Happiness and wellbeing are the desired outcomes of positive psychology" (Seligman 1999, p.559).

The potentially relevant literature is extensive. The cost of replacing productive staff choosing to leave has led to a considerable body of research into retention and could well be of interest; after all, keeping people at their best would seem like a logical goal to avoid people leaving an organisation. Yet retention research is also an example of the interwoven nature of the literature. It picks up on the psychological contract, job satisfaction and commitment to name just a few of the relevant concepts. It is in that overlap of research and concepts that 'being at your best' appears to exist – where there are consistencies of definitions, descriptions and applications. In particular, it seems to me that 'best' is located in the overlap between three major factors – Performance, Engagement and Commitment – as the following diagram illustrates:

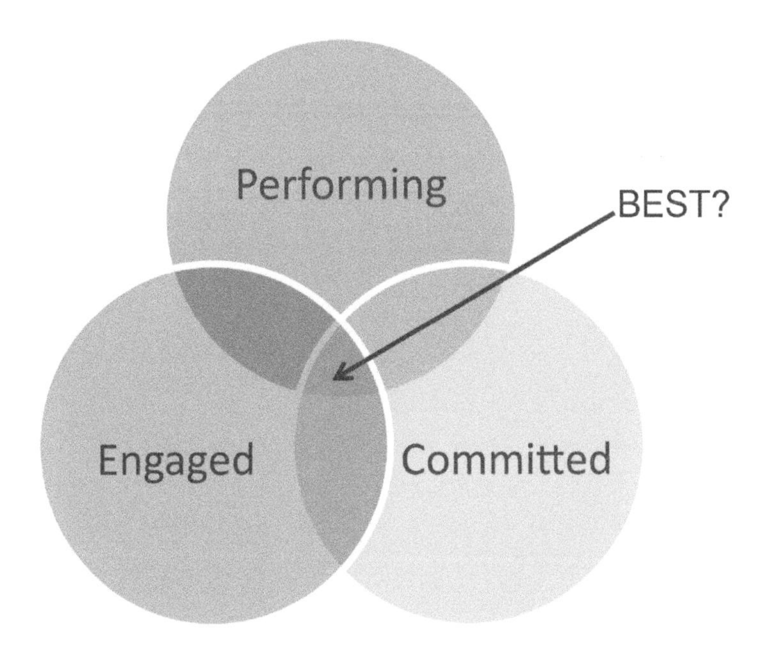

Figure 1: The location of 'best' in the academic literature

Performance

Traditionally organisations use competency descriptions and measurements to communicate performance expectations. Competencies relate to the behaviours required for success. Many organisations have put considerable investment into defining these competencies. They are often applied in recruitment and although some make the effort to utilise them for development, this tends to be more difficult to transition into the wider organisation context. The challenge of working with competencies is that having defined them, they quickly become 'out of date' in rapidly changing work environments.

Griffin et al. (2007) proposed a very helpful framework for defining performance in changing environments. They suggested three key areas are involved: Proficiency, Adaptivity, and Proactivity. These factors would appear key to successful performance in changing environments and are clearly relevant in today's fluctuating economy and work context. The recent economic downturn saw 2.7 million people made redundant in the UK (Office of National Statistics 2008–2012). Those left in the workplace needed to deal with the changing structure (adaptable) whilst still producing (proficient). With fewer people in the workforce there is greater focus on efficiency and that is where proactivity becomes essential – the ability to spot how things can be improved and make that happen. Griffen et al. (2007) take the model further to suggest that these elements are all required on an individual, team and organisational level to ensure success. Performance is therefore more complex than a simple set of competencies people need to possess.

Another term that forms a part of the performance literature is 'potential'. This describes the stretch in performance possible for each individual. It has proved quite a challenging issue in both research and practice. One of the questions that we regularly ask our clients who are attempting to identify high potential individuals is, "potential for what?" That question focuses the process of identifying potential. The Corporate Leadership Council (CLC, 2005) conducted a review of the literature in the area and defined three consistent elements of potential: Ability, Aspiration and Engagement. Once again the literature and the conversational evidence points to internal characteristics (in terms of elements of engagement and aspiration – a desire to achieve more) and behavioural elements (in terms of ability and what is produced as a result of being engaged).

There are a number of useful models of potential currently used in business. The tri-partite model developed by YSC emphasises the role of Judgment, Drive and Influence when looking for high potential (YSC, 2014). A closer inspection of each of the three dimensions reveals the role of learning agility in developing potential in each of the three elements. Lombardo and Eichinger (2000) argued that "learning from experience is how a person demonstrates what is termed high potential" (p. 321). De Meuse et al. (2010), working with the Korn Ferry group, noted individual characteristics that are a pre-requisite for learning agility – experience, self-awareness and an ability to handle complexity. The Korn Ferry model identifies different areas of learning agility – Mental agility, People agility, Change agility and Results agility – and distinguishes between specialist and general management potential – going some way in helping to answer the question, 'potential for what?'

Engagement

Engagement forms part of the CLC model of potential and is a separate field of research in itself. Mihaly Csikszentmihalyi's prolific work around the concept of Flow focuses on complete engagement where individuals have greater awareness and are more in touch with their emotions. "Life means to experience – through doing, feeling and thinking" (Csikszentmihalyi, 1997, p.8). This definition of life provides more support for considering being at our best in terms of what we do (behaviour) and what we feel (internal). Using the Experience Sampling Method where a pager signals a command to participants to answer questions in a book they carry with them, Csikszentmihalyi found flow was reported when individuals were doing their favourite activity. The activities varied but there was consistency in having clear goals, immediate feedback and skills that were balanced to action opportunities. When these conditions are in place, flow is experienced – a state of joy, creativity and total involvement. Csikszentmihalyi's work has clear implications for the workplace and provides further clarity around what individuals are feeling and experiencing (internal aspects) alongside what they are doing (behavioural elements) when they are at their best.

Schaufeli and Bakker (2000) also note the role of both internal factors and external behaviours in engagement, suggesting "engagement as behaviour – driving energy in one's work role – is considered the manifestation of psychological presence, a particular mental state". This manifestation or link between feelings or state and behaviour may not always be quite so straightforward. Farndale et al.'s (2011) study provides some indication of what work engagement means in practice for individuals and organisations. They identify four different domains of engagement and the factors that drive them:

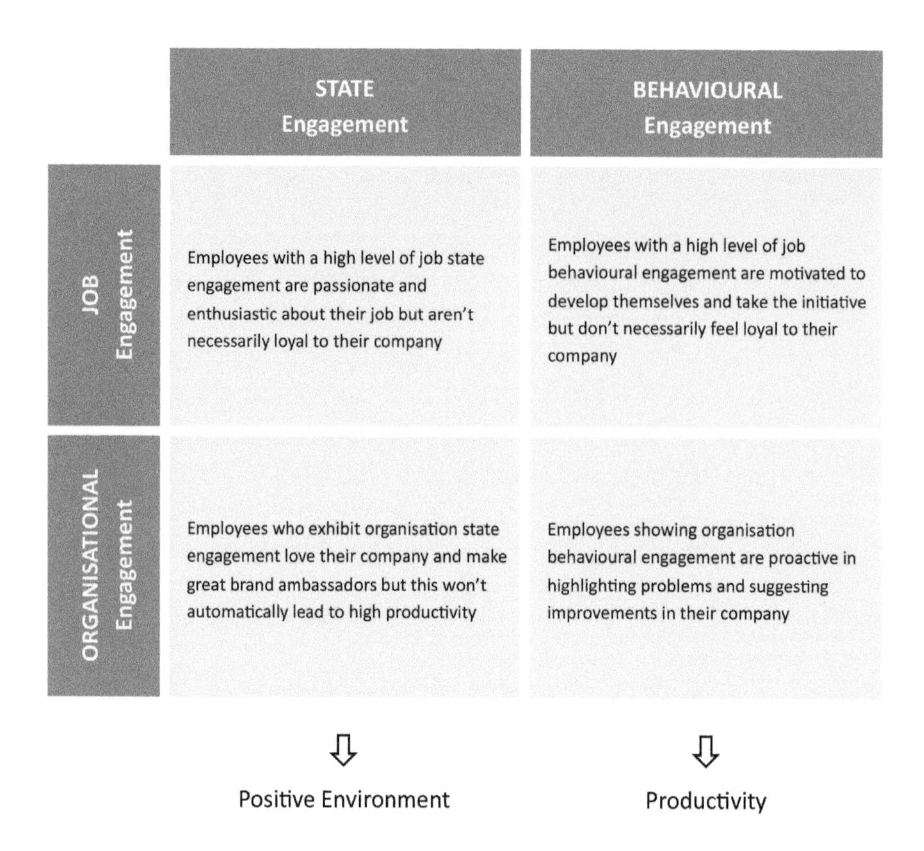

Figure 2: Representation of Farndale et al. (2011) Engagement Domains

What is interesting is that Farndale et al. (2011) highlight that it is essential to be clear about what types of engagement are being measured and which are important for the company, given differences in operating contexts. They draw a distinction between job engagement and organisation engagement. An individual may be engaged in their activities and in their role but may not necessarily be engaged by or with their organisation. This could go some way to explain why we see people move from company to company but still doing the similar roles. The other distinction they make is around the difference between an individual's psychological state (their perception and indeed feelings towards the job or organisation) and what they actually do. From an organisation's perspective, behavioural engagement may have more obvious advantages as it is related to increased productivity whereas state engagement plays a role in creating a positive working environment. For individuals, state engagement contributes to work being experienced as more pleasant. However, Farndale et al. (2011) note that state engagement does not necessarily lead to behavioural engagement. For example, individuals may be talking passionately about their job (a sign of job state engagement) but are not necessarily motivated to develop themselves or take the initiative (job behavioural engagement). So there may be other influential factors that are needed to ensure all four engagement domains are high, if that is indeed possible. Farndale et al. (2011) continue to interrogate their wealth of data to understand the links and influences on both state and behavioural engagement.

One model that goes some way to demonstrating the complexities of engagement is Bakker and Demerouti's (2007) Job Demands-Resources Model of Engagement. It distinguishes Engagement as 'Vigor, Absorption and Dedication' going further to identify the individual and job resources required to achieve these. The model highlights the role of the internal characteristics (psychological capital) of Self Efficacy, Resilience, Optimism and Hope. This model has since been further researched and applied to a range of concepts and in a number of contexts including human thriving (Spreitzer et al. 2010), employee burnout (Halbesleben, 2010) and workaholism (Taris, 2010). It therefore represents a useful overview of the psychological processes and behaviour characteristics involved in engagement.

Commitment

The 'dedication' that forms part of the model's description of engagement relates to the Commitment literature. Commitment in itself is both a feeling or internal characteristic and a behaviour. Swailes (2004) links organisational commitment to behaviour and retention. He notes that employers see it as leading to behavioural intentions and actions such as the willingness to take on extra activities or organisational citizenship behaviours. Meyer et al. (2004) suggest that commitment is actually a component of motivation which involves internal characteristics often demonstrated in behaviours. Motivation can be related to a specific activity and it is also a term used to describe general drive. In most of the literature, a feeling of commitment

to one's work relates to general drive which is likely to manifest itself in activities that demonstrate a focus on achieving goals.
Key to understanding what it means to be at your best in work is therefore clarification of the internal characteristics (or feelings) that are experienced and the external activity (or behaviours) that are exhibited when people are at their best.

The research study

I had the opportunity to work with a retail organisation looking to understand what was going on in three of their department stores that were producing unexplained results. All the stores were part of a new format for the company – all had been in existence for less than three years. Performance was forecast based on a range of socio-economic, geographic and stock profiles. But one very new store was outperforming any expectation or forecast. Another store had, for two years running, been at the top of the employee satisfaction survey (top in both the new format and in the traditional format stores). Whilst the manager was seen to be incredibly effective he was also responsible for another store and the staff survey results were not the same. The third store was actually the very first new format store to open and had experienced a number of initial challenges. Historically it had not performed to expectations but recently performance had changed. Whilst there had been turnover of staff within that store, a large proportion of staff had been there since day one and were the longest serving new format staff members, despite experiencing all those initial challenges.

The research had been inspired by the conversations and the recurring themes that came from the resulting discussions. The social constructionist view that meaning is socially constructed through words and symbols has therefore influenced the research approach, right from the beginning. The research therefore needed to explore the words and symbols used in the specific context, so I observed and interviewed the members of staff in each of the stores. This is reflective of Sarantakos's (1998) description that, "Social phenomena exist not 'out there' but in the minds of people and their interpretations." (p. 36). Understanding how the individuals interpret their work and working environment will help to get to the bottom of the unexpected outcomes in these stores. As anecdotal evidence and existing literature all point to both feelings and behaviours being involved in being at one's best, I looked at these two angles when structuring my investigations.

I interviewed the staff in the three stores:

i. The store with the highest performance (237% of target)
ii. The store that was the top of the employee survey for two years running (engaged)
iii. The store that was improving in both performance & survey results and had the longest serving staff (commitment)

The interviews were kept simple and open, without specific mention of feelings and behaviours, in order to elicit natural language and conversation with the individuals. The key questions were:

- What attracted you to the job?
- What were your first impressions?
- What do you enjoy most?
- What would you like more of?
- What does a great day look like?

I interviewed 42 staff across the sites and at all levels from manager to shop assistant. The interviews lasted between 20 and 90 minutes depending on their availability and how talkative the individuals were. After interviewing, I used Nvivo software to code the themes. Using software avoided the risks inherent in manually coding and counting of occurrences. It also allowed me to interrogate the data more thoroughly – looking at the words coded under each theme to ensure each theme was distinct and looking for themes that consistently came up together. I based the themes on internal characteristics (feelings) and behaviours. The consistency of the findings was very interesting.

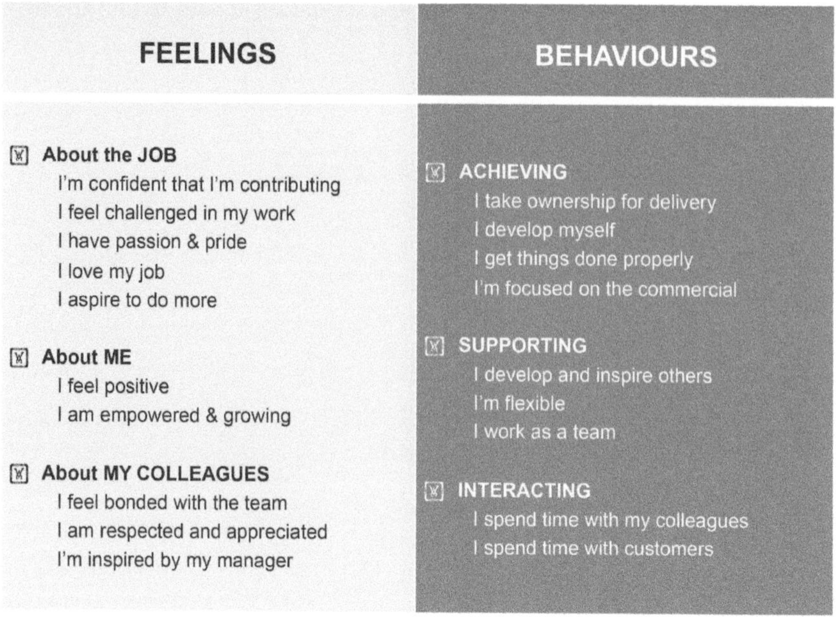

FEELINGS	BEHAVIOURS
About the JOB I'm confident that I'm contributing I feel challenged in my work I have passion & pride I love my job I aspire to do more	**ACHIEVING** I take ownership for delivery I develop myself I get things done properly I'm focused on the commercial
About ME I feel positive I am empowered & growing	**SUPPORTING** I develop and inspire others I'm flexible I work as a team
About MY COLLEAGUES I feel bonded with the team I am respected and appreciated I'm inspired by my manager	**INTERACTING** I spend time with my colleagues I spend time with customers

Figure 3: Overview of interview themes

In order to ensure the themes were each distinct, the words used or coded for each theme were checked and compared. There were no significant similarities between the words coded for different themes suggesting that each was discrete and distinct from the others.

All of the themes occurred across each of the sites, although not necessarily all the themes in every interview. The most common themes were 'taking ownership for delivering' (*behaviour* such as solving problems or following up on promises made), 'passion and pride' (*feelings* such as being proud to say where they work), 'confident that I am contributing' (*feeling* they are able to deliver) and 'developing and inspiring others' (*behaviour* such as role modelling or helping others to learn). These are reflective of both the anecdotal conversations I had prior to this research and the existing literature.

When considering which themes most commonly occurred together within the same interview, it was that of feeling 'inspired by my manager' and having 'bonded with the team'. Whilst of course there is no cause and effect here, it is interesting to note that individuals who reported feeling inspired by their manager also talked about how well they had bonded with their colleagues. Looking at which themes commonly occurred together within the same interview three broad clusters came through the analysis. These could be termed:

- Contributing (e.g. "I am confident I am contributing"; "I'm focused on the commercial")
- Inspiration (e.g. "I'm inspired by my manager"; "I'm empowered and growing")
- Developing (e.g. "I develop myself"; "I am challenged").

The consistency of themes across all stores did not immediately identify what was making the three target stores stand out from others in their particular ways. There were, however, some nuances between the themes noted in each of the three different stores – the most common themes in each store can be seen below:

	All stores	High Commitment Store	High Engagement Store	High Performance Store
1	I take ownership for delivery	I develop and inspire others	I have passion and pride	I take ownership for delivery
2	I have passion and pride	I aspire to do more	I take ownership for delivery	I have passion and pride
3	I'm confident I am contributing	I take ownership for delivery	I develop and inspire others	I am confident I am contributing
4	I develop and Inspire others	I feel challenged	I work as a team	I spend time with customers

Figure 4: Most common themes

This closer inspection of the combination of the most common themes in each of the stores helps to draw out the distinct characteristics of each context. The most common theme overall, "I take ownership for delivery" also appeared in the top four themes for each of the stores, suggesting this is the stable theme that ties them together. Of the top four themes identified in all stores, all except "I'm confident I am contributing" appeared in at least two of the stores. That was a particular theme in the High Performance store more than in any of the others. Also, uniquely, in the top four for that store was "I spend time with customers". Uniquely in the top four themes for the High Engagement store was "I work as a team". For the High Commitment store it was both "I aspire to do more" and "I feel challenged". These nuances and indeed similarities are interesting to note and provide greater depth to our understanding of what was going on in these contexts. However, the prevailing message is the overall consistency of themes across the three contexts.

One surprise that came up from the research was actually from a conversation starter activity that I used in the interviews. I gave the individuals a sheet of words that related to values (e.g. wealth, health, family, fun, achievement) and asked them to highlight which were important to them personally. This is a simple technique I have used before in career transition coaching to get people to think about what is important to them or what they value. I then asked them which of these values were fed or supported by their work. Between 61% and 100% of the words highlighted as important to them were also supported by their work and there was an overall average of a 93% match. This struck me as unusually high and some might suggest the high level could be due to a priming effect. However, in other contexts such as coaching (and indeed in other case studies since) such a high level is not seen despite a similar questioning process. This connection between what an individual values and the work he or she was doing provides another theme or element to understand what being at your best in work really means. Values are often used as a point of differentiation in company marketing and communications. However, their definition and what that means in practice often requires further clarification. Burke (2000) associated the alignment of organisational and individual values with improved job satisfaction, productivity and profitability. Given the findings during the interview and the relevant literature, values are therefore likely to play a role in being at one's best in work.

This might modify the tentative definition we developed to now say: 'Being at your best in work' is a term that means individuals feel they are contributing, inspired, developing and connected to what they value; and they behave in a way that reflects this.

Implications

What we are beginning to see is a picture of what being at your best involves. In the above retail context:

i. Feelings and behaviours clustered around:-
    a. Contributing
    b. Inspiration
    c. Developing
ii. A conscious connection between what individuals value and their work.

Now of course, these results are in just one study, but the sheer consistency of findings suggests some tentative implications. This study was the starting point for my PhD research and further studies have been undertaken and are currently underway. Whilst it is still early days, I can confirm that all the themes are recurring in these other organisations. The most common themes differ slightly, as one would expect, according to the context. In terms of the values connection, there have been varied results. In studies with teams that are perceived as the best in the organisation, but with acknowledged challenges and difficulties, there appears to be a lower level of connection between individual values and the perception that their work supports those values (Addicott). It may therefore be more helpful to explore reasons why there is a disconnection in order to understand when individuals are not currently quite at their best.

The understanding from this case study (and the indications from the subsequent investigations) has implications for coaching and supporting managers:

Use more focused, exploratory questions in coaching

When a coachee is vague about their particular development focus, having a structure for exploring their context is helpful. My research suggests two ways to help that exploration. On a broad basis, we can explore with individuals how much they are contributing, how inspired they are feeling and how much they are developing in order to focus their thoughts and clarify their development goals. Alternatively, if we want to explore on a more detailed level, we could use these specific themes: feelings about their job, themselves and their colleagues; what they are doing around achieving, supporting and interacting. If there are particular problems to work through, exploring values and those which individuals may perceive as not supported by their work may be another helpful tool in the coaching process.

Giving managers a structure for performance management conversations

Performance management often focuses purely on objectives achieved or not achieved. We can help managers make these conversations have greater impact by encouraging them to explore an employee's feelings and behaviour in more detail: feelings about their job, themselves and their colleagues, and what they are doing around achieving, supporting and interacting. Again, using the broader clusters (contributing, inspiration, developing) can provide managers with a structure for the conversations around employees' contribution, about how inspired they feel and what they are doing to develop themselves and others. Another way to improve the impact of the conversations is for managers to explore the potential barriers to each of the three elements and how these can be overcome. The discussion around values and how employees can be supported in their work could be one way of overcoming those barriers. Adding these elements to a performance management conversation can be quite tricky and managers are likely to need support in how to do so naturally.

Design more effective development interventions for managers

Knowing what 'being at your best' is likely to involve can inform the design of development interventions such as workshops or training programmes. We can ensure that contributing, developing and inspiration are all included. This may simply be about how we position or frame activities for individuals. The most common pairing of themes being that of feeling 'inspired by my manager' and having 'bonded with the team' points to the need for manager development to focus on inspiring and creating a bond between members. This means considering at every stage the impact of how they supervise, structure the work and what they do and say on the team dynamics.

References

Addicott, C. M. *The role of feelings, values and behaviours in being at your best in work.* PhD Thesis, in preparation.

Bakker, A. B., & Demerouti, E. (2007). The Job Demands–Resources Model: State of the art. *Journal of Managerial Psychology, 22*, 309-328.

Burke, R. (2000). Do Managerial Men Benefit from Organizational Values Supporting Work–Personal Life Balance? *Women in Management Review, 5*(2), 81-87.

Corporate Leadership Council (2005). *Realizing the full potential of rising talent (volume 1): A quantitative analysis of identification and development of high-potential employees.* Washington, DC: Corporate Executive Board.

Csikszentmihalyi, M. (1997). *Finding flow: The psychology of engagement with everyday life.* New York, NY: Basic Books.

De Meuse K. P., Dai G., & Hallenbeck, G. S. (2010). Learning Agility: A Construct Whose Time has Come. *Consulting Psychology Journal: Practice and Research, 62*, 119-130.

Cass Business School, Tilburg University, Cranfield University (2011). *A study of the link between Performance Management and Employee Engagement in Western multinational corporations operating across India and China – Final Report.* London, Netherlands, Cranfield: Farndale, E., Hailey, V. H., Keliher, C., & van Veldhoven, M.

Griffin, M. A., Neal, A., & Parker, S. K. (2007). A New Model of Work Role Performance: Positive Behavior in Uncertain and Interdependent Contexts. *Academy of Management Journal, 50*(2), 327-347.

Halbesleben, J. R. B. (2010). A meta-analysis of work engagement: relationships with burnout, demands, resources and consequences. In A. B. Bakker & M. P. Leiter (Eds.), *Work Engagement: A Handbook of Essential Theory and Research* (pp.102-117). East Sussex: Psychology Press.

Lombardo, M. M., & Eichinger, R. W. (2000). High Potentials as High Learners. *Human Resource Management, 39*(4), 321-329.

Meyer, J. P., Becker, T. E., & Vandenberghe, C. (2004). Employee Commitment and Motivation: A Conceptual Analysis and Integrative Model. *Journal of Applied Psychology, 89*(6), 991-1007.

Office for National Statistics (2008-2012). *Labour Market Statistics*. Retrieved from http://www.ons.gov.uk/.

Sarantakos, S. (1998). *Social Research.* Hampshire and London: Palgrave Macmillan.

Schaufeli, W. B., & Bakker, A. B. (2010). Defining and Measuring Engagement: Bringing clarity to the concept. In A. B. Bakker & M. P. Leiter (Eds.), *Work Engagement: A Handbook of Essential Theory and Research* (pp.10-24). East Sussex: Psychology Press.

Seligman, M. E. (1999). The president's address. *American Psychologist, 54*(8), 559-562.

Spreitzer, G. M., Lam, C. F., & Fritz, C. (2010). Engagement and human thriving: Complementary perspectives on energy and connections to work. In A. B. Bakker & M. P. Leiter (Eds.), *Work Engagement: A Handbook of Essential Theory and Research* (pp.132-146). East Sussex: Psychology Press.

Swailes, S. (2004). Commitment to Change: Profiles of commitment and in-role performance. *Personnel Review, 33*, 187-204.

Taris, T. W., Schaufeli, W. B., & Shimazu, A. (2010). The push and pull of work: The differences between workaholism and work engagement. In A. B. Bakker & M. P. Leiter (Eds.), *Work Engagement: A Handbook of Essential Theory and Research* (pp. 39-53). East Sussex: Psychology Press.

YSC (2014). *High potential identification and development: JDI Model.* Retrieved from http://www.ysc.com.

BUSINESS PSYCHOLOGIST AS PERFORMANCE CONSULTANT

Nigel Harrison

Business Psychology is a broad church and I guess all of us work in different ways. I want to share my experiences of working as a Business Psychologist in large global businesses and as an independent Performance Consultant.

What is Performance Consulting?

Put simply, Performance Consulting (PC) is a series of questions to ask a client: to turn them away from instant solutions like *"We need a training course"*; to examine the real needs behind the request; and, crucially, to quantify the business benefit from any solution.

The key questions are:

- Who is this for?
- What is happening now?
- What do we want to happen?
- What is the cost of the gap?

The PC role can be played by anyone from HR, Learning & Development (L&D) or IT who receives requests for solutions. Organisations typically train all their HR Business Partners and L&D Partners/Relationship Managers in a common approach called 'Front-end analysis' in the USA.

The PC approach is derived from Mager and Pipe's work on Performance Technology and was developed in 1995 by US authors Robinson and

Robinson in *Performance Consulting*. I have championed the approach in the UK in: *Improving Employee Performance* (part of the Sunday Times' *Creating Success* series), *How to be a True Business Partner by Performance Consulting* and *How to deal with Power and Manipulation by Performance Consulting*.

My experiences are personal, opinionated and anecdotal. Read them at your own risk; they are not intended to be research-based facts. I have worked with some of the biggest companies in the world in the Financial Services, Technical and Pharmaceutical business sectors, and for Governmental and Academic organisations. The examples I give are real but, to avoid sharing information within my non-disclosure agreements, disguised.

To give you an idea of their sources, I have helped the following businesses to adopt a Performance Consulting approach:

- LloydsTSB, HSBC, Central European Bank, Thomson Reuters
- Nokia, Ericsson, Qualcomm, Xerox
- AstraZeneca, Johnson and Johnson, GSK
- The Cabinet Office, London School of Economics and The International Labour Organisation.

The case for using a Performance Consulting approach

UK Training departments have been undergoing a transformation in the last few years of recession and slow growth. Training budgets are no longer an act of faith. Lean-minded executives scrutinise them just like every other part of the organisation's expenditure. The result has been massive cuts in traditional training and growth in e-learning, informal learning and Performance Consulting.

What are the big issues I deal with as a Business Psychologist?

This may surprise you, but my main value to the corporate client is to help them avoid jumping to conclusions too quickly and from implementing people solutions that are bound to fail.

In *Thinking, Fast and Slow,* Daniel Kahneman (2013) explains the difference between fast thinking, which is intuitive, and slow thinking which is diagnostic and based on evidence.

My clients live in complex systems and are under pressure to find instant solutions. Quick fixes abound. Let me give you some examples (which we'll look at later in more detail):

- A sales director says to the Chief Learning Officer, *"We have agreed a budget of £650,000 for more sales coaching next year".*
- An HR director for a major bank agrees to recruit 150 new lenders in order to meet the bank's targets next year.
- An HR specialist agrees to help terminate an employee because he regularly leaves the production line 15 minutes early.
- An HR director agrees to outsource recruitment because the line managers are fed up with the time taken to recruit replacement staff.

Would it interest you to know that in all these cases none of the solutions would have been effective? In fact, all would have involved an investment in cost, time and energy that probably would have made the original problem worse. In medical terms, they are all cases of malpractice. In these cases, the Learning & Development and HR 'professionals' did not diagnose the real problems and merely accepted the order.

You might think this is unusual, but leading consultants think that 60% of an organisation's problems are caused by previously implemented solutions. When I ask my clients, they think this is an under-estimate and it is more like 70-80%. Tony Law at BP came up with the term 'solutioneering' to describe this tendency.

More recently David Wilson described the 'Conspiracy of Convenience'. This beautifully illustrates the closed-loop system of order-taking, which used to be prevalent in large organisations. Training was seen as a good thing and executive boards allocated a percentage of their turnover to employee development as an act of faith. Held in a central budget, training was often seen as free by the line manager. Individuals started to expect training as a perk and as relaxation from the daily grind.

Training Needs Analysis often consisted of a senior manager stating, *"They need sales training"*. A more junior manager would then take the order to design and deliver an excellent off-site training course. Evaluation consisted of 'happy sheets' at the end of the course and of measuring whether the training budget had been spent.

Can you see any flaw in this system?

At the time not many people could, because everyone benefited from this conspiracy:

- Senior managers did not have to face up to their involvement in current performance problems.
- Training Managers received a budget and a feeling of doing something worthwhile.
- Trainers enjoyed running inspiring courses.
- Trainees enjoyed the time off work, some personal development, valuable networking and of course the food!

With so many people colluding in this fantasy, there is no wonder the 'Training Conspiracy' existed for so long.

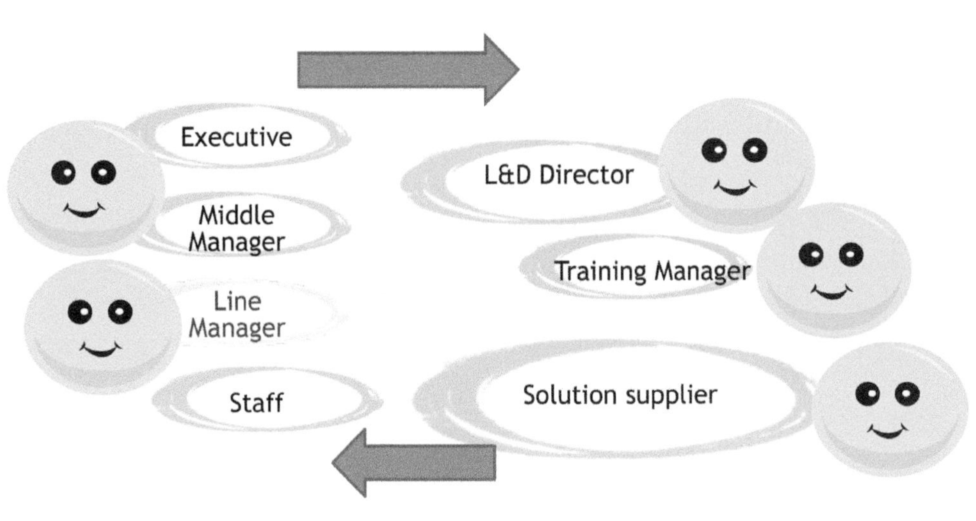

Figure 1: The "Conspiracy of Convenience"

The missing element of diagnosis

What is missing from this model is any element of diagnosis. Line managers are assuming that the solution is training. Training Managers see their roles as providers of solutions. No one is challenging the fundamental performance problem. The same solutioneering and order-taking model exists for HR and IT, and indeed for any solutions provider.

Heuristics

Learning directors are not the only people who jump to conclusions too early. We all do it. We need a fast way of thinking to cope with the complex world around us. Daniel Kahneman (2013, p. 12) warns:

"The essence of intuitive heuristics [is]: when faced with a difficult question, we often answer an easier one instead, usually without noticing the substitution".

If we add to this fast thinking bias, the normal defence mechanisms to stress, such as denial, avoidance and projection onto others, we can start to see the enormous pressures on busy executives to jump to quick solutions.

Let's go through the example (above) of the HR director who agrees to outsource recruitment because the line managers are fed up with the time taken to recruit replacement staff. This was not the complex question that the CEO faced. Unable to hit their service targets, his line managers blamed the fact that they had unfilled vacancies and not enough staff to handle the workload. Furthermore they blamed HR for the fact that it took 18 months to fill a vacancy. An interesting corollary was that, by operating short staffed, they reduced their costs and actually hit their cost-reduction targets. The CEO was exasperated and warned the HR director that she must outsource recruitment to solve the problem. His senior managers seemed satisfied that at last HR was getting the blame and something was being done.

I was approached to help the HR director with this problem, which she thought was leading potentially to a very expensive mistake. More later ...

What role does the Business Psychologist play?

i. The first attribute I brought to the problem was independence.
ii. I had a problem-analysis process (Performance Consulting).
iii. I had wide experience in solving people problems.
iv. As a Chartered Psychologist, I was committed to tell the customer my professional perception of the truth even if it was against my commercial self-interest.
v. I was also committed to empower the client to solve their own problems, rather than to leave them dependent on me or one particular solution.

To paraphrase thought leader Chris Argyris, the role of the consultant is to:

- Have a process.
- Know where you are in that process.
- Act like a mirror to the client.
- Be authentic at all times.

So what consulting interventions did I make in the case of *"Let's outsource recruitment"*? A first practical step was to run a series of one-day problem-analysis sessions with senior managers and HR wherein we took a diagnostic approach to identify the real problems, their causes and appropriate solutions.

As usual there was not one simple problem but many. To deal with this, we drew a systemic model of everyone's involvement in recruitment, the processes involved, timescales etc. This revealed that the HR part of the issue only accounted for three months of the delay in replacing staff. Much of the remainder was down to poor administration by line managers and lack of manpower planning by the senior managers themselves.

One of the key reasons for the performance problem was poor pay for key staff and lack of career opportunities, leading to high wastage rates. The line managers had not identified who the key players were and had no plans to retain them. They merely blamed HR for long term vacancies and an inability to meet customer service targets, while at the same time they received tacit approval for keeping costs low.

There were many pay-offs for jumping to the solution that HR recruitment should be outsourced, mainly that the spotlight on performance would temporarily be shifted away from the managers themselves.

My intervention was to be the independent consultant with a process. I literally made the protagonists take a blank sheet of paper and re-consider the problem using a diagnostic process. By roughly midday, everyone agreed that the original solution would not actually solve the problem. We then re-framed the question to: "*How do we retain more of our key staff?*"

The first step in answering this new question was to ask: "*Who are our key staff?*" Drawing a diagram of who is involved is a non-threatening way of creating a systemic model *with* the client. In this case we drew a model of a typical court including everyone involved from a crime being detected until sentencing. I then asked who the key players were in the successful performance of this system. We identified five key roles needed to maintain the efficiency of the process. They had originally challenged me by saying that this could not be done, as every work unit was different. By challenging them back with persistent open questions such as "*Who does this?*" "*What do they do?*" I annotated the systemic model to identify the five key roles for achieving the team's targets based on their key performance indicators. The other roles were less critical. This was a revelation to the managers and energised them for action by making their task so much more achievable.

We spent the remainder of the day on realistic solutions that were within the managers' control to keep the key players from leaving. The first action was to give them some personal attention by sending all the line managers out to talk to them about their personal goals, satisfaction and feelings about the job. We also asked them to find out their ideas about job enrichment and what would make them stay.

My consulting intervention took about seven days. It involved five one-day problem-analysis workshops for the key stakeholders around the country, so that they 'bought into' the re-framing of the problem and the new solutions.

The most immediate result of my consulting intervention was to stop the expenditure of £6 million for the outsourcing recruitment programme. Once the senior managers had faced up to the real problem (and avoided the expensive solutioneering), they were quite capable of implementing the solutions themselves.

The three practical steps for Performance Consulting

Engagement

- Build trust and rapport with the client.
- Treat the presenting problem as a starting point.
- Draw a systemic model *with* the client so you see the world though their eyes.
- Use the system diagram to understand the complexity of their issues.
- Build trust and rapport by forensic active listening whilst drawing the rich picture.

Problem analysis

- Use 'gap analysis' to help the client identify and face up to the real problem.
- Use persistent open questions to probe beneath generalisations.
- Expose metrics around the current and desired performance.
- Quantify the cost of the performance gap.

Solutions design

- Investigate a wide range of causes for the performance gap around knowledge, skill, motivation, environment and self-image.
- Brainstorm possible solutions to all of these causes.

- Pick those that will give best return for minimum effort.
- Commit the client and yourself to defined actions with dates.

Who is involved?

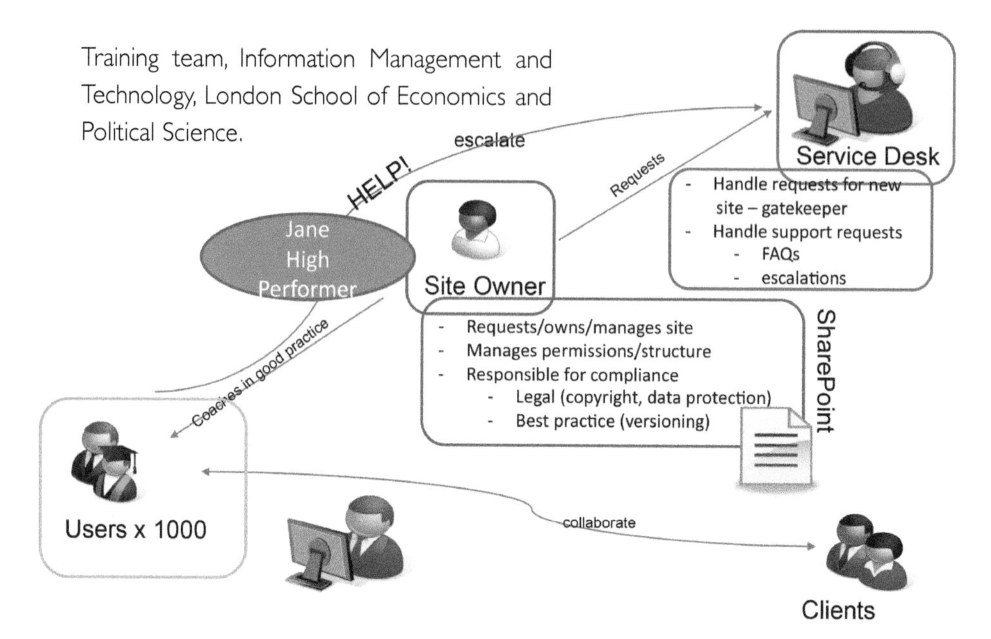

Figure 2: A typical "Who is involved diagram".

How do we investigate causes of performance problems?

There is actually quite a lot of useful theory that tells us how to investigate the cause of any problem. In 1978, Thomas Gilbert found that people do not perform because of a combination of things, usually in this order:

i. Inadequate information or reference material.
ii. Poor working environment or inadequate tools.
iii. Poor incentives.
iv. Lack of knowledge.
v. Lack of skill.
vi. Poor motivation.

Another key concept in Performance Consulting is the idea of quantifying the performance gap. I first came across the idea in the Learning Technology work of Mager and Pipe, who published *Analysing Performance Problems* in 1970. Their approach involved analysing performance discrepancies. The big thing I took from their complicated flow charts was the importance of comparing the existing performance with the desired performance and then quantifying the gap.

In 1995, Robinson and Robinson published *Performance Consulting – Moving Beyond Training*. Their approach has three main stages with ten steps.

As a practising consultant I tried to use the approaches above, but found them too unwieldy to 'hold in my head' when conversing with my clients. In 2000, Kogan Page asked me to write a short paperback aimed at managers called *Improving Employee Performance*. In it, I introduced a simplified seven-step process:

i. What is the problem?
ii. Who is involved?
iii. What is happening now?
iv. What do we want to happen?
v. What is the cost of the gap?
vi. What are the causes and potential solutions?
vii. Action planning.

The process is summarised in the diagram on the following page. (You can download a free copy from www.performconsult.co.uk)

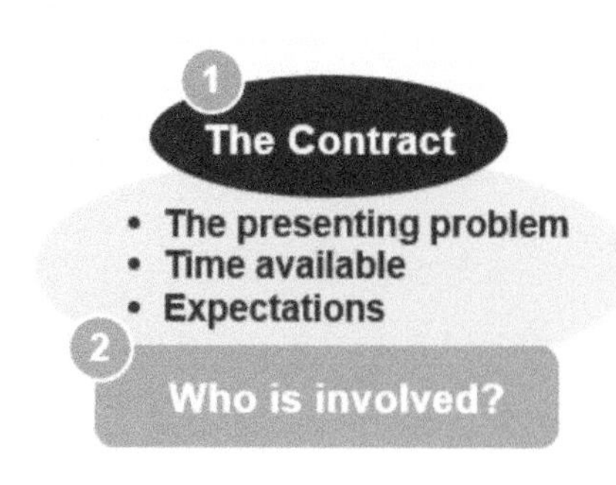

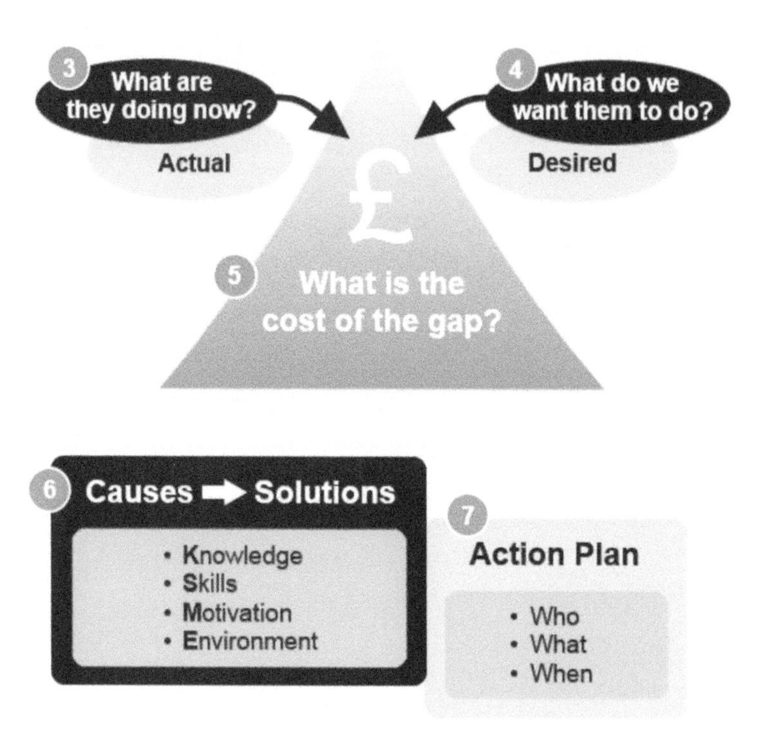

Figure 3: The 7-Step Performance Consulting diagram
by Nigel Harrison (2008)

In 2008, I used my experience of training several hundred internal Business Partners in Performance Consulting as the basis of another practical paperback, *How to be a True Business Partner by Performance Consulting* from which the above diagram is drawn. Topics included:

- What does it mean to be a business partner?

- The skills needed to be an effective partner.
- The irrational organisation.
- What sort of relationship do our clients really want?
- Building your resilience to overcome setbacks.

Thinking Traps

Much of my role as a Business Psychologist is about making psychological theory practical and useful for internal consultants working in HR, L&D, IT. My external role is to give them the support, confidence and credibility to challenge these long-held assumptions and beliefs:

- HR, L&D and I.T. are solutions providers.
- When a client asks for something it is the order.
- It is our role to take orders.
- When the client says: "we just need this" that is what they need.
- When the client says they have no time to discuss it, they have no time.
- It is not our job to develop the business case for company investment.

Common thinking traps:

- Jumping to conclusions – solutioneering.
- Tunnel vision – Your mind automatically taking shortcuts and not seeing the bigger picture.
- Personalising – seeing it as 'my' problem.

You will have your own favourite "thinking traps", patterns of behaviour learnt over time that work for you. For example, you may be a glass half-empty person or be convinced that all senior managers are useless. When you receive an e-mail from a client you might automatically think that something is wrong or when you are in a meeting your 'inner voice' might constantly be saying, "I need to come up with a solution".

Hints to avoid 'thinking traps':

- Pause (Breathe).
- Listen to your "inner voice", but don't react to it immediately.
- Hold back from jumping into your thinking trap.
- Gather more data.
- Break the situation into:
  - Who is involved?
  - What is happening now?
  - What do we want to happen?
- Ask yourself: "What is real?"

Performance Consulting in Action

Let's look at another of the examples I've already outlined.

Remember the sales director who says to the Chief Learning Officer (CLO), "*We have agreed a budget of £650,000 for more sales coaching next year*"?

In this case, the CLO was suspicious. An external supplier's sales coaching had excellent feedback from the senior managers. Their bosses were very enthusiastic, but had it had a real impact on performance? The CLO asked me to run a one-day problem-analysis session with some of the Sales Directors and some of his learning specialists just to check that this was a suitable investment.

For my intervention I prepared a blank wall covered with flip charts, which I would later ask the ten stakeholders to face. The CLO introduced the session by saying that I was an external consultant, hired to help them take a fresh look at the problem before they commissioned more sales coaching.

After covering aims and ground rules and sharing the problem-analysis process, I asked simple, open questions in order to draw the systemic model, for example:

- What do you sell?
- Who do you sell to?
- And who does that?
- What outputs do they produce?
- How many do they do at the moment?

After then asking the group what was the desired performance of this system, we moved on to the key issues stopping the people involved in the system from performing, for example:

- Lack of time.
- Short term budgets.
- Incentives linked to old products.
- Five different sales processes across Europe.
- Senior Managers not taking time to coach their subordinates.
- Long-winded sales induction training that was not relevant to the job.

About mid-morning, I eventually asked the question: *"Would more sales coaching help to close this performance gap?"* The managers' answer was a resounding no, because they said they already did not have enough time to coach. We jointly agreed that the priority issues were:

- The different sales processes.
- Out-of-date incentives.
- Too much top-down reporting robbing the sales managers of time.
- A slow and ineffective sales induction training programme.

The group of senior managers and sales specialists agreed among themselves what the key actions were to move forward. We managed to stop the expenditure of £650,000 to the coaching company and to re-direct the investment into the new, slick sales induction, which used significant amounts of online flexible learning.

In this case my intervention cost two days' consulting and immediately saved the company £650,000 – not to mention the positive effects of helping them focus on the right things to do to achieve European sales targets worth several millions.

How far has Performance Consulting been adopted in the UK?

David Ulrich first modelled business partnership in the USA as a route for HR to play a strategic role in business 20 years ago. Since then his model has both been developed and adopted by many organisations across the world.

The benefits of this approach are that it allows centralisation and cost-reduction of shared corporate resources, while the client has a one-stop-shop for internal suppliers. The job of the Business Partner is to help analyse the client's needs and contract with appropriate suppliers. When the role works well, the business partner is respected, stops a lot of solutioneering and helps to prioritise a set of realistic requirements for suppliers.

Most UK organisations have adopted the Business Partner model. They have converted HR and L&D Specialists into Business Partners, and some organisations have adopted Performance Consulting as their approach for initial meetings with clients. Charles Jennings even claimed that Performance Consulting is the number one theme for UK L&D in 2014.

What is holding us back?

Historically many L&D departments worked as a closed system with no links to the system that actually produces business performance. Many L&D managers and HR stay in the 'safe' side of the tracks as 'order-takers' and 'specialist' providers. Just changing their name to Business Partner or Learning and Performance Consultant is not going to change this overnight.

Reality and fantasy in organisations

At the end of my Performance Consulting workshop, I stress that the process is a rational diagnostic one. But I also stress that, in my opinion, most organisations are emotional power-ridden places, where some decisions are made based on fantasy rather than adult rationality.

What about my earlier example of the HR director for a major bank, who agrees to recruit 150 new lenders in order to meet the bank's targets next year?

I am sorry to say that we did not catch this one in time. The HR department rushed into panic mode and focused all its resources on an intensive recruitment programme. They found it very hard to find the required talent. Those who did join had six-month notice periods to work. When they arrived, they needed company induction and coaching to adjust to the new bank and its sector. This all demanded the high-performing lenders' time, meaning that the bank fell further behind its target, missing it by more than if they had done nothing at all. In this case, a well-meaning and conscientious HR Director had acted as an 'order-taker' and ended up being the scapegoat.

As a Psychologist, I believe that most of us use defence mechanisms to protect our fragile self-image. Commonly, we project blame onto others. We are in denial about problems and we avoid difficult messages that mean that we have to change.

As Performance Consultants, this avoidance and projection appears to us as solutioneering: the desire to move quickly to solutions (that do not involve us in changing), instead of facing up to our own problems and the need to change.

Synthesis of solutions

We don't just help clients to face up to their problems and leave them to it. A key part of the Performance Consulting process is to work with the clients to build powerful combined solutions to solve the real problems. This is where much of the expertise in psychological theory and solutions comes in. It is important to simplify the theory and work with the client towards workable, elegant solutions.

As Steve Jobs (2012, p. 110) said: "Simplicity is the ultimate sophistication. When you first look at a problem, it seems easy because you don't know that much about it, then you get into the problem and you see it's really complicated and you come up with all these convoluted solutions.

Most people stop there. But the key is to keep going until you find the underlying principle of the problem and sort of come full circle with a beautiful, elegant solution that works".

He could have been talking about Performance Consulting.

Knowledge is useless until it is used

Writing this has allowed me to reflect on 30 years' experience of working as a Business Psychologist and Performance Consultant. What conclusions do I draw and what does it mean for Business Psychology?

My Masters in Occupational Psychology from Birkbeck, University of London, gave me a wide range of theory and models, which in turn allowed me to see that no one model is true. This gave me the confidence not to be too closely aligned to one set of solutions.

No one in the business world will pay you to tell them about theory. What they want is practical application of theory to help them solve their performance problems. So, in addition to theory and knowledge, I believe we also need practical relationship and consulting skills.

In addition we need a problem analysis and consulting process. It does not really matter which one as long as you can use it, know where you are in the process and help the client through it in an authentic way.

My list is not finished yet, because even given theory, knowledge, skills and process, the business will still not work with you unless you have rapport, credibility and trust. This usually means that you need to have similar business experience to them – you need to be involved in marketing, selling and invoicing from your own business, for example – or to have played 'real' roles in 'real' business like those of your clients. In my case, I worked in Personnel and then Training for large global companies, before starting my own business and then working for a range of large clients.

Finally, we need to be brave.

Much of the value we add is helping clients face up to their own problems when it would be cognitively less demanding to follow easier solutions. Organisations pretend to be rational places, but power, status, influence and manipulation are just under the surface. As Business Psychologists, we often feel the discomfort from challenging a common fantasy. We suffer projected anger and rejection, as well as positive life-enhancing surges of energy from working with our clients as partners. Finally, we do not leave our clients dependent on us, which means that they often need to grow away from us.

It is a challenging, valuable and important role.

Please contact me if you would like a free abridged download from *"How to be a True Business Partner by Performance Consulting"* nigel@performconsult.co.uk.

References

Block, P. (1981). *Flawless Consulting.* San Diego, CA: Pfeiffer and Co.

Gilbert, T. F. (1978). Human Competence: Engineering Worthy Performance. *NSPI Journal, 17*(9), 19-27.

Harrison, N. (2014). *How to deal with Power and Manipulation by Performance Consulting.* Sheffield, England: Performance Consulting UK Ltd.

Harrison, N. (2008). *How to be a True Business Partner by Performance Consulting.* Sheffield, England: Performance Consulting UK Ltd.

Harrison, N. (2000). *Improving Employee Performance.* London: Kogan Page.

Jennings, C. (2014). *Top Five Trends in L&D in 2014.*Retrieved from https://www.702010forum.com/Posts/view/top-five-trends-in-l-d-in-2014.

Jobs, S. (2012).*The Man who thought different*. London: Karen Blumenthal Bloomsbury.

Kahneman, D. (2013). *Thinking, Fast and Slow.* New York, NY: Farrar, Strauss and Giroux.

Mager, R. F., & Pipe, P. (1970). *Analysing Performance Problems.* Atlanta, GA: Belmont, CA: Fearon Pitman Publishers.

Robinson, D. G., & Robinson, J. C. (1995). *Performance Consulting.* San Francisco, CA: Berret-Koehler Publishers.

Ulrich, D. (1997). *Human Resource Champions.* Boston, MA: Harvard University Press.

Wilson, D. (2014). *Charles Jennings – Crystal balling with Learnnovators.* Retrieved from http://learnnovators.com/interview/charles-jennings-crystal-balling-learnnovators/.

RAISING THE BAR AND MAKING BUSINESS PSYCHOLOGY MATTER

Steve Whiddett

The purpose of Business Psychology is "to attain effective and sustainable performance for both individuals and organisations" (ABP purpose statement, 2014). This purpose will not be fulfilled by focusing our energies on promoting, selling or seeking opportunities to use our tools and techniques.

Too often interventions in organisations appear driven by knowledge of tools and techniques rather than by an understanding of the causes of performance issues (Solvik & Heller, 2007). These interventions are attractive because they offer quick responses, addressing issues that are easy to see and relatively easy to deal with. Business Psychology's benefits come from interventions driven by what is necessary to do and by addressing what is not so easy to see. However, like taking medicine or eating our greens, doing what is necessary can be a challenge that makes easier alternatives more attractive (Iyengar, 2010; Kahneman, 2012) and consequently more popular.

To deliver the benefits of Business Psychology we need to understand and manage the challenges to doing what is necessary and resist just doing what is easier. These can be significant challenges, but they can be overcome. In overcoming them we can fulfil our purpose and develop our reputation for being the resource that organisations turn to for interventions that deliver both short and long term benefits.

These challenges reflect normal patterns of human behaviour. People pay attention to issues that they believe warrant immediate action and people's actions are affected by how they feel (Frijda, 1986). Such patterns can be seen in client behaviour and also our responses. Clients appear confident requesting interventions that have an observable impact on current, visible issues – even if that impact might be short lived. However, they appear less willing to accept advice that relates to addressing the less evident causes, especially when there will be no immediately detectable benefits from dealing with them. We can compare this with fire-fighting and fire-prevention. A fire is a visible symptom of a problem, a set of conditions, and addressing the fire has observable, immediate and obvious results. Fire prevention stops new fires occurring by avoiding or removing the conditions that create fires. Prevention therefore has no observable, obvious immediate or future outcome. Similarly in business, addressing causes would prevent symptoms from recurring yet might not create new and observable outcomes; evidence for efficacy is the lack of something rather than the creation of something.

These challenges favour responding to clients' requests to deal with symptoms they have identified, using tools and techniques that they want and that alternative providers are ready to supply if we choose not to. Agreeing to these requests may do some good short term, but is unlikely to deliver sustainable benefits for the client or their provider and it is not doing Business Psychology. Our metaphorical fire is seen as the problem. Once it is put out the problem is deemed to have been resolved – even though the conditions that created it might still exist. A professional fire-fighting team would carry out a causal investigation and take action to prevent a further fire. Our practice needs to include fire prevention even when fires need to be put out; we can and should do both.

We can address the challenges to doing Business Psychology by understanding and managing the influences on our approach. To help with this I am presenting a model that enables practitioners and clients to:

- see the symptoms and causes of issues more clearly;
- identify what is necessary to do and increase confidence in doing it;
- maximise the benefits from doing Business Psychology.

Influences that encourage symptoms focused interventions

A key influence on symptoms focused interventions appears to be an assumption that our primary interest is in people. This shows in our alignment with professions that focus on people, e.g. human resources, personal development and training. This person-centric position places attention on, and an almost complete devotion to, what we can do to people rather than what we can do for people. This attention is encouraged and maintained with frequent redefining of observable people issues, an expanding supply of tools and techniques related to these issues and the people centred models we use. Following this approach we come to be seen as people experts not performance experts.

Generally, attitudes, skills and knowledge (ASKs) have been used in job descriptions, and when job performance doesn't meet expectations tools and techniques based on ASKs are called on to address the mismatch. As criteria became more sophisticated behaviours were included (Boyatzis, 1982; Whiddett & Hollyforde, 2003) and tools and techniques evolved based on hybrid criteria. Appraisals and performance management processes focus on the person – what people are expected to do, what people achieve and how people may need to be improved. Goals are set for the person, the person's progress is monitored, feedback is given on the person's performance and how the person performed is reviewed and evaluated. Performance improvement focuses on developing people and on activities designed to change the person.

Business psychology is about attaining effective and sustainable performance for the person and the organisation, i.e. doing something for the person not necessarily to the person. This shifts attention away from making people more able to deal with stress or more skilled at managing their own behaviour and onto making work settings less stressful and developing organisational cultures that encourage and support appropriate behaviour.

Business psychology needs to focus and keep its attention on effective and sustainable performance for the person and the organisation, which requires attending to the range of influences that can affect performance outcomes. Few models in popular practice help to do this. Many of the influences on performance, whether or not intentional, are rarely included in practice models. ASKs may be included, but not the influences that might limit their use. Behaviours might be included, but not the influences that encourage or discourage them. Goals and tasks might be included, but not the influences that help or hinder their achievement. Clear expectations about performance are essential to enable performance to be assessed, managed or changed and yet expectations are frequently vague or not understood. Outcomes are considered separately from, or with no reference to, the behaviours that would produce them and behaviours are considered separately from, or with no reference to, the outcomes they are intended to produce. These models can be useful in matching tools and techniques to the symptoms of performance issues (or rather the person displaying the symptoms) but they do not help to identify or address the causes.

Many of these models are like a speedometer informing us of road speed. Relying on a speedometer to manage performance implies that performance is just about road speed. A speedometer focuses interventions on tools and techniques that can affect road speed, such as the accelerator or brake, and how we use them. If we consider road speed along with engine speed, engine temperature, oil pressure, air temperature, fuel consumption, vehicle direction and passenger comfort then performance becomes more complex and more meaningful. Our tools and techniques for managing road speed aren't sufficient for managing this more complex notion of performance. Information about influences acting upon this new view of performance such as driving conditions, legal restrictions, vehicle characteristics, driver characteristics and deadlines are needed to establish a sufficient understanding of expected and actual performance. We need this breadth and depth of understanding to help identify which influences require attention if we are to manage performance. A dashboard of instruments is needed to help us achieve sustainable performance for the vehicle and its passengers.

Business psychology needs something like a dashboard to focus our attention on the influences that contribute to performance.

The dashboard that I use combines the science of human behaviour with experience of the world of work gained through many years of consultancy practice and business management. Its focus is sustainable performance. It covers all factors that can contribute to that performance and it is simple – but not simplistic. It shows what business psychology is about and can help express why investing in fire prevention and not just fire-fighting is essential for sustainable performance. This model emphasises that being performance experts includes, but is not limited to, being people experts. It takes us from being narrow knowledge experts assisting in aspects of Human Resources management to a role that might be better described as a business performance process consultant (as suggested by Schein, 1999).

Indicators of performance are at the centre of the dashboard and influences on performance surround them (Figure 1). The dashboard provides a holistic view of a situation and recognises the person as just one source of the influences on performance within it.

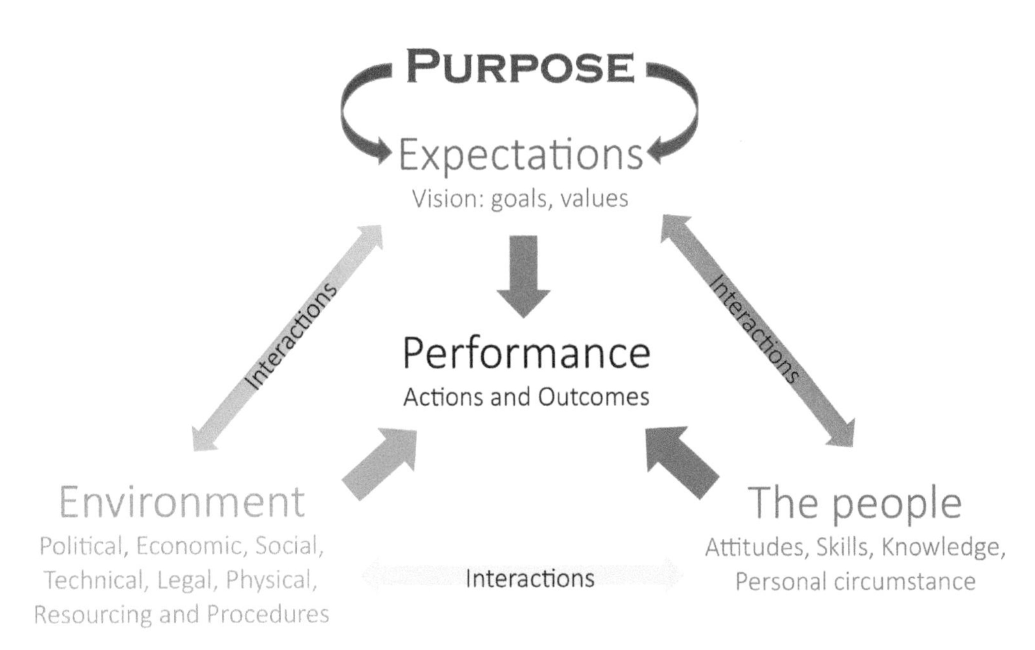

Figure 1: The Situation Dashboard

This dashboard also provides a reminder that influences on performance interact with each other. If influences in the environment inhibit or do not support expectations, performance will not fulfil those expectations. If the environment supports expectations but not the person then again, performance will not be what is needed. If the person is not matched to the expectations even a perfect environment may not produce the desired performance. If the person does not have the ASKs required for working in the available environment then outcomes and behaviours will not be the ones needed to fulfil the expectations. Of these potential causes of performance issues only the last two are likely to warrant an intervention primarily targeted at the person. Even in these cases interventions can be made to address performance without changing the person, as illustrated in case studies below. If we only think of performance management as people management we adopt a simplistic model and will miss opportunities to address substantial performance issues.

The dashboard represents a situation made of influences that interact to create observable outcomes and behaviours. It also draws attention to something easily overlooked when deciding on an intervention: that what is observed can be judged very differently depending on the position of the observer. The individual who sets expectations, the person expected to deliver, other individuals within the situation and external observers may all see the same outcomes and behaviours yet have different views about why they are happening and what to do about them. The driver in the car, the passenger, an automotive engineer and an external observer – say a police officer – may each develop different theories about why a car is performing as it is and what should be done about changing its performance. A dashboard can help develop a common understanding of what is happening in a situation and why. When there is no consensus about interventions to improve performance this is especially important as decisions can then at least be made knowing which influences are being given priority.

To help communicate the essential themes in this dashboard, I use a model that likens performance to light. Three primary light colours – blue, green and red – combine to create white light. From the situation dashboard, three sets of influences, expectations (represented by blue), the environment (green) and the person (red) combine to create outcomes and behaviours that are needed (white).

Figure 2: The Model – where we see performance

Wherever the person interacts with the environment or expectations there will be outcomes and behaviours (within the dashed area).

- Outcomes and behaviours that are needed will be produced when the environment supports the expectations and both support a person with the necessary ASKs and personal circumstances (the white area).
- Unwanted outcomes and behaviours will be produced when the person and environment support each other but do not support or are not supported by the expectations (the yellow area).
- Unwanted outcomes and behaviours will also be produced when the person and expectations support each other but are not supported by the environment (the magenta area).

Unwanted outcomes and behaviours are often undesirable.

Ideally, the three sets of influences will overlap to a high degree, and there will be minimal overlap between just two sets. The model can be presented as a Venn diagram to illustrate how good or poor a situation is, judged by the proportion of outcomes and behaviours that contribute to fulfilling the expectations. In Figure 3, the overlap between sets of influences represents the degree to which they support each other and shows the consequent outcomes and behaviours.

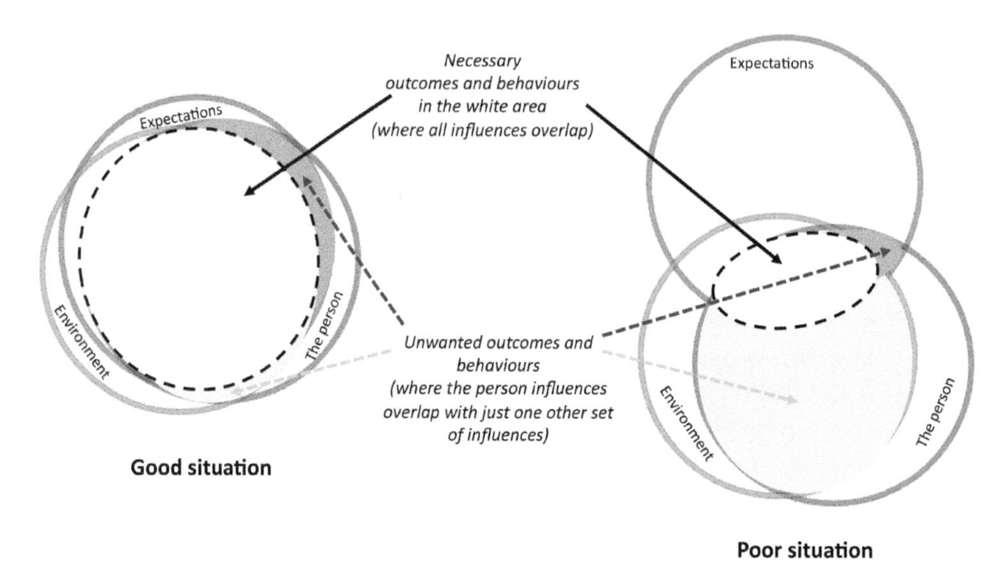

Figure 3: Good and Poor Situations

Unwanted outcomes and behaviours that do not contribute to expectations may be problematic in themselves. They are also symptoms of more substantial problems within the situation, i.e. support issues between the expectations, the environment and the person.

The Model in Action

This model can be used to explore performance in any type of situation including hypothetical situations. Specific expectations, environment and person influences will vary depending on the type of situation as shown in the case studies below.

The ability to use the model to describe what 'should be' and use it again to describe 'what is' can be very useful when diagnosing a performance issue and when attempting to change a situation to make it more productive.

By comparing two views of a situation we can:

- understand why outcomes and behaviours that were needed didn't occur (A and B were needed and did not happen or were not to a necessary standard);
- understand why unwanted outcomes and behaviours happened (A and B were needed but D or E occurred when D or E were not wanted);
- clarify and differentiate between symptoms and causes;
- target interventions appropriate to symptoms and/or causes.

To illustrate these points here are a few short case studies. In these case studies, influences contributing to outcomes and behaviours provide a more complete understanding of the situation and enable us to identify interventions that can address causes and not just the apparent issue, the symptoms. These situations, which are not unusual, show that interventions to address unwanted outcomes and behaviours, while apparently reasonable, would not have resolved the causes or prevented the situations from reoccurring.

In each case the situation to be addressed is described briefly then represented using the model. I focus on one set of influences at a time to highlight how each contributes to understanding the situation within the case study and choice of interventions. In practice, attention would be given to the whole dashboard.

We start by looking at expectations as these set challenges for performance in situations (Vroom, 1964). Expectations prescribe what is to be achieved and what performance is likely to be judged against. The most common and significant problems generated by expectations are when they are unrealistic, unclear or ambiguous. Unrealistic expectations are those that are not supported by the environment or the ASKs or personal circumstances of people expected to fulfil the expectations. Unrealistic expectations show in problems with the outcomes and behaviours of those who are eventually 'punished' for not fulfilling them.

In a situation where we do not know what is expected of us or we are presented with ambiguous expectations we might either seek clarity or have to make assumptions. Asking for clarity can mean challenging senior people to make explicit something that they may think they have already made clear, so relying on assumptions can feel preferable (Bandura, 1977; McClelland, 1985).

This first case study deals with unclear or ambiguous expectations.

To address underperformance in its regional operations, a housing association asked for help to redesign its appraisal system and retrain appraisers.

The unwanted outcomes and behaviours: consistently poor performance across regions, poor appraisal ratings in all regions, high number of uncompleted job and regional goals (and consequently not delivering corporate goals) and disputes over appraisal ratings.

The apparent issue: poor appraisal process and skills in managing performance. This view was reinforced with evidence from an internal survey which highlighted difficulties using the appraisal process, compared goals set versus goals achieved and uncovered widespread dissatisfaction with the appraisal documentation.

I helped to redesign the appraisal materials and developed training programmes for reviewers and reviewees. I was then asked to pilot the training in one region prior to rolling the programme out nationally.

The first training event was for the most senior managers in the pilot region. During the training I used the model to help the managers describe how they aligned local expectations (goals for the region) with national strategic goals and how they ensured local expectations were realistic. The managers could not complete the task. It became clear that local expectations were based on the managers' beliefs about the services they should provide locally and were not based on corporate goals or corporate resourcing.

The main causes of poor performance were: a mismatch between local and strategic goals; and local goals that were not supported by local operating conditions and head office resourcing.

Senior managers did not (or would not) recognise that they had a role to play in managing alignment between local and strategic expectations. The new appraisal process and the training would have had little if any long term effect on performance had this situation not been addressed. I used the model to help the managers see that they were setting up situations that would fail. A workshop exercise helped managers clarify their roles in aligning local goals at all job levels with strategic goals. A substantial goal setting and strategy alignment module was added to the training for all managers. Additionally on-the-job support was provided through action learning sets facilitated by appraisal change champions. These interventions had the desired effect and following evaluation of the revised pilot the programme was rolled out nationally.

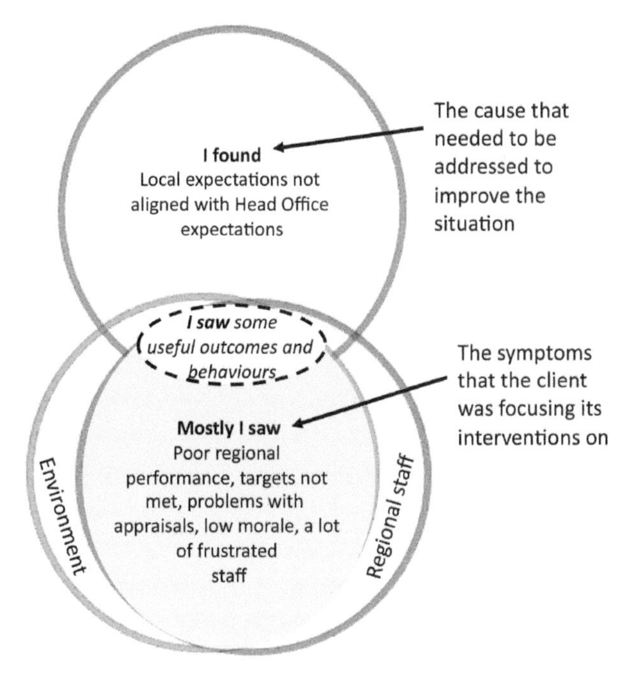

Figure 4: The Housing Association Situation

Successes happen when the environment supports both the expectations and the individuals working to fulfil those expectations (Thierry & Koopman-Iwema, 1984). If the environment does not support expectations then those expectations are unrealistic. Nevertheless, individuals may, incorrectly, be seen as responsible for not fulfilling the expectations. If individuals have the necessary ASKs to fulfil expectations but the environment inhibits use of their ASKs, individuals may, again incorrectly, be seen as responsible.

A private equity firm bought a successful but underperforming manufacturing company with the intention of improving its performance and value. The firm had concerns about the company's ability to fulfil their expectations and appointed a new chief executive to help make improvements and to prepare the company for sale. I was brought in to help develop the ability of the management team to deliver a new strategy.

The unwanted outcomes and behaviours: strategic business development was not happening and managers tended to behave more as operational than strategic managers, giving priority to looking after their individual areas of responsibility.

The apparent issue: lack of ability in the management team.

I reviewed past reports and noted their strategies had been based on clear, well-reasoned expectations (goals) and that the business development goals in these strategies had not been acted on. The 30+ members of the senior team were keenly focused on the company's core competences of designing and manufacturing highly specialised equipment and that is what they delivered.

I provided a process by which team members could identify behaviours needed when working to fulfil each of the goals in the new strategy. Team members were then asked to identify existing environmental (structures, systems, resourcing etc.) and personal influences (e.g. ASKs) that might inhibit use of the behaviours and achievement of the goals. The team identified their operating style, meeting arrangements and the management structure as not supporting some necessary behaviours and strategic business development goals. The team acknowledged that behaviours relating to supporting colleagues, sharing information, openness to ideas and capitalising on others' strengths were necessary but lacking in the way the team worked. These were behaviours that the team members' ASKs suggested they should be able to use.

The main cause of not delivering business development goals was identified as a work environment that did not support or promote the use of ASKs that were needed and that team members already had.

Changes were made to reporting lines, ownership of goals and how meetings were conducted. Service level agreements were developed between individual managers that depended on each other's roles or departments. Behaviours changed and there was a greater focus on business development goals and on engaging with and supporting colleagues. Developing the ability of the management team was achieved by changing their environment and not by directly changing the individuals. The private equity firm bought the company for $140m and sold it two years later (within 18 months of this intervention) for $375m.

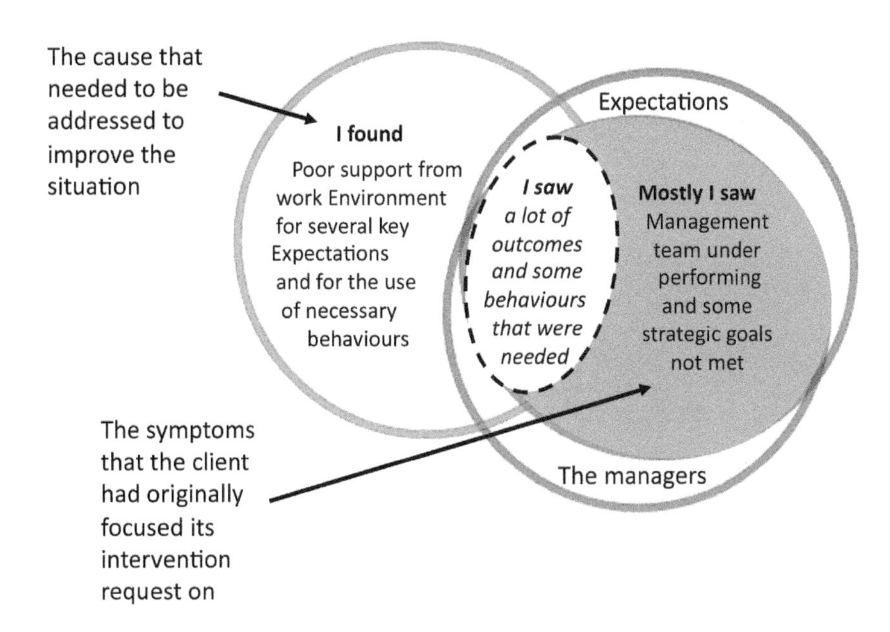

Figure 5: The private equity firm's manufacturing company situation

A telephone call centre had a retention problem. Staff turnover, a very visible measure, was out of control, with recruiters working full time to fill vacancies.

The unwanted outcomes and behaviours: poor performance, low morale, disengaged staff, people leaving shortly after being recruited.

The apparent issue: disengagement and poor motivation.

The HR team was asking for help to develop an intervention that would motivate and reengage staff. People-focused interventions were being used, such as individual rewards to motivate staff.

I interviewed new recruits and those who were about to leave.

The main cause of staff turnover was, ironically, the recruitment process, an environmental factor.

The recruitment process gave job applicants an inaccurate picture of the job and work conditions. This contributed to new recruits' beliefs about what they would experience and how they would be supported by the company. Once these beliefs were proven invalid new recruits became disengaged and many resigned. A new recruitment process was developed based on actual job demands and the true work environment. This provided applicants with realistic job previews and a pre-application self-assessment process based on descriptions of working conditions and tasks. A simulation of the work environment was included in the assessment stage. Staff turnover quickly dropped to close to the industry average.

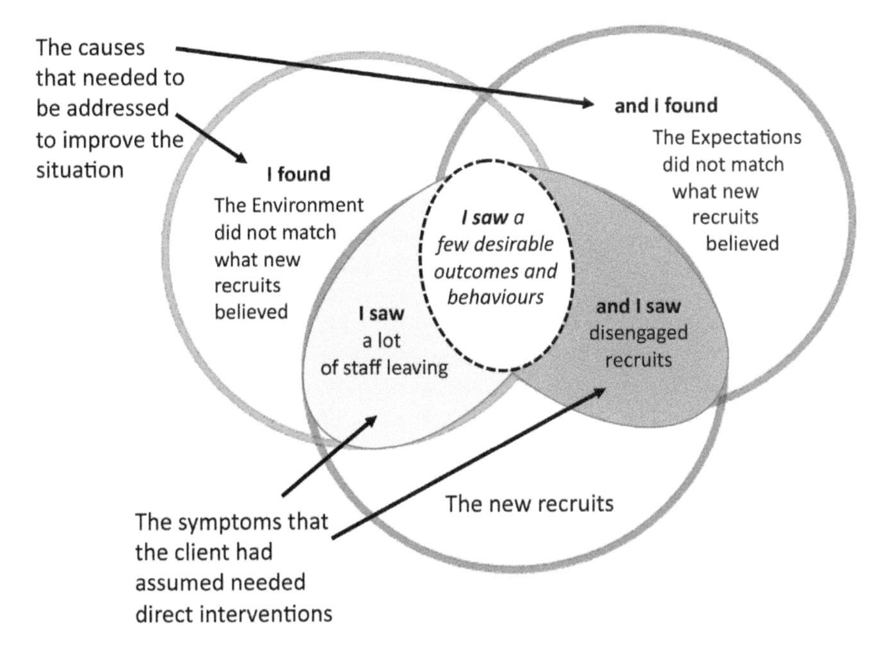

Figure 6: The call centre situation

If the environment supports both the expectations and the use of ASKs required to fulfil them, we need to look at the person trying to fulfil the expectations when performance is not as expected. The most likely cause will be a lack, or inhibited use, of some necessary ASKs. Even so, the cause may not always be obvious and the solution need not involve developing or replacing the person.

While working with a regional authority I observed but was unable to intervene in this next situation. The authority was trying to respond to significant cuts in its funding. Department heads had been asked to produce plans to show how their departments could be managed to balance departmental costs with reduced incomes and without affecting essential services.

The unwanted outcomes and behaviours: after several months, plans had not been produced and managers appeared reluctant to cooperate with the request.

The apparent issue: managers' reluctance to commit to a way of working that they felt they were being forced to comply with.

The authority provided guidelines for producing plans and individual counselling to help the managers, but this did not improve the situation.

The main cause of delays in producing plans was neither attitude nor motivation.

Most departments were administered, scheduling tasks and overseeing budgets, rather than managing costs and efficiency. Business plans and the principles behind them were unfamiliar to these managers. The help provided had been to structure the necessary information to produce a plan, but no support had been given for how to gather the information. Managers lacked the skills to analyse departmental functioning or to recognise and diagnose inefficiencies. During the next 18 months new operating principles were introduced in parallel with significant cost reductions made through redundancies. These interventions were designed to take direct action on costs and the inactivity of managers. Managers effectively received new parameters for the operation of their departments, which addressed the symptoms. Managers still lacked the knowledge and skills to manage, rather than administer, the cause of the issues.

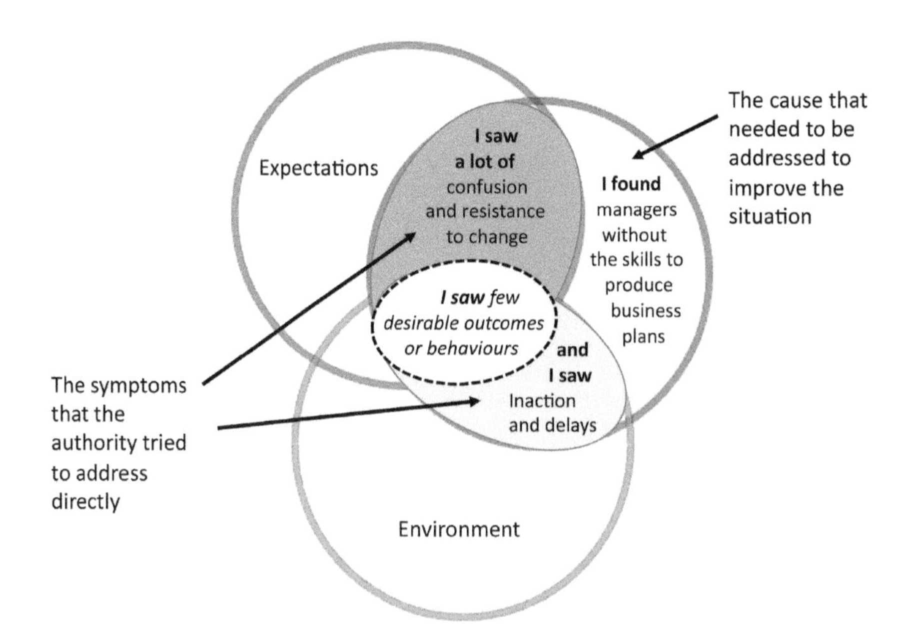

Figure 7: The regional authority situation

Here is an example of using the model to look ahead to match existing staff to future job demands. As part of a major change programme a water company embarked on the redesign of some of its jobs. A consultancy created job designs based on tasks required to produce desired outputs. The new jobs were based on similarities in the skills and knowledge required to complete tasks. I was asked to help design a process to assess the suitability of applicants for one of the new jobs. The majority of applicants would be staff in existing jobs that were to be phased out.

The unwanted outcomes and behaviours: inefficient working and unacceptable behaviour from some existing job holders.

The apparent issue: job tasks were not organised for efficient performance and some job holders had attitudes that were not suited to some key tasks.

Expectations for the future situation: the job designs and assessment process would enable the majority of current job holders to be identified as suitable for the new jobs and individuals with attitudes not suited to the new jobs could be identified.

The consultancy provided me with its task descriptions for the jobs but not the skills and knowledge requirements. I agreed to do the work, provided I could include field based research to identify the ASKs required for the job rather than the desk-based deductive approach employed by the consultancy. Using a multi-method job analysis approach I explored task demands with a sample of employees who already completed or managed some of the new-job tasks in their existing jobs. It became apparent that a few physical skills would inhibit some existing job holders from completing tasks in the new job that they were able to complete successfully in their existing jobs. For example, the new job would require people to visit construction sites to collect information that they would then use to produce construction drawings and work plans. In existing jobs staff produced construction drawings and work plans based on information provided by colleagues in other roles. The new job could not be fulfilled by individuals with impaired vision or restricted mobility. However, individuals with impaired vision or restricted mobility were performing well on many of the tasks that would be required in the new job.

The unwanted outcomes and behaviours: potential for the job design to limit unnecessarily the number of existing staff that could be considered suitable for the new jobs.

The cause: the way in which the jobs had been designed.

The organisation accepted my analysis and together we produced new job designs that avoided potential unfair treatment of existing staff and improved the pool of candidates from which it could draw in future recruitment programmes.

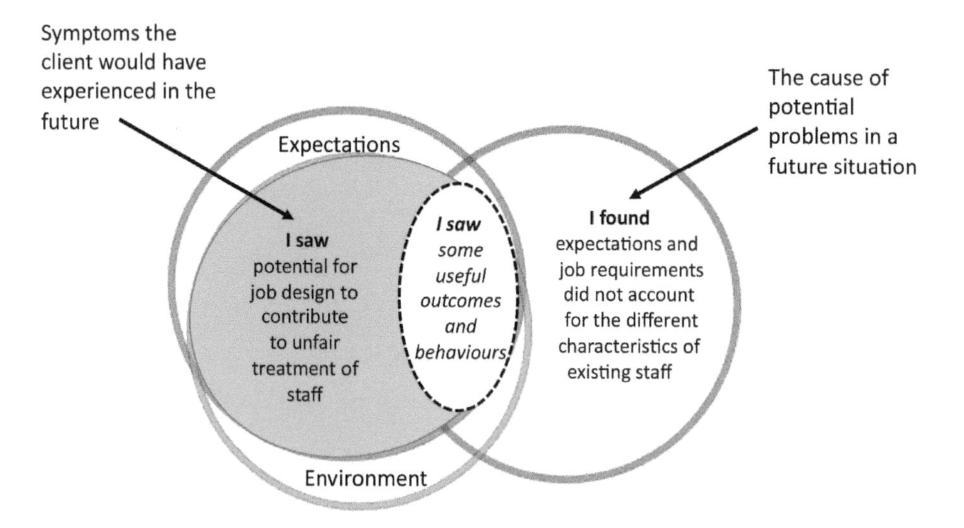

Figure 8: The Water Company's potential situation

These case studies have focused on mis-matches between expected outcomes and behaviours and those that were actually observed. In each example the intervention to address the apparent issues or symptoms would not have resolved the underlying and less obvious cause. It is in our nature to give attention to the fire and once it is out to move on to put out other fires. The model was an essential tool in identifying interventions that dealt with symptoms and the dissonance in situations that contributed to them – the causes.

The model can also help to understand and deal with behaviours and outcomes that are unwanted, even when these appear to make little sense. This is particularly important when unwanted behaviours and outcomes are damaging, such as emotional outbursts, bullying, surprising resignations, reckless decisions and damage to property and equipment. Often these behaviours and outcomes are tolerated unless they are considered too serious to ignore, in which case 'the offender' may be punished. Again, treating the symptom without necessarily addressing the cause.

When influences create more dissonance than the person in the situation can cope with, outcomes and behaviours may have little if anything to do with trying to fulfil others' expectations. Outcomes and behaviours that appear more emotional than rational can indicate that the person in the situation is choosing actions to make them feel more in control or to relieve how they feel (Goleman, 1996). Outcomes and behaviours in these situations can prove damaging for the person and for the organisation as they are often motivated by feelings with little if any conscious direction. The dark side of personality might be assessed using our tools. This model can help organisations to identify, manage and possibly avoid situations that could contribute to unwanted outcomes and dark side behaviours (Kaiser, LeBreton, & Hogan, 2013; Whiddett, 2015).

This final case study positions the consultant as an external observer of a situation working to limit dark side behaviours. The consultant must not be limited to the views of those who set expectations, the person required to fulfil those expectations or people trying to deal with the outcomes and behaviours. The external observer must seek to understand these different views and help those who hold them to create and manage situations for mutual benefit.

NHS Primary Care Trusts (PCTs) throughout England, once responsible for the majority of NHS spending, were abolished on the 31 March 2013 and replaced by new types of organisations. The changes were not wanted by many working in the PCTs, but an Act of Parliament enforced them and there was an expectation that individuals within the PCTs would help make the changes happen.

Staff from PCTs could transfer to roles in the newly formed organisations or other parts of the NHS if those roles were similar to their PCT role. They could also apply through a recruitment process for other roles in the new organisations. Alternatively they could opt for voluntary redundancy or early retirement.

Central government dictated expectations to the existing management teams and the people expected to help with the changes waited to hear what would happen to them.

The unwanted outcomes and behaviours: staff focused on their own short term needs, staff not assisting with changes and some actively disengaged from the process.

Staff were brought gradually into the change using the model to show individuals: the problematic outcomes if changes did not happen; what was happening and what was intended; how helping with the changes could help individuals deal with their own feelings while influencing their own futures (using the model to show how individuals can affect situations and how situations can affect individuals).

The senior management teams were helped to set realistic expectations, take control of their operating environments and shape the future of their organisations by using the legislation as a framework. Managers were supported in contributing their knowledge and skills to the design of the new organisations. Individuals at all levels contributed to the design of new jobs and in shaping the recruitment and reassignment processes. They were then helped to make effective use of these processes for their own benefit, as job applicants, and the benefit of the new organisations. The evolving organisations passed all central government assessments. The new organisations' potential clients had been helped to influence some expectations for the new organisations, e.g. their values and operating principles. Management teams engaged with the change and some became strong advocates for the new expectations and new performance indicators. Staff representatives supported the change work and many joined the project's lead team.

Conclusion

Fires present an understandable need for action and completing that action provides demonstrable evidence that something worthwhile has been done. Fire prevention requires an activity that, if successful, is unlikely to produce an observable result. Organisations do not want fires. They want their expectations to be met. We have a role, I say responsibility, to show organisations that when they have a fire it is an indication, a warning, that their expectations are at risk of failing. By all means help to put out the fire, but keep the organisation focused on that message, 'your expectations are at risk of failing'. Show them how Business Psychology can help them identify and address that risk. A holistic model of situations will help us and our clients to see and focus more clearly on the causes of performance issues, not just the symptoms.

Workplaces are not renowned for challenges to senior colleagues, or even between peers at senior level, about why issues arise. Instead, some remedial attention is often given to the symptomatic outcomes and behaviour of issues. This is like tapping the glass on a speedometer dial to see if the reading might change to show what we want it to show or bending the speedometer needle to make it fit expectations. Bending the speedometer needle to point at 60mph when the car is actually travelling at 80mph does not change the speed of the car. Addressing indicators changes appearances, not performance. We can and must draw attention to the shortcomings of dealing only with indicators, the symptoms, and the dangers in ignoring causes. This model can help identify what is necessary to do and so increase our confidence and the confidence of others in doing it.

Business Psychology is able to account for the complexities of situations and performance, but we need help to maintain this high level view when faced with the challenges that arise from normal patterns of human behaviour. We should not commit unquestioningly to the views of those who set expectations. We must not limit ourselves to the views of those who want only to put out a fire. They have more than enough supporters who share that short term view. We should seek to understand these views and the views of people in the situation. Looking beyond symptoms to explore and understand the complexities of performance is essential to delivering the substantial benefits of Business Psychology.

This model should not prescribe nor constrain the path we follow. I offer it as a compass to guide the path and actions we each choose to fulfil our purpose.

References:

Association for Business Psychology (2014). *What is business psychology?* Retrieved from http://www.theabp.org.uk/about/what-is-business-psychology.aspx.

Bandura, A. (1977). *Social Learning Theory*. New Jersey: Prentice-Hall.

Boyatzis, R. E. (1982). *The Competent manager: A model for effective performance*. Chichester: John Wiley & Sons.

Frijda, N. H. (1986). *The Emotions: Studies in emotion and social interaction*. Cambridge: Cambridge University Press.

Goleman, D. (1996). *Emotional Intelligence*. London: Bloomsbury Publishing plc.

Iyengar, S. (2010). *The Art of Choosing*. London: Little Brown.

Kahneman, D. (2012). *Thinking, Fast and Slow*. London: Penguin.

Kaiser, R. B., LeBreton, J. M., & Hogan, J. (2013). The Dark Side of Personality and Extreme Leader Behavior. *Applied Psychology: An international Review, 64*(1), 55-92.

McClelland, D. C. (1985). *Human Motivation*. Glenview, Il: Scott, Foresman.

Schein, E. (1999). *Process Consultation Revisited*. Reading, MA: Addison-Wesley.

Solvik, P., & Heller, F. (2007, January). *The Tavistock's approach towards an integration of social sciences.* Paper presented at the British Psychological Society's Division of Occupational Psychology Annual Conference, Bristol, UK.

Thierry, H., & Koopman-Iwema, A. M. (1984). 'Motivation and satisfaction'. In Drenth P. J. D., Thierry H., Willems, P. J., & de Wolff C. J. (Eds.), *Handbook of Work and Organizational Psychology* (pp. 253-290). Chichester: John Wiley & Sons Ltd.

Vroom, V. (1964). *Work and Motivation*. Chichester: John Wiley & Sons Ltd.

Whiddett, S. (2015). *Headlines, Headaches and the Human Condition*. Kibworth Beauchamp: Matador.

Whiddett, S., & Hollyforde, S. (2003). *A Practical Guide to Competencies: How to enhance individual and organisational performance*. London: Chartered Institute of Personnel and Development.

5

SECTION

Looking Ahead

LOOKING AHEAD INTRODUCTION

Pauline Grant

The pace of change in the world of work and its impact on the demands of working life has been a recurrent theme. Also impressive is our growing understanding of how people operate, individually and collectively. This has moved a long way since I studied psychology as an undergraduate. We now know that our brains are not static computers that are fixed by our genes and early experiences, but that they continue to evolve functionally in response to the challenges we place before them and the repeated practice we engage in.

Having covered some background to current practice and the thinking that has informed Business Psychology to date, it is now time to wonder about where this all might take us. We therefore conclude this book with a look at some of the more recent learning that will inevitably inform evolving Business Psychology practice, and also some emerging themes that arise from social research or that represent changes in technology.

The section starts with Fiona Murden's thoughtful assimilation of the lessons from neuroscience. She both captures important insights and debunks some persistent myths. Whilst some of her conclusions might be unsettling, it can only be a good thing to have the opportunity to consider potentially controversial implications before being confronted with them in practice. Mike Crimes challenges us to consider a model of selling expertise that supports clients' learning and independence rather than protecting intellectual property. He points to where this is already beginning to happen as well as explaining how the context is likely to become more amenable to this approach. Janey Howl embraces the virtual world where, for various reasons, people are spending increasing amounts of time. She alerts us to the opportunities this offers in the areas of coaching and development as well as identifying specific routes that practitioners and clients can pursue. Finally Jan de Jonge reminds us that well-being is now a mainstream topic in corporations, and he provides a rationale for this being firmly on the business agenda for the future. He gives an overview of current approaches together with their limitations, and invites Business Psychologists to play a more integrated role for the benefit of individual and corporate clients.

LOOKING AHEAD – MEET THE AUTHORS

Fiona Murden has worked in business psychology since 2002. She works predominantly with senior leaders and executive boards in coaching, leadership development, team development and understanding how to better leverage the power of people. Passionate about educating the wider population about how the brain works, she believes we are a long way off fully leveraging our understanding of psychology in all areas of life and business so is currently in the final stages of writing a book for the lay person on neuropsychology.

Mike Crimes, a Principal Business Psychologist, has been on the UK Leading Specialist Register across four areas of Occupational Psychology since 1999. With over 15 years organisational development experience, he has designed and implemented assessment and development centres in public and private sectors. He was previously a strategic advisor and people specialist working across different geographies and a senior business partner developing actionable talent management strategies. Mike recognises that people performance relies on workplace wellbeing, effective alignment to business goals, development of the right skills, motivation and commitment.

Janey Howl is a Psychologist, Coach, Facilitator, Mentor, and Writer helping global business leaders and their teams to achieve extraordinary results. A long-time associate of Ashridge Business School, she encourages clients to become authentic leaders who take strategic action and communicate courageously. Her aim is to hardwire new habits, through mastery of tools such as mindfulness and storytelling that enable clients to develop the skills in cognitive processing, emotional connectivity and resilience that deliver significant organisational outcomes and happier personal lives.

Jan de Jonge is a Business Psychologist and owner of People Business Psychology ltd, founded in 2012. His specialities are within business psychology consultancy, assessment and development, coaching, mediation, design and delivery of training. Jan advises on well-being at work and performance and competency management, and focuses on C-suite and management development consulting. Besides 'psychology', Jan worked in the Dutch police and as a sales negotiator, and set up and ran a successful translation company. He is active in local Federation of Small Businesses (FSB) and CIPD branches.

THE BRAINS BEHIND BUSINESS – AN OVERVIEW OF CUTTING EDGE NEUROSCIENTIFIC RESEARCH AND ITS IMPACT ON BUSINESS PSYCHOLOGY IN PRACTICE

Fiona Murden

The history of neuroscience dates back as far as the ancient Egyptians, with evidence that they had knowledge about the systems of the brain. Over the centuries significant contributions have been made to the field with milestones including René Descartes' 17th century proposal of the dualist separation of mind and body and in the 19th Century Franz Gall's theories that personality was related to certain structures within the brain. Despite these contributions it wasn't until the 1970s and 80s that the field of neuroscience really began to impact our understanding of the brain. The introduction of technologies such as MRI (Magnetic Resonance Imaging), PET (Positron Emission Tomography) and Computerised Axial Tomography (CAT scanning) allowed neuroimaging to make significantly more research possible.

In the 1990s our access to the workings of the brain made another substantial step forward when neuroscience began using fMRI (functional Magnetic Resonance Imaging), which detects changes in blood flow that take place in response to neural activity. This has allowed scientists to see activity in the brain as opposed to merely viewing static images. Current interest in neuroscientific research is being fuelled by initiatives such as the 'Brain Activity Map Project' launched in 2013 by the Obama administration. With $300 million worth of funding, this project aims to map the activity of every neuron in the human brain. The focus is already allowing dramatic steps forward in our understanding of mental disorders such as depression, neurological diseases such as Parkinson's and the neurological pathways involved in conditions such as autism. An invaluable by-product of this research is an understanding of how normally functioning neurological circuits operate.

Whilst advances are flying along in the field of neuroscience, its application to business psychology has been less extensive and at times a little spurious. This has been particularly evident where certain 'neuromyths' have taken hold in common culture and been applied in the workplace. Take the beliefs that some individuals are 'right brained' and some 'left brained', that our behaviour is fixed because brain pathways are laid down at birth and that we only use 10% of our brain. These 'facts' are unfounded yet an intervention has been designed around them, for example coaching people to accept certain behaviours which are 'part of who they are'. Our advancing knowledge of neuroplasticity challenges beliefs that were once tightly held. The neural networks are not, as we once thought, created a certain way never to be changed. The prefix 'neuro' has also been added to some approaches (e.g. Neuro Linguistic Programming). This gives the illusion of scientific rigour and adds the mystery of brain science which deters the layperson from questioning its validity. However, extensive research has found such interventions to be lacking in any empirical validity. Consequently the more discerning stakeholder has become sceptical of other findings claiming to be based on neuroscience.

If leveraged effectively, neuroscience has huge potential to add credibility to our field through a variety of means. Firstly, it provides us with the ability to eliminate and refine theories through direct insight into the brain mechanisms involved. This concentrates our attention on areas which have the greatest impact on the practice of business psychology. Secondly, it creates the opportunity to increase accurate measurement of psychological interventions and consequently ROI (Return on Investment). Historically it has been nearly impossible to link cause and effect of the work we do but research within businesses using methods such as neuro-imaging combined with self-report and observation offer a more robust link (e.g. research at Standard Life by Dr Linda Shaw). Thirdly, it provides us with a more convincing psychological framework (as opposed to theory alone) from which to create the buy-in of 'sceptical' business leaders. Whilst we know that behavioural interventions are invaluable, many CEOs doubt their validity. Fourthly, it opens up the possibility of having an impact on broader areas of the business psychology market. For example, our advancing knowledge of risk appetite and its neurological precursors can enable us to add valuable contributions in the financial service sector and other industries in which risk is an area of high focus.

How is Neuroscience Being Applied to Business Psychology

There is a wide range of approaches that could be taken in order to apply our growing insights. One popular framework is that of the emotional and rational functions as being independent yet co-existing areas of the brain. The advances being made in neuroscience have fuelled this approach together with the increasing popularity of evolutionary psychology. In very crude terms neuroscience has allowed us to see that emotions relate to the limbic system and rational thinking resides predominantly in the frontal lobes of the brain. The limbic system, a brain structure we share with animals and with our ancient ancestors, is primitive and responds in an automatic manner. As a consequence it enables us to function and survive in the world through unconscious emotional drivers, impressions and intuitions which happen quickly. This allowed our ancestors the best opportunity to quickly escape from danger or to exert energy in order to obtain food. The frontal lobes represent part of our advanced brain structure, which developed at a later stage of evolution. This area of the brain enables us to consciously reason, have beliefs, make choices and exert self-control. Although higher primates and other animals have this outer layer of cortex, it is the size in humans that separates us from the animal kingdom.

Neuroscience has allowed us to see that when we are under threat a significantly higher level of blood flow goes to the primitive brain than the advanced brain. For example, areas involved in emotional processing such as the amygdala, posteromedial orbital cortex and the ventral anterior cingulate cortex show an increased blood flow during emotion-related tasks (MacDonald, 2008). Concurrently neural activity is decreased in cognitive processing areas of the brain when someone is reacting emotionally to a situation. As a result, in certain situations we are more or less hijacked by our primitive brain, meaning that being advanced does not equate to being in control.

With our advanced brain comes an ability to infer things and project potential meaning. Hence we will often perceive something to be a threat which in reality isn't life-threatening and our 'primitive brain' runs away with this thinking, causing us to react in emotional ways to seemingly inconsequential stimuli. This is a problem in all walks of life, but is largely dismissed in business which is viewed as a predominantly rational setting. For example coming in to work to find someone sitting at your desk can cause upset at a level that is not consciously acknowledged; after all, it's silly isn't it? In primitive times this would have represented an invasion of territory and consequently pose a threat to survival. Although it's no longer a threat and a simple request to move would solve the issue, the brain is wired to have us believe otherwise. Consequently the primitive brain triggers a series of emotional reactions, releasing chemicals which can then skew the perception of interactions which ensue. This is a vast oversimplification, but provides a useful starting point for the application of neuroscientific insights in a way people understand.

Within the framework of the primitive and advanced brain we can see how certain factors influence and impact individuals with regard to a broad range of areas. Factors such as leadership, group membership, motivation, reward, risk appetite, resistance to change and a need for status are territorial drivers in relation to job role and office layout. They all impact on tiredness and stress, on performance and psychological well-being. These areas and more, that we may not even have considered, are relevant for us to address as Business Psychologists. In the remainder of this article we will look at a few of these areas, namely leadership, group membership and motivation, and we will look anew at mindfulness.

Although hundreds of theories exist on leadership, it is known that to be a truly successful leader two areas are of key importance: the faculty to make effective decisions and the ability to build effective relationships.

The area of decision-making is traditionally viewed as a purely rational function devoid of emotion, but we can use neuroscience to illustrate how this belief and therefore everything based on the premise is faulty. Research carried out by Nobel prize winner Daniel Kahneman in the 1970s is now supported by neuroscientific insights. Kahneman (2011) proposed that decision-making is based on certain heuristics which create unconscious short cuts (in the primitive brain) rather than conscious and rational step-by-step processing alone (in the advanced brain). Whilst these heuristics may be quicker than the rational thinking of the 'advanced' brain, they introduce the risk of uncertainty and emotional biases. These biases are then unconsciously 'covered up' as we post-rationalise the decisions we have made.

The influence of the unconscious is demonstrated in a number of other circumstances and is particularly evident when decision-making involves taking risks. Where risks are involved, the emotions experienced depend on different cognitive appraisals. What neuroscience has shown us is that these appraisals then generate distinctive cognitive and motivational tendencies that influence judgements and decisions (Kugler, Cooper, & Nosek, 2010). Ultimately these decisions are open to influence by numerous factors including the individual's appraisal of a situation (based on personality and past experience), personal preferences and emotion. Therefore, in a whole range of situations, decision-making becomes far from rational, and in fact heavily flawed and unpredictable.

Taking emotion as an example, research has shown that if a risk and uncertainty involves placing a financial 'bet' on a randomising device such as putting money on a national lottery or the roll of a dice, people's mood will effect what they do. Both fearful and angry people will place a smaller bet on a lottery outcome than people who are in a normal mood. Those who are fearful will be especially risk averse (Kugler, Connolly & Ordonez, 2010). Taking a business scenario, if a boss has just openly fired someone on the trading floor of a bank, traders who perceived this as a personal threat and became fearful will become more risk-averse in the trades they place for however long that mood lasts. The same situation may make other traders angry (due to differences in personality and past experience) which will also make them risk averse in the trades they place, but less so than the person who was scared by the incident. The outcome of the day's trading is therefore impacted by factors which reach beyond a rational appraisal of the economic circumstances surrounding the trades. Neuroscience tells us the mechanisms by which this is happening, which in turn will enable us to more accurately pin-point the variables and conditions involved. Such knowledge is incredibly powerful and can be applied beyond banking to other areas of high risks. For example, if applied effectively it could not only mitigate a repeat of the 2008 financial crisis, but also help to prevent a repeat of the Deep Water Horizon oil spill of 2010, which had a severe environmental and economic impact.

Neuroscience is also helping to evolve our thinking when it comes to the key leadership aspect of 'relationships'. Whilst common sense and centuries of history have shown positive relationships result in better outcomes, we can find it hard to quantify this in a way that is relevant to the business world. Leaders generally acknowledge the power of relationships, but when put under pressure will focus on bottom line results as opposed to the less tangible relational aspects. This is generally because relationships and their impact are so difficult to quantify; after all shareholders want numbers and results not platitudes and promises.

Through neuroscience we are able to measure the positive impact of relationships on organisational outcomes which could very well help to shift the focus. For example, in 2011, Boyatzis examined the neural substrates activated in experiences with leaders who were good at relating to followers (resonant leaders) and those who were not (dissonant leaders). They found that subjects recalling specific experiences with resonant leaders significantly activated 14 regions of the brain, specifically arousing areas associated with attention and relationships. Whereas recalling experiences with dissonant leaders activated only 6 areas of the brain and actually deactivated 11, specifically narrowing attention and initiating negative emotions. This of course has significant and damaging consequences. Negative emotions lead to cognitive, emotional and perceptual impairment, which in turn limits an employee's ability to make accurate rational decisions (i.e. cognitive decision-making) and causes them to have an inaccurate and overly negative view of their environment and others' actions (i.e. perceptual inaccuracies and related emotional impairment). This skewed perception affects how they respond which in turn has an impact on bottom line results. For example, if a store manager loses his temper with an employee on the shop floor, that employee is then more likely to make cognitive errors such as putting a price through the till incorrectly. They are also more likely to perceive others, including the customers, as being negative to them which in turn will mean they react more negatively to others. This could then decrease sales as a result of a bad customer experience. Neuroscience provides a robust mechanism by which to demonstrate these pathways and consequences in a concrete manner. Without sound evidence, the links between mood and bottom line results are usually brushed aside due to the vague and inconclusive nature of the connections.

Recent findings not only help us to prove where positive relationships impact bottom line results but also how to do something about it. For example, neuroscience is uncovering a myriad of ways in which centuries-old practices such as mindfulness help people to function more effectively. Research has proven that mindfulness practice helps people to more effectively regulate emotion and raises individuals' levels of self-awareness (e.g. Farb et al., 2007). Leveraging such approaches can help people to learn to regulate their emotions. Consequently when a person finds someone sitting at their desk they can acknowledge and successfully process the emotion. This then minimises negative fall-out such as a disgruntled reaction or a negative mood (which in a leader can then affect their followers).

Mindfulness has also been shown to increase our ability to focus attention (Nataraja, 2008) which improves decision-making. A combined understanding of what mindfulness can do and why we need to do it (in order to manage our primitive brain so that we can optimise the output of our advanced brain) can drive a range of positive initiatives. Indeed, mindfulness is already having significant impact in Silicon Valley, with companies such as Google, Ebay, Twitter and Facebook investing heavily in mindfulness practice. If this gains momentum in the cutthroat world of financial services, and other more traditional industries not so readily disposed to innovative approaches, it could have hugely significant benefits.

Group membership has been the focus of psychological research for decades with the majority of papers being written about teamwork within the organisational context. The multitude of factors involved makes it notoriously difficult to isolate the mechanisms involved in behaviour relating to a group, which means that it is hard to offer interventions that have a guaranteed impact. However, neuroscience, in the context of evolutionary psychology, is helping us to understand more in this complex area. We've known since the days of Milgram and Zimbardo that people conform to group norms, but the reasons why have largely eluded us. Recent papers such as that written by Miller (2014) have illuminated a variety of factors influencing obedience, such as the participants' identification with authority, in more detail. When this is analysed in the context of neuroscience the richness increases further. For example, we look at the primitive brain as triggering behaviours that were essential to our ancestors. Rejection from a group made it incredibly difficult for our ancient ancestors to survive, hence the brain developed chemical pathways to enhance conformity and assure group membership. Experiments using fMRI have shown that conformity of opinion activates the rostral cingulate zone and the ventral striatum, a brain circuit relating to reinforcement learning. This reinforcement learning means that an individual's judgments are adjusted in line with group opinion. When someone doesn't conform to the group, the brain evaluates it as an error and consequently adjusts behaviour (Klucharev et al., 2009).

Neuroscience has shown that the need to conform is reinforced by the reward centres of the brain (Campbell-Meiklejohn et al., 2010) creating two strong pathways to encourage the need to 'toe the line'. As this is happening at a predominantly subconscious level (in the primitive brain) people are often unaware that they are altering their behaviour or being influenced by others. Yet they may be aware of feeling uncomfortable or hurt if they are excluded from a group situation such as a meeting or project group. As the reason is unclear, while they will try to move on, they may well be unable to shake off the emotions which will in turn impact their interaction with others.

At an individual level raising awareness of these mechanisms of behaviour and applying neuroscience to well-known phenomena could (among other things) help people to stand up for what they believe in, be less influenced by popular opinion and better handle being excluded from a group. This could also notably help mitigate 'group think' which has historically led to disasters such as The Bay of Pigs Invasion. This is just one example of where faulty decision-making came about from a need to conform and resulted in a failed military invasion of Cuba in 1961. The aim was to overthrow the dictator Castro. However, such was the influence of conformity amongst the group responsible that they overlooked a simple analysis of Castro's military power. Consequently the 1400 invaders were vastly outnumbered and Kennedy, the US President at the time, was left asking, "How could I have been so stupid?"

A commonly cited business example of groupthink is the financial decline faced by Marks and Spencer in the late 1990s. Having traded as a successful leading retailer for nearly 100 years, Marks and Spencer became overly confident and assured of its own infallibility. The board believed that their traditional business plan was so robust that they did not need to take notice of increasingly innovative competition. They proactively discouraged non-executive influence at board level which exacerbated conformity of thinking and prevented the opportunity for divergent thinking or questioning of the judgements being made. In effect, the board's arrogance led it to ignore, deny and rationalise any sign that suggested it was no longer leading the way. As a consequence, M&S shares had fallen by almost 50 percent by the turn of the century. Some argue that the retailer has yet to fully recover from the impacts of this faulty decision-making.

Other examples of groupthink in business include the collapse of SwissAir in 2001, the significant fall of British Airways' share price in the late 1990s and the Enron scandal in 2001. Understanding the neuroscience behind groups could not only help to raise awareness of such phenomena, but also mitigate the negative outcomes which occur on a smaller scale across a range of organisations daily. From a positive perspective an improved understanding could also be used to enhance employee engagement, assist the people aspects of mergers and acquisitions and effectively facilitate culture change.

Neural imaging is also providing more detailed information on dopamine pathways and their influence on reward and motivation. These pathways originally existed as a means to ensure our survival and they are therefore in parts of our brain that are not controlled at a conscious level. Yet the implications in the workplace are highly relevant. For example, it has been found that people with a greater dopamine response in the striatum and ventromedial prefrontal cortex put more effort into tasks, even when it is less possible to succeed. These are areas of the brain that relate to motivation and reward. In effect, such people's increased motivation to achieve not only impacts decision making, but also performance (Treadway et al., 2012). This suggests that individual differences occur in how people respond to tasks at a neural level and gives strength to the argument that people are motivated in different ways. It also demonstrates the need to understand other ways to trigger the reward centres of the brain for people who find it difficult to persist when things get tough.

There is an ethical consideration to these advancements in our understanding, in this case motivation versus manipulation. If we are more able to release the potential for triggering the reward centres, when does it move from motivation (i.e. encouraging employees) to manipulation (i.e. controlling employees)? This highlights the need to develop our ethical guidelines around the approaches we use.

Our growing understanding of what we can and cannot change can inform workplace policy. When it comes to the individual we can and should educate and create interventions that optimise natural pathways and ways of operating. For example, clearer evidence of the negative impact of tiredness on the brain should help us to design shift work more effectively at a policy level. Although we currently know the adverse effects of mental fatigue on task performance and everyday activities, we are only just beginning to uncover the neurocognitive mechanisms that underlie the effects. Illuminating these mechanisms could significantly help the health and safety of workers in key roles such as medical professionals and other emergency workers, where others' lives are dependent on their performance. Also, at an individual level, helping people to understand why they respond more emotionally in certain situations (a greater reliance on primitive drivers under stress for example) could raise levels of awareness and therefore help them to manage their own behaviour.

Although this article has only covered certain aspects of neuroscience and its impact, what is clear is that the research offers a hugely significant contribution to the work we do as Business Psychologists. Mechanisms of measurement via neuroimaging in academic and research settings can be generalised to enable more accurate intervention in workplace environments. They provide a means of educating people as to why we behave in certain ways and a tool for persuading businesses of the importance of interventions. Potential future advances of neuroscience could influence our practice even more significantly.

At the extreme end of the spectrum, ethically dubious practice could also arise, for example, scanning a job applicant's brain rather than using psychometrics to match them to a role. Professor Verbeke, who heads the department of neuro-economics at Erasmus University, Rotterdam, predicts that brain scans will replace job interviews in as little as 5 years' time. Whilst interviews are unlikely to be as endangered as Professor Verbeke predicts, his suggestion of using brain scanning to eliminate candidates with psychopathic tendencies from senior leadership roles (revealed to be a real issue amongst leaders by research conducted by Psychologist, Robert Hare) could become a reality. However, it is questionable whether such a procedure would be accepted by candidates, or enforced by organisations seeking to woo as opposed to scare off elite business leaders. Such measurements may, however, creep through the system when dealing with less senior individuals and, according to Verbeke's predictions, this may not be too far off.

Another example of future applications could be seeking to change people's moral judgements to align with the values of an organisation through methods such as 'non-invasive transcranial magnetic stimulation' (see research by Rebecca Saxe, Department of Brain and Cognitive Sciences, MIT). The existence of such procedures demands that professional ethics be continually updated in line with the advancing technologies. This is no simple task as ethical guidelines need to provide a detailed classification of the morals and values that are acceptable and unacceptable when using brain scanning for non-medical purposes. Ultimately this will help to guard against misuse.

Other potential techniques for applying advances in neuroscience could be used with less controversy. For example neuroscientist Christopher deCharms has presented a technique called Neuroimaging Therapy. This measures a person's brain activation patterns using real time fMRI and enables people to be trained to control the patterns of activation inside their own brain. This can help people to better focus attention or control emotional reactions (deCharms et al., 2004). Such techniques could be applied to activities such as coaching in order to assist behavioural change.

Another approach MIT Professor Ed Boyden highlighted is the concept of optogenetics. Optogenetics aims to control the activity of specific sets of brain cells using light. Boyden (2011) has been able to use light to 'photoactivate' certain areas in the brain in animals to overcome specific neural mechanisms such as the memory of fear. Although not yet explored in human studies, Boyden has shown that dopamine neurons can be activated in a similar manner to drive learning (Kim et al., 2012). Whilst advances in this area will initially be used to treat brain disorders and to develop therapies for those who have experienced trauma, there are projected opportunities for its use in business psychology.

To end, it is worth restating that despite all of the wonder and excitement of neuroscience and its wealth of potential applications it does not give us all the answers. Our understanding of neural mechanisms is still not crystal clear; every individual brain is different, making exact mapping difficult and, furthermore, pathways can change (due to neuroplasticity). Also, whilst the technologies such as fMRI are an amazing advancement they only provide a view of blood flow not actual neurotransmission. This assumes that blood flow provides us with a direct interpretation of which areas of the brain are active and implicated in different behaviours and outcomes. Additionally the use of fMRI is not pragmatic at an everyday level. Not only is it expensive but it also requires a high level of expertise in order to operate and interpret outcomes and is too cumbersome to be used in ordinary workplace settings.

What is certain is that the knowledge that we do have should be handled responsibly with the ethics and scientific consideration that, as experts, we are duty-bound to bring. Dispelling myths and concentrating on areas where we know there is relevant application is essential. Educating people about the way our brains work and teaching them how to optimise the advantages and limit the pitfalls at an organisational and individual level will help to create a vast range of benefits. Neuroscience could ultimately help us to seed significant changes in the way we look at behaviour within organisations, potentially as a positive starting point for the broader population.

References

Boyatzis, R. (2011). *Neuroscience and the link between inspirational leadership and resonant relationships*. Ivey Business Journal, online January/February 2011. Retrieved from http://iveybusinessjournal.com/topics/leadership/neuroscience-and-leadership-the-promise-of-insights.

Boyden, E. (2011, March). *A light switch for neurons*. Presented at Ted Talks. Retrieved from http://www.ted.com/talks/ed_boyden?language=en.

Campbell-Meiklejohn, D. K., Bach, D. R., Roepstorff, A., Dolan, R. J., & Frith, C. D. (2010). How the opinion of others affects our valuation of objects. *Current Biology, 20*(13), 1165-70.

deCharms, R. C., Christoff, K., Glover, G. H., Pauly, J. M., Whitfield, S., & Gabrieli, J. D. (2004). Learned regulation of spatially localized brain activation using real-time fMRI. *Neuroimage, 21*(1), 436-443.

Farb, N. A. S., Segal, Z. V., Mayberg, H., Bean, J., McKeon, D., Fatima, Z., & Anderson, A. K. (2007). Attending to the present: Mindfulness meditation reveals distinct neural modes of self-reference. *Social Cognitive and Affective Neuroscience, 2*(4), 313-322.

Kahneman, D. (2011). *Thinking, fast and slow*. London: Penguin Books Ltd.

Kim, K. M., Barratta, M. V., Yang, A., Lee, D., Boyden, E. S., & Fiorillo, C. D. (2012). Optogentic Mimicry of the Transient Activation of Dopamine Neurons by Natural Reward Is Sufficient for Operant Reinforcement. *PLos One,* 7(4), e33612. doi: 10.1371/journal.pone.0033612.

Klucharev, V., Hytonen, K., Rijkema, M., Smidts, A., & Fernandez, G. (2009). Reinforcement learning predicts social conformity. *Neuron, 61*(1), 140-151.

Kugler, T., Connolly, T., & Ordonez, L. D. (2010). Emotion, decision, and risk: Betting on gambles versus betting on people. *Journal of Behavioural Decision Making, 25*(2), 123-134.

Kugler, M. B., Cooper, J., & Nosek, B. A. (2010). Group-based dominance and opposition to equality correspond to different psychological motives. *Social Justice Research, 23*(2-3), 117-155.

MacDonald, K. B. (2008). Effortful control, explicit processing, and the regulation of human evolved predispositions. *Psychological Review, 115*(4), 1012-1031.

Miller, A. G. (2014). The Explanatory value of Milgram's obedience experiments: A contemporary appraisal. *Journal of Social Issues, 70*(3), 558-573.

Nataraja, S. (2008). *The blissful brain: Neuroscience and proof of the power of meditation.* London, UK: Gaia Books Ltd.

Treadway, M.T., Buckholtz, J. W., Cowan R. L., Woodward, N. D., Sib Ansari, R., Baldwin, R. M., Schwartzman, A. N., Kessler, R. M., & Zald, D. H. (2012). Dopaminergic mechanisms of individual differences in human effort-based decision-making. *The Journal of Neuroscience, 32*(18), 6170-6176.

'SOLUTIONS PRACTICE' IN ASSESSMENT AND DEVELOPMENT: A MINDSET TRANSITION WITHIN A SEA OF BUSINESS CHANGE AND UNCERTAINTY

Mike Crimes

The clouds were dark, the tornado hit, and it became evident very quickly that ... *"We're not in Kansas anymore..."* (*The Wizard of Oz*, 1939).

The impact of the 2008 economic downturn on the management consultancy marketplace has been significant, and people assessment and development practice is no exception. However, recent evidence from the Management Consultancies Association (MCA) indicates that firms are spending more money on management consultants to improve functions in order to boost efficiency and savings. Alan Leaman, chief executive of the MCA, believes the UK's consulting industry is both "*resilient and agile,*" and recently stated: *"While most private sector clients are not confident enough to undertake major projects, they are often developing their capacities, processes and systems so that they are ready for an upturn when it materialises."*

Human Resources (HR) and recruitment processes are not immune to this streamlining, and technological developments in the marketplace reflect this. Furthermore, advances in people processes, whether in recruitment or development, are responding to wider societal and global changes. And change in business can be rapid and unpredictable. Consequently, in order to align to this new business ether of technological advance and rapid change, people assessment and development practices need to be flexible.

Successful Business Psychology practitioners can respond to this by ensuring that people assessment and development processes can evolve in real time, creating sustainability within continually moving business targets.

I propose a potential strategic change in the assessment and development of employees that I call *Solutions Practice*. This idea represents a mindset transition that can enable assessment and development (A&D) tools to break free from the bonds of copyright and address the moving target of rapid change driven by a wider business backdrop. Critically, A&D practice needs to drive a 'creative destruction' in which old technologies, products and practice go into terminal decline and new ones emerge that encapsulate the challenges businesses now face.

Putting a new materials ownership philosophy within the key strategic shifts in assessing and identifying development needs creates its own complexity. The intention is to clear the mists and outline:

- the context – the wider backdrop and key factors driving global business practice;
- how the present climate has shaped the A&D requirement;
- how A&D practice could potentially evolve by giving managers more control;
- how to align A&D training to the evolved materials;
- the potential that the technological present and future hold for devolution of copyright in relation to A&D materials.

Key Factors Driving Global Business Practice

People A&D practice, along with all types of external management consulting, now requires a much greater emphasis on return on investment. "*There is a tremendous interest in return on investment (ROI) these days, and many clients want to know the payoff of a consulting project – because of the high cost for consulting projects and because consulting has a tarnished image*" (Phillips, 2001). From a strategic perspective, this requirement is driven by the need to deliver *'more for less'* so the cost of A&D is at the forefront of budget holders' minds.

In terms of the *more*, Josh Bersin, a Forbes contributor from Deloitte, states how in the future the needs for talent, skills and capability will become global. Consequently it becomes important to source and recruit people globally as well as build networks across the world to attract people. He further predicts integrated capability development (i.e. continuous improvement) will replace training, and performance management systems will be re-designed to link recognition and reward directly to strategy. In terms of the *less*, cost effectiveness can be achieved by flexible tools and techniques that are purpose built to evolve with the business.

Josh Bersin's predictions are arguably critical factors to be considered in improving employee engagement. A recent Gallup survey (*October 8, 2013 – Worldwide, 13% of Employees Are Engaged at Work*) showed that the bulk of employees worldwide, 63%, are "not engaged" and are less likely to contribute to organisational goals. More interestingly, the survey found 24% are "actively disengaged," indicating they are liable to spread negativity to co-workers. In rough numbers, this translates into 900 million not engaged and 340 million actively disengaged workers around the globe.

This point is further evidenced by the growth in wellbeing at work strategies (Warr, 2007) and in positive psychology, which was described by the American Psychological Association as the *"darling of the popular press"*. Positive psychology also made the cover of *Time* (Jan. 17, 2005) and featured in other media such as *The Washington Post* (2002), UK *Sunday Times Magazine* (2005) and even a six-part BBC series (2006). There is very real justification for this focus in the UK. Stress and other mental health conditions are among the main causes of employee absence according to the Chartered Institute of Personnel Development (CIPD) Absence Management Survey 2006, and the Health and Safety Executive estimates that stress costs business £3.8 billion a year.

Having examined the factors driving a renewed people focus in organisations, we now turn to the external recruitment marketplace. There is undoubtedly a larger pool of talent to select from. According to the Organisation for Economic Cooperation and Development, emerging economies are investing in education on a massive scale. In EU countries student numbers more than doubled to 1.7 million between 2000 and 2010. Such trends make selection processes even more critical in identifying individuals with the right skills, and employers need to become more effective at getting the people–to–business fit right. Assessment centres, with clear business simulation goals and objectives that reflect the reality of the business environment, have been evidenced to deliver higher validity in terms of person fit.

Enabling businesses to *'own'* and *'control'* A&D materials has the potential to significantly improve their adeptness in decision making. Tools that are devoid of copyright restrictions allow the development of widespread parallel forms that align directly to the strategic and operational issues. This approach creates consultancy opportunities through a new ethos, one led by management and supported by Business Psychology practitioners. It is a true sharing of knowledge and best practice within which a self-managed and viral learning agenda can evolve whilst potentially reducing costs associated with the bespoke design of materials.

How the Present Climate has Shaped Assessment and Development Requirements

Cost reduction and service delivery transformation are two sides of the same coin. Industry leaders face the twin pressures of reducing spending and providing more customer-focused services. This involves looking at new ways of managing business processes, and people A&D is no exception.

The expectation of achieving the 'right fit' remains even if recruitment and development spend is reduced. Changing the prevailing model to bespoke A&D process design delivers greater value for money. Giving in-house professionals more power to align materials directly to their needs, and to adapt them as these needs change, allows flexibility. This is organisation rather than consultant led, with the consultant supporting from the sidelines when required. Solutions Practice materials can be *'self-replicating and evolving'* through clear and educated instruction allowing HR and training departments to own and maintain the quality of their person-fit decision making. A Solutions Practice minimises external consultancy involvement and so tackles the pressure to reduce spending head-on.

Solutions Practice represents a good communication platform to position evolved A&D practices to employees as part of a wider engagement agenda. Employers can change materials to reflect their business and control their own internal marketing. Managers can confidently 'sell' internal A&D practice with key messages, such as: *'activities that reflect the business environment you operate in,' 'culturally aligned development activities,' 'real challenges that will help you develop and progress,' 'topical subject matter to challenge your leadership skills,' 'goal orientated, so management and leadership approaches can be clearly observed'*. Articulating such a narrative around A&D helps to gain people's buy-in to the processes they may go through to progress in the company.

This point is effectively illustrated in bespoke assessment centre design and implementation at the Department for Transport 2001–2007. Each year the design of the annual senior and middle management assessment centres focused on a different business simulation backdrop. Backdrops spanned a broad range of challenging subjects, from developing country transport initiatives to environmental crime prevention. The success of these events, based on annual feedback reports, was driven mainly by two factors: communication forums where participants received clear instruction of what to expect during the assessment, i.e. key logistics overview and exercise practice, and the flexibility built into the subject matter. The HR and training teams were taught to evolve and amend their assessment materials, be they individual assessment centre exercises, for *ad hoc* recruitment events or full event portfolios. (An event portfolio consists of a combination of exercises relating to the same backdrop.) The assessment materials bank increased as parallel forms of individual exercises and event portfolios were created and applied to new business areas. Strategic changes within the organisation were reflected in the business simulation materials. Equally, more immediate development drives such as leadership, communication skills and project management were woven into the subject matter as required.

Engagement statistics are now a common feature of many FTSE 250 corporate reports (e.g. Grant Thornton, 2011) and underpin new performance and competency models that drive A&D practice. Business simulations need to reflect these challenges to ensure that people recruited or promoted are the right fit for the business.

Assessment and development materials also need to reflect the organisational culture they are applied to in order to maintain face validity – perceived credibility. The main levers to achieve culture change are organisational development combined with leadership and management development (Ogbonna & Harris, 2000). These two activities are regarded as mutually dependent and reinforcing. Assessment and development centres can play a key role in both strategic agendas by weaving leadership and organisational challenges into the exercises and materials. This also applies to assessment/development centres undertaken in an online environment.

All bespoke assessment work undertaken for the Department for Transport between 2001 and 2007 involved the creation of fictitious cultural challenges that were played out within the exercises. These included role-plays incorporating performance and relationship issues arising from different cultural norms. This gave a purpose and credibility to the backdrop that participants perceived as very real and relevant, and this was reflected in the feedback.

Of further importance is the symbiotic value backdrop. Core organisational values underpin culture and changes in employee behaviour (see O'Tool, 1996). These values need to be clearly identified and understood to further drive the effectiveness of A&D. In designing numerous assessment centres, across all key government departments, clearly defining values as well as competencies was the norm. The style of an individual's approach to an exercise was more often than not considered in assessing their performance e.g. whether the participant showed integrity, passion, respect for others and honesty and whether they engendered trust.

Professionals working inside an organisation are part of their own culture and values backdrop. Their thinking reflects the cultural nuances and unwritten laws better than external consultants. Consequently, with the right self-managed instruction in place, this instinctiveness can ensure assessment and development challenges reflect the *true nature* of the business.

In the public sector there has never been a stronger strategic reason to re-invent A&D practice so that it becomes less consultant-centric. Billions are being cut from budgets, and the majority of Central Government has closed its doors to all but essential recruitment and development activity. In the UK today we are set to embark upon some of the largest and most fundamental public sector spending changes in our history. The Office for Budget Responsibility says cuts to services are key to the government's aim of generating a budget surplus. Steep cuts in government spending over the next six years will shrink state services back to a level not seen since 1948, according to the government's spending watchdog, and will require new thinking to operate with substantially lower resources.

The public sector has been an important market for management consultancy, the second largest after financial services. The total expenditure by the public sector on outside expertise was £70bn from 1997 to 2009 (Hall & Campbell, 2006). It is clear that the substantial reduction in this market represents a great deal of pain for Business Psychology A&D practice unless significant savings can be delivered, paralleled with solid measurable return on investment. Exercise materials that can be owned and evolved by these departments will contribute significant savings by reducing external consultancy fees. For example, a Solutions Practice *editable assessment event template* would attract a fixed fee of £750. This can be changed by internal management or professionals to reflect the specific circumstances, modified to produce parallel forms and used indefinitely, all within the fixed fee.

This contrasts with an 'off the shelf' unit cost approach (i.e. fee per exercise per person), where any required changes to materials are managed externally for a fee, which is sometimes significant. Typically, 4 'off the shelf', single use exercises are used in an assessment centre. At a cost of £75 per exercise, (or £300 per person assessed) an assessment centre of 12 people has a materials cost of £3,600. Consultancy fees are charged when materials require editing or designing on a bespoke basis. Solutions Practice is also more flexible than enforcing licensing agreements, allowing professionals to access materials when they need them by breaking down the protective intellectual property (IP) barrier.

Private companies also use assessment and development centres. According to the CIPD's 2004 survey on 'Recruitment, Retention and Turnover', 34% of employers used assessment centres when recruiting managers, professionals, and graduates. However, recent studies have evidenced a lowering of validity. Personal observations and trends in how organisations employ this approach reveal a number of factors at work:

- Pressure to reduce costs has led to cutting corners and less regard for following best practice;
- The use of unqualified assessors who lack the proper credentials;
- Irrelevant competency frameworks based on talent models that have not been updated to reflect the business world post 2008;
- Outdated, off the shelf, materials that cannot be changed, even though they do not reflect the nature and functional purpose of the organisation.

Furthermore, administering assessment/development exercises to people in live settings, the current norm, does not reflect the nature of today's virtual, device-heavy, technological environments.

These factors provide further evidence of the need for new thinking and having the courage to abandon outmoded, protectionist agendas around A&D intellectual property. It forces Business Psychology practitioners to re-think the support and training required to operate with a more collaborative consultancy style. This less invasive consulting relationship creates a meaningful dialogue around the approaches in-house professionals want to use and allows clients to make informed choices about the support they need.

How Assessment and Development Practice could Potentially Evolve by Giving Managers More Control

Creative Commons licenses provide an easy way to manage the copyright terms that attach automatically to all creative material under copyright. This requires a delegative mindset and trust in the capability of the internal professionals that are responsible for people assessment and development. They can strengthen their people assessment knowledge through supervised live practice. However, these in-house professionals need to have the right competencies, and to demonstrate positive behaviours and values. Key competencies include logistical and organisational talents, problem solving, analytical skills and the ability to communicate with and understand a wide range of people. Key behaviours/values include objectivity, judgement, empathy and a sense of ethics.

For a Solutions Practice to be effective requires clear instructions for editing materials, and more focus on the assessment design process in A&D training programmes. Time and effort must be invested in evaluating assessment skills and expertise before allowing complete access to the intellectual property, supervised in the early stages of release. The focus here is on the background and experience of the in-house professional, identifying skills and abilities that relate directly to professional body and consultancy Strategic Guidelines on Best Practice.

Specifically it becomes important to identify levels of:

- HR and commercial awareness – knowledge of employment law and cost management;
- Information technology usage – for clients to put exercises online;
- Coaching and mentoring experience – giving feedback is a critical aspect of people assessment;
- Managing people information – relating to security and storage of information;
- Managing process change – reflecting any change of business strategy in the assessment currency and language;
- Resourcing and talent planning – getting the right number of people with the right skills at the right time;

- Learning and development knowledge – to ensure assessment challenges are proportionate and measureable;
- Performance and reward management – so people performance change can be embedded effectively;
- Employee engagement and employee relations involvement – so that buy-in to A&D processes can be achieved through the right communication.

The person may have to analyse information quickly, especially if there are large numbers of participants and tight deadlines, and use it to make robust decisions. They also need to have the capability to influence and gain commitment from different quarters and to work collaboratively. There may be a wide range of stakeholders involved with different ideas on where to focus energy.

It may be possible to assess these areas through a formal online application, where questions around experience of the above areas can be asked. Responses can be validated through informal dialogue. Once signed off, key in-house professionals and management staff would have access to a secure area of a website where they can download materials and instructions, any time and from anywhere, for a single fee.

If unrestricted editing is to be allowed, professionals need to understand competency and behavioural semantics and know how to design effective business simulations. The emphasis relating to business simulation is being able to design a narrative with challenges that both reflect the organisation and are appropriate in terms of the targeted employee group.

Given the objective to help instil enlightened decisions across A&D practice when faced with global goals, support might be required to manage assessments across different locations, or indeed countries and consequent time zones.

However, as consultants, we have to ask:

- Do we have time, skills and resources to provide and manage the development that may be needed by in-house professionals?

- Are we convinced that the key person wanting unrestricted access is an unbiased decision maker?
- Does this person have time to take on the learning challenge?
- Does Solutions Practice supply what he or she wants to achieve in terms of A&D practice?

Reduced cost and increased flexibility creates a potentially wider market for these advanced approaches, the Small/Medium Enterprise (SME) marketplace being a case in point. Links are being generated between universities and SMEs, following high competition for graduate placements in larger and more established organisations. Applying a more flexible business model to advanced recruitment and development methods has the potential to fuel these partnerships.

Nevertheless, it is important to understand why people may want to avoid such a strategy and not lose control of their intellectual property. Material could be diluted and misused. A lack of expert knowledge could lead to best practice being compromised or equality legislation breached which in turn could lead to legal challenges and damage to corporate reputation. These are very strong arguments against this approach.

It is easier to design and write business simulation content that is *written in stone* than to produce content that is flexible, where key parameters can be manipulated to reflect the diversity within any given organisation. As management scientists who understand people assessment and development extremely well it would be relatively straightforward – even fun – for us to write content. A stronger, more flexible approach is to provide material templates with guided editable parameters, controlled by the individuals who are living and breathing the business context.

A significant number of programmes in the market impart A&D design knowledge in the classroom – AD&C Ltd, SHL, Talent Q and OPC to name but a few providers. Further, some are already allowing flexibility in material editing. Criterion Partnership's Criterion Attribute Library of 46 personality scales effectively allows managers to build their own personality assessment tool. Cesim adopt a module approach to business simulations, in which each has vastly different agendas, goals and objectives for the participant. They can change narrative details in relation to market structure, area names and currencies as well as take out or add decisions to be made in relation to the subject matter.

Business HR teams are likely to enhance their skills by engaging in the A&D Solutions Practice project to the point where they can apply the approaches with confidence. Embedding our practices within everyday organisational functions and processes creates opportunities for Business Psychologists to support the business as the practice becomes mainstream. Business Psychologists consequently can make better use of their time and skills by creating *aerial* views of A&D practice, enabling a more strategic and long term consulting agenda.

There are several initial questions that need to be asked to ascertain if this approach is appropriate:

- Are there key stakeholders within the business who can be allowed unrestricted access to A&D IP?
- Does release of materials to these stakeholders create an opportunity for them to embed assessment and development centre practice for hiring and promotion decision making?
- Is the investment in this approach likely be worthwhile – will the company save money in the long term?
- What are the consulting support opportunities?

How to Align Assessment and Development Training to the Evolved Materials

The learning instructions surrounding the materials used in assessment and development are a critical component of successful Solutions Practice. They need to be clearly articulated for the user to implement the key processes. Any professional given unrestricted rights to change materials also needs explicit guidance in relation to ethics and best practice.

Furthermore, A&D documentation needs to explain the operational logistics that are critical to implementation, i.e.:

- Participant familiarisation;
- Assessment timetables;
- Participant contact communications;
- Feedback logistics.

There needs to be a clear explanation of competency/behavioural definition and how to assign positive and negative indicators to business simulation narratives. Documentation should outline the type, nature and purpose of the A&D exercises, and include an explanation of the behavioural assessment process, using ORCE (Observe, Record, Classify and Evaluate).

Users need to understand how to prepare and present candidate data in accurate behavioural terms, supported by relevant examples, in any formal candidate discussions. They will need clear instructions and a template to write a candidate report outlining strengths and development needs against individual competencies and exercise types. An organisational A&D code of practice can guide internal best practice which can be shared through Online Forums and Secure Knowledge Houses, where people A&D knowledge and expertise can be exchanged and disseminated.

Business Psychologists will need to be prepared to provide adequate support to enable clients to maintain the skills required to implement a Solutions Practice, as well as providing the materials templates and instructions. This ongoing communication and monitoring helps to crystallise relationships, facilitates learning success and builds trust. In the early stages, it is important to take time to review all stakeholder edited materials, especially where competence/behavioural scoring frameworks are re-defined.

Turning now to the nature of copyright, there is growing evidence, given the current progress of new technologies, that 19th century notions of copyright, patent and intellectual property are fast becoming obsolete. Attempting to enforce a copyright regime on the information stratosphere is at best problematic. Constraints on assessment and development materials such as business simulation narratives, pictures or videos, will come to be seen as arbitrary and outmoded.

It has been argued that intellectual property law has an unfortunate tendency to *"disable critical thought"* (Lessig, 2004). The key argument for retaining IP copyright is that it gives credit to the person who originally designed the materials. This can be addressed by the creation of core editable templates under a brand identity that is clearly referenced in all parallel form designs. Businesses can add their own branding and logos alongside the overarching identity. Hosting sites could potentially lead to an explosion of online business simulation materials as any given templates are transformed, improved and morphed into new works. Virtual A&D practice would evolve far more quickly.

A parallel factor is publication of assessment and development materials. Services that make it easier for would-be authors to publish their own materials can give impetus to more sharing of knowledge since it is owned by and under the control of the authors, and not centralised publishing houses.

What Potential the Technological Present and Future Holds for Devolution of Copyright in Relation to Assessment and Development Materials

Vic Hartley, of the Institute for Employment Studies, points out that organisations rely today on remote communication across geographic separation. He considers that for assessment to be valid, and development planned around real world working, these organisations need to reflect the changing ways of interaction by measuring the things that are important (Hartley, 2007).

Organisations rely today on remote communication across global locations. If assessment practice is to evolve, A&D processes need to be aligned to real world working, which is becoming increasingly globalised. A group or role play interaction can now be facilitated and assessed online and remotely. There are many organisations across Europe that have technical solutions to virtual A&D practice. These range from online In-Box exercises (AD&C Ltd) to online assessment centre logistics and administration (OptimHOM – Portugal), right through to arenas where people can interact virtually. Releasing materials from editing constraint has the potential to make a significant contribution to this new environment.

Breaking down copyright by creating editable materials enables management and HR to align documentation to their proprietary software and so helps to further their virtual A&D agenda. In traditional A&D centres, all stakeholders are present at the live venue with the inherent costs of senior management downtime, room hire, participants' travel and accommodation. Virtual approaches reduce the cost per participant by significantly decreasing the need for physical attendance at a set venue, date and time. Many organisations are currently adopting a virtual approach, including, KPMG, Development Dimensions International (DDI), The Scala Associates, Hudson, Fenestra and Mercer.

Business Psychologists have enabled employers to make a quantum leap forward in A&D practice, creating enormous time and cost savings. Now the technology to automate laborious and costly processes gives us more time to examine how we can modernise the assessment material narrative. The key strategic aims are not only to improve the realism, i.e. face validity, of the business simulation backdrops. More clearly, we can address how to weave assessment tasks around the changing competency and behavioural parameters to improve predictive validity. We want to differentiate between participants on the basis of metrics that reflect real world business issues in the present climate: rapid change; unpredictability; more for less; self-development; and flexible working attitudes. Designing and creating materials free of editing restriction can help to realise these goals more rapidly.

Taking these principals forward into business requires bold thinking and a clear agenda around the implementation of A&D processes. Helping clients to uncover the subtler, less superficial and often more important attributes required in a given role is the foundation for them to align an editable assessment template that truly predicts performance.

Clients need to be provided with exercise templates, self-contained instruction and, most importantly, the provision of editable parameter guidelines. When positioning a flexible A&D service to clients, it is important to ensure that the non-copyrighted material:

- Is different from restricted material in both purpose and focus;
- Includes a comprehensive set of individual exercises and full event portfolios *(i.e. combination of different exercises linked to the same backdrop subject matter),* to choose from;
- Includes a suite of different types of exercises;
- Contains all of the administrative and scoring materials needed to manage an assessment event;
- Is accessible and easy to change;
- Is built on behaviours that are flexible and adaptive;
- Enables meaningful conversations around performance;
- Purchasing these materials can be managed by fixed fee.

The lifting of copyright restriction can be controlled by the use of *'Creative Commons Attribution-Non Commercial Licensing'.* Applying this license with clients in relation to A&D materials leads to the following terms and conditions in law:

Clients are free to

- Share — copy and redistribute the material in any medium or format
- Adapt — remix, transform, and build upon the material

The licensor cannot revoke these freedoms as long as clients follow the license terms.

Under the following terms:

i. Attribution — They must give appropriate credit, provide a link to the license, and indicate if changes were made. They may do so in any reasonable manner, but not in any way that suggests the licensor endorses them or their use;
ii. Non-Commercial — They may not use the material for commercial purposes, i.e. they cannot re-sell material.

Long term, materials will evolve as clients create new versions of either individual exercises or full assessment event portfolios. An online library can be built, where clients can download the latest versions of the individual exercises or full event portfolios they have purchased, without incurring additional charges. This is similar to how some online apps operate. In addition, materials can be developed by Business Psychologists to reflect new subject areas as well as current thinking and best practice about assessment parameters.

ADEPT® – Assessment and Development Event Portfolio for Talent is a living example of these practices. ADEPT® is over 2,500 pages of assessment and development template material that, under *Creative Commons Attribution-Non Commercial Licensing,* is not controlled by copyright. This is the largest amount of A&D materials released in this way in the UK to date. Any person, who completes the application stage, can download a full A&D event portfolio or choose from the range of exercises. All materials can be used indefinitely. More importantly, if they don't fit the business culture or corporate standards exactly they can be edited without restriction.

Many clients are looking to save money. As Business Psychologists if we cling to outmoded protectionism we do not evolve our services. A business model centred on helping clients find the right person in a given context leads to short termism. A more enlightening business model of knowledge sharing and flexibility is required. By strategically supporting and promoting more self-sufficiency we create a new kind of involvement and consultancy relationship, a new and different type of dialogue that is fit for the present climate.

Tell me and I'll forget, show me I may remember, involve me and I understand – Chinese Proverb.

References

Azar, B. (2011). Positive psychology advances, with growing pains. *American Psychological Association 42*(4), 32-36. Retrieved from http://www.apa.org/monitor/2011/04/positive-psychology.aspx

Bodell, L. (2012). *Kill the company: End the Status Quo, Start an Innovation Revolution.* Brookline, MA: Bibliomotion.

Chartered Institute of Personnel and Development (2004). *Recruitment, Retention and Turnover. A Survey of UK and Ireland* (Reference 2983). London, England: Conway, N., & Taylor, S.

Chartered Institute of Personnel and Development (2006). *Annual Survey Report. Absence Management* (Reference 3776). London, England: Willmott, B.

Deloitte Consulting (2013). *Predictions for 2014. Building a Strong Talent Pipeline for the Global Economic Recovery – Time for Innovation and Integrated Talent and HR Strategies*. Oakland, CA: Bersin, J.

Gallup (2013). *Worldwide, 13% of Employees are Engaged at Work.* Washington, DC: Crabtree, S. Retrieved from http://www.gallup.com/poll/165269/worldwide-employees-engaged-work.aspx.

George, W. (2003). *Authentic Leadership: Rediscovering the Secrets to Creating Lasting Value.* San Francisco, CA: Wiley.

Grant Thornton (2011). *Corporate Governance Review. A Changing Climate: Fresh Challenges Ahead.* London, UK: Lowe, S. Retrieved from http://www.grant-thornton.co.uk/pdf/corporate_governance.pdf

Hall, B., & Campbell, M. (2006, August 7th). Public Sector Consultants to Cost £20bn. *The Financial Times.* Retrieved from http://www.ft.com/cms/s/0/f4829964-25b0-11db-a12e-0000779e2340.html#axzz3aV23Bmjj.

Harter, J. K., Schmidt, F. L., & Keyes, C. L. (2002). Well-being in the Workplace and its Relationship to Business Outcomes: A Review of the Gallup Studies. In C. L. Keyes & J. Haidt (Eds.), *Flourishing: The Positive Person and the Good Life* (205-224). Washington D.C.: American Psychological Association.

Hartley, V. (2007). *Adapting assessment and development to the changing nature of work*. Institute for Employment Studies. Retrieved from http://www.employment-studies.co.uk/system/files/resources/files/op4.pdf

International Task Force on Assessment Centre Guidelines (2009). Guidelines and Ethical Considerations for Assessment Centre Operations. *International Journal of Selection and Assessment 17(3),* 243-253. Retrieved from http://onlinelibrary.wiley.com/doi/10.1111/j.1468-2389.2009.00467.x/epdf.

Keyes, C. L. M., & Haidt, J. (Eds.) (2002). *Positive Psychology and the Life Well-Lived.* Washington, D.C.: American Psychological Association.

Cameron, K. S., & Quinn, R. E. (2011). *Diagnosing and Changing Organisational Culture: Based on the Competing Values Framework.* San Francisco, CA: Wiley.

Lessig, L. (2004). *Free Culture: How Big Media Uses Technology and the Law to Lock Down Culture and Control Creativity*. New York, NY: Penguin.

Migration Policy Institute (2013). *Attracting and Selecting From the Global Talent Pool: Policy Challenges.* Washington, DC: Demetrios G. P., & Sumption, M.

Murphy, N. (2009). Recruiters Back On-Line Psychometric Testing. *Assessment and Development Matters 1* (1: Spring), 29-31.

Ogbonna, E., & Harris, L. C. (2000). Leadership style, organisational culture and performance: empirical evidence from UK companies. *International Journal of Human Resource Management 11*(4), 766-788.

O'Tool, J. (1996). *Leading Change: The Argument for Values-based Leadership*. New York, NY: Ballantine Books

Phillips, J. (1997). *Return on Investment in Training and Performance Improvement Programs*. Houston, TX: Gulf Publishing Company.

Phillips, J., Stone, R., & Pulliam Phillips, P. (2001). *The Human Resources Scorecard: Measuring the Return on Investment.* Woburn, MA: Butterworth-Heinemann.

Povah, N., & Povah, L. (2009). Impact of the Current Climate on Assessment Centre Practice. *Assessment and Development Matters, 1* (1; Spring), 32-34.

Smith, M., & Smith, P. (2005). *Testing People at Work: Competencies in Psychometric Testing*. Oxford: Blackwell.

Thorpe, R., & Holloway, J. (2008). *Performance Management Multi-Disciplinary Perspectives.* Hampshire, UK: Palgrave Macmillan.

Warr, P. (2007). *Work, Happiness and Unhappiness.* London: Lawrence Erlbaum Associates.

Woodruffe, C. (2000). *Development and Assessment Centres: Identifying and Assessing Competence* (Third Edition). London: CIPD.

COACHING IN THE DIGITAL AGE

Janey Howl

The gift of the digital age is the creation of new ways of connecting and communicating. The ability to transcend time zones and traditional boundaries transforms our personal relationships and ways of doing business at a pace faster than we can learn.

Coaching, a tried and tested methodology for enhancing performance, defining purpose and alleviating anxieties, is the offspring of the preceding information age. Media would have us believe that in our wonderfully technologically connected world, levels of anxiety, alienation and angst are increasing. The premise of a link between anxiety and technology is plausible, but unproven. What is certain is that there are stressful demands unique to the digital age (Hampton et al., 2015). These include the expectation to be 'on' 24/7, the perceived need to cultivate a social media persona, the expectation of an implausible number of 'friends' in the digital space, the crimes of cyber space – including bullying, defamation, identity theft – with little chance of retribution. Do we accept that stress is simply the price we choose to pay for the myriad opportunities of technology? What antidote does coaching offer for the concomitant stresses of the digital age? How well equipped is the coaching profession to meet the demands of the digital age?

Consider the nature of coaching in the digital age. José is Spanish. He lives in California and travels the world in his role as President of Global Brands for a German organisation. He is preparing to come to a UK business school for a residential module on leadership development. It is his first 'meeting' with his coach.

Figure 1: Coaching connection in the digital age
(reprinted with permission)

Coaching in a Digitally Connected World

Welcome to coaching in the digital age. José is speaking in English, his third language, whilst thinking in his native Spanish, searching for answers to questions he has never considered from a woman he has never met. All that connects them across the barriers of language, of space, of time zones, of culture, is the technology of the digital age and the skills of the coach.

The coach's challenge is to engage with the essence of the client, to grasp his unique talents and potential, to understand his immediate challenges and business environment, to help him give voice to his aspirations and his self-limiting beliefs. Sixty minutes later, José has gained personal insight, placed trust in his coach, identified the first steps in developing his leadership capability, is committed to take action and has discovered a newfound enthusiasm and energy for his visit to the UK business school.

So, what do we coach in the digital age? How do we coach in the digital age? What is the impact of new tools such as apps, avatars and virtual environments on coaching?

What Do We Coach in the Digital Age?

Organisational Outcomes

Organisations want results; results that place extraordinary demands on cognitive processing, emotional connectivity and human resilience. The labels vary but, in the author's experience, essentially organisations invest in the development of three things: Strategic Action; Communication; and Authentic Leadership.

Strategic Action

The outputs of effective leadership are strategic action. Leaders must be able to cut through complexity and ambiguity with speed and clarity, making ever more, ever faster, consistently high quality decisions in a world on information overload. According to Eric Schmidt, executive chairman of Google, every 48 hours human beings create as much information as the entire output of humanity from the dawn of civilisation up to 2003 (referenced in St. John's, 2013 *The Power Habits System*). And yet, as Professor Eddie Obeng (2012) says, "we spend our time responding rationally to a world which we understand and recognise but which no longer exists".

Communication

Leaders must be masters of communication. The ability to connect with hearts and minds across all platforms is key to managing virtual teams, leveraging performance, influencing and motivating others, engaging with stakeholders, and generally making things happen. In the digital age, 'all platforms' includes the intimacy of one-on-one, the showtime of large-scale conference presentations, and the robust dialogue of 'town hall' discussion forums, team meetings, board discussion, client negotiations and other diverse interactions. Leaders are also increasingly expected to have a strong social media presence, with a Twitter account and blog often being minimal requirements. Do not forget that, as well as being almost permanently on 'transmit', leaders are also expected to be masters of 'receive'; coaching is expected to equip clients with great listening skills.

Authentic Leadership

Only leaders with real vision, passion, purpose and integrity will survive the remorseless scrutiny of the digital age. In *Energy Leadership*, Bruce Schneider (2008) argues that successful authentic leaders are those who "energetically resonate at a level of success". This is particularly important in the digital age because resonance goes way beyond language; energy is contagious and has instant global impact. Schneider (2008) distinguishes catabolic and anabolic energy. At the cellular level, catabolism usually refers to a breakdown of complex molecules, while anabolism is the opposite. In referencing a person's catabolic or anabolic energy, Schneider is making a broader statement about destructive and constructive forces within a person, asserting that a person's thoughts, beliefs and behaviours all have energetic force too. Authentic leaders not only have positive anabolic energy, they infect others with positive energy in all their interactions and have the ability to cause energetic shifts at all levels of the organisation. Schneider (2008, p.15) claims "nearly 85 percent of all so-called leaders are actually catabolic, thereby destroying the energy and momentum of the people around them and the company as a whole." Whilst this percentage will vary both between and within organisations, most readers will identify with the boss or colleague who saps energy and motivation, and seek to avoid those toxic individuals whose negativity is contagious.

At our basic molecular level, we are energy; particles in a constant state of flux. Energy is not just physical; it is also a psychological, emotional and spiritual force that we manifest in the world, determining how we 'show up' to others. Energy is the source of the vibration that attracts and repels others. We all resonate at different frequencies, and seek out those with similar resonance. Giving out 'good vibes' is key to success. Although it is often an unconscious process, the CEO of a recent client company explained to the board his choice of consultant for a major organisational intervention by saying "She really resonated".

There is one other generic coaching requirement, never stated but always implied. It is the expectation that leaders of our multinational corporations should display the unbounded resourcefulness of timelords; plugged in 24/7, ready to travel the globe at a moment's notice. When the representatives of a leading oil company go to negotiate drilling rights, culpability and accountability with the governments or dictatorships of far-flung countries they travel in person. It is interesting to observe in a variety of business meetings and indeed coaching, that most intimate and personal of development tools, flourish in virtual space. And yet, for complex business negotiations, the personal touch, the tangible experiences of eyeball-to-eyeball contact, the physical handshake, and the smell of fear, are considered to be non-negotiables.

Personal Outcomes

Executive coaching clients usually share their employer's aspirations for developing skills in key aspects of the job. But in the author's experience there are almost always two things that a client wants more than excellence at work. The *first* is time and the *second* is quality of life, or what was once called work–life balance. The very concept of 'balancing' requires a constant vigilance that triggers adrenalin in a perpetual risk/survival mode; a level of intensity and attention that is simply not sustainable. Many executives operate permanently in a low level fight or flight mode; out of touch with feelings, and perpetuating thought patterns that reinforce stress and anxiety. They are often profoundly disconnected from the natural rhythms and relationships of daily human life, whilst being totally plugged in to the rituals of the digital age – most notably the learned 21st century reflex of constant and simultaneous checking of several communication devices. One of the many inherent paradoxes of the digital age is that its defining connectivity frequently comes at the cost of an increasing disconnect from both human relationships and from experiencing life's opportunities and challenges in the present moment.

Every client is time-poor in a 24/7 digital universe. Our European clients, finishing emails before they go to bed and waking up to an influx from America, struggle to find an off switch. The very idea of managing time seems misguided at best, and delusional at worst. In a world of abundance, time is possibly the only finite human resource. As coaches we seek simply to raise awareness of the consequences of choices, and to help our clients make better choices.

The Coaching WHAT

So what are the coaching outcomes that will meet the needs, and satisfy the expectations, of both commissioning organisations and clients themselves? The author concentrates on five key areas to deliver a fast, lasting positive impact: Authentic Leadership; Communication; Strategic Action; Energy; and Freedom from Angst. Having identified WHAT to coach to enable humans to thrive in the digital age, the coach's challenge is to establish the HOW.

How do we Coach in the Digital Age?

It is the coach's responsibility to discern the best tools for achieving client outcomes. The communication tools of the Digital Age are numerous – Skype, Lync, WebEx, Telepresence, Google Hangout, Yammer, Facebook, Twitter, Dropbox, GoToMeeting, Adobe Connect – and ever increasing. Most clients will use a variety of these tools in their everyday lives and be expected to regularly master new ones. It is therefore essential for coaches to not only be alert to tools that enhance the coaching experience *per se*, but also to understand the communication tools and media of the digital age. How else can they help clients to perform effectively, to be healthy and fulfilled, or to develop mastery of the new skills of presence and communication in virtual environments? Of particular interest to coaches is the use of technology in the form of apps, avatars and virtual learning environments, and digital-age-appropriate coaching methodologies.

Lessons and Challenges from Apps

There is a plethora of apps, many of them free and all available 24/7, to transform multiple aspects of personal and business life, including fitness, nutrition, career, life balance, spirituality, relationships, career and finances. They variously promise to deliver "ah-ha moments", to provide "holistic focused personal service," to help you "raise your game" or "take control of your life". The co-creation of a "happier, more accomplished and fulfilling lifestyle" was once the unique selling point of an accomplished coach.

Apps have a successful track record in helping to set and achieve targeted goals, for instance using reinforcement to create new habits or providing public accountability and communities of support. Apps use a multiplicity of psychological models and coaching tools – positive reinforcement, solution focus, Appreciative Inquiry, scaling questions, GROW (Goal-Reality-Options-Will), to provide self-directed learning *par excellence*. The simple efficacy of such tools challenges perceived wisdom regarding the true value-add of the executive or life coach.

Learning from Avatars

The use of virtual world software has the ability to transform learning and ways of doing business in organisations. Online, on-screen technology enables both direct and remote working, generating individual or team outputs that can be saved and shared. Some applications, for example ProReal™, involve a fantasy landscape incorporating metaphor and symbols to create a multi-perspective narrative and visual representation of any situation. Others simulate a real business environment.

Virtual World

ProReal™, a tool developed for coaches, consultants and business leaders, enables participants to provide a visual representation of their world, or a specific situation, and explain it to others, as a way to offer insight and stimulate conversation. The scenarios are used to clarify understanding, share ideas, identify problems, and consider options for change and development. ProReal™ is being used in organisations around the world, as well as within the UK National Health Service, prisons and therapeutic communities, to enhance human communication and performance, to ramp up staff engagement, to understand the customer perspective, to provide a visual aspect to remote coaching and to effect culture change.

Case Study: Business Strategy

ProReal™ was used in an intervention with an international consulting firm that was in the process of implementing significant change and the formulation of a new business strategy. This involved reassessing markets, realigning service lines, rebranding, cost cutting, and staff redundancies. There was an abundance of conflicting priorities, vested interests, and toxic history in the organisation. It was a place where careers thrived by playing the game, doing down colleagues and avoiding, at all costs, telling the truth or addressing poor performance. The use of avatar technology enabled unprecedented levels of disclosure and openness between teams of disparate individuals with conflicting interests.

The participants were in the same room together, but they were telling the truth about management and colleagues in an online version of 'reality', by using avatars to position key players in a virtual landscape of mountains, rivers, fields and roads, and using symbolic 'props' such as castles, clocks, bombs and books, to tell the organisational story and identify its challenges.

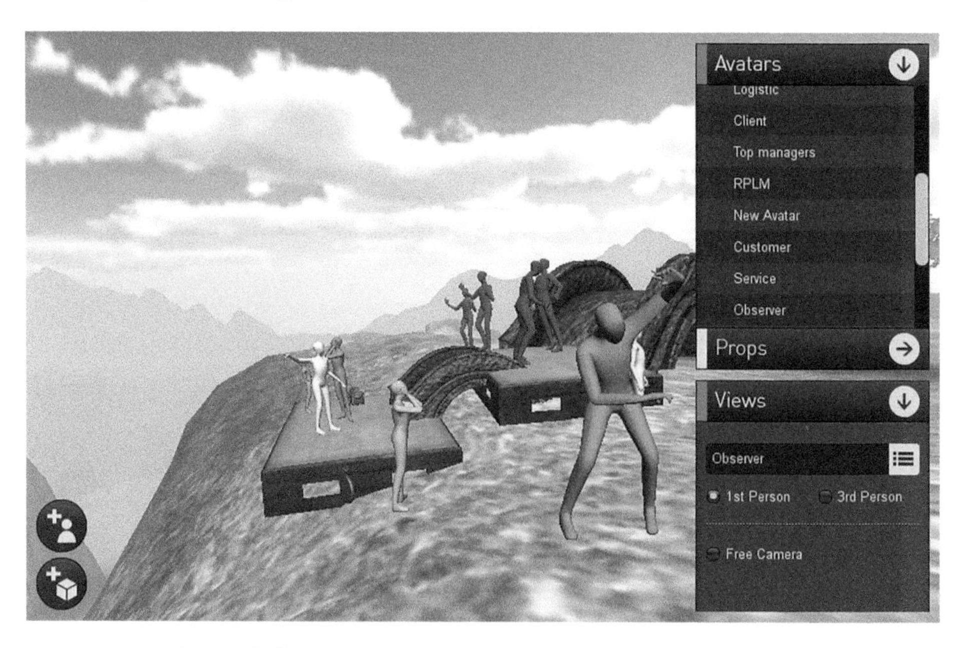

Figure 2: Organisational reality via avatar representation (reprinted with permission)

And what a revealing story they told. The leadership team inhabited the tower of the castle, guarding the treasure chest; the finance team were in the dungeon counting pots of gold; the majority of consultants (individually named in identified team clusters) were fighting each other in the courtyard; various named mavericks were on solo missions attempting to penetrate the leadership tower without being killed by colleagues; business support staff were barely keeping their heads above water, swimming circles in the castle moat. The drawbridge was firmly up. The cavalry glimpsed on the far horizon, represented potential partners in a merger or acquisition. Clients were represented as a group of forlorn individuals, forgotten and abandoned, on the banks of a river far from the castle. Armies of competitors were marching at speed to seize the castle.

The creation of a visual and narrative representation was used as a diagnostic tool to tell the organisational story. The use of metaphor and symbols provided a meaningful and non-contentious way of describing issues and opportunities. Many of the traditional organisational interventions of Business Psychologists are characterised by conflict and personal attachment to individual versions of organisational 'truth'. In the ProReal™ world, multiple perspectives are captured, as the software makes it easy for participants to incorporate each other's views, making adjustments as a team to the shared screen representation until they have a picture that satisfies everyone.

The granular data brought simplicity to a complex situation, enabling the facilitators to dive deeper into specific situations to find out what was really going on. The use of avatars and props was perceived as playful; they made the intervention enjoyable and memorable for participants.

The software created the basis for a shared language and memory that went on to form the foundation for a collective vision that placed client experience at the heart of the business.

Virtual Business Environment

Qube™, the brainchild of Professor Eddie Obeng, is a virtual learning and working business environment. Participants achieve real business outcomes via a series of facilitated or self-driven workshops, conferences, meetings and project activities in virtual space, using pre-loaded tools and techniques. Qube™ is genuinely simple and intuitive to use, enabling 'participants' to move around, physically interacting, working shoulder to shoulder, brainstorming with whiteboards and sticky notes, and opening and working on documents together. The 'participants' are gender-neutral Qubot™ avatars, with webcam displays for heads to simulate face-to-face conversations. Visit www.pentaclethevbs.com for further information.

Benefits of Avatars and Virtual Environments

Qube™ is a highly effective business tool with the capability to gather colleagues, clients, suppliers and partners together to solve problems, deliver projects and develop innovations, without travel time, costs, or carbon footprint. Business Psychologists are frequently challenged to help clients to work effectively in virtual teams. Qube™, for example, was recommended to a client as the possible answer to the needs of a Sales Director based in Delhi, responsible for the entire Asia/Pacific region, managing a team who work from home and traverse the continent for monthly team meetings.

The ProReal™ world of avatars and props is an artificial landscape that helps people to see the world through other people's eyes. The process of "Mentalization", identified by Fonagy et al. (2002), enables us to perceive and interpret human behaviour in terms of intentional mental states – a fundamental skill for effective communication and influencing. The use of symbols and avatars creates a universal language. This is an advantage not just in global organisations where people are often conducting business in their second, third, or even fourth language. In a world that favours the articulate Extravert communicator, ProReal™ also creates space for Introverts to tell their stories.

Fundamentally, ProReal™ is a medium for individuals and organisations to tell stories that recreate the past or rehearse possible futures. It is a powerful, tangible reminder of the truth of Bryant McGill's (2012) assertion, in *Voice of Reason*, that "The world, as it is, is not a permanent reality, but is a temporary product of our choices as creators." Effecting change through understanding choices and consequences is the *raison d'être* of coaches, whether working with individuals, or teams of people, whether facilitating personal development or organisational change.

Early research by the developers David Tinker and Andrew Jackson, working in collaboration with the boards and management teams of diverse organisations, confirms the potential for the use of avatars and virtual business environments to supplement, and in some cases supersede, the traditional tools of business psychology in delivering quality and timely organisational outcomes (visit http://www.ProReal.co.uk for further information). For example, a core skill of the Business Psychologist is the ability to make sense of the web of interconnected relationships that represents an organisation. Virtual reality software enables unconscious social mapping to be brought quickly and accurately to conscious awareness so that the complexities of organisational dynamics, politics, structures and systems can be expressed, shared and explored. Similarly, for facilitators in the business of capturing a picture of current organisational reality and promoting a better vision for the future, the software creates a visual representation that provides an opportunity for coaching, prioritising and shared problem-solving.

Avatars offer psychological credibility in the digital age in that they have high face validity, are enjoyable to use and transcend some of the barriers of language and culture (Lieberman et al., 2007; Suler, 2004). Virtual environments enable people to experiment safely with alternative versions of the future and potentially eliminate the resistance to change, which often represents a major block to coaching progress. There is, however, no definitive evidence of the efficacy of avatar representation relative to traditional coaching methods for eliciting clients' stories of their imagined, possible futures. Nor, indeed, is there empirical evidence of the extent to which the skill of the coach or facilitator influences the outcomes of interventions using technology.

With a focus on delivering key client outcomes, the coach is likely to coach some of the outward manifestation of subcomponents; for example, leadership presence, influencing skills or stakeholder engagement. However, this is unlikely to be sufficient, for authentic leadership, like happiness, comes from within. The Dalai Lama proposes that true happiness is a stable sense of serenity, calm and contentment that does not depend upon external factors or circumstances, and is cultivated by the development of conducive attitudes and actions (The Dalai Lama & Cutler, 1999). Much the same could be said of authentic leadership. And it takes time, dedication and practice to change the habits of the leader's mind; that is the coaching challenge. The most successful coaches of the 21st century are those who hardwire new habits of both being and doing. The author recommends five master multitasking coaching tools for the digital age. They are Mindfulness, Play, Energy, Grit and Storytelling. In reconnecting people with the ancient wisdom of heart and soul, they create the energy and fluidity that are essential for flourishing in the digital age.

Tool 1: Mindfulness

Mindfulness, a concept and practice inherited from the Buddhist tradition, has found its way into mainstream psychology and medicine, and is increasingly becoming viewed as an important business tool. Jon Kabat-Zinn, a Western Buddhist practitioner from the University of Massachusetts Medical School, describes it (2012) as "paying focused attention on purpose, without judgment, to the experience of the present moment". The author's professional practice demonstrates that coaching mindfulness creates the opportunity for clients to become fully present in their own lives. Innovative practitioners include Tobyn Tribbeck and Andy Puddicombe, who are both dedicated teachers of mindfulness, celebrating its efficacy in providing the essential focus, attention and concentration required for meeting the relentless demands of an infinitely connected world. Visit www.prezentmind.com and www.headspace.com for leading edge applications of mindfulness.

Mindfulness is less about spirituality and more about concentration. It is the ability to quieten your mind and focus your attention on the present, dismissing any distractions that come your way. Choosing, and learning to control focus of attention leads to significant clarity of thought and much better and faster decision-making. By simply noticing what we do not usually notice, because our heads are too busy in the future or the past – thinking about our to-do list or going over what has already been said and done – we train our attention 'muscle' and become mentally fitter.

The benefits of mindfulness training are not just behavioural; they are physical too. Mindfulness training helps people to change how they think, feel and act at a basic neural level. George Dvorsky, Chairman of the Board for the Institute of Ethics and Emerging Technologies and a prolific commentator on the impact of cutting-edge science and technology on human performance and experience, cites numerous scientific studies that demonstrate the efficacy of mindfulness. In particular is the ongoing research of John Denniger of Harvard Medical School. Studies consistently show improved connectivity inside the brain's attentional networks with neural activation patterns undergoing a leftward shift in frontal asymmetry, an activity pattern associated with positive emotional states. Clinical trials prove the efficacy of mindfulness practice in alleviating a variety of mental and physical conditions including anxiety, stress and depression. They also point to improving the ability to handle emotions, increasing resilience and generating a positive outlook on life. See Davis and Hayes (2011) for a practice review.

Tool 2: Play

Silicon Valley, the headquarters of Google, of Facebook, of Apple, crackles with the creative energy generated by a working environment that encourages play. The great innovative dotcoms understand that the benefits of playfulness at work are measured in increased productivity, higher job satisfaction, better teamwork, greater workplace morale and reductions in absenteeism and staff turnover. A popular feature of our Board Retreats is the opportunity for spontaneous play. Clients connect with self and each other through shooting basketball hoops, doing jigsaws, playing table tennis, strumming guitars, playing Connect, or draughts, or chess.

Remember your childhood self and the intensity with which you played? How you forgot time until hunger, or the dying of the light, brought you back to earth? In play we find purpose. Play is hard work, and yet it is in play that we find rest – a stop to the almost ceaseless background chatter of our minds, the soundtrack to our busy lives.

Forget fun. Fun is contrived. Fun frequently takes planning, and requires effort. Play, on the other hand, is spontaneous, of and in the moment, taking us out of our contrived selves into authenticity where we discover passion and purpose. After all, as George Bernard Shaw so eloquently reminds us, we do not stop playing because we get old: rather we get old because we stop playing.

Coach your clients on how to play – play hard. For it is in play that they will connect with their creative energy to fuel the accomplishment of their goals, boost energy and vitality, increase resistance to disease, and ward off stress and depression. Play silences the inner critic that is the enemy of innovative problem-solving. Encourage your clients to reclaim their inner child and set aside regular quality playtime free from electronic devices.

Tool 3: Energy

Energy is the source of potential output. The achievement of personal potential requires currency in the form of being plugged into the universal grid that is the digital age and resonating at the appropriate frequencies. This requires consistent and extraordinary physical, mental and spiritual input. Coaches who enable clients to make energetic shifts also give them the power to change their world. They support clients in the creation of the fundamentals of good energy: quality nutrition and hydration; adequate sleep; exercise; rest; and play. They coach on non-toxicity in relationships, purpose at work and a life outside. Coaches help clients to create the habits of inspiring thoughts: the clean language and healthy self-talk that characterise and fuel an abundant life force.

Tool 4: Grit

The digital age has changed not only our experience of time, but also the possibilities of our lives. It used to take a lifetime to establish a reputation; now you can go viral on YouTube in an instant, the same instant that it takes to trash a reputation, with or without evidence. Andy Warhol famously said that everyone would be famous for fifteen minutes. Timelines for fame and fortune, in a world where everyone can be famous every fifteen minutes, are transformed. Remember how long it used to take to publish a book, to produce and distribute music, to communicate in writing, to be a consumer, to interact and meet up with people.

The notion that something requires effort can be shocking to a "because I'm worth it" generation reared on instant gratification and shielded from failure by a world in which even school sports days are frequently non-competitive events. Grit – defined as "sustained perseverance and passion for long-term goals" – is a relatively new construct (Duckworth et al., 2007), identified by Martin Seligman's research team at the University of Pennsylvania (Peterson & Seligman, 2004), the home of positive psychology. Grit, a non-cognitive trait, accounts for 4% of variance in success outcomes (Duckworth et al., 2007; Duckworth & Seligman, 2005). That 4% is the difference between mediocrity and brilliance, between cruising and flying, between just ticking over and vibrant energy, between vague discontent and fulfilment. Seligman's studies demonstrate that it is grit – rather than talent, intelligence, or education – that best predicts success.

Although it takes intelligence and talent to set a far-reaching goal and drive relentlessly towards it, they are not enough. Ability and talent frequently shut down in the face of adversity. Grit never quits. As grit is both a skill and an attitude, it is eminently coachable. An effective tool for cultivating an attitude, and a habit, of grit is via the Thirty Days Challenge. The client chooses a life-enhancing (or performance-enhancing) activity and undertakes to do it every single day for thirty days. Challenges reflect client diversity. For example, take a lunch break, Bikram Yoga, reading a bedtime story, clearing the email inbox, alcohol abstinence, no gossiping, journaling, follow-up on delegated tasks, walking, drinking two litres of water, returning all phone calls, getting up twenty minutes earlier, giving constructive feedback to the team or saying "thank you". Acquiring grit in one area, any area, of life is hugely beneficial as clients realise they can accomplish what they set their minds to. A series of Thirty Days Challenges supports clients in developing the grit that will sustain them on the long path to the accomplishment of significant business and life goals.

Grit is often particularly relevant for clients in the critical 'manager to leader' transition zone, where the talent that got them there is no longer enough. It is a lonely exposed place where new leaders learn to abandon the comfort zone of reliable trusted skills, such as 'do-it-myself', and acquire new ones, all in the face of public scrutiny and the risk of career derailment.

Tool 5: Storytelling

A basic coaching skill is that of 'coaching the client, not the story', a powerful reminder to avoid getting caught up in the dramas and noise of clients' busy lives. However, coaches working with the concept of Authentic Leadership and other similarly complex business challenges will recognise the value of mastery of Storytelling as a valuable coaching tool in the digital age. Narrative Psychology is identified with the "storied nature of human conduct" (Sarbin, 1986) and its assertion that people are influenced more by their constructs of the world than by an objective reality. It has taught us that human activity and experience are filled with 'meaning' and stories, rather than logical arguments or lawful formulations. Scientists, including James Pennebaker of the University of Texas, have evidenced that the generation of narrative coherence – that is making sense of the story arc of our lives – improves health and wellbeing on a range of objective measures, including immune function (see Pennebaker & Seagal, 1999; Smyth & Pennebaker, 2008).

Dan McAdams, an American Northwestern University psychology professor who has spent the past decade systematically and quantitatively studying stories, demonstrates how redirecting narratives, an approach known as story editing, can have amazingly powerful long-term effects (see McAdams, 2006). This is also the experience of professional coaches. Coaches' accounts of successful client interventions demonstrate that stories are a powerful source of self-persuasion, which not only help people to create something that is meaningful and sensible out of the chaos of our lives, but also to shape our future. Coaching techniques such as solution focus, Appreciative Inquiry and 'what if' questions inspire clients to create their imagined futures, to tell better stories, to create the narrative that shapes behaviour; the narrative that drives how they perform at work and that ultimately determines how they live their lives.

The Future of Coaching

The Digital Age has created a world without frontiers, an unbounded universe where there is no such thing as too much information. Clients, and indeed coaches themselves, are struggling with the limits of time, energy, knowledge and belief. As technological innovation multiplies we are all required to upgrade our operating systems, to become ever more efficient human beings. The rising generation of "digital natives" (Prensky 2001a) – Generation Y – do indeed have distinctly different behaviours, values and attitudes from previous generations. In particular, they are detached from institutions and particularly well networked with friends. The world has changed and, as the world shifts, so too must our paradigms.

What then is the essence of coaching? At heart, coaching is an intimate conversation, whether with a single individual or several people, that leads to behavioural change. In an age where social robots with simulated empathy are created to alleviate loneliness, an age in which we increasingly expect more from technology and less from each other, the real relationship and deep listening of the coaching experience will become ever scarcer. Digital communication already encourages us to sacrifice conversation for mere connection. As the Psychologist and cultural analyst Sherry Turkle (2012) reminds us, "what technology makes easy is not always what nurtures the human spirit."

If the digital age is still in its infancy, then the scientific evidence for the efficacy of its new technology and tools for personal and organisational development is in the early gestation period. Herein lies an opportunity, indeed an obligation, for Business Psychologists to undertake rigorous empirical investigation to shape the future of the digital age.

Conclusion

Back in 2005 when *Business Psychology in Practice* was published, we coached on raising your game. Now we strive also to transform our own game, our core skills, our assumptions and tools, our business practice, our models of human potential and organisational growth, in order to help business leaders to do the same. Technology gets a bad rap for disconnecting us from each other and making human interaction less personal. It threatens mediocre coaches with extinction as they run the risk of replacement by app. But the thing is this: as coaches in the digital age we can choose to invent new coaching methodologies, to embrace multi-disciplinary scientific discovery, to reconnect with ancient wisdom, to apply futurist thought and seize the opportunity to transform human happiness and success on an unprecedented global scale.

References

The Dalai Lama & Cutler H. C. (1999). *The Art of Happiness: A Handbook for Living*. London: Hodder and Stoughton.

Davis, D. M., & Hayes, J. A. (2011). What are the Benefits of Mindfulness? A Practice Review of Psychotherapy-Related Research. *Psychotherapy, 48*(2), 198-208.

Duckworth, A. L., Peterson, C., Matthews, M. D., & Kelly, D. R. (2007). Grit, perseverance and passion for long-term goals. *Journal of Personality and Social Psychology, 92*(6), 1087-1101.

Duckworth, A. L., & Seligman, M. E. P. S. (2005). Self-Discipline Outdoes IQ in Predicting Academic Performance of Adolescents. *Psychological Science, 16*, 939-944.

Fonagy, P., Gergely, G., Jurist, E. L., & Target, M. (2002). *Affect Regulation, Mentalization and the Development of the Self*. New York, NY Other Press.

Hampton, K., Rainie L., Lu, W., Shin I., & Purcell, K. (2015). *Psychological Stress and Social Media Use*. Retrieved from http://www.pewinternet.org/2015/01/15/psychological-stress-and-social-media-use-2/ on 24 May 2015.

Kabat-Zinn, J. (2012). *Mindfulness for Beginners: Reclaiming the Present Moment and Your Life.* Colorado: Sounds True Inc.

Lieberman, M. D., Eisenberger, N. I., Crockett, M. J., Tom, S. M., Pfeifer, J. H., & Way, B. M. (2007). Putting Feelings Into Words: Affect Labeling Disrupts Amygdala Activity in Response To Affective Stimuli. *Psychological Science, 18*(5), 421-428.

McAdams, D. P. (2006). *The Redemptive Self: Stories Americans Live by.* New York, NY: Oxford University Press.

McGill, B. (2012). *Voice of Reason: Speaking to the Great and good Spirit of Revolution of Mind.* Florida: Paperlyon.

Obeng, E. (2012). TEDGlobal 2012, *Smart failure for a fast-changing world.* Retrieved from https://www.ted.com/talks/eddie_obeng_smart_failure_for_a_fast_changing_world on 8 June 2015.

Pennebaker, J. W., & Seagal, J. D. (1999). Forming a Story: The Health Benefits of Narrative, *Journal of Clinical Psychology*, *55* (10), 1243-1254.

Peterson, C., & Seligman, M. E. (2004). *Character Strengths and Virtues: A Handbook and Classification.* New York, NY: Oxford University Press.

Prensky, M. R. (2001a). Digital Natives, Digital Immigrants Part I. *On the Horizon (MCB University Press), 9*(5), 1-6.

Sarbin T. R. (Ed.) (1986). *Narrative Psychology: The storied nature of human conduct.* New York, NY: Praeger.

Schneider, B. D. (2008). *Energy leadership: Transforming your workplace and your life from the core* (4th ed.). Hoboken, NJ: John Wiley & Sons.

Smyth, J. M., & Pennebaker J. W. (2008). Exploring the Boundary Conditions of Expressive Writing: In Search of the Right Recipe. *British Journal of Health Psychology, 13*(1), 1-7.

St. John, N. (2013). *The Power Habits System – The New Science for Making Success Automatic.* Illinois: Nightingale Conant.

Suler, J. (2004). The Online Disinhibition Effect. *Cyberpsychology and Behavior, 7(*3), 321-326.

Turkle, S. (2012). TED2012, *Connected, but alone?* Retrieved from http://www.ted.com/talks/sherry_turkle_alone_together on 10 October 2014.

Further Reading

Beck, M. (2012). *Finding your way in a wild new world: Five steps to fulfilling your true calling*. London: Piatkus.

Carroll, S. (2011). *From Eternity to Here: The Quest for the Ultimate Theory of Time.* London: Oneworld Publications.

Gray, J. (2013). *The Silence of Animals: On progress and other modern myths.* Colchester: Penguin.

Howl, J. (forthcoming, 2016). *Self Talk: Coaching the Inner Critic.*

Prensky, M. R. (2012). *From Digital Natives to Digital Wisdom: Hopeful Essays for 21st Century Learning*. California: Sage.

WELL-BEING IN ORGANISATIONS: THERE IS MORE WE CAN DO

Jan P. de Jonge

If the most important reason for people to be in work is to earn a living, then one of the key conditions for employment to be sustained successfully, apart from satisfactory performance, may well be people's level of mental well-being at work. It has been widely found that being in work in itself has many advantages. Apart from an income, it offers personal fulfilment, job satisfaction and sense of mastery and achievement. Work, then, on balance, is generally good for our level of well-being (e.g. Black, 2008; Van Stolk et al., 2014; National Institute for Health and Clinical Excellence (NICE), 2009). Yet, the world of work can also be where well-being is damaged. It is where illness, stress, conflict, anxiety and depression can originate. Indeed, in the UK between 2007 and 2008, an estimated 13.5 million working days were lost to stress-related absence, with a consequential national cost of work-related stress at around £4 billion per year (Health and Safety Executive (HSE), 2009). Mental illness in the UK that affects work efficiency costs £15 billion per year; the estimated annual cost of absenteeism is £8 billion. Prevention and early identification of problems should save employers some 30% of that amount (NICE, 2009).

In this article, I discuss the key developments in the way mental well-being at work has been addressed in recent years in the UK, by way of policy, guidelines and available support, after which I offer my knowledge and experience of what works in terms of further promoting well-being in work. The role that professional practitioners in the field of business psychology can play is also discussed. Apart from many sources of research in this field, my personal opinions are based on my experience in providing support and advice to some 200 clients who, in various ways and for various lengths of time, have struggled with their personal (mental) well-being at work while retaining their jobs. These clients were referred to a national mental health charity tasked to provide advice and guidance to people in employment. They were often referred to this 'job retention service' by their GP, although in some cases, people requested this support directly. I will point to those aspects where my personal opinion on how to promote well-being at work differs from, or is complementary to, other sources of advice or guidelines that are available.

Key developments

In recent years, mental health and well-being has received a lot of attention in the UK – or, at least, more than previously. The reasons for this may relate to an increased focus within British society on mental health and well-being brought about, at least in part, by the economic downturn of recent years. Both central government, through policies and legislation, and other advisory bodies have been giving attention to mental health and well-being at work. This is sometimes as part of a wider debate accessing various perspectives on, and aspects of, well-being (e.g. the report in 2011 by the Office for National Statistics (ONS) on 'Measuring What Matters').

In 2007, the Health Work Wellbeing Executive/Department of Work and Pensions (DWP) commissioned PricewaterhouseCoopers to review the business case for workplace wellness programmes in the UK. The Foresight Project on Mental Capital and Wellbeing, commissioned by the Government Office for Science reported in 2008. This aimed to identify the opportunities and challenges facing the UK in the next few decades and implications for people's 'mental capital' and 'mental well-being'. It offered a broad framework for further analysis and policy development. The public health white paper Healthy Lives, Healthy People (Department of Health (DofH), 2010) was the first public health strategy to give equal weight to both mental and physical health, with emphasis on well-being at work and 'working well'. The Chartered Institute of Personnel and Development (CIPD) and mental health charity Mind have jointly issued practical, specific guidance on managing and supporting mental health at work (CIPD and Mind, 2011).

New legislation (notably the Equality Act 2010) has been introduced to prevent discrimination based on, among other things, a person's mental health. Along with its Management Standards, the HSE offers its 'Management Standards Indicator Tool', an online freely accessible questionnaire with acceptable reliability (Kerr, McHugh & McCrory, 2009). This questionnaire aims to give organisations an indication of how their workforce rates their performance in managing work-related stress. The questionnaire can be used on its own or be included in other measurement tools. Similarly, in 2010, with sponsorship from the DofH, Investors in People (IIP) introduced its Health and Wellbeing Good Practice Award, based on the 'Health and Wellbeing Framework'. This Good Practice Award to an extent overlaps with the well-established Investors in People Standard first launched in 1991 (IIP, 2010), which is similarly awarded upon assessment of five indicators (Planning, Supportive Management, Evaluation, Work-life balance and Supportive Culture). Engage for Success in 2014 reported on the increasing interest in both employee engagement and well-being in the UK and in the 'global developed economies'.

In its 2014 paper, Engage for Success refers to research by Robertson Cooper's founding directors, which showed that measures of both well-being and employee engagement correlated with those of employee performance. Specifically, well-being works to significantly strengthen performance. Several compelling case studies are described in which well-being and engagement campaigns are shown to bear fruit in terms of improved customer satisfaction, reduced sickness and improved reported levels of well-being. Similarly, the CIPD (2012) advises that well-being is closely linked to sustained employee engagement, which affect performance of both employees and organisations.

It could be argued that the increased currency of the topic of 'well-being' in our society has been in tandem with a similar increase in the attention that mediation has gained, featuring as an approach to resolve workplace issues with a lower threshold than litigation. Many workplace problems where mental health and well-being is (potentially) at stake lend themselves to mediation. Examples of such problems are conflicts between members of staff and management, poor communication and when there is misunderstanding of the need for support.

In my experience, a significant proportion of 'well-being at work' issues are suitable for a mediation process. In essence, mediation can be seen as a structured approach, embedded in policy, to addressing conflict through increased and better direct communication within the organisation. Better communication in this context often boils down to intervening earlier and being more open, without feeling restricted by or being apprehensive of the legal rules and ramifications of engaging in such communication. Organisations such as the Advisory, Conciliation and Arbitration Service (ACAS) and the CIPD have published guides about mediation in the workplace (e.g. ACAS, 2013) in recent years. The recommendation of early support and intervention is a central theme in many reviews (e.g. Van Stolk et al. in their 2014 RAND Europe report) and my own experience confirms this. Responsiveness, both by employers and external support providers, is key. Business psychology and human resource practitioners have a relevant role to play here in designing and implementing processes and policies that promote responsiveness that is both pragmatic and prompt.

The increased attention for well-being at work is also underpinned by the Quality Standard for Service User Experience in Adult Mental Health and the related Guideline published in 2009 by NICE on promoting mental well-being at work. Currently, neither this Standard nor the Guideline are legally binding for health care providers. There is a move, however, towards elevating these into legislation. Adopting the definition that is used by the Foresight Project on Mental Capital and Wellbeing project, the NICE guideline defines well-being at work as a "dynamic state, where one can develop one's potential, work productively and creatively, build strong and positive relationships, and contribute to the community" (NICE 2009).

According to the definition, mental well-being is enhanced when the individual is able to fulfil personal and social goals and achieve a sense of purpose in society. The guideline offers specific recommendations on how line managers should promote the well-being of employees and respond to any well-being concerns. At an organisational level, it recommends that a strategic and coordinated approach should be taken to promote employee well-being and manage risks. The guideline also recommends that employers, trade unions and other employee representatives should provide opportunities for flexible working (which may take several forms) and promote a culture that supports it. A final key recommendation within this NICE guideline is that relevant parties, such as business sector representative bodies and others involved in national programmes and initiatives, should support micro, small and medium-sized businesses, through offering a range of support, advice, tools and approaches in order to promote well-being.

Many other initiatives and organisations have been created in recent years, at levels varying from local to national and beyond, that aim to address well-being-at-work issues, such as Business in the Community (BITC). This outreach charity, established in 1982, invites businesses to commit to improving and publically reporting on their employee well-being. Many UK businesses are members of this charity. It has its own 'Workwell Model', developed within the business sector, which identifies actions it recommends employers to undertake to promote 'wellness' and engagement. Through engaging business in its Workwell Campaign, BITC aims to improve well-being and business performance.

In 2008, the NHS-funded 'Improving Access to Psychological Therapies' (IAPT) programme was launched. This pan-England programme offers interventions approved by NICE for treating people with depression and anxiety disorders, for example Cognitive Behavioural Therapy, counselling and employment advice. The IAPT programme also includes employment retention services focusing on offering advice and guidance to people in employment who are experiencing problems with their well-being. Referrals to IAPT job retention services can be made by GPs, other primary and secondary healthcare professionals, occupational health services and by individuals themselves who are seeking support.

In its first three years the IAPT programme treated over a million people, whilst 45,000 people moved off sick pay and benefits (IAPT, 2012). It is now in its second phase where, as part of the government's national mental health strategy 'No health without mental health,' £400 million was committed for the 4-year period up to 2015. Recently the IAPT programme has put trials in place as part of a gradual development of a payment-by-results approach, as opposed to a focus on an activity or needs-based system (Health and Social Care Information Centre, 2014). In a strict Payment-by-Results (PbR) approach, providers of mental health and job retention support services are paid according to outcomes instead of activity or service provided. For instance, a patient moving off Statutory Sick Pay and back into active work constitutes an outcome for the service provider. According to the DofH, in a PbR system, "commissioners pay healthcare providers for each patient seen or treated, taking into account the complexity of their needs" (DofH, 2013). Although the PbR approach is meant to improve overall quality of service provision, its impact is as yet unknown and, given the quoted PbR system definition, it is unclear whose outcomes are being evaluated for funding purposes: provider-based outcomes ('outcomes' referring to 'activity') or outcomes recognisably to the benefit of the patient.

Since its inception, the IAPT job retention services have been provided at local level by charities and other independent providers on the basis of contracts with councils and NHS trusts. Many local IAPT-based job retention programmes have been overstretched, with waiting lists for applicants to use the service as referring agencies have increased their level of referrals to advisors. These job retention activities in some specific cases seem to have been more successful when the service user, the IAPT advisor and the employer worked together to address the needs and perceptions of the service user, whilst also attending to the perspective of the employer. In this sense, such effective approaches are similar to a transparent mediation approach, where 'both sides' are heard by a third, mediating party.

An example of a partly government-funded initiative is the 'Time to Change' pledge, where individuals and businesses sign up to a pledge to end the stigma and discrimination around mental health at work. The programme, run by the charities Mind and Rethink Mental Illness, is funded by the DofH, Comic Relief and Big Lottery Fund, and has received over £23 million in funding. The initiative encourages open conversation about mental health and equality for people with mental health problems. Over 62,000 pledges have been registered, though only 200 are from organisations that have also submitted an action plan. Examples range from local councils and central government departments to universities and, although less well represented, private companies, with a range of programmes and activities. A clear result of the 'Time to Change' initiative has been significant positive changes in public and employers' attitudes to mental health and workplace practices. However, compared to the public and third sectors, the impact of this initiative on private-sector employers appears less clearly in evidence.

The City Mental Health Alliance (CMHA) is an example of a recent private-sector initiative. Employers in the City of London formed a coalition in 2013 with the aim of breaking down the stigma attached to mental health problems and helping to improve mental health amongst its employees. Some well-known banks and other companies in the financial and legal services sector are founding members of the Alliance that aims to create a culture of openness and enable practical steps employers can take. It focuses on common stress-related mental health conditions and encourages employers to adopt policies to support their staff's mental well-being. It may be too early to say to what extent the aims of more 'local' sector-specific initiatives like the CMHA are being met, although they appear to have great potential in reshaping attitudes to, and management practices around, well-being in larger organisations. In 2014, Dame Carol Black warned that national productivity is at risk if companies ignore employee health and that they need to invest more in staff well-being (People Management, 2014). Referred to as "the last workplace taboo" (Aston, 2014) there still seems to be a 'culture of silence' around mental health amongst some business leaders. However, improvements in awareness, attitudes and understanding (BITC, 2014) suggest this could soon change. In its Absence Management survey for 2014 the CIPD, in partnership with healthcare provider Simplyhealth, reports a fall in absence levels since 2013. The report identified an increase amongst its survey respondents in line manager capability to identify and manage mental health and well-being issues amongst staff

(CIPD, 2014b), although the majority of surveyed organisations have not (yet) increased their focus on employee well-being. In July 2014, the UK DWP announced that its new Health and Work Service in England and Wales would be delivered by Health Management Limited, a MAXIMUS company. Employees on sick leave will receive support to help them return to work by providing them with an occupational health assessment when they reach, or are expected to reach, more than 4 weeks' sickness absence.

Most referrals will come from GPs, but also from employers that do not have access to occupational health programmes. As part of the service, a 'return-to-work plan' will be shared with their employer and GP. More general health and work advice will be available to GPs, employees and employees via telephone and a website. It is unclear to what extent this new service will cooperate with the IAPT employment retention service mentioned earlier. The Organisation for Economic Cooperation and Development (OECD 2014) points out that extensive research suggests that productivity loss is caused by people remaining at work with work-related stress or mental ill-health (often described as 'presenteeism'); this may be an even bigger issue than that represented by sickness absence due to mental health and well-being issues, but does not seem to be clearly acknowledged in recent policy changes.

What works to promote employees' well-being at work?

It is clear from the key developments and sources referred to above that a growing proportion of organisations sees well-being as an area of human resource management to focus on and invest in. Examples of initiatives, especially in larger organisations, are the appointment of well-being or wellness champions, personalised counselling, and programmes in which employees are involved early on in the planning process. More organisations are also starting to realise the importance of line managers' skills and their awareness of their role in influencing and promoting well-being amongst employees. Several pieces of research confirm that training of line managers is effective in improving the mental health of employees (e.g. Black, 2008; Hassan et al., 2009). Research conducted as part of the Foresight Mental Capital and Wellbeing Project demonstrates that poor-quality line management is detrimental to mental health (Barling & Carson, 2008). Organisations that address both well-being and sustainable employee engagement may prove to be more successful in terms of absence levels, staff retention and productivity.

Based on the evidence from research and initiatives mentioned above, and my case work with some 200 individual employees in a local IAPT job retention service, the following seem to be characteristics of effective approaches to well-being at work.

- Staff feel involved in the design of the approaches to their well-being or have a say in how these approaches are implemented in daily practice. This is where engagement of staff is closely related to well-being.
- Senior management visibly champions and drives the approach that is implemented across the organisation.
- Job retention policy is geared towards providing guidance on simple, active steps to be taken when staff experience well-being issues. For example, ensuring that these steps are introduced during the induction ('on-boarding') of new staff may have a positive effect. Inductions are an important formative stage at which the organisational culture and approach to well-being is expressed to new staff. In these inductions, the importance of a sustained work-life balance and appropriate workloads could be emphasised. A better understanding of the longer-term effects of poor practices, and a subsequent recalibration of organisational culture may be needed in some organisations.
- Employees (including managers) who are trained to detect well-being issues respond more quickly and effectively when problems emerge. This applies to individuals' self-awareness and capacity to 'self-diagnose', as well as where colleagues play a role in creating awareness and providing initial support. Well-being has a place within the organisational culture and practices, influencing the entire employment cycle, from recruitment, selection and on-boarding to when staff leave the organisation.
- Organisations that frequently and systematically monitor well-

being, as a factor in how their staff perform, do better at preventing and addressing well-being issues at work.

- An impartial and trained ear can reduce periods of absence if made available quickly and action-oriented solutions are identified. In my experience, those individuals whose well-being is at stake are not always as vocal about that as they would wish to be.

The SLH Group, a housing provider in the north of England, has won several awards for its health and well-being initiatives. Elements of their successful efforts include employees having a say in the organisation's personalised well-being service, an annual payment to employees that they are expected to use to promote their personal health and well-being, the availability of a personal life coach, and nutrition advice. Clear gains have been achieved, including a reduction of sickness absence to less than half the level measured under a year earlier and increased levels of well-being (SLH, 2014). The CEO of the organisation reports that health and well-being has become such a priority at SLH that the first question managers now ask in monthly one-to-ones with employees is about their personal well-being.

The role of business psychology in achieving further improvements

It is important that employers are ready, by default, to assume a sense of urgency where well-being approaches are concerned. In its recent manifesto ahead of the 2015 general election, mental health charity Mind urges the next government to mandate the NHS to make 'talking therapies' available within 28 days of referral. This may not be ambitious enough. Van Stolk et al. (2014) also concluded this in their report to the DWP and the DofH: early access is important.

Programmes at national level will be more effective if they are more integrative. An example is the existence of, on the one hand, the IAPT employment advisory services, overseen by the NHS and commissioned by local Clinical Commissioning Groups (CCGs), and, on the other hand, the new DWP-led Health and Work Service; both services have a role to play in supporting individuals' well-being and their return to work. A greater focus on how these services could offer a more aligned, integrated service (where mental health services and employment services are seen as two sides of the same coin) would increase the effectiveness and efficiency of overall support given to individuals. Research has also pointed to this need for increased integration between treatment and employment services, to improve outcomes in both areas. C. Black (personal communication, June 23, 2014) also identifies this need for integration, emphasising that mental health and well-being often goes hand in hand with providing support for people to gain and maintain employment.

Business psychology practitioners could play a bigger role in helping GPs and their Practices to deal more effectively with well-being at work issues as presented by their patients. I worked with many IAPT referred clients who felt that their engagement as patient with their GP was restricted to being given a sick note, or a 'fit' note, for several weeks' duration, without the causes of the well-being issues being sufficiently addressed or advice being given on how their well-being-at-work issues might be addressed. Creating a greater awareness amongst GPs of the existence of the employment retention services within the wider IAPT programme, and integrating this service more closely within daily practices at GP surgeries, is important in this context. Such creation of awareness should be coordinated and funded in line with strategic long-term programmes at national level, rather than be dependent on small-scale, ad-hoc local initiatives, commissioned as they are by separate CCGs or other contracting parties (e.g. local councils).

Although well-being at work has gained more attention as a topic in recent years, and the government has introduced or supported initiatives, employers are 'conspicuously absent from the policy process' (OECD, 2014). As yet, only a small proportion of employers use existing tools and support to help their awareness of work-related stress and actions that could prevent and reduce it. Despite the well-being business case being evident (Van Stolk et al., 2014), it seems that employers need to be incentivised or, some may argue, compelled to focus on prevention and rehabilitation.

A model for well-being at work

When thinking about the drivers of well-being in the world of work, it can be useful to look at this from a 'needs' perspective: what are people's general needs in the context of their work? Maslow's Hierarchy of Needs (Maslow, 1943) is a familiar framework that sets out the progressive levels of an individual's needs. The model below is an extension of Maslow's hierarchy, turned on its head to show where the largest incremental gains can be obtained in terms of employees' engagement and well-being.

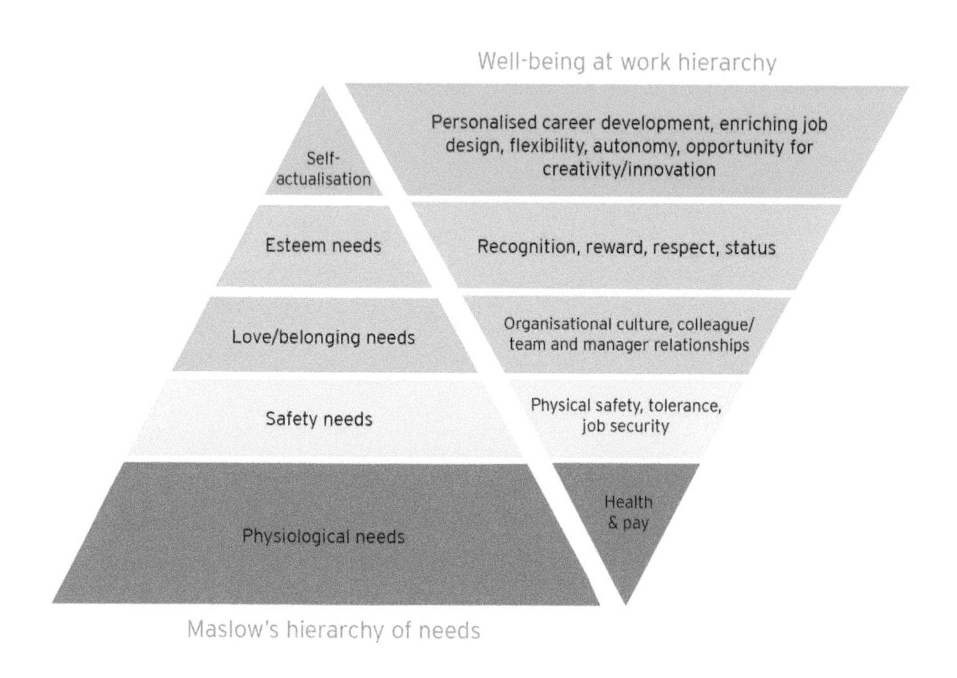

Figure 1: Well-being at work hierarchy.

The top of this inverted well-being at work model is about improving employees' full potential, their creativity, using their individual strengths. Organisations that focus on well-being look at personal and career development, training to increase competence, opportunities for innovation and creative thinking, job design for challenging work, flexibility and autonomy. Looking at well-being through this lens highlights the need for a joined-up approach that incorporates culture, policies and management. Well-being is not just about showing appreciation for staff and, for instance, supporting physical fitness; it should be treated as an organisation-wide continuous activity and a Key Performance Indicator (KPI) that is measured with the same importance, urgency and frequency as financial indicators. Such KPIs would be, for instance, the availability of an impartial and trained ear who helps to reduce periods of absence if made available quickly, through a focus on action-oriented solutions agreed with the employee(s). In our culture (and reinforced by national policy), the apparent habit of observing a four-week waiting period as criterion before more actively addressing a person's return to work may often be too long, especially where well-being problems are involved. In my experience, a period of 'time out' for the employee may merely serve to delay the cause being addressed and thus further postpone any improvement in their well-being

Using a clearly communicated approach that permeates through the organisation may give a framework not only for measure well-being, but also for constructing organisation-wide initiatives to improve well-being. Business psychology practitioners are ideally positioned to play a more prominent role in building such frameworks. As external and independent advisors, we can offer an eye for the intersection of immediate commercial and operational factors at play within organisations and the issues around well-being, its causes, measurement and possible solutions. They have the ability and expertise to design, help implement and monitor a joined-up, sustainable, actionable approach from which employers and employees are alike bound to benefit.

References

ACAS & CIPD (2013). *Mediation: An approach to resolve workplace issues* [online]. London: ACAS. Retrieved from http://www.acas.org.uk/media/pdf/2/q/Mediation-an-approach-to-resolving-workplace-issues.pdf.

Aston, L. (2014, April 3). Mental health: the last workplace taboo. *Guardian professional*. Retrieved from http://www.theguardian.com/sustainable-business/mental-health-taboo-workplace-employers.

Barling, J., & Carson, J. (2008). *State-of-Science Review: SR-C3. The Impact of Management Style on Mental Wellbeing at Work. Foresight Mental Capital and Wellbeing Project*. London: The Government Office for Science. Retrieved from http://webarchive.nationalarchives.gov.uk/20140108144555/http://www.bis.gov.uk/assets/foresight/docs/mental-capital/sr-c3_mcw.pdf.

Black, C. (2008). *Working for a Healthier Tomorrow. The Stationary Office (TSO)*. Retrieved from http://www.dwp.gov.uk/docs/hwwb-working-for-a healthier-tomorrow.pdf.

Black, C., & Frost, D. (2011). *Health at work – an independent review of sickness absence. The Stationary Office (TSO)*. Retrieved from http://www.dwp.gov.uk/docs/health-at-work.pdf.

Business in the Community (2014). *Mental health: We're Ready to Talk: Rethinking the approach to mental wellbeing in the workplace*. Retrieved from http://www.bitc.org.uk/our-resources/report/mental-health-were-ready-talk.

Chartered Institute of Personnel and Development (2012). *Emotional or transactional engagement – does it matter? Research insight*. London: CIPD. Retrieved from http://www.cipd.co.uk/binaries/emotional-or-transactional-engagement_2012.pdf.

Chartered Institute of Personnel and Development (2014a). *CIPD manifesto for work. A policy programme to champion better work and working lives*. Retrieved from http://www.cipd.co.uk/binaries/cipd-manifesto-for-work-july_2014.pdf.

Chartered Institute of Personnel and Development (2014b). *Absence Management. Annual survey report 2014. CIPD in partnership with Simplyhealth*. Retrieved from http://www.cipd.co.uk/hr-resources/survey-reports/absence-management-2014.aspx.

Chartered Institute of Personnel and Development, Health and Safety Executive, & Investors in People (2009). *Line management behaviour and stress at work*. Retrieved from http://www.dwp.gov.uk/policy/welfare-reform/sickness-absence-review/.

CIPD & MIND (2011). *Managing and supporting mental health at work: disclosure tools for managers. Guide*. Retrieved from http://www.cipd.co.uk/binaries/managing-and-supporting-mental-health-at-work-disclosure-tools-for-managers_2011.pdf.

Department of Health (2010). *Healthy Lives, Healthy People: Our strategy for public health in England*. Retrieved from http://tinyurl.com/healthyliveshealthyPeople.

Department of Health (2013). *Mental Health Payment by Results Guidance for 2013-14*. Retrieved from https://www.gov.uk/government/uploads/system/uploads/attachment_data/file/232162/Mental_Health_PbR_Guidance_for_2013-14.pdf.

Department for Work & Pensions (2013). *Fitness for work: the Government response to 'Health at work – an independent review of sickness absence'*. London: Department for Work & Pensions.

Department of Work and Pensions (2014). *Health and Work Service supplier announced*. Retrieved from https://www.gov.uk/government/news/health-and-work-service-supplier-announced.

Engage for Success (2014). *The evidence: Wellbeing and Employee Engagement*. Retrieved from//www.slideshare.net/engage4success/wellbeing-and-employee-engagement-the-evidence-whitepaper.

Government Office for Science (2008). *Foresight Mental Capital and Wellbeing Project. Final Project report – Executive summary*. London: The Government Office for Science.

Hassan, E., Austin, C., Celia, C., Disley, E., Hunt, P., Marjanovic, S., Shehabi, A., Villalba-van Dijk, L., & Van Stolk, C. (2009). *NHS Workforce Health and Wellbeing Review: Health and Wellbeing at Work in the United Kingdom*. Retrieved from http://www.rand.org/pubs/technical_reports/TR758.html.

Health & Social Care Information Centre (2014). *Improving Access to Psychological Therapies Payment and Pricing System*. Retrieved from http://www.hscic.gov.uk/iapt.

Health & Safety Executive (2004). *Working together to reduce stress at work: a guide for employers*. Retrieved from www.hse.gov.uk/pubns/indg424.pdf.

Health & Safety Executive (2009). *How to tackle work-related stress: A guide for employers on making the Management Standards work*. Retrieved from http://www.hse.gov.uk/pubns/indg430.pdf.

IAPT – Improving Access to Psychological Therapies (2012). *IAPT three-year report: The first million patients*. Retrieved from http://www.iapt.nhs.uk/silo/files/iapt-3-year-report.pdf.

Investors in People (2010). *Why should you be improving health and wellbeing? The answer is in the question*. Retrieved from http://www.healthwellbeingstandard.com/media/Health-and-Wellbeing-Good-Practice-Award-Leaflet-ROI.pdf.

National Institute for Health and Clinical Excellence (2009). *Promoting mental wellbeing at work. NICE public health guidance 22.* Retrieved from http://www.nice.org.uk/guidance/ph22/resources/guidance-promoting-mental-wellbeing-at-work-pdf.

Kerr, R., McHugh, M., & McCrory, M. (2009). HSE Management Standards and stress-related work outcomes. *Occupational Medicine, 59*, 574-579.

Maslow, A. H. (1943). A Theory of Human Motivation. *Psychological Review, 50*(4), 370-396.

OECD (2014). *Mental Health and Work: United Kingdom*. Mental Health and Work. Retrieved from http://www.oecd.org/employment/emp/mentalhealthandwork-unitedkingdom.htm.

The Office for National Statistics (2011). *Measuring what matters. National Statistician's Reflections on the National Debate on Measuring National Well-being*. Retrieved from http://www.ons.gov.uk/ons/index.html.

People Management (2014 April). The Big Lesson; We need a well-being revolution'. p. 8.

PriceWaterhouseCoopers LLP (2008). *Building the business case for wellness.* Retrieved from https://www.gov.uk/government/uploads/system/uploads/attachment data/file/209547/hwwb-dwp-wellness-report-public.pdf.

Royal College of General Practitioners (2012). *Preparing the Future GP: The Case for Enhanced GP Training*. London: Royal College of General Practitioners.

SLH (2014). *The SLH Group scoops top award for employee's health and wellbeing.* Retrieved from http://www.slhgroup.co.uk/about-us/news/the-slh-group-scoops-top-award-for-employee-s-health-and-wellbeing/.

Van Stolk, C., Hofman, J., Hafner, M., & Janta, B. (2014). *Psychological Wellbeing and Work; Improving Service Provision and Outcomes.* Retrieved from https://www.gov.uk/government/publications/psychological-wellbeing-and-work-improving-service-provision-and-outcomes.